Management of Heterogeneous and Autonomous Database Systems

The Morgan Kaufmann Series in Data Management Systems

SERIES EDITOR, JIM GRAY

Management of Heterogeneous and Autonomous Database Systems, Edited by Ahmed Elmagarmid, Marek Rusinkiewicz, and Amit Sheth

Database Modeling and Design, Third Edition, Toby J. Teorey

Web Farming for the Data Warehouse, Richard Hackathorn

Object-Relational DBMSs: Tracking the Next Great Wave, Second Edition, Michael Stonebraker and Paul Brown with Dorothy Moore

A Complete Guide to DB2 Universal Database, Don Chamberlin

Universal Database Management: A Guide to Object/Relational Technology, Cynthia Maro Saracco

Readings in Database Systems, Third Edition, Edited by Michael Stonebraker and Joseph M. Hellerstein

Understanding SQL's Stored Procedures: A Complete Guide to SQL/PSM, Jim Melton

Principles of Multimedia Database Systems, V. S. Subrahmanian

Principles of Database Query Processing for Advanced Applications, Clement T. Yu and Weiyi Meng

The Object Database Standard: ODMG 2.0, Edited by R. G. G. Cattell and Douglas K. Barry

Introduction to Advanced Database Systems, Carlo Zaniolo, Stefano Ceri, Christos Faloutsos, Richard T. Snodgrass, V. S. Subrahmanian, and Roberto Zicari

Principles of Transaction Processing, Philip A. Bernstein and Eric Newcomer

Distributed Algorithms, Nancy A. Lynch

Active Database Systems: Triggers and Rules For Advanced Database Processing, Edited by Jennifer Widom and Stefano Ceri

Joe Celko's SQL for Smarties: Advanced SQL Programming, Joe Celko

Migrating Legacy Systems: Gateways, Interfaces, and the Incremental Approach, Michael L. Brodie and Michael Stonebraker

Database: Principles, Programming, and Performance, Patrick O'Neil

Atomic Transactions, Nancy Lynch, Michael Merritt, William Weihl, and Alan Fekete

Query Processing for Advanced Database Systems, Edited by Johann Christoph Freytag, David Maier, and Gottfried Vossen

Transaction Processing: Concepts and Techniques, Jim Gray and Andreas Reuter

Understanding the New SQL: A Complete Guide, Jim Melton and Alan R. Simon

Building an Object-Oriented Database System: The Story of O_2, Edited by François Bancilhon, Claude Delobel, and Paris Kanellakis

Database Transaction Models for Advanced Applications, Edited by Ahmed K. Elmagarmid

A Guide to Developing Client/Server SQL Applications, Setrag Khoshafian, Arvola Chan, Anna Wong, and Harry K. T. Wong

The Benchmark Handbook for Database and Transaction Processing Systems, Second Edition, Edited by Jim Gray

Camelot and Avalon: A Distributed Transaction Facility, Edited by Jeffrey L. Eppinger, Lily B. Mummert, and Alfred Z. Spector

Readings in Object-Oriented Database Systems, Edited by Stanley B. Zdonik and David Maier

Management of Heterogeneous and Autonomous Database Systems

Edited by
Ahmed Elmagarmid
Marek Rusinkiewicz
Amit Sheth

Morgan Kaufmann Publishers, Inc.
An Imprint of Elsevier
San Francisco, California

Senior Editor   Diane D. Cerra
Director of Production and Manufacturing   Yonie Overton
Assistant Production Editor   Julie Pabst
Copyeditor   Judith Brown
Illustration   Cherie Plumlee
Composition   Ed Sznyter, Babel Press
Proofreaders Jennifer McClain and Christine Sabooni
Indexer   Bruce Tracy
Cover Design   Ross Carron Design
Cover Image   ©PhotoDisc, Inc.
Printer   Courier Corporation

Morgan Kaufmann Publishers, Inc.
Editorial and Sales Office
340 Pine Street, Sixth Floor
San Francisco, CA 94104-3205
USA
Telephone   415/392-2665
Facsimile   415/982-2665
Email   *mkp@mkp.com*
WWW   *http://www.mkp.com*
Order toll free   800/745-7323

Library of Congress Cataloging-in-Publication Data is available for this book.
ISBN-13: 978-1-55860-216-8   ISBN-10: 1-55860-216-X

Contents

Preface

These pages have been long in coming. This project was initiated in 1992, and since then we've seen many iterations and revisions. We hope the final product meets the need of the community and fills a gap in the literature. Multidatabase systems have been the subject of research for over 25 years. There seems to be no fading in the interest of researchers to find better ways to integrate information and knowledge systems more efficiently and effectively. A sign of the success achieved in this area is the availability of commercial tools that provide mechanisms to integrate databases, file systems, and knowledge bases.

This book consists of contributed chapters with original material, commissioned specifically to create a comprehensive resource on this topic. We began by compiling a list of topics of interest and invited leaders in the field to contribute specific chapters. The book consists of 11 chapters, most of which have multiple authors. In total there are 17 contributors and three editors. The book covers fundamental issues and concepts such as autonomy, semantics, and languages. It also covers the major research subtopics and techniques, including schema integration and translation, transactions, and similarity and dissimilarity in the structure of data and its use across multiple databases. There are numerous references and citations to the literature.

The book can be divided into three parts. The first two chapters give an overview and cover introductory material. The second part contains five chapters, generally focusing on logical or intentional issues. The chapters provide details on representational issues, semantic issues, schema integration, and languages. The last part, which includes four chapters, covers system-level issues with emphasis on data consistency and transactions. These chapters discuss replication issues, concurrency control, models, and recovery. Chapter 8 covers broad issues that can fit into transactional issues as well as those that are handled by schema descriptions.

Chapter 1 provides a tutorial on the subject as a whole. It covers terminology and attempts to shed some light on how conflicting and multiple terms were introduced. It also defines an architecture for heterogeneous databases, covers research issues at large, and gives a synopsis of research prototypes and tools. It sets the stage for the rest of the book, where individual chapters detail concepts briefly discussed in Chapter 1. This chapter is written by Bouguettaya, Benatallah, and Elmagarmid.

Chapter 2 provides an overview of autonomy by Elmagarmid, Du, and Ahmed. This chapter covers design and implementation as well as administrative issues. The major goal of this chapter is to discuss the impact of autonomy on schema integration, query processing, query execution, and transaction management. Autonomy is one issue that has received a lot of attention in the literature. We felt it was worthy of a whole chapter.

Chapter 3 on semantic similarities between entities in databases is written by Kashyap and Sheth. It describes how to identify objects in different databases that are semantically related yet schematically different. The chapter discusses the need to capture more knowledge about the objects in order to capture the relationships between the objects. In the opinion of the authors, simple mathematical tools do not suffice and knowledge of the context, domain, and uncertainty of objects must be harnessed in order to relate such objects.

Chapter 4 on the resolution of representational diversity is related to the previous chapter. This chapter is written by Hammer and McLeod. It addresses a pervasive problem faced when attempting to share information across databases: It discusses, among other concepts, how to determine relations between sharable objects across databases and how to detect representational differences.

Chapter 5 by Ram and Ramesh provides comprehensive coverage on schema integration. Schema integration refers to the process of generating integrated schemas from multiple existing schemas. These schemas represent the semantics of the databases being integrated and are used as input to the integration process. The chapter sheds some light on the confusion related to this subject and view integration. A framework for schema integration is presented in this chapter as well. This chapter is supported by a number of illustrations that help clarify these issues.

Chapter 6 by Czejdo and Gruenwald discusses schema and language translation. This chapter describes how to export schemas in the process of building a global schema and provides a description of schema transformations between source and target schemas. This chapter covers techniques for efficient translation of subqueries into local data manipulation languages. Schema translations into relational, ER, functional, and object-oriented models are briefly described, and a final example is provided. Issues related to language translations such as using intermediate languages, rule-based languages, and general query transformation systems are covered.

Chapter 7 by Missier, Rusinkiewicz, and Jin provides an in-depth coverage of multidatabase query languages. Specifically, it provides a description of an MSQL+ approach. The chapter covers fundamental issues related to multirelational algebra and the development of multidatabase query languages including evaluation strategies and update constructs.

Chapter 8 on interdependent database systems, written by Karabatis, Rusinkiewicz, and Sheth, provides a comprehensive coverage of multidatabase consistency and interrelated data across heterogeneous databases. The chapter uses a system, Aeolos, to describe a specification framework for interdependencies. The goal of this chapter is to model the relationships and consistency requirements between independent data objects. Correctness of the specifications and verification of correct relationships between these objects are given. The chapter also describes an execution model for transactions that can be used to maintain mutual consistency between interdependent data.

Chapters 9, 10, and 11 cover transaction management. Chapter 9, by Chrysanthis and Ramamritham, overviews the problem of parallel execution of transactions in the absence of knowledge of global system states. The chapter describes various correctness criteria that are used to reason about autonomous histories that heavily impacted one another. In Chapter 10, Barker and Elmagarmid describe several architectures for modeling transactions. Chapter 11, which is written by Veijalainen and Wolski, covers issues of reliability in multidatabase systems. This chapter provides comprehensive coverage of architecture for reliable global transaction execution, a discussion of failure types, and a formal recovery model.

We hope that readers find this a valuable resource for learning about over a decade of research in managing heterogeneous databases.

Ahmed Elmagarmid
Marek Rusinkiewicz
Amit Sheth

1

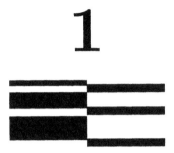

An Overview of
Multidatabase Systems:
Past and Present

Athman Bouguettaya
Boualem Benatallah
Ahmed Elmagarmid

Introduction

Organizations all over the world rely on a wide variety of databases to conduct their everyday business. Large organizations use databases on a variety of platforms, including mainframes, workstations, and servers configured for a corporate intranet. Historically, the databases are usually designed from scratch if none is found to meet the organization's requirements. This has led to a proliferation of databases obeying different sets of requirements for modeling identical or similar world objects. In many instances, and because of a lack of an organized conglomeration of databases, users typically create their own pieces of information that may be present in existing databases.

As organizations have become more sophisticated, pressure to provide information sharing across dissimilar platforms has mounted. At the same time, advances in distributed computing and networking, combined with the affordable high level of connectivity, are helping to make information sharing across databases a reality.

Databases are typically managed by different database management systems (DBMSs) running on heterogeneous computing platforms. The challenge is to give users the sense that they are accessing a single database that contains almost everything they need while preserving the integrity and investments of the preexisting environment [BS95]. In such systems, it is necessary not only to provide uniform access to all data and resources but also to allow databases to cooperate by exchanging data and synchronizing their execution seamlessly.

This emerging need to provide organization-wide access to data and software resources is creating a demand to interconnect previously isolated software systems. An end user in a heterogeneous computing environment should be able not only to invoke multiple existing software systems and hardware devices but also to coordinate their interactions. These systems may run autonomously on different computers, may be supported by different operating systems, may be designed for different purposes, and may use different data formats.

However, any successful solution to the interconnection and cooperation of preexisting autonomous and heterogeneous databases will have to address two fundamental issues: autonomy and heterogeneity. There are different types of autonomy and heterogeneity. Early research overlooked the problem of autonomy, and emphasis was put on solutions to heterogeneity [HBP94]. Autonomy issues were largely ignored due to the poor networking infrastructure that existed in the 1970s and early 1980s. In addition, most prototypes were designed for intracorporate database sharing, which minimized the issue of autonomy.

The heterogeneity problem cuts across all layers of a database management system. Early efforts focused on the schema level. Traditional distributed database techniques were used to cope with other aspects of heterogeneity (e.g., concurrency control). As a result, the first approach proposed relied on the integration, or fusion, of component databases at the schema level [BLN86]. A later research approach was proposed that catered to more autonomy and flexible bridging of heterogeneity. This approach is called the *federated* approach [HM85]. However, the drawback is twofold: first, the partial integration is done on demand with little system support; and second, database administrators acting on behalf of users, process the integration manually, making the integration a repetitive process. The other approach that favored autonomy over heterogeneity is the *multidatabase language* approach [HBP94]. In this approach, users are responsible for integrating the schemas they need for their application. Support is provided by a multidatabase language that contains all the syntactic constructs needed for accessing and manipulating disparate and autonomous databases. This, of course, relieves database administrators and puts the onus on users to locate and integrate the pieces of schemas that are needed. Additionally, support for reuse was not a primary objective of this approach.

Schema integration usually involves a process of translation that is done manually, automatically, or both. This process may involve the translation of query languages or the mapping of a schema from one data model to another. The latter model was usually a canonical model [SP94, BLN86, AT93]. Early work involved research into techniques that could perform semiautomatic translation to and from the *entity-relationship* (ER) model [SKS97, HNSD93]. CASE tools were developed to translate ER diagrams into relational schemas. Almost invariably, early canonical schemas were relational, and therefore translations were done to the relational model.

Traditionally, concurrency control, recovery, and deadlock management techniques originally developed for distributed databases were also used in multidatabase systems. As a result and until the late 1980s, little research was conducted in the area of transactional support for multidatabase applications [DE89]. More complex and richer applications and the proliferation of different techniques led the push for alternative global methods to deal with the transactional support in multidatabase systems. [Mos85] was the first to propose the concept of multilevel nested transactions. Since then, several techniques and models have been proposed to address the need for advanced applications in multidatabase environments [SYE+90].

With the advent of the Internet, intranets, and affordable network connectivity, business reengineering has become a necessity for modern corporations that want to stay competitive in the global market. The process of reengineering includes the automation and support of workflow processes. Because of the rich set of documents and interactions, new paradigms are needed [She96]. The use of advanced transaction techniques to model workflows shows promise for dealing with the sophisticated type of constraints that exist in such environments [PDBH97]. However, more work is needed to lay the theoretical foundations of workflows and define optimal models of implementations [She96].

Most of the existing multidatabase systems (MDBSs) are research prototypes. Some commercial systems, such as Ingres, UniSQL, Sybase, and Oracle

[HBP94], provide limited support for multidatabase functions. A good summary of research issues in multidatabase systems is given in [SYE+90]. In this chapter, we first discuss the terminology related to multidatabase systems (Section 1.1). We then discuss the architecture of multidatabase systems and present a taxonomy of such systems (Section 1.2). Then we concentrate on some critical issues addressed in this book (Section 1.3), including query languages and data model translation, schema integration, multidatabase modeling, local autonomy, concurrency control, and crash recovery. We are not concerned with issues related to heterogeneity at hardware and operating system levels. In Section 1.4, we present an overview of various multidatabase systems. Section 1.5 summarizes the main topics of the chapter.

1.1
Terminology

There is unfortunately no consensus on the terminology used in the area of multidatabases. In this section, we present a set of definitions used in this chapter. These definitions, to a large extent, are consistent with the terminology used in the majority of work in the area.

1.1.1 Distribution

In many environments and applications, data is *distributed* among multiple databases. These databases may be stored on one or more computer systems that are either centrally located or geographically distributed but interconnected by a communication medium. Data may be distributed among the multiple databases in different ways. These include, in relational terms, vertical and horizontal partitions. Multiple copies of some or all of the data may be maintained. These replicas need not be identically structured.

Benefits of data distribution include increased availability, reliability, and improved access times. In a distributed DBMS, distribution of data may be induced; that is, the data may be deliberately distributed to take advantage of these benefits.

1.1.2 Heterogeneity

It is important to note that heterogeneity is independent from the physical distribution of data. Information systems or databases may be located in remote geographical locations and still be homogeneous [OV91]. We say that an information system is *homogeneous* if the software that creates and manipulates data is the same at all sites. Furthermore, all data follows the same structure and format (data model) and is part of a single universe of discourse. In contrast, a *heterogeneous* system is one that does not adhere to *all* the requirements for a homogeneous system. This means that any dissimilarity at any level in the information system design and implementation requires that the system be called heterogeneous. In this respect, heterogeneity can happen at all levels of the database system. For instance, different sites may use different languages to write applications, different query languages, different models, different DBMSs, different file systems, etc. The more dissimilar the two systems are, the more difficult it is to bridge that heterogeneity.

1.1.3 Autonomy

The organizational entities that manage different database systems are often *autonomous*. In other words, databases are often under separate and independent control. Those who control a database are often willing to let others share the data only if control is retained. Thus, it is important to understand the aspects of autonomy and how they can be addressed when a database is a member of a network of databases or shares its data with remote users. The different aspects of autonomy are summarized as follows [SL90]:

- *Design autonomy:* Local databases choose their own data model, query language, semantic interpretation of data, constraints, functions/operations support, etc.

- *Communication autonomy:* Local databases decide when and how to respond to requests from other databases.

- *Execution autonomy:* The execution order of transactions or external/local operations is not controlled by foreign DBMSs. Local databases do not need to inform any other DBMS of the execution order of local or external operations. A component database doesn't distinguish among local and global operations.

- *Association autonomy:* Local databases can decide how much of their functions/operations (e.g., `project`, `select`, `join`) and data to share with certain classes of users. The release of statistical information, such as costs, efficiency, and execution speeds of processing information, is also determined by individual databases; thus, global query processing and optimization may be difficult. Local databases have the ability to associate or disassociate themselves from the network of databases.

1.1.4 Interoperability

Interoperation implies the ability to request and receive services between the interoperating systems and use each others' functionality. A limited form of interoperation is that of data exchange whereby a system may be able to periodically send data to another recipient system. Interdependency implies that data and functions in different systems are related or dependent on each other, although the end user or the application may not be aware of this relationship or dependency. Thus, the management of interdependent data implies the enforcement of multidatabase consistency constraints [ASSR93]. More generally, we consider information systems to be interoperable if the following conditions are met [BGML+90, SYE+90, SSU91]:

- They can exchange messages and requests

- They can receive services and operate as a unit in solving a common problem

The above conditions suggest that for information systems to be interoperable, they must have the following features:

- Use of each other's functionality

- Client-server abilities

- Communication despite incompatible internal details of components

- Distribution

- Extensibility and ease of evolution

1.2
Architecture of Heterogeneous Distributed Databases

Information systems that provide interoperation and varying degrees of integration among multiple databases have been termed multidatabase systems [HBP94], federated databases [HM85], and more generally, heterogeneous distributed database systems. An attempt to relate some of the frequently used terms, using the fundamental dimensions of distribution, heterogeneity, and autonomy, was presented in [SL90]. The term federated database system is used to imply the role of the autonomy as discussed in [SL90]. Other perspectives and overviews can be found in [EP90, OV91, BE96, HNSD93, LMR90, Lit94].

Effective sharing and use of data and functions can be achieved in different forms. Common forms include integration, interoperability, interdependency, and exchange. As with the other terminology, there is no general agreement in the interpretation nor a consistent use of these terms. We propose to use these terms in the context of heterogeneous distributed database systems (HDDBSs) in the following manner. Data integration generally implies uniform and transparent access to data managed by multiple databases. A mechanism to achieve this is an integrated schema that involves all or parts of the component schemas that are integrated. In HDDBSs, it is not necessary to have a single (global) integrated schema in the entire system. Sheth and Larson [SL90] clearly talk about the possibility of multiple integrated schemas (called federated schemas) in a federated database system and give examples of systems that support multiple integrated schemas.

The taxonomy presented below classifies the existing solutions in three categories: global schema integration (Section 1.2.1), federated databases (Section 1.2.2), and multidatabase language approach (Section 1.2.3). These categories are presented according to how tightly integrated the component systems are. Historically, there has always been a trade-off between sharing and autonomy. This trade-off can be succinctly stated as follows: the more sharing, the less autonomy. For instance, the use of schema integration increases data sharing dramatically while reducing database autonomy to almost nothing. Other classifications and reference architectures are proposed in the literature [SL90, LMR90, BE96]. For example, Hurson and Bright [BE96] classify the architectures of a multidatabase system in five categories: distributed databases, global schema multidatabases, federated databases, multidatabase language systems, and interoperable databases.

1.2.1   Global Schema Integration

Global schema integration was one of the first attempts at data sharing across HDDBSs. It is based on the complete integration of multiple databases in order to provide a single view (global schema) [SP94]. [BLN86] provides a thorough survey on schema integration, comparing twelve methodologies.

The advantage of this approach is that users have a consistent, uniform view of, and access to, data. Users are unaware that the databases they are using are heterogeneous and distributed. Multiple databases logically appear as a single database. However, global schema integration has several disadvantages:

- It is hard to automate because it is difficult to identify relationships among attributes of two schemas and to identify relationships among entity types and relationship types. The general problem of integrating relational schemas has been proven to have no general solution. Human understanding is required to solve many types of semantic, structural, or behavioral conflicts.

- Autonomy, especially association autonomy, is often sacrificed to solve semantic conflicts. All databases involved need to reveal all information about their conceptual schemas or data dictionary, as the global integration process requires full prior semantic knowledge. Sometimes, this process may even require a local database to alter its schema to ease integration.

- If there are more than two databases, several integration methods exist: either consider all schemas at once or consider two at a time and then combine them at the end. Depending on the order in which schemas are integrated, only incomplete semantic knowledge is used at each step. As a result, some semantic knowledge may be missing from the final global schema unless integration is done in one step and has considered all export schemas simultaneously. It is hard to prove correctness of a global schema—i.e., whether it represents completely all the information in all given schemas—due to context-dependent meanings.

It should be obvious by now that global schema integration is both time consuming and error prone. It is not suitable for frequent dynamic changes of schemas, as the whole process of integration may need to be redone [BPK95]. As a result, it does not scale well with the size of the database networks.

Partial schema unification/combination in [HM93] is similar to schema integration to some extent. It requires each local database to provide some semantic information (real-world meaning) of its sharable objects in a local lexicon and structural information using metafunctions. The system provides an intelligent advisor (sometimes human), which will identify similar/related sharable objects and answer users' queries. Therefore, users do not have to understand each individual database schema. A partial schema unification, similar to merging and restructuring in schema integration, is used to identify new supertypes and subtypes, and inherited functions must be created along with value types for new functions. In general, partial schema unification cannot be easily automated.

1.2.2 Federated Database Systems (FDBSs)

The aim of the FDBS architecture is to remove the need for static global schema integration. It allows each local database to have more control over the sharable information, i.e., more association autonomy among independent databases in a cooperative environment. Control is, therefore, decentralized in FDBSs. The amount of integration does not have to be complete as in global schema integration, but it depends on the needs of the users, as FDBSs may be either tightly or loosely coupled systems. Note that FDBSs are a compromise between no integration and total integration. A typical FDBS architecture would have a common data model (CDM) and an internal command language. It relies on the following types of schemas and processors:

- *Local schema*: The conceptual schema of a component database, expressed in the data model of component DBMSs.

- *Component schema*: A local schema is translated to the common data model of the FDBS. This alleviates data model heterogeneity. Thus it eases negotiation, schema integration (for tightly coupled), and specification of views/queries (for loosely coupled). Each local database should store one-to-one mappings between the local data model and CDM schema objects during schema translation.

- *Transforming processor*: Using the one-to-one mappings between local and CDM schema objects obtained from the schema translation, command- and data-transforming processors translate commands from the internal command language to local query language, and data from local format to CDM format. The transforming processor sits between local and component schemas and is provided by each database.

- *Export schema*: Each database can specify the sharable objects to other members of the FDBS. Each database contains access control information (i.e., only specific federation users can access certain information). As a result, association autonomy is maintained.

- *Filtering processor*: Using the access control information specified in the export schema, a filtering processor limits the set of allowable operations submitted to the corresponding component schema. It acts as a semantic integrity constraint checker and access controller, sitting between component and export schemas, and is provided by each database.

- *Federated schema*: Can be a statically integrated schema or a dynamic user view of multiple export schemas. The integrated schema is managed and controlled by the FDBS administrator if the FDBS is tightly coupled. The view is managed and controlled by users if the FDBS is loosely coupled. There can be multiple federated schemas, one for each class of federation users.

- *Constructing processor*: Using the distribution information stored in the federated dictionary, the constructing processor performs query decomposition from one federated schema to one or more export schemas and merges data produced by several processors into a single data set for another single processor, i.e., negotiation and schema integration. This is provided by the FDBS.

- *External schema*: It is mainly for customization when the federated schema is very large and complicated. It is another level of abstraction for a particular class of users/applications, which only require a subset of federated schema. It contains additional integrity constraints and access control information. This schema is not needed for loosely coupled FDBSs but is essential for those that are tightly coupled. The data model of an external schema can be different from that of a federated schema; thus a transforming processor for command and data translation is required.

- *Data dictionary*: It contains external, federated, and export schemas. In a tightly coupled system, component and local schema objects are also sometimes contained. Mappings between schemas (e.g., external and federated schemas, federated schema and its export schemas) are also stored in the data dictionary of the FDBS as distinct objects. Other information such as statistics and heuristics for query optimization, and schema-independent information such as functions for unit/format transformations, network addresses, communication facility, etc., are also stored in the data dictionary.

The five-level schema of the FDBS architecture is extended from the standard three-level schema architecture of a single database to give explicit interfaces for supporting distribution, heterogeneity, and autonomy dimensions of a multidatabase environment. Component, export, and federated schemas are all in the CDM. They are managed and controlled by the corresponding component database administrator. The structure of an FDBS data dictionary is not described in the literature, but it is obviously complex, as it stores many levels of schemas and mappings and other information. Locating the right information in the FDBS data dictionary becomes a problem [SYE+90]. The level of integration and services in an FDBS depends on how tightly or loosely coupled the component DBMSs are.

Loosely Coupled FDBSs

It is the user's responsibility to maintain and create the federation schema in loosely coupled FDBSs. No control is enforced by the federation system or federation administrators. Creating a federated schema corresponds to creating a view against relevant export schemas. In that respect, each user must be knowledgeable about the information and structure of the relevant export schemas in order to create views. Federated schemas here are dynamic and can be created or dropped on the fly. Multiple federation schemas are supported. These systems assume highly autonomous read-only databases and cannot support view updates. Loosely coupled systems have these advantages:

- Different classes of federation users have the flexibility to map different or multiple semantic meanings among the same set of objects in export schemas by using dynamic attributes.

- Loosely coupled systems can cope with dynamic changes of component or export schemas better than tightly coupled systems because it is easier to construct new views than to create global schemas from scratch. However, the detection of dynamic changes in an export schema by some remote databases may be difficult to achieve in an overloaded network, as triggers may introduce too many broadcast messages.

Some of the disadvantages of loosely coupled FDBSs are

- If two or more independent users access similar information from the same component databases, they create their own mappings/views and don't know if the others have done the same mappings/views. Thus, there is a potential for duplicate work in view creations and the understanding of the same export schemas. Another difficulty is understanding export schemas when the number of schemas is large.

- Due to multiple semantic mappings between objects, view updating can't be supported well. This can create difficulty.

Tightly Coupled FDBSs

Federation administrators have full control of the creation and maintenance of federated schemas and access to export schemas in tightly coupled FDBSs. The aim is to provide location, replication, and distribution transparency. The tightly coupled FDBSs support one or more federated schemas. A single federated schema helps maintain uniformity in the semantic interpretation of multiple integrated component data. Multiple federated schemas are harder to maintain, as multiple constraints from multiple export databases are difficult to enforce and could lead to inconsistencies in semantics.

Forming a single federated schema is really doing global schema integration on all export schemas. However, view updates can be at least partially supported if FDBS administrators fully understand and define all mappings and resolve all semantic conflicts during schema integration. This is somewhat similar to solving the view update problem in centralized or distributed DBMSs. Disadvantages of tightly coupled systems are

- FDBS administrators and component DBAs negotiate to form export schemas. During negotiation, FDBS administrators may be allowed to read the component schemas without any data access. This clearly violates autonomy.

- Once a federated schema is created, it is rarely changed (i.e., static). When there are changes in the export/component schemas, integrations need to be done from scratch for each federated schema.

1.2.3   Multidatabase Language Approach

The multidatabase language approach is intended for users of a multidatabase system who do not use a predefined global or partial schema. Preexisting heterogeneous local DBMSs are usually integrated without modifications. Information stored in different databases may be redundant, heterogeneous, and inconsistent. These problems occur when component systems are strongly autonomous. Multidatabase language systems are more loosely coupled than the previous classes covered in the previous section.

The aim of a multidatabase language is to provide constructs that perform queries involving several databases at the same time. Such language has features that are not supported in traditional languages. For instance, a global name can be used to identify a collection of databases. Queries can specify data from any local participating database.

The system MRDSM and its MSQL language take the aforementioned approach [LMR90, HBP94, Lit94]. The relational data model is used as the

CDM. This system has been designed to operate on databases implemented using the MRDS (Multics Relational Data Store) DBMS.

Databases that cover the same subject are grouped under a collective name (e.g., restaurants, airlines) using the MSQL language. Interdatabase dependencies with respect to data semantics, privacy, and integrity are specified in the dependency schemas.

One major criticism of the multidatabase language approach is the lack of distribution and location transparency for users [BGML+90], as users have to find, a priori, the right information in a potentially large network of databases. Users are responsible for understanding schemas and detecting and resolving semantic conflicts. The multidatabase language provides adequate operators and expressive constructs for users to perform the resolution of semantic conflicts at various abstraction levels. Some of the interesting features of the MSQL language are global naming, interdatabase dependencies, and interdatabase queries.

In general, in this approach, users are faced with the following tasks: finding the relevant information in multiple databases, understanding each individual database schema, detecting and resolving semantic conflicts, and performing view integration.

1.3
Research Issues in Multidatabase Systems

In this section, we present some of the issues in multidatabase systems that are relevant to several database levels. We discuss these issues from two basic perspectives: application and database system. The former deals with query languages and data model translation, schema integration, and multidatabase application modeling. The latter deals with system autonomy, concurrency control, and crash recovery.

1.3.1   Schema and Language Translation

An important feature of a multidatabase system is the support of translation between local and global data models. Over the years, several data modelings have been used to design universes of discourse: hierarchical, network, relational, semantic, and object-oriented models [SKS97]. Mapping between data models used at local and global levels has been the focus of much research in multidatabase systems. In general, when integrating heterogeneous databases, local schemas are translated to a common data model. This allows for resolving syntactic heterogeneity that is the result of different data models. For example, in the Multibase [HBP94] system, the components are relational and network databases, and the common data model follows the functional model. It is usually expected that the modeling power of the common data model is richer than the models followed by the component databases. The relational model has frequently been used as a common data model of multi-database systems with relational, hierarchical, and network databases. Since the entity-relationship model has been the overwhelming tool for conceptual modeling, early efforts in data modeling translation research focused on the transformation to and from the ER model [SKS97, Joh94]. Recently, there has been a shift to using the object-oriented model as the focal model through which other models have to be translated to or from [BE96, AT93]. The shift has been spurred on by the fact that the object-oriented model can be used as a tool for both design and implementation. The ER model lacks the latter part, although attempts have been made to use CASE tools to automatically generate schemas.

Another type of mapping is between access languages—that is, the translation of commands (e.g., queries) from one language (e.g., query language) to another. Different languages are used to manipulate data represented in different data models. Even when two DBMSs support the same data model, differences in their query languages (e.g., QUEL and SQL) or different versions of SQL supported by two relational DBMSs can contribute to heterogeneity. Most of the existing multidatabase prototypes provide some support for translation from the global access language to the local access language. If the local system has more expressive capabilities than the global system, the latter system does not use the extra features. However, if the global system is more expressive than the local system, the translation processor must take into account this difference. For example, a routine programmed using the local system can be associated to a function supported at the global level and not supported at the local level. As pointed out in [SL90], the previous types of mapping provide data model transparency. Data structures and commands used by one system are hidden from the other systems. Data model transparency hides the differences in query languages and data formats.

1.3.2 Schema Integration

An organization may have multiple DBMSs. Different departments within the organization may have different requirements and may select different DBMSs. When purchased over a period of time, they may be different due to changes in the technology. Whether each DBMS has a different underlying data model or not, there are still many ways to model a given real-world object. Different perspectives and views of data can lead to different representation (structure and constraints), different meaning, and so on. This aspect is referred to as schematic (or structural) and semantic heterogeneity. This includes differences in naming, structure, format, missing or conflicting data, and interpretation of data.

Different data models provide different structural primitives (e.g., the information modeled using a relation in the relational model may be modeled as a record type in the CODASYL model). If the two representations have the same information content, it is easier to deal with the differences in the structures. For example, an address can be represented as an entity in one schema and as a composite attribute in another schema. If the information content is not the same, it may be very difficult to deal with the difference. Similarly, some data models (notably semantic and object-oriented models) support generalization (and property inheritance), while others do not. Even if the same data model is used, different but equivalent modeling constructs can be used to represent the same concept. For example, an attribute `position` of type `employee` in one schema is modeled as entity subtypes `secretary` and `manager` under the supertype `employee` in another.

Integrity constraints for the same class of objects can also be specified differently. For example, it could be the case that either deleting the last employee of a department will not delete the department in one schema or deleting the last employee of a department will delete the department in another schema. Two data models may also support different types of constraints. For example, the set type in a CODASYL schema may be partially modeled as a referential integrity constraint in a relational schema. CODASYL supports insertion and retention constraints that are not captured by the referential integrity constraint alone. Triggers (or some similar mechanism) must be used in relational systems to capture such semantics.

Naming conflicts occur when semantically identical data items are named differently (i.e., synonyms) or semantically different data items are named identically (i.e., homonyms) [BE96]. For example, an attribute `size` for dresses and trousers may mean different things. In general, homonyms are easier to detect than synonyms. The *alias* capability in the access language and global schema constructs is usually used to resolve homonyms. The help of a thesaurus/semantic dictionary is required to detect synonyms. Missing or conflicting data occurs when semantically identical data items have some attribute values that are different or missing in some data sources.

The term *semantic heterogeneity* has been used to characterize a discrepancy about the meaning, interpretation, or intended use of the same or related data [SL90]. It is important to understand the distinction between the semantic and the structural/representational (i.e., schematic) issues. First note that schematic differences between objects are usually of interest only when the objects have some semantic similarity. The problem of differences in understanding the same information comes primarily from the diversity in geographical and organizational aspects [Mad96]. A case of geographical differences occurs when different currencies are used in different countries. For instance, the value 200 for attribute `money` is understood as 200 `Marks` for a German receiver. In the United States, it would be understood as 200 `dollars`. Subtle differences can arise even if the currency name is embedded in the schema. For instance, several countries use the dollar currency, including the United States, Canada, and Australia. If the proper context is not understood, the wrong information may be conveyed. For instance, the value of the U.S. dollar is currently more than the Australian dollar. A case of organizational differences occurs when two organizations define the same concept differently. For instance, a credit rate is defined differently depending on whether the Citibank or Chase database is being accessed. Although there has been a lot of research in this area, the current solutions do not address the issues of automatically processing or manipulating semantics [BE96].

1.3.3   Multidatabase Consistency and Dependencies

Consider two traditional "stovepipe" insurance applications, one handling claims processing, underwriting and actuarial accounting, and subscriber accounting for insurance company A, and the second handling the same functions for insurance company B. For the sake of simplicity, assume that each application is homogeneous and uses a single database system. Now consider what happens if the two companies merge. Presumably, they would want to coordinate their data processing for various reasons. They want to know what clients the two companies have in common. They may also want to minimize duplication of effort by (gradually) isolating certain functionalities to one system or the other.

Now consider the single issue of recognizing common insurance subscribers. What this amounts to is developing some notion of unique identity that spans the subscribers in system A and the subscribers in system B. At a minimum, users of the two systems will want to be able to relate an update to a subscriber in system A with a corresponding, semantically equivalent subscriber in system B. For example, if a specific subscriber in system A is discovered to be submitting fraudulent claims, the users of the two systems will want their claims-processing subsystems to automatically reevaluate any outstanding claims that may have been submitted by this subscriber to system B.

Some sort of triggering or alerting mechanism will have to be used to notify system B that system A has discovered a potential problem. In order to more quickly detect future problems, a constraint may have to be specified that encompasses both database systems, controlling the relationship between claims in system A and claims in system B; this constraint may indicate, for example, that a subscriber cannot report to company A that he has had heart transplant surgery in April and then report to company B that he has had double bypass surgery in May. In other words, a wide class of fraud-detecting constraints that exist in the individual systems may have to be extended to include both systems.

What this section is meant to present is the fact that interconnecting diverse information systems is, in the current state of the art, a highly manual process. This is because most of the interconnection requirements of a multi-information system application are highly application specific. The goal of many emerging products is to automate as much as possible the construction of interinformation system connections.

An important issue is the data-centric view of information management. The problem is how to capture the specification of semantically related data stored in different databases and maintain consistency in a multisystem application and multidatabase context. The key component is to specify and enforce consistency of interrelated data stored in databases managed by different DBMSs and different application systems. Recent research on active databases [Sto94] and interdependent data [ASSR93, Elm92] reflects a tentative effort to address this issue. In essence, the framework for modeling interdependent data uses data dependency descriptors to capture structural dependency among related data stored in different databases. Consistency requirements involve both temporal, state components and procedures to restore the consistency of related data.

1.3.4   Workflow Management Systems

A workflow management system (WfMS) captures the application (activity) semantics as related to the dependencies among operations performed by multiple components. This dimension is closely related to the extended transaction model [Elm92]. It can also be used to support multisystem transactional workflows (also called task-flows or operation-flows) [AS96]. In addition, it may include the semantics of operations/transactions such as commutativity, one-sided commutativity of operations, or the levels of inconsistencies that can be tolerated by an operation. Managing a workflow involves the specification and support of dependencies among the operations performed by different systems and databases to support a multisystem application.

Workflow systems are receiving more attention because they facilitate the operations of enterprises by coordinating and streamlining business activities. The need for automated support as well as operational models that allow workflow applications to coordinate units of work—according to business-defined rules and routes—are becoming indispensable for the proper management of businesses.

Despite its usefulness and popularity, workflow technology is still lacking in maturity. It does not scale well, has limited fault tolerance, and lacks reliability, availability, and interoperability [AAM97, WS96]. When the first generation of workflow systems was developed, the main emphasis was on sharing, routing, and cooperation. Moreover, the requirements for workflow management systems in heterogeneous and autonomous systems currently far exceed the capabilities provided by existing products [WS96].

Until recently, the traditional approach to workflow management has been based on extensions of advanced transaction models (ATMs) [She96]. For example, advanced transaction models such as Sagas [GMS87] and Flex [DE89] have been implemented to handle semantic failures in IBM's FlowMark [MAGW95].

Flexible transactions and polytransactions are used to specify intertask dependencies, which control workflows in order to create a transaction model that supports long-lived flow-through processing. These transaction models have a strong theoretical basis. Solutions to problems such as correctness, consistency, and recovery have been proposed [BE96]. However, these models are specific to databases. They are too data-centric, making them hard to use for modeling the rich requirements of today's organizational processes. Indeed, it is important to remember that workflows are made up not only of data but also of processes. It is argued in [She96] that it would be useful to incorporate transactional semantics such as recovery, relaxed atomicity, and isolation to ensure reliable workflow executions.

1.3.5 Transaction Processing

In a database system, several users may read and update information concurrently. Undesirable situations may arise if the operations of various user transactions are improperly interleaved. Concurrency control is an activity that coordinates concurrently executed operations so that they interfere with each other in an acceptable way. Some of the prototype implementations of multidatabase systems described in the literature [HBP94] only allow retrieval operations in a heterogeneous environment, because updates present serious problems in areas such as concurrency control, logging, and security. Recently, much attention has been focused on providing support for updates that span multiple autonomous database systems. A key step in achieving this goal is global concurrency control, which has been discussed in [Pu88, ED90, LE90, MRB+92].

Designing a concurrency control strategy for a heterogeneous database environment is more difficult than designing one for its homogeneous counterpart, primarily because we must deal not only with the data distribution but also with heterogeneity and autonomy of the underlying databases. In a tightly coupled distributed database system, there is only one concurrency controller to certify and/or produce schedules. The concurrency controller has access to all the information it needs in order to produce and/or certify the schedules. In addition, it normally has control over all the transactions running in the system. By contrast, multidatabase systems must deal with problems caused by the autonomy of multiple local systems. First, local concurrency controllers (LCCs) are designed in such a way that they are totally unaware of other local database systems (LDBSs) and of the integration process (design autonomy) [LE90]. Second, the global concurrency controller (GCC) needs information about local executions in order to maintain global database consistency. However, the GCC has no direct access to this information and cannot force the local concurrency controllers to supply it (communication autonomy). Another complication is that LCCs make decisions about transaction commitments based entirely on their own considerations. LCCs do not know or care whether the

commitment of a particular transaction will introduce global database inconsistency. In addition, a GCC has no control over the LCCs at all. For example,
a GCC cannot force an LCC to restart a local transaction, even if the commitment of this local transaction will introduce global database inconsistency
(execution autonomy).

Research in this area followed two paths: ensuring serializability in
MDBSs [MRB⁺92] and developing correctness criteria that are relaxed notions of serializability (e.g., quasi-serializability [DE89], two-level serializability
[MRKS91], etc.). A significant work on ensuring global serializability in MDBSs
was developed in [Pu88]. [Pu88] describes multidatabases in terms of a hierarchy of superdatabases. The serial ordering of each local transaction is represented by *o-elements* (order-elements). O-elements are distinct time/operations
in each transaction that will indicate the serialization order of committed transactions for a particular protocol (e.g., time stamp in a time-stamping protocol,
the start of shrinking phase in a two-phase locking protocol, etc.). For every
pair of transactions T1, T2, o-element(T1) precedes o-element(T2) if T1 precedes T2 in the schedule. Each global transaction is associated to an *o-vector*,
which consists of one or more o-elements, with each o-element representing a
subtransaction. The full autonomy is dilated in this approach, as it requires
the participation of local DBMSs in informing the superdatabases of the logical
order of transactions at their sites. [MRB⁺92] use o-elements without requiring
any modification in the existing local DBMS. They have reduced the problem
of global serialization by serializing the o-elements at each local DBMS. Using
this reduction, traditional concurrency protocols can be used to ensure serializability in MDBSs. [MKS97] propose a mechanism that extends existing
approaches for ensuring serializability in the context of hierarchical MDBSs.

Other significant research argues that serializability does not work well
in heterogeneous distributed database environments [DE89]. Some models use
correctness criteria that allow component databases to have inconsistent data
with some known and approved range (bounded inconsistency) in order to increase concurrency [PLC91]. Other approaches are based on the assumption
that integrity constraints between data stored in autonomous local DBMSs can
be ignored. Examples of these approaches include quasi-serializability [DE89]
and two-level serializability [MRKS91, MRKS92, OAB94]. [DE89] define an
execution as quasi-serializable if it is equivalent to a quasi-serial execution in
which global transactions are executed sequentially and all local executions are
serializable. When there are no direct interdatabase dependencies, the quasi-
serializability constitutes a simple and relatively easy way to enforce correctness
criteria for concurrent execution of multidatabase transactions. However, when
these assumptions are not satisfied, traditional criteria based on serializability
are necessary. To assure multidatabase consistency in this case, the MDBS
must deal with both direct and indirect conflicts. Direct conflicts that involve
only the subtransactions of multidatabase transactions can easily be handled
by the MDBS's concurrency control mechanism. However, indirect local con-

flicts involving local transactions are extremely difficult to detect. Since the MDBS is not aware of local transactions and the indirect conflicts that may be caused, it cannot determine whether an execution of arbitrary global and local transactions is serializable.

[GRS94] proposed a scheme under which the subtransactions of the global transactions are required to perform special data manipulation operations at each LDBS. This approach is based on the concept of providing *tickets* at local sites. This ensures that either the subtransactions of each multidatabase transaction have the same relative serialization order in all participating LDBSs or they are aborted. In [RELL90], instead of requiring local systems to report their serialization orders to the MDBS, additional operations are incorporated in all the subtransactions of global transactions that create direct conflicts at each LDBS. Thus, the execution order of the incorporated operations can be observed by the MDBS. The LDBS's concurrency control mechanism will then guarantee that either the execution order of the incorporated operations is consistent with the serialization order of the subtransaction they belong to, or, if not, the conflict will be resolved by the local concurrency control mechanism.

If the execution order observed by the MDBSs is inconsistent with the order in which the subtransactions obtain their tickets or the local execution becomes nonserializable, it is not allowed by the LDBS's concurrency control. Therefore, indirect conflicts can be resolved by the local concurrency control, even if the MDBS cannot detect their existence. The tickets can be used to maintain global consistency by validating global transactions using the global serialization graph. To guarantee global serializability, the tickets allow global transactions to commit only if their relative serialization order is the same in all participating LDBSs.

As pointed out before, the main source of difficulty in applying the traditional transaction management techniques to these environments is the previously discussed requirement of local autonomy. Another major problem is the potential for long-lived transactions, which make many basic techniques developed in the context of centralized databases (strict locking, two-phase commit, etc.) totally inapplicable. There have been several attempts to overcome the inadequacy of traditional transaction concepts and the limitations of serializability as a basic correctness criterion for the concurrent execution of transactions spanning multiple and autonomous systems. An idea that has received much attention as a means for overcoming the above mentioned difficulties is the concept of nested transactions [Mos85]. However, the notion of nested transactions as proposed by Moss does not address the autonomy of local systems. Garcia-Molina developed a notion of Sagas [GMS87], which rejects serializability as a basic correctness criterion. [RELL90] proposed an extended transaction model that allows the composition of flexible transactions consisting of mutually dependent subtransactions. This approach requires a redefinition of the notion of successful executions of transactions, their scheduling, and their commitment. In [Elm92], the proposed model includes both subtransactions that may be compensated for and subtransactions that may not be compensated for. The Distributed Object Management (DOM) project at GTE [Elm92] uses a mixed model to create complex transactions from simple components. This includes multitransactions for long-lived activities, nested transactions, compensating transactions, and contingency transactions. Watcher and Reuter [Sto94] proposed the ConTract model to build large applications from short ACID transactions as an application-independent service.

1.4
Multidatabase Prototypes

Several multidatabase prototypes have been developed over the last few years [BE96]. Recently, some commercial products have been extended to support multidatabase functions. Examples of commercial multidatabase systems include Sybase, Oracle, Ingres/Star, and UniSQL/M [HBP94]. Other examples of multidatabase prototypes and projects are OMS [BE96], Pegasus [ASD+91, AAK+93], Carnot [WCH+93], HKBMS [BE96], OMNIBASE [REMC+88], FBASE [Mul92], Interbase [ME93, BE96], CIS/OIS [BE96, GCO90], DOMS [NWM93, MHG+92, Elm92], VODAK [KDN90, BE96], A La Carte [BE96], FINDIT [MBP95, BPK95]. Information Manifold [LRO96], and Thor [LDS92]. Some of the existing systems support the full functionality of a multidatabase, whereas others support only specific functionality. In this section, we will briefly review some representative multidatabase projects in industry and academia. This is in no way an exhaustive list of projects. The systems presented here serve as a means of demonstrating how some of the aforementioned issues are being partially handled in practice. Parts of the discussion presented here are more exhaustively covered in [BE96].

Sybase's Open Client and Open Server extend Sybase to support heterogeneous distributed databases. No global model or schema is enforced. Sybase provides two multidatabase languages: Transac-SQL and Visual Query Language (VQL). Using these languages, users can, for example, qualify a relation name with a database name or define multidatabase views, interdatabase queries, and interdatabase manipulation dependencies. Oracle also provides a multidatabase language called SQL*PLUS. This language offers statements that qualify a relation within a database, define aliases for relations or databases, and define interdatabase queries. The distributed database manager SQL*STAR allows multidatabase operations to be available to distributed databases. Ingres/Star is a software layer for transparent access to Ingres distributed systems. It allows the definition of virtual external multidatabase schemas over Ingres or non-Ingres SQL databases. Unlike Sybase, this system does not support interdatabase dependencies. Users are also not allowed to formulate multidatabase queries to the actual databases directly. Instead, a multidatabase query is formulated over an external multidatabase whose elements are the tables referenced in the query. UniSQL/M is another commercial multidatabase system. The query language SQL/M is an extension of ANSI SQL with object-oriented modeling. This system uses global virtual classes to integrate heterogeneous entities from relational and object-oriented schemas. The major focus of this system is schema and data conflict resolution among component databases. For example, naming conflicts are handled by using renaming operations.

Pegasus is a multidatabase prototype that provides access to native (controlled by Pegasus) and external (not controlled by Pegasus) autonomous databases. It uses the functional and object-oriented language HOSQL (Heterogeneous Object SQL) [ASD+91] as the common data definition and manipulation language. HOSQL is used to define the imported Pegasus global schema in terms of imported types and functions. New object identifiers are generated for instances of each imported type. Schema integration is supported by defining equivalence relationships between objects and creating supertypes of various types defined in different databases. Name conflicts are resolved using aliases. Semantic and behavioral conflicts among functions in different databases are reconciled using functions written in HOSQL or any general-purpose language (foreign functions). Identity conflicts are handled by allowing users to specify equivalences among objects. Query optimization in Pegasus is either cost or heuristic based, depending on the availability of statistical data. The OMS project is an interoperability framework developed for Xerox information systems. It also uses an object and functional common data model called FUGUE. An extended transaction model that supports cooperation between transactions and user-specified correctness is proposed.

The OMINIBASE system uses a knowledge base to resolve relation name ambiguity, DBMS incompatibility, and inconsistencies in participating databases. The knowledge base contains information about local databases, relation attributes, attribute domains, and necessary conversions. Information about attribute names, aliases, types, measurement units, corresponding domains, and conversions into canonical form is stored. This information is also used whenever implicit or explicit data conversions are required by a global query. The system's knowledge base contains this information and a corresponding set of rules. The inference engine uses the rules stored in the knowledge base to remove ambiguity from a global query and to derive an efficient query evaluation plan. OMNIBASE also supports extended transaction models. The Carnot project addresses the integration of distributed and heterogeneous information sources (e.g., database systems, expert systems, business workflows, etc.). It uses a knowledge base called Cyc to store information about the global schema. The InfoSleuth project [B+97] is the successor of Carnot and presents an approach for retrieving and processing information in a dynamic Web-based environment. It integrates agent technology, domain ontologies, and information brokering to handle the interoperation of data and services over information networks. Information Manifold is a system that provides uniform access to collections of heterogeneous information sources on the World Wide Web. It provides a high-level query system to describe the contents and capabilities of information sources using a knowledge base with a rich domain model. The focus of this system is the efficient execution of high-level queries over several information sources. [LRO96] proposed the algorithms to create executable plans for given descriptions and queries. As in InfoSleuth, a centralized knowledge base is used for describing the information space.

The VODAK project is mainly concerned with the dynamic integration of heterogeneous and autonomous information sources. The common data model, called VML (VODAK Model Language), is object-oriented. The export schemas of the local systems are defined by means of metaclasses. To overcome structural heterogeneity, the corresponding local subschemas are identified and then adapted to each other. This is done by augmenting transformations so that the subschemas become isomorphic (e.g., generate roles of a class, introduce additional abstractions, etc.). A graphical representation of schemas is also provided. A declarative approach is used for resolving structural conflicts by performing graph operations on the schema graph. Users can define the correspondence between schemas, and the augmenting transformations are automatically generated. The proposed heterogeneous transaction model presents many innovative ideas, including the fact that local systems export methods instead of read-write operations. In addition, language constructs are provided to define subtransactions. The model also provides semantic-based serializability. The Interbase system provides a global interface for accessing a variety of local systems, including SAS, Sybase, Ingres, DB2, and Unix utilities. It uses the InterSQL language as both a query language and a transaction specification language. InterSQL is based on FSQL (Federated SQL) developed in the FBASE project, which is a federated heterogeneous object database system. Interbase uses the extended transaction model Flex, and InterSQL provides facilities to allow users to define Flex tasks and appropriate commitment methods. Translation and integration are not supported in FBASE and Interbase.

DOMS (Distributed Object Management System) is an object system that is used to integrate native objects and external autonomous and heterogeneous systems. The implemented prototype is used for connecting Apple Macintosh Hypercard applications, the Sybase relational DBMS, and the ONTOS object DBMS. With regard to transaction management, the DOMS approach is to propose a parametric model that would capture the capabilities of most extended transaction models. OIS (Operational Integration System) and CIS (Commandos Integration System) are generalized integration tools that provide application environments with a global interface for accessing data in heterogeneous sources (e.g., file systems, information retrieval systems, etc.). These systems propose an operational mapping approach, which is based on defining correspondence between operations instead of defining correspondence between data elements. On top of each local system, an object-oriented view is defined as a set of operations (operations on objects and classes) on a set of abstract data. The operational mapping is defined as the implementation of these operations in terms of the operations of the local systems. In this way, each local system must provide an interface in the form of an implementation for a predefined set of operations. The A La Carte toolkit provides an extensible object-oriented framework that can be used to integrate a set of heterogeneous DBMSs. The focus is on the modeling of transaction management services as a set of objects of a special type.

The FINDIT project addresses issues of interoperability in very large multidatabases. It aims to achieve scalability through the incremental discovery and formation of interrelationships between information repositories. Clusters (groups) of information repositories are established through the sharing of high-level meta-information, and individual sites join and leave these clusters at their discretion. Cluster formation and maintenance, as well as the exploration of the interrelationship structure, occurs via a special-purpose language called Tassili. Tassili provides constructs for educating users about the available space of information, for finding the target databases that are most likely to hold the required type of information, and for connecting to databases and performing remote queries. The process is enabled by the introduction of a layer of metalevel software that surrounds each local DBMS, which knows a system's capabilities and functionality. An object-oriented approach is used for the description of the metalevel. WebFINDIT, the successor of FINDIT, provides a framework for sharing structured data on the Web [BB97]. The WebFINDIT prototype has been implemented using the latest in object technology, including CORBA as a distributed computing platform (SUN's NEO), SUN's Java, and Database Connectivity Gateways to access native databases. Different off-the-shelf database systems (mSQL, Oracle, Ontos, and ObjectStore) have been used as a test bed.

Thor is an object distributed DBMS. It aims to allow programs written in different languages to share Thor's objects. Transaction management in Thor is similar to the traditional transaction management in a distributed database system. The two-phase commit is used as a commitment protocol. The concurrency control is based on objects instead of pages or segments. Thor's main strength is its emphasis on system performance (e.g., object-caching, physical storage). Thor is different from other systems described here in that it does not support the integration of preexisting systems. The HKBMS is another system that differs from other projects; it does not consider the integration of heterogeneous DBMSs, but rather emphasizes the integration of multiple heterogeneous rule-based systems and a database system. An implemented prototype of this system consists of three expert systems (written in CLIP, PROLOG, and C) and an Ingres DBMS. At the global level, HKBMS uses OSAM* (Object-Oriented Semantic Association Model), which integrates semantic modeling with the object-oriented paradigm.

Recent projects such as TSIMMIS [PGMW95] and DISCO [TRV96] are based on wrapper/mediator architectures [Wie92]. TSIMMIS is a system for semistructured information source integration. To this end, the common object information exchange model EOM and the query language LOREL are proposed. They propose rules for query reformulation to resolve mismatch in the querying of different data sources. An important functionality of TSIMMIS is the automatic generation of translators and mediators. The DISCO project uses an extension of ODMG-93 and OQL [Cat94] as a common data model and query language. They provide support for unavailable information sources and transparent addition of new information sources. The answer to a query may include data from available information sources and another query for the remaining unavailable information sources. Tables 1.1 and 1.2 summarize some of the systems discussed in this section. The multidatabase function, the common data model, and global access interface are presented in Table 1.1. Translation, integration, and transaction issues are presented in Table 1.2. The summary provided in these tables is based on those presented in [BE96].

1.5
Summary

This chapter provides a general overview of research in multidatabase systems. It defines the relevant terminology, discusses the architecture, and presents a taxonomy of multidatabase systems. The most important issues are reviewed. Finally, several prototypes are described as a means of demonstrating how various issues are handled in practice.

Bibliography

[AAK+93]   J. Albert, R. Ahmed, W. Kent, M. Ketabchi, W. Litwin, A. Rafii, and M. Shan. Automatic importation of relational schemas in Pegasus. In *Proceedings IEEE RIDE-IMS*, April 1993.

[AAM97]   G. Alonso, D. El Abbadi, and C. Mohan. Functionality and limitations of current workflow management systems. *IEEE Expert*, 1997.

[AS96]   G. Alonso and H. Schek. Research issues in large workflow management systems. In *Proceedings of the NSF Workshop: Workflow and Process Automation in Information Systems*, May 1996.

TABLE 1.1
Multidatabase features.

System	Type	Components	CDM	GAI	Key Features
Pegasus	Complete system (loosely coupled)	Information systems of various data models	Iris data model, functional and object-oriented	HOSQL (extension of OSQL)	Treatment of conflicts, foreign functions, query optimization
VODAK	Complete system (loosely coupled)	Database systems	VML (VODAK Model Language), object-oriented	VML	Use of metaclass, new ideas for transaction management, and declarative approach for resolving conflicts
CIS/OIS	Integration tool (tightly coupled)	File systems, databases, information retrieval, etc.	Abstract data model (CIS), integration data model (OIS), object-oriented	QL, extension of a functional-based language	Operational mapping
OMS	Integration framework (loosely coupled)	Engineering information systems	FUGUE model, functional and object-oriented	Extension of a functional-based language	Cooperative transaction and user-specified correctness
DOMS	Complete system (loosely coupled)	Database systems, hypermedia, application programs, etc.	FROOM (Functional Relational Object-Oriented Model)	Extension of a functional-based language	Complete framework for distributed object architectures
Carnot	Complete system (loosely coupled)	Database systems, knowledge-base systems, and process models	Instead of CDM, it uses a knowledge base called Cyc	GCL (Global Context language), based on extended first-order logic	Use of a knowledge base for database integration
FINDIT	A system for data sharing in large multidatabases (loosely coupled)	Heterogeneous databases and object-oriented metainformation repositories (called co-databases)	Object-oriented	Tassili (special-purpose functional and object-oriented language)	Provides architectural constructs for the discovery of information interrelationships in large multidatabases
Thor	Distributed DBMS that provides sharing of objects among heterogeneous distributed systems (loosely coupled)	Not applicable	Based on Argus, object-oriented	Based on Argus	A different approach for handling heterogeneous information (sharing information in the form of Thor's objects), performance issues
FBASE	Integration framework (tightly coupled)	Database systems	Object-oriented	FSQL (Federated SQL)	Limited global language
Interbase	Complete system (tightly coupled)	Database systems and Unix utilities	Object-oriented	InterSQL (based on FSQL, also provides transaction specification)	Use of an extended transaction model, language support for transaction specification, treatment of commitment
A La Carte	Integration framework (tightly coupled)	Database systems	Not applicable	Not applicable	Use of object-orientation for transaction management services
HKBMS	System that integrates expert systems with a database system (loosely coupled)	Many heterogeneous expert systems with a database system	OSAM* (Object-Oriented Semantic Association Model)	Natural language based	Integration of expert systems with a database

TABLE 1.2
Translation, integration, and transaction management issues.

System	Translation	Integration	Transaction
Pegasus	During importation, automatic translation of relational models	Importation (virtual classes), conflicts (domain mismatch, naming, schema mismatch, and object identification)	Not supported
VODAK	During importation, uses metaclasses (implement interfaces modeling local systems)	Uses metaclasses to map the modeling constructs of local systems to the CDM. Uses the graphical representation of the local schemas to identify structural correspondences among them and then applies augmentation operations	Three-level open-nested transactions. The interface of local systems is considered in terms of methods instead of r/w operations, semantic (commutativity based) serializability
CIS/OIS	Operational mapping	Not supported	Not supported
OMS	Not discussed	Importation (virtual classes, an object-algebra is defined with a set of functions that generate new sets of objects from existing ones)	Nested transactions
DOMS	Not discussed	Importation (an object-algebra is defined with a set of functions that generate new sets of objects from existing ones)	Programmable transactions
Carnot	Special frames are defined for common information sources	Uses axioms to express mapping between two expressions that have equivalent meaning	User-specified correctness (provides a language based on ACTA for defining relationships between the subtransactions)
FINDIT	A special database (called co-database) is used as a repository to map types of information from local databases to co-databases	Integration happens at the metatype level	Not supported
Thor	Not applicable	Not applicable	Objects are the basis for concurrency control, commit protocol (2PC), optimistic concurrency control, primary copy for replication
FBASE	Performed by special servers		Not supported
Interbase	Performed by special servers	Not supported	The Flex extended transaction model; language support for transaction specification; an elaborate treatment of commitment at the subtransaction level
A La Carte	Not applicable	Not supported	Properties and dependencies of different transaction models are part of the system metamodel; the functionality of the transaction management of each component is modeled as a set of objects
HKBMS	Not discussed	A function graph is defined to describe relationships between variables referenced in the rules of the component systems; value conflicts are resolved by the administrator	Not supported

[ASD+91]   Rafi Ahmed, Phillipe De Smedt, Weimin Du, William Kent, Mohammad A. Ketabchi, Witold A. Litwin, Abbas Rafii, and Ming-Chien Shan. The Pegasus heterogeneous multidatabase system. *IEEE Computer* 24(12):19–27, December 1991.

[ASSR93]   P. C. Attie, M. P. Singh, A. Sheth, and M. Rusinkiewicz. Specifying and enforcing intertask dependencies. In *Proceedings of the 19th VLDB Conference*, pages 134–143, 1993.

[AT93]   P. Atzeni and R. Torlone. A metamodel approach for the management of multiple models and the translation of schemes. *Information Systems* 18(6), June 1993.

[B+97]   B. Bohrer et al. Infosleuth: Semantic integration of information in open and dynamic environments. In *Proceedings of the ACM International Conference on Management of Data (SIGMOD)*, 1997.

[BB97]   B. Benatallah and A. Bouguettaya. Data sharing on the web. In *Proceedings of the First International Enterprise Distributed Object Computing Workshop—EDOC'97*, October 1997.

[BE96]   Omran Bukhres and Ahmed K. Elmagarmid, editors. *Object-Oriented Multidatabase Systems: A Solution for Advanced Applications*. Englewood Cliffs, NJ: Prentice Hall, 1996.

[BGML+90]   Yuri Breitbart, Hector Garcia-Molina, Witold Litwin, Nick Roussopoulos, Marek Rusinkiewicz, Glenn Thompson, and Gio Wiederhold. Final report of the workshop on multidatabases and semantic interoperability. In *First Workshop on Multidatabases and Semantic Interoperability*, November 1990.

[BLN86]   C. Batini, M. Lenzerini, and S. B. Navathe. A comparative analysis of methodologies for database schema integration. *ACM Computing Surveys* 18(4):324–364, December 1986.

[BPK95]   A. Bouguettaya, M. Papazoglou, and R. King. On building a hyperdistributed database. *Information Systems, an International Journal* 20(7):557–577, 1995.

[BS95]   Michael L. Brodie and Michael Stonebraker. *Migrating Legacy Systems: Gateways, Interfaces, and the Incremental Approach*. San Francisco: Morgan Kaufmann, 1995.

[Cat94]   R. Cattell, editor. *The Object Database Standard: ODMG-93.* San Francisco: Morgan Kaufmann, 1994.

[DE89]   Weimin Du and Ahmed K. Elmagarmid. Quasi serializability: A correctness criterion for global concurrency control in InterBase. In *Proceedings of the 15th International VLDB Conference*, pages 347–355, 1989.

[ED90]   A. Elmagarmid and W. Du. A paradigm for concurrency control in heterogeneous distributed database systems. In *Proceedings of the Sixth International Conference on Data Engineering*, February 1990.

[Elm92]   A. Elmagarmid, editor. *Database Transaction Models for Advanced Applications.* San Mateo, CA: Morgan Kaufmann, 1992.

[EP90]   A. Elmagarmid and C. Pu, editors. Heterogeneous databases: Special issue. *ACM Computing Surveys* 22(3), September 1990.

[GCO90]   R. Gagliardi, M. Caneve, and G. Oldano. An operational approach to the integration of distributed heterogeneous environments. In *Proceedings of the IEEE PARBASE-90 Conference*, 1990.

[GMS87]   H. Garcia-Molina and K. Salem. SAGAs. In *Proceedings of the ACM Conference on Management of Data (SIGMOD)*, pages 249–259, 1987.

[GRS94]   D. Georgakopoulos, M. Rusinkiewicz, and A. Sheth. Using tickets to enforce the serializability of multidatabase transactionns. *IEEE Transactions on Knowledge and Data Engineering*, February 1994.

[HBP94]   A. R. Hurson, M. W. Bright, and H. Pakzad. *Multidatabase Systems: An Advanced Solution for Global Information Sharing.* Los Alamitos, CA: IEEE Computer Society Press, 1994.

[HM85]   D. Heimbigner and D. McLeod. A federated architecture for information systems. *ACM Transactions on Office Information Systems* 3(3):253–278, July 1985.

[HM93]   J. Hammer and D. McLeod. An approach to resolving semantic heterogeneity in a federation of autonomous, heterogeneous database systems. *International Journal of Intelligent and Cooperative Information Systems* 2(1):51–83, March 1993.

[HNSD93]   D. K. Hsiao, E. J. Neuhold, and R. Sacks-Davis, editors. *IFIP DS-5 Semantics of Interoperable Database Systems*. New York: Elsevier Science, 1993.

[Joh94]   P. Johanneson. A method for translating relational schemas into conceptual schemas. In *Proceedings of the 10th International Conference on Data Engineering*, 1994.

[KDN90]   M. Kaul, K. Drosten, and E. J. Nuehold. Viewsystem: Integrating heterogeneous information bases by object-oriented views. In *Proceedings of the Sixth International Conference on Data Engineering*, pages 2–10, 1990.

[LDS92]   B. Liskov, M. Day, and L. Shira. Distributed object management in thor. In *The International Workshop on Distributed Object Management*, 1992.

[LE90]   Y. Leu and A. Elmagarmid. A hierarchical approach to concurrency control for multidatabase systems. In *Second International Symposium on Databases in Parallel and Distributed Systems*, July 1990.

[Lit94]   W. Litwin. *Multidatabase Systems*. Englewood Cliffs, NJ: Prentice Hall, 1994.

[LMR90]   W. Litwin, L. Mark, and N. Roussopoulos. Interoperability of multiple autonomous databases. *ACM Computing Surveys* 22(3):267–293, September 1990.

[LRO96]   A. Levy, A. Rajaraman, and J. Ordille. Querying heterogeneous information sources using source descriptions. In *Proceedings of the 22nd International VLDB Conference*, 1996.

[Mad96]   Stuart E. Madnick. Are we moving toward an information superhighway or a tower of Babel? The challenge of large-scale semantic heterogeneity. In *Proceedings of the 12th International Conference on Data Engineering*, pages 2–8. Los Alamitos, CA: IEEE Computer Society Press, 1996.

[MAGW95]   C. Mohan, G. Alonso, R. Gunthor, and X. Wang. Exotica: A research perspective on workflow management systems. *Data Engineering Bulletin* 18(1):19–26, March 1995.

[MBP95]   S. Milliner, A. Bouguettaya, and M. Papazoglou. A scalable architecture for autonomous heterogeneous database interactions. In *Proceeedings of the VLDB Conference (VLDB)*, September 1995.

[ME93]   J. G. Mullen and A. K. Elmagarmid. InterSQL: A multidatabase approach to federated databases. In *The 1993 Workshop on Database Programming Languages*, 1993.

[MHG⁺92]   F. Manola, S. Heiler, D. Georgakopoulos, M. Hornick, and M. Brodie. Distributed object management. *International Journal of Intelligent and Cooperative Information Systems* 1(1), March 1992.

[MKS97]   S. Mehrotra, H. F. Korth, and A. Silberschatz. Concurrency control in hierarchical multidatabase systems. *VLDB* 6(2), 1997.

[Mos85]   J. E. B. Moss. *Nested Transactions: An Approach to Reliable Distributed Computing*. Cambridge, MA: MIT Press, 1985.

[MRB⁺92]   Sharad Mehrotra, Rajeev Rastogi, Yuri Breitbart, Henry F. Korth, and Avi Silberschatz. The concurrency control problems in multidatabases: Characteristics and solutions. In *Proceedings of the ACM SIGMOD International Conference on Management of Data*, pages 288–297, June 1992.

[MRKS91]   S. Mehrotra, Rajeev Rastogi, Henry F. Korth, and Avi Silberschatz. Non-serializeable executions in heterogeneous distributed database systems. In *Proceedings of the First International Conference on Parallel and Distributed Systems*, December 1991.

[MRKS92]   S. Mehrotra, R. Rastogi, H. F. Korth, and A. Silberschatz. Relaxing serializability in multidatabase systems. In *Proceedings of the Second International Workshop on Research Issues on Data Engineering: Transaction and Query Peocessing*, 1992.

[Mul92]   J. G. Mullen. Fbase: A federated objectbase system. *International Journal of Computer Science and Engineering* 7(2), April 1992.

[NWM93]   J. R. Nicol, C. T. Wilkes, and F. A. Manola. Object orientation in heterogeneous distributed computing systems. *IEEE Computer* 26(6), June 1993.

[OAB94]   M. Ouzzani, M. Atroun, and N. Belkhodja. A top-down approach to two-level serializability. In *Proceedings of the 20th International Conference on VLDB*, 1994.

[OV91]   M. Tamer Özsu and Patrick Valduriez. *Principles of Distributed Database Systems*. Englewood Cliffs, NJ: Prentice Hall, 1991.

[PDBH97]   M. Papazoglou, A. Delis, A. Bouguettaya, and M. Haghjoo. Class library support for workflow environments and applications. *IEEE Transactions on Computers* 46(6), June 1997.

[PGMW95]   Y. Papakonstantinou, H. Garcia-Molina, and J. Widom. Object exchange across heterogeneous information sources. In *Proceedings of the International Conference on Data Engineering*, 1995.

[PLC91]   C. Pu, A. Leff, and S. F. Chen. Heterogeneous and autonomous transaction processing. *IEEE Computer* 24(12):64–72, December 1991.

[Pu88]   Calton Pu. Superdatabases for composition of heterogeneous databases. In *International IEEE Conference Management of Data*, pages 548–555, 1988.

[RELL90]   M. E. Rusinkiewicz, A. K. Elmagarmid, Y. Leu, and W. Litwin. Extending the transaction model to capture more meaning. *ACM SIGMOD Record* 19(1):3–7, March 1990.

[REMC+88] M. Rusinkiewicz, R. El-Masri, B. Czejdo, D. Georgakopoulos, G. Karabatis, A. Jamoussi, K. Loa, and Y. Li. OMNIBASE: Design and implementation of a multidatabase system. *Distributed Processing Technical Committee Newsletter* 10(2):20–28, November 1988.

[She96]   A. Sheth, editor. *Proceeding NSF Workshop: Workflow and Process Automation in Information Systems*, May 1996.

[SKS97]   A. Silberschatz, H. F. Korth, and S. Sudarshan. *Database System Concepts (Third Edition)*. New York: McGraw-Hill, 1997.

[SL90]   A. Sheth and J. Larson. Federated database systems for managing distributed, heterogeneous, and autonomous databases. *ACM Computing Surveys* 22(3):183–236, September 1990.

[SP94]   S. Spaccapietra and C. Parent. View integration: A step forward in solving structural conflicts. *IEEE Transactions on Knowledge and Data Engineering* 6(2), April 1994.

[SSU91]   A. Silberschatz, M. Stonebraker, and J. F. Ullman. Database systems: Achievements and opportunities. *Communications of the ACM* 34(10), October 1991.

[Sto94]   M. Stonebraker, editor. *Readings in Database Systems*. San Francisco: Morgan Kaufmann, 1994.

[SYE⁺90]   P. Scheuermann, C. Yu, A. Elmagarmid, H. Garcia-Molina, F. Manola, D. McLeod, A. Rosenthal, and M. Templeton. Report on the workshop on heterogeneous database systems. In *SIGMOD Record*, volume 19, pages 23–31. New York: ACM, December 1990.

[TRV96]   A. Tomasic, L. Raschid, and P. Valduriez. Scaling heterogeneous databases and the design of disco. In *Proceedings of the International Conference on Distributed Computer Systems*, 1996.

[WCH⁺93]   D. Woelk, P. Cannata, M. Huhns, W. Shen, and C. Tomlinson. Using carnot for enterprise information integration. In *The Second International Conference on Parallel and Distributed Information Systems*, 1993.

[Wie92]   G. Wiederhold. Mediators in the architecture of future information systems. *Computer* 25(3):38–49, March 1992.

[WS96]   D. Worah and A. Sheth. What do advanced transaction models have to offer for workflows? In *Proceedings of the International Workshop in Advanced Transaction Models and Architectures (ATMA)*, 1996.

2

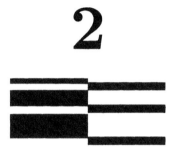

Local Autonomy
and Its Effects on
Multidatabase Systems

Ahmed Elmagarmid
Weimin Du
Rafi Ahmed

Introduction

During the last few decades, large organizations have used numerous database systems that were designed to run in isolation. The database systems are usually heterogeneous and do not cooperate with each other. It has become apparent that great improvements in productivity will be gained if the systems can be integrated—that is, made to cooperate with each other—to support global applications accessing multiple databases. This has motivated the study of multidatabase systems (MDBSs).

An MDBS is a federation of preexisting database systems (called local database systems, or LDBSs). An MDBS is the natural result of shifting priorities and needs of an organization that wants to create larger databases using heterogeneous database systems it has acquired. For many applications, an MDBS is an attractive alternative to using a set of database systems because it supports global applications accessing multiple, heterogeneous databases. An MDBS is different from a traditional homogeneous distributed database system in that it interconnects LDBSs while allowing existing applications developed on each of the LDBSs to continue working without modification.

System Model

Figure 2.1 shows a general MDBS model. The system consists of a global database management system (GDBMS) and a set of LDBSs. Each LDBS has a local DBMS (LDBMS) managing a local database. The GDBMS has its own database containing integration information, such as a global system catalog. Local databases are integrated in the sense that a single global schema is constructed from local schemas exported by the underlying LDBSs. Global queries against the global schema can then be submitted to the GDBMS to access data stored in multiple local databases. Local queries may also be issued directly to each LDBMS without consulting the GDBMS. The GDBMS is responsible for maintaining the global schema, decomposing global queries into subqueries executable by each LDBMS, coordinating executions of the subqueries, and ensuring consistency of the MDBS.

Compared with traditional distributed database systems such as R* [S+84], an MDBS has the following special characteristics.

- LDBSs are preexisting database systems and therefore are usually heterogeneous. There are two levels of heterogeneity. At the system level, LDBMSs may support different data models (e.g., relational, hierarchical, object-oriented), employ different query optimization strategies and different concurrency protocols (e.g., two-phase locking, time-stamp ordering), etc. At the data level, information may be represented differently, e.g., explicitly as a data item in one LDBS or implicitly as a relationship between two data items in other LDBSs.

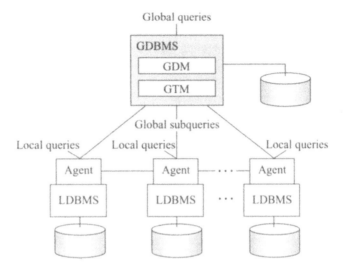

FIGURE 2.1
Multidatabase system model.

- A GDBMS usually has limited resources. This may be due to the lack of access to either system information or system operations of underlying LDBMSs that are essential for GDBMSs to execute global queries correctly and efficiently. For example, LDBSs may not export their cost models to the GDBMS, making good global query optimization challenging. LDBMSs usually do not allow the GDBMS to access their internal data structure, such as index trees. Because of this limitation, the GDBMS must submit global subqueries to LDBMSs in string format, rather than more efficient internal query trees, resulting in inefficient execution.

- Local queries may be independently submitted to LDBMSs without informing the GDBMS. Local queries may interact with subqueries submitted by the GDBMS in any of the ways allowed by the LDBMSs, making coordination of subquery executions difficult.

Local Autonomy

Local autonomy results from the fact that LDBSs are designed, developed, and administered independently. Informally, local autonomy in an MDBS defines the ability of each LDBS to control accesses to its data by other LDBSs, as well as the ability to access and manipulate its own data independently of other LDBSs.

It is desirable to preserve local autonomy in MDBSs. First, because an LDBS was originally an independent database system, it may have had many application programs developed on it. Such applications should continue to be executable in an MDBS. Second, LDBSs often belong to different organizations that maintain full control over their data. It is desirable for these organizations to retain a high degree of control within MDBSs.

Local autonomy makes it possible to add a database system to an MDBS and just as easily take one away. Further, because of local autonomy, supporting global applications in MDBSs is both much more difficult and quite different from supporting them in homogeneous database systems. The lack of understanding of local autonomy and its effects has greatly hindered the study and development of MDBSs.

Local autonomy can be better understood by discussing its requirements and the ways it could be violated [GPZ86, CR93, CR94a].

We distinguish between design and execution aspects of local autonomy. *Design autonomy* refers to the ability of an LDBS to choose its own design with respect to issues such as data model, query language, and transaction processing strategy. *Execution autonomy* refers to the ability of an LDBMS to decide whether and how to execute queries without distinguishing between regular local queries and global subqueries submitted by the GDBMS. For example, an LDBMS should be free to abort a global subtransaction to resolve a local deadlock.

From the GDBMS's point of view, local autonomy takes several different forms. The most obvious one is heterogeneity (a consequence of design autonomy). Other forms include refusing to provide the service necessary for the GDBMS to do the job and insisting on doing things that may result in either inefficient execution of global queries or an inconsistent MDBS.

From an LDBS's point of view, autonomy can be violated in three different ways: being modified (both systems and data) to behave differently (*violation through modification*), being forced to do things it was not originally designed to do (*violation through proscription*), or being prevented from doing things it was originally able to do (*violation through prescription*). For example, local autonomy is violated through modification if local data has been either reorganized or modified to make it consistent with data at other sites. Similarly, local autonomy is violated through proscription if the GDBMS assumes or requires that LDBMSs provide local serialization order to ensure global serializability. Local autonomy is also violated through prescription if the GDBMS ensures global database consistency only if local transactions do not update replicated data.

There are two general approaches to deal with problems caused by local autonomy when implementing a system. The *pessimistic approach* avoids violating local autonomy by either reducing functionalities of the global system or imposing restrictions on ways global functions are implemented. For example, global queries may not be allowed (or allowed in a limited way) to access some local data in order to avoid undesired interactions with local transactions. In contrast to the pessimistic approach, the *optimistic approach* compromises local autonomy to some extent but tries to detect and deal with possible problems afterward.

In general, it is impossible to support global applications in a consistent and efficient way without compromising local autonomy. For example, the GDBMS cannot ensure mutual consistency of a replicated MDBS if each LDBMS updates local copies of replicated data independently without informing the GDBMS. In practice, each MDBS has its own autonomy requirements, determined not only by the willingness of LDBSs to cooperate but also by functionalities the GDBMS provides. For an MDBS, autonomy requirements are not all equally important. For example, it might be reasonable to add an agent at each LDBS to identify updates to replicated data by local queries. However, it is generally impractical to expect LDBMSs to change their concurrency control strategies.

Pessimistic and optimistic approaches described above are each suitable to specific types of problems. For example, if similar information has been stored in several LDBSs but in different forms, the only thing the GDBMS can do is to retrieve the data from all sites and resolve the inconsistency (i.e., the optimistic approach). On the other hand, the GDBMS should always be pessimistic on committing a global subtransaction, unless compensation of committed transactions can be easily performed at LDBSs. Sometimes, both approaches can be applied (e.g., concurrency control), and the decision should be made based on actual application environments (see Section 2.3).

Outline

Processing global queries that access multiple LDBSs takes place in three major phases. First, the LDBSs must be integrated so that a global schema is constructed. This phase occurs only once[1] for a given set of LDBSs and is usually called *schema integration*. Second, each global query must then be decomposed and translated into a set of subqueries that can be executed by each LDBMS. This phase is known as *query processing* and is needed once for each global query. The last phase, called *query execution* or *transaction management*, executes the previously produced global subqueries, along with possible local transactions at local sites.

In the next three sections, we discuss the three phases, with emphasis on the effects of local autonomy. We discuss problems caused by local autonomy and present existing and possible solutions for some of them. Section 2.4 summarizes the chapter.

---

[1] The global schema may have to be updated infrequently to reflect changes of local schemas.

2.1
Schema Integration

One approach to an MDBS is to provide a single uniform and unified interface for multiple autonomous and heterogeneous LDBSs. Even though the motivations for integration may differ from domain to domain, many of the underlying issues are common to a broad range of applications. We have discussed various types of local database autonomy, which can require a spectrum of conformation to the underlying LDBMSs and impose a variety of constraints on the modification of the data and schema in the LDBSs.

A three-layered schema [SAD⁺95] framework facilitates the integration of heterogeneous systems. The first layer contains the native schemas of the LDBSs. The second layer contains an imported schema that is directly transformed from the schema of LDBSs into the data model of the global system; the imported schema still reflects the native idiosyncrasies of underlying systems. The third layer is a conceptual unified schema, which defines a consistent set of rules and constructs at a higher level of abstraction in order to manage the integrity, uniformity, access, and manipulation of shared information. The unified schema conceals the incongruence among LDBSs that arises as a result of their local autonomy.

We must distinguish integration technology from interfacing technology (e.g., a simple access capability through gateways). The key difference between them is the integrity and resolution of data and schematic conflict. Database autonomy, data integrity, and schematic discrepancies are the overriding issues in the integration approach, whereas they cause little problem in the interfacing approach. Consequently, while a two-schema approach suffices for the interfacing approach, a three-schema approach is highly desirable in the integration approach.

The object-oriented approach can be valuable in integrating heterogeneous systems, but it is not a panacea. The conceptual advantages of object-oriented approaches must be backed up by the implementation of considerable interface support. Current research on object-oriented database systems addresses some of these issues, but little work exists that combines both elements of object-oriented research and heterogeneous distributed DBMS research.

A comprehensive discussion of a spectrum of representational heterogeneity is presented in Section 4.2. Because of the large number of issues and variables involved, a comprehensive solution to the problem of integrating distributed heterogeneous information systems has remained an elusive dream. Many schema integration techniques have been proposed, which provide solutions to some of the problems. An overview of these techniques is given in Chapter 5.

2.1.1   Heterogeneous Data Models

Conceptual data model heterogeneity is a direct consequence of the database design autonomy of local DBMSs. At the first step in integration, local database schemas are transformed into the data model construct of the central system. Some underlying data models may not be entirely incompatible; for example, the mapping of underlying relational databases into a semantic object-oriented model does not pose unresolvable problems. Relations that represent entities can be mapped into user-defined types (classes), while relationships expressed by foreign keys can be mapped into associations among classes; information about inclusion dependencies can also provide hints for creating supertype-subtype relations [AAK+93].

However, consider the process of mapping a pair of child-parent segments in a hierarchical data model. In semantic models, these associations are invariably bidirectional, whereas in hierarchical models, they are inherently unidirectional. Generally, logical pointers can be defined in the program control block (PCB) of hierarchical DBMSs to express bidirectional associations. However, local autonomy precludes such schema changes in the underlying system, and query translation must take care of the traversal from the child to the parent. On the other hand, if logical pointers have been used to express such associations, the mapping technique must recognize that the two pairs of unidirectional associations are essentially a single pair and hence must be translated into two classes with a bidirectional association.

2.1.2   Resolution of Schematic Discrepancies

Schematic discrepancies arise when a given data modeling concept is expressed using data modeling constructs in different underlying LDBMSs [KIGS93, BLN86]. These differences may be in structure, data types, or in semantic concepts, which reflect autonomy in the design of schema for a universe of discourse. Semantic proximity or aproximity is discussed in Section 3.2. In order to resolve these conflicts and provide a capability to access and manipulate data in heterogeneous LDBSs, a unified schema should be defined with powerful semantic constructs. The design of such a system requires that a data definition language be used that is more expressive than that of local databases; furthermore, this language must be capable of resolving the conflicts and discrepancies in the schemas of these LDBSs. The capability for defining abstract types (virtual classes) [ASD+91, KIGS93, Mot87, DH84] has been deemed important for resolving schematic conflict. The definition of abstract types derives the collection of attributes and functions (methods), and materializes the instances of the abstract type from underlying types in the imported schema.

One of the most common schematic conflicts is the *missing* attribute in similar entities in the imported schema. The solution is to define an abstract type that contains an aggregation of attributes from the underlying types and returns null for those instances that originate from the type that has the missing attribute. However, the query that explicitly retrieves those object instances that have null value for the attribute must not retrieve instances from the type that has the missing attribute, since the attribute itself is undefined rather than the values being unavailable.

Schematic conflicts that relate to conflicting names, data types, units, and precision have obvious solutions, such as renaming and isomorphic conversion of data types and units in the unified schema [KIGS93]. However, update remains a problem if two underlying types use nonisomorphic domains, such as using letters and numbers to express the attribute grade of a course.

Conflicts in attribute representation arise when the domain of semantically similar types, say T_1 and T_2, are incompatible (e.g., the domain of T_1's attribute is a user-defined type A, whereas that of an equivalent attribute of T_2 is a primitive type). The solution that is generally proposed is that a uniquely valued attribute of A, which must be compatible with the domain of the attribute of T_2, is chosen to be represented at the abstract type level. However, there is a loss of information—information that represented an explicit association between T_1 and A.

In an extreme case of local autonomy, each LDBS may insist on viewing the unified schema in terms of its own native schema constructs. In [KLK91], a second-order language extension, which allows variables to range over data as well as metadata (types, functions, relations, database names), has been proposed to deal with schematic discrepancies and provide these views. An interesting feature of this proposal is the dynamic view capability: the number schema constructs (e.g., types, classes, relations, functions) dynamically change corresponding to changes in the data values in some underlying database. However, in such an extension, both the automatic query and update translation have to be compromised.

2.1.3   Reconciliation of Data Values

Local DBMSs evolve independently and may model overlapping universes of discourse. Therefore, even without an abstract type, instances of two types in the imported schema may semantically represent the same real-world object. A language facility provides the specification of conditions under which two object instances are considered equivalent [SAD+95]. Note that a circularly defined object equivalence relationship may lead to the equivalence of the object of the same type. This violates the native semantic autonomy of the underlying database and also exacts a severe run-time performance penalty.

As mentioned before, the data constructs in the imported schema layer faithfully reflect the LDBSs; such a reflection includes discrepancies in data values. A critical task of the integration mechanism is the reconciliation of disparate data values of identical attributes of similar classes. A reconciliation of these data values can be performed by applying an aggregate function (e.g., max, min, sum, avg, etc.) or a DBA-supplied reconciler routine on these values. The update of an abstract type's attributes, however, is not always feasible.

2.1.4   Query and Update Translation

The central system must be capable of taking a single query against the unified schema, decomposing it against various LDBSs, and translating and executing the queries in an optimal way.

Due to local autonomy, underlying DBMSs may have different query processing capabilities; for example, hierarchical and network DBMSs do not support aggregate functions and group-by. Therefore, the central query processor must perform those operations that are not available in the underlying DBMSs. Another example is a query that involves a self-join operation on a class that has been mapped from a hierarchical or network database. The autonomy of these systems disallows such operations, and hence they must be performed by the central query processor in the postprocessing phase.

In MDBSs, the integration technology and the translation methods employed in constructing a unified schema are essentially similar to a view mapping problem. Views are generally defined within database systems using the facilities of the system's DML, but view update techniques, in spite of their long history, have met with limited success [DB82, BS81]. Several resolution and reconciliation mechanisms defined in Sections 2.1.2 and 2.1.3 are simply not updatable. Some can be updated only through the imported schema; for example, if an aggregate function is used to reconcile disparate data values, the abstract type in the unified schema cannot be updated, as it has to be decomposed to two or more values. The types in the imported schema, however, are updatable in this case.

2.2
Query Processing

There are four major steps in processing an MDBS query: compilation, unification decomposition, optimization, and translation.

First, an MDBS query is compiled and transformed into an internal form. At the unification decomposition step, integrated data items are replaced with corresponding local data items, along with necessary inconsistency resolution functions. The query tree is then optimized. The optimized query tree is analyzed, and all subtrees local to a single LDBS are identified. Finally, an executable query tree is constructed by translating each identified subtree into a subquery that is executable by the underlying LDBMS.

The compilation and translation steps are either straightforward or similar to those of traditional database systems. In this section, we study problems related to the other two steps.

2.2.1   Unification Decomposition

The main purpose of unification decomposition is to determine at both compile and run time how integrated data can be constructed and which local

data should be used for its construction. The problem could be very complicated, as local data at different sites may be equivalent to each other, according
to the integration criteria. Because it affects system performance, the issue is
significant. For a reasonably complicated MDBS, a simple query that accesses
a local data item at one LDBS may have to access an arbitrary number of data
items at other LDBSs, due to either direct or indirect equivalence relationships.

The difficulty of unification decomposition is mainly due to the fact that
LDBMSs may autonomously update local data, thus affecting equivalence relationships between data at other LDBSs. Consider, for example, three local
data items d_1, d_2, d_3 at three different LDBSs. Suppose that d_1 is directly
equivalent to d_2, but not to d_3, and d_2 is equivalent to d_3. Whether d_1 is indirectly equivalent to d_3 (assuming equivalent is a transitive relation) depends
on the existence of d_2. As a consequence, unification decomposition is often
performed at run time.

There is no easy solution to the problem, as it is inherent in MDBSs.
The only thing that can be done is to distinguish between simple and complex
problems. Simple unification decomposition should be performed at compile
time whenever possible. Language constructs should also be provided to avoid
complex unification at schema integration time or to issue warnings when possible complex unification has been identified. Unfortunately, research in this
area is still very preliminary. But this is an important and difficult issue that
deserves more attention.

2.2.2   Optimization

The query optimization problem can be stated as follows: Given a query
Q, an execution space E consisting of all execution plans that compute Q, and
a cost function C that is defined on E, find an execution plan $e \in E$ that is of
minimum cost using some search strategy.

Clearly, the general query optimization problem is the same in both
regular and multidatabase systems. In practice, however, how this general
paradigm can be implemented in the two environments is very different due to
the autonomy of LDBSs.

The effects of local autonomy are manifested in both cost function and
execution space aspects of MDBS query optimization.

First, the GDBMS may not have complete cost information about global
subqueries to do the global optimization. For example, cost formulas of
LDBMSs, which are essential to global query optimization, are usually not
known to the GDBMS. Even if the cost formulas are available, the GDBMS
still lacks the ability to obtain run-time cost parameters, such as data buffer
size, that are needed in estimating costs of global subqueries.

Second, execution spaces have different shapes in traditional database
systems and MDBSs. For example, sort-merge and hash joins are more often
favored to implement global joins in MDBSs. Since each LDBMS is an inde-

pendent and autonomous DBMS, the GDBMS can only interact with it via its Application Programming Interface (e.g., at SQL level). In other words, the GDBMS is unable to access internal data structure and functions of the underlying LDBMSs. Clearly, an overhead is associated with each LDBS access. Although the overhead is not significant in a single access, it dominates the cost of operations that require repeated LDBS access. As a consequence, a nested loop join can become expensive and cannot be expected to outperform a sort-merge and hash join unless the outer table is very small.

This change of execution space has an indirect impact on the search strategies of global query optimization, especially with respect to response time. Since sort-merge and hash joins provide good interoperator parallelism in a balanced (e.g., bushy) query tree, but bad response time in an unbalanced (e.g., left deep) query tree, the widely used optimization in homogeneous database systems that searches only left deep join trees works poorly in MDBSs. New searching strategies have to be developed to cope with the problem.

Estimating Costs of Global Subqueries

One solution to the unknown cost problem is to use a logical cost model that views the cost on the basis of the logical execution of global subqueries. In other words, the cost of a given subquery is estimated based on logical characteristics of the LDBMSs, the data, and the subquery. More specifically, the cost of a single table query Q is

$$\text{Cost}(Q) = C_0 + C_1 + C_2$$

where C_0 is the initialization cost, such as processing the query and setting up the scan; C_1 is the cost to find qualifying tuples including locking overhead, doing the get-next operation, amortized I/O cost, and all other overhead incurred per tuple of the scan; and C_2 is the cost to process selected tuples such as projection.

To a large extent, C_0 depends only on LDBMSs, C_1 depends on the table being accessed, and C_2 is a function of the number of tuples the query returns. For a given LDBMS, the above cost model can be refined as

$$\text{Cost}(Q) = c_0 + c_1 * \|R\| + c_2 * \|R\| * s$$

where $\|R\|$ is the cardinality of the table being accessed, s is the selectivity of the query, and c_0, c_1, and c_2 are cost coefficients.

Note that both $\|R\|$ and s are logical characteristics of the query and the table it accesses and are known to the GDBMS. Therefore, costs of global subqueries can be estimated if the three cost coefficients are known for the given LDBMS.

Fortunately, cost coefficients can be easily derived through a calibration process. The idea is to run a suite of specially designed calibration queries on a specially designed calibration database on the LDBS, which are then calibrated and the costs recorded. Replacing Cost(Q) in the above logical cost model with the actual values results in a linear function of c_0, c_1, and c_2. Cost coefficients can be obtained by solving a set of such equations for different $\|R\|$ (tables being accessed) and s (queries accessing the tables) values.

Note that the above logical cost model is general enough to estimate costs of not only single table queries but also more complicated ones containing joins. For example, the cost of a nested loop join can be estimated using the costs of primitive queries in a similar way, as in traditional database systems. The cost model and calibration approach can also be extended to estimate costs of queries on nonrelational database systems [DKS92].

Reducing Global Query Response Time

Two major factors contribute to the poor response time of left deep join trees in MDBSs: sequential execution of joins and the fact that sort-merge and hash joins do not produce any result until the subordinate joins produce all results. Since the latter factor is inherent in sort-merge and hash joins, response time of MDBS queries can only be improved by performing joins concurrently (i.e., in bushy join trees).

The problem can be solved by extending the search space to include bushy join trees. This, however, will greatly increase the complexity of optimization. For a query with n joins, there are $\frac{1}{n+1}\binom{n}{2n}$ different bushy join trees. It is clearly impossible for an optimizer to do an exhaustive search on such a large execution space (e.g., for $n > 10$).

The other approach, proposed in [DSD95], is to first choose a left deep join tree that is of minimum total cost. The resulting left deep join tree is then further optimized with respect to response time.

For a given left deep join tree, there are many equivalent bushy join trees. Finding the best bushy join tree that is equivalent to the original left deep join tree is as difficult as the original optimization problem of finding the best execution plan from scratch. A feasible approach is attempting to improve response time without sacrificing total cost. This can be achieved incrementally starting from the original left deep join tree. An incremental strategy is easy to implement if the increment is small, but it requires an algorithm to dynamically determine the next step. Different algorithms can be developed (see, e.g., [DSD95]); however, each is more suited to a certain type of query tree. In general, the algorithms will not guarantee that the final execution plan is optimal with respect to response time.

2.3
Transaction Management

An important notion in databases, a *transaction*, is a sequence of reads and writes against a database. A transaction has the following properties:

- *Consistency:* A transaction is a consistent unit of database access; that is, if executed without interference from other transactions, it transforms a database from one consistent state to another.

- *Atomicity:* A transaction is an atomic unit of database access; that is, it is either completely executed (i.e., committed) or not executed at all (i.e., aborted).

- *Durability:* A transaction is a persistent unit of database access; that is, if a transaction commits, all its effects are made permanent.

Figure 2.1, at the beginning of the chapter, shows a general model of transaction processing in MDBSs. The GDBMS consists of two components: a global data manager (GDM) and a global transaction manager (GTM). A global transaction is first decomposed into a set of subtransactions by the GDM, according to the availability of data. The GDM, together with data managers of LDBMSs, is also responsible for checking authorization, which prevents illegal access to local databases. The GTM is responsible for the submissions and executions of global subtransactions. To preserve local autonomy, an agent is superimposed on top of each LDBMS. An agent is an interface between the GDBMS and an LDBMS and controls executions of global subtransactions at the site.

2.3.1   Concurrency Control

The global concurrency controller is a component of the GTM that coordinates execution of global subtransactions at different sites so that global consistency is maintained. The conventional approach to concurrency control is to execute transactions in some serializable way. An execution of a set of transactions is serializable if it is equivalent to a sequential execution of the transactions.

The difficulties of global concurrency control in MDBSs are mainly due to the lack of information about and control over local executions. As shown in Example 2.1, local transactions may introduce indirect conflicts between two global subtransactions at a site. It is generally unknown to the GTM if and how two global subtransactions may conflict at a site. The only thing the GTM can do to avoid or resolve such undesirable conflicts is to delay or abort global subtransactions.

EXAMPLE 2.1
Let G_1 and G_2 be two global transactions. Suppose that they read data items a and b at site S_0, respectively. Let $G_{1,0}$ and $G_{2,0}$ be subtransactions of G_1 and G_2 at S_0, respectively.
$$G_{1,0} : r_1(a)$$
$$G_{2,0} : r_2(b)$$

Let L be a local transaction concurrently executed with $G_{1,0}$ and $G_{2,0}$ at S_0.

$L : w_l(a)w_l(b)$

Let E_0 be a local execution of $G_{1,0}$, $G_{2,0}$, and L. Three serialization orders of $G_{1,0}$ and $G_{2,0}$ are possible:

None,   if $E_0 : w_l(a)w_l(b)G_{1,0}(a)G_{2,0}(b)$;

$G_{1,0} \rightarrow G_{2,0}$, if $E_0 : r_1(a)w_l(a)w_l(b)r_2(b)$; or

$G_{1,0} \leftarrow G_{2,0}$, if $E_i : w_l(a)r_1(a)r_2(b)w_l(b)$.

Although execution orders of G_1 and G_2 are the same in all three cases, their serialization orders are different. The same result can be obtained for the other combinations of G_1 and G_2 (i.e., G_1 reads a and G_2 writes b, G_1 writes a and G_2 reads b, and G_1 writes a and G_2 writes b).

Global concurrency control is one area in which both pessimistic and optimistic approaches can be applied. In general, the pessimistic approach avoids possible inconsistencies by delaying submissions of global subtransactions and therefore results in lower concurrency. The optimistic approach resolves undesired interactions afterward and therefore may have to abort many global transactions.

Another important issue in global concurrency control is the knowledge of executions that LDBMSs schedule. From the GTM's point of view, the following five types of local schedules are distinguished [BGMS92].

- *Serializable.*

- *Strongly serializable:* A schedule is strongly serializable if it is serializable and the serialization order of any two nonoverlapped transactions is consistent with their actual execution order.

- *Sp-schedule:* An sp-schedule is a strongly serializable execution, and the serialization order of a transaction can be determined by a designated operation (called serialization point, e.g., lockpoint) of the transaction.

- *Strongly recoverable:* A schedule is strongly recoverable if it is an sp-schedule and a transaction will not commit until all transactions that conflict with it and precede it in serialization order have committed.

- *Rigorous:* A schedule is rigorous if it is strongly recoverable and an operation will be executed only if it does not conflict with any preceding operations of uncommitted transactions.

Many concurrency control protocols have been proposed that generate serializable schedules (e.g., two-phase locking, time-stamp ordering, optimistic, and serialization graph). Most of them generate only sp-schedules, except the serialization graph approach, and can be easily modified to generate only strongly recoverable schedules.

Both pessimistic and optimistic protocols can be designed that do not violate local autonomy (through prescription). For performance reasons, however, local autonomy may be intentionally violated (through proscription). Most proposed protocols assume certain properties of LDBMSs in order to achieve a higher degree of concurrency. There is clearly a trade-off between the performance and autonomy requirements. In general, the more we know about the underlying LDBMSs, the higher concurrency can be achieved. For example, some concurrency control protocols perform much better if all LDBMSs schedule only rigorous local execution. On the other hand, the more we assume about the LDBMSs, the more likely that a new LDBMS will not meet the requirements.

Many global concurrency control protocols (both pessimistic and optimistic) have been proposed. They are discussed below, with emphasis on the assumptions they make about local schedules and the global concurrency they provide.

Pessimistic Approaches

The pessimistic approach relies on LDBMSs to schedule global subtransactions properly. Therefore, knowledge about LDBMSs is essential, not only to guarantee global serializability but also to provide a higher degree of global concurrency. In general, the pessimistic approach is more suited to MDBSs whose underlying LDBMSs generate only strict local schedules or at least strongly serializable schedules.

Site graph [BS88] and altruistic locking [AGMS87] are two early protocols that only require strongly serializable local execution. The basic idea of both protocols is to avoid concurrent execution of two global transactions at more than one site. Site graph is similar to the serialization graph protocol but at a higher level of granularity (site and transaction). It detects possible conflicts at a global level and resolves them by delaying one or more (entire) global transactions. Altruistic locking improves concurrency by preventing overlapping at each site. If two global transactions G_1 and G_2 both access sites S_1 and S_2, G_2 may start its subtransaction at S_2 before G_1 finishes its subtransaction at S_1. But if G_2 follows G_1 at S_1, it must also follow G_1 at S_2.

The top-down protocol assumes all local executions are sp-schedules [DEK91]. Concurrency is improved because two conflicting global transactions do not have to run sequentially at local sites as in the site graph and altruistic locking protocols. Global transactions may overlap as long as the serialization points are executed in a consistent order at all local sites.

Strongly recoverable local executions [BGRS91] are only special cases of sp-schedules, in which serialization points are simply commitment operations. Therefore, all protocols that work for sp-schedules (e.g., top down) also work for strongly recoverable local executions (with fixed serialization points). Note that this will not improve concurrency, as commitment operations are the last operations of each transaction.

Global concurrency can be greatly improved if all local schedules are rigorous. [BGRS91] presented a protocol that ensures global serializability by
controlling the commitment of global transactions. More specifically, the GTM
will not schedule the commitment of a global transaction until all previous operations of the same transaction have completed their execution. Concurrency
is improved because regular operations can be scheduled concurrently.

Optimistic Approach

The key to the success of the optimistic approach is the accurate detection
of undesired conflicts between global transactions. The assumption is that two
global transactions may not conflict even though they could in general. Therefore, the general knowledge of LDBMSs is not as useful as in the pessimistic
approach. As a consequence, the optimistic approach is more suited to the
general case where few assumptions can be made about local executions.

[Pu88] presented a general optimistic model for superdatabases. The idea
is to detect inconsistent global schedules by comparing the execution order of
serialization points of each global transaction.

The optimistic ticket protocol [GRS91] further enhanced the above general
model by developing a technique that effectively obtains the serialization order
of global transactions at run time. The idea is to create a special data item
(called a ticket) at each local site. All global transactions are required first
to read the value of the ticket, which is incremented after each use. A global
execution is inconsistent if any two global transactions read inconsistent ticket
values from more than one site.

The main problem with optimistic ticket protocol is that it introduces
direct conflicts between every pair of global transactions that access a common
site, resulting in many global transaction aborts. On the other hand, it seems
necessary to introduce the conflicts, otherwise the GTM may not be able to
resolve inconsistencies even if it detects them. Consider, for example, the last
case of Example 2.1. G_2 conflicts with G_1 after the execution of $w_l(b)$. If
both G_1 and G_2 have been committed before $w_l(b)$, the only way to resolve
the conflict is to abort local transaction L. This, however, violates execution
autonomy through proscription.

2.3.2   Commitment and Recovery

Commitment and recovery are other activities of the GTM that guarantee atomicity of transactions and ensure that failures do not corrupt persistent
data. To guarantee that the subtransactions either all commit or all abort, a
two-phase commit (2PC) protocol is often used. In the first phase of the protocol, subtransactions that finish their execution successfully enter the "prepare-
to-commit" state and send messages to the coordinator, which then makes the
global commitment decision. The transaction commits if all subtransactions
are in the prepare-to-commit state; otherwise, it aborts. In the second phase,

the coordinator sends the decision to all LDBMSs, which in turn carry out the decision on subtransactions.

In MDBSs, global transactions may fail due to system failures, communication failures, or transaction aborts. Note that global transactions may be aborted by both the GDBMS (e.g., due to global deadlocks) and underlying LDBMSs (e.g., due to local deadlocks). Since LDBMSs ensure atomicity and durability of both local transactions and global subtransactions, the GDBMS needs only to ensure that a global transaction either commits or aborts at all sites.

One problem with commitment of global transactions is that LDBMSs usually do not support the prepare-to-commit operation. Without this operation, the GDBMS will not be able to guarantee that the same decision is made by LDBMSs for subtransactions belonging to the same global transaction. The problem can be addressed either by submitting a compensating transaction to overcome the effect of a committed subtransaction [LKS91, MR91] or by resubmitting aborted subtransactions [WV90, BST90, MRB+92].

The problem with the first approach is that not all transactions can be compensated, especially after their results have been read by other transactions. It is also difficult to write compensating transactions in MDBS environments because a compensating transaction depends on not only the original transaction but also other transactions executed in between. Information about these transactions (especially local ones), however, may not be available to global users.

The problem with resubmitting aborted subtransactions is that local transactions may be executed between the failed subtransaction and the resubmitted subtransaction. As a result, the database state that the resubmitted subtransaction sees after the local transactions have been executed may be different from the one seen by those that completed the transaction successfully without resubmission. This may cause problems, as the values the resubmitted subtransaction wrote may depend on the values read by other subtransactions. One way to deal with this is to impose restrictions on local executions, e.g., do not allow local transactions to update the data that is readable or updatable by global transactions [WV90, BST90]. Obviously, this violates local autonomy through prescription. Another approach is to send the result of a subtransaction to other subtransactions of the same global transaction only after the subtransaction has completed successfully. This may cause performance problems because subtransactions of the same global transaction, but at different sites, may have to be executed sequentially.

There is an ongoing debate among researchers on whether LDBMSs will provide a prepare-to-commit operation for the transactions. The addition of the new operation greatly simplifies global commitment and recovery but violates local autonomy through proscription. For example, existing local applications may have to be rewritten to incorporate the prepare-to-commit operation. Without the operation, global commitment and recovery will be very difficult. The difficulties are primarily due to the conflict between the consistency requirements of commitment and autonomy requirements of LDBSs.

2.3.3   Replication Control

Data replication is an effective way of sharing data in MDBSs. Replication increases data availability in the presence of failures and reduces data retrieval costs by allowing local applications to read otherwise "remote" data efficiently. The GDBMS, together with agents at local sites, is responsible for the consistency of the global database.

Maintaining the consistency of replicated MDBSs, however, is much more difficult than not only that of traditional distributed databases but also that of nonreplicated MDBSs. Since local queries may access replicated data, they are no longer "local transactions." In replicated MDBSs, we distinguish among three different kinds of transactions. A *global transaction* is submitted to the GDBMS and accesses data (both replicated and nonreplicated) from multiple sites. A *basic local transaction* is submitted to an LDBMS and only updates nonreplicated data at the site. Local applications that do update replicated data are called *replica-update transactions*.

One difficulty in maintaining consistency in replicated MDBSs is that replica-update transactions may update local copies of replicated data. Clearly, it is impossible for the GDBMS to ensure the global consistency without being aware of replica-update transactions. The general solution to the problem is to submit replica-update transactions to the agent instead of to the LDBMS directly. The agent will identify replica-update transactions and propagate updates to relevant sites. Note that although this approach violates local autonomy through modification, it can be justified, as it is the only way to address the problem.

Replica-update transactions must be processed differently from global transactions, for performance reasons. To LDBS users, replica-update transactions are still local applications. It is usually unacceptable to ask local users to wait for the time-consuming 2PC process. Consider, for example, a bank customer who withdraws money from his account at his home branch in San Francisco. The bank clearly cannot ask him to wait until the update is propagated to a replica of his account at the headquarters in Los Angeles. Another disadvantage of 2PC is that local user requests may be refused simply because the remote replica is not available at the moment.

A general solution to the problem is the *primary copy* approach originally proposed in [Sto79]. The idea is to designate a primary copy for each replicated data item. An update to a replicated data item is performed in two steps. First the primary copy is updated and the update is committed. The second step propagates the update to other copies as a different global transaction. The approach fits naturally to MDBSs but has consistency problems. Since update propagation is performed and committed independently of the original transaction that updates the primary copy, coordination of global transactions and replica-update transactions that originated from different sites is challenging (see Example 2.2).

EXAMPLE 2.2
Consider a replicated MDBS consisting of two LDBSs. Let a and b be two replicated data items belonging to the two LDBSs, respectively. Consider a replica-update transaction that updates the primary copy of a and reads the nonprimary copy of b at one site, and another replica-update transaction that updates the primary copy of b and reads the nonprimary copy of a at the other site. If the two transactions were issued independently at about the same time, they might result in the following nonserializable execution:

$$E_1 : r_{t1}(b)w_{t1}(a)w_{t2}(b)$$
$$E_2 : r_{t2}(a)w_{t2}(b)w_{t1}(a)$$

Both pessimistic and optimistic approaches have been proposed to deal with the problem. The basic idea of the pessimistic approach proposed in [DEKB93] is to impose restrictions on the accessibility of global and replica-update transactions so that some of the undesirable conflicts are avoided while others can be resolved at run time. For example, global transactions are only allowed to access primary copies of replicated data, and replica-update transactions are only allowed to update replicated data belonging to their home sites. It has been shown that the restrictions avoided most, but not all, undesirable conflicts.

The optimistic approach proposed in [JDEB94] takes advantage of information derived from the commit protocol and uses it to detect and resolve improper conflicts between global and replica-update transactions. The protocol guarantees one-copy serializability by ensuring that the serialization order of two conflicting transactions is consistent with the order in which they enter the prepare-to-commit state if one of them is a replica-update transaction.

Another important feature that differentiates a replicated MDBS from traditional replicated database systems is that replication may result from integration. Consider, for example, two LDBSs containing similar information. Two data items representing the same information are managed independently by two LDBMSs before integration. After integration, the two independent items become two copies of the same replicated data. They both must be primary copies, as local applications have been developed to update the data. The approaches described above do not handle this case very well, as they all assume a single primary copy. It is still not clear how the consistency of replicated data with multiple primary copies can be maintained.

2.4
Summary

It is local autonomy that makes MDBSs unique and challenging. In this chapter, we have tried to provide a better understanding of local autonomy by discussing how it affects various issues of MDBSs. The focus is on the problems, not the solutions, although solutions are also briefly discussed.

The three major MDBS areas covered are schema integration, query processing, and transaction management. Many other areas (e.g., security) are also closely related to and greatly affected by local autonomy. Unfortunately, little research has been conducted, and it is still not clear what the autonomy requirements are in other areas and exactly how local autonomy affects them. Even in the areas the research addresses, many autonomy-related issues remain open or untouched.

Bibliography

[AAK⁺93] J. Albert, R. Ahmed, W. Kent, M. Ketabchi, W. Litwin, A. Rafii, and M. Shan. Automatic importation of relational schemas in Pegasus. In *Proceedings IEEE RIDE-IMS*, April 1993.

[AGMS87] R. Alonso, H. Garcia-Molina, and K. Salem. Concurrency control and recovery for global procedures in federated database systems. *Quarterly Bulletin IEEE Technical Communications on Database Engineering* 10(3):5–11, September 1987.

[ASD⁺91] Rafi Ahmed, Phillipe De Smedt, Weimin Du, William Kent, Mohammad A. Ketabchi, Witold A. Litwin, Abbas Rafii, and Ming-Chien Shan. The Pegasus heterogeneous multidatabase system. *IEEE Computer* 24(12):19–27, December 1991.

[BGMS92] Y. Breitbart, H. Garcia-Molina, and A. Silberschatz. Overview of multidatabase transaction management. *VLDB Journal* 1(2):181–239, October 1992.

[BGRS91] Y. Breitbart, D. Georgakopoulos, M. Rusinkiewicz, and A. Silberschatz. On rigorous transaction scheduling. *IEEE Transactions on Software Engineering* 17(9):954–960, September 1991.

[BLN86] C. Batini, M. Lenzerini, and S. B. Navathe. A comparative analysis of methodologies for database schema integration. *ACM Computing Surveys* 18(4):324–364, December 1986.

[BS81]   F. Bancilhon and N. Spyratos. Update semantics and relational
            views. *ACM Transactions on Database Systems* 6(4), 1981.

[BS88]   Y. Breitbart and A. Silberschatz. Multidatabase update issues.
            In *Proceedings of the ACM SIGMOD International Conference
            on Management of Data*, pages 135–142, 1988.

[BST90]   Yuri Breibart, Avi Silberschatz, and Glenn R. Thompson.
            Reliable transaction management in a multidatabase system.
            *Proceedings of the ACM SIGMOD International Conference on
            Management of Data*, pages 214–224, 1990.

[CR93]   P. Chrysanthis and K. Ramamritham. Impact of autonomy
            requirements on transactions and their management in hetero-
            geneous distributed database systems. In *Proceedings DBTA
            Workshop on Interoperability of Database Systems and Database
            Applications*, 1993.

[CR94a]   P. Chrysanthis and K. Ramamritham. Autonomy requirements
            in heterogeneous distributed database systems. In *Proceedings
            of the Conference on the Advances on Data Management*, pages
            283–302, 1994.

[DB82]   U. Dayal and P. Bernstein. On the correct translation of update
            operations on relational views. *ACM Transactions on Database
            Systems* 7(3), 1982.

[DEK91]   W. Du, A. Elmagarmid, and W. Kim. Maintaining quasi seri-
            alizability in HDDBSs. In *Proceedings IEEE Data Engineering*,
            1991.

[DEKB93]   W. Du, A. Elmagarmid, W. Kim, and O. Buhkres. Supporting
            consistent updates in partially replicated multidatabase systems.
            Very Large Data Bases 2(2), 1993.

[DH84]   U. Dayal and H. Hwang. View definition and generalization
            for database integration in a multidatabase system. *IEEE
            Transactions on Software Engineering* 10(6):628–644, 1984.

[DKS92]   W. Du, R. Krishnamurthy, and M. Shan. Query optimization in
            a heterogeneous DBMS. In *Proceedings VLDB*, 1992.

[DSD95]   W. Du, M. Shan, and U. Dayal. Reducing multidatabase query re-
            sponse time using tree balancing. In *Proceedings ACM SIGMOD*,
            1995.

[GPZ86]   V. Gligor and R. Popescu-Zeltin. Transaction management in distributed heterogeneous database management systems. *Information Systems* 11(4):287–297, 1986.

[GRS91]   D. Georgakopoulos, M. Rusinkiewicz, and A. Sheth. On serializability of multidatabase transaction through forced local conflicts. In *Proceedings of the Seventh International Conference on Data Engineering*, pages 314–323, 1991.

[JDEB94]   J. Jing, W. Du, A. Elmagarmid, and O. Buhkres. Maintaining consistency of replicated data in multidatabase systems. In *Proceedings IEEE Distributed Computing Systems*, 1994.

[KIGS93]   W. Kim, C. Injun, S. Gala, and M. Scheevel. On resolving semantic heterogeneity. *Distributed and Parallel Databases* 1(3), 1993.

[KLK91]   R. Krishnamurthy, W. Litwin, and W. Kent. Language features for interoperability of databases with schematic discrepancies. In J. Clifford and R. King, editors, *Proceedings of the ACM SIGMOD*, pages 40–49. New York: ACM, May 1991.

[LKS91]   E. Levy, H. Korth, and A. Silberschatz. An optimistic commit protocol for distributed transaction management. In *Proceedings of the ACM SIGMOD Conference*, pages 88–97, May 1991.

[Mot87]   A. Motro. Superviews: Virtual integration of multiple databases. *Transactions on Software Engineering* 13(7), 1987.

[MR91]   P. Muth and T. Rakow. Atomic commitment for integrated database systems. In *Proceedings of the Seventh International Conference on Data Engineering*, pages 296–304, April 1991.

[MRB+92]   Sharad Mehrotra, Rajeev Rastogi, Yuri Breitbart, Henry F. Korth, and Avi Silberschatz. The concurrency control problems in multidatabases: Characteristics and solutions. In *Proceedings of the ACM SIGMOD International Conference on Management of Data*, pages 288–297, June 1992.

[Pu88]   Calton Pu. Superdatabases for composition of heterogeneous databases. In *International IEEE Conference Management of Data*, pages 548–555, 1988.

[S⁺84]   P. Selinger et al.   The impact of site autonomy on R*: A
            distributed relational DBMS. *Database—Role and Structure*,
            1984.

[SAD⁺95]   M. Shan, R. Ahmed, J. Davis, W. Du, and W. Kent. Pega-
            sus: A heterogeneous information management system. *Modern
            Database Systems*, 1995.

[Sto79]   M. Stonebraker. Concurrency control and consistency of multiple
            copies of data in distributed INGRES. *Transactions on Software
            Engineering* 3(3), 1979.

[WV90]   A. Wolski and J. Veijalainen.   2PC agent method: Achieving
            serializability in presence of failures in a heterogeneous multi-
            database. In *Proceedings of the IEEE PARBASE-90 Conference*,
            pages 321–330, 1990.

3

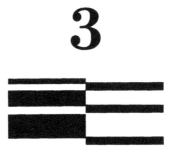

Semantic Similarities
Between Objects
in Multiple Databases

Vipul Kashyap
Amit Sheth

Introduction

Many organizations face the challenge of interoperating among multiple independently developed database systems to perform critical functions. With high interconnectivity and access to many information sources, the primary issue in the future will not be how to efficiently process the data that is known to be relevant, but which data is relevant.

Some of the best known approaches to dealing with multiple databases, discussed in Chapter 1, are tightly coupled federation, loosely coupled federation, and interdependent data management [SL90, She91a]. A crucial task in creating a tightly coupled federation is that of schema integration (e.g., [DH84]). A crucial task in accessing data in a loosely coupled federation [LA86, HM85] is to define a view over multiple databases or to define a query using a multidatabase language. *In performing any of these crucial tasks, and hence in any approach to interoperability of database systems, the fundamental question is that of identifying objects in different databases that are semantically related and then resolving the schematic differences among semantically related objects.* Classification taxonomies of schematic differences appear in [DH84, BOT86, CRE87, KLK91, KS91]. (See [KS] for a further discussion.) However, purely schematic considerations do not suffice to determine the semantic similarity between objects [FKN91, SG89].

Wood [Woo85] defines semantics as "the scientific study of the relations between signs and symbols and what they denote or mean." We consider these to be aspects of *real-world semantics* (RWS) of an object. In this chapter, we focus on the techniques and representational constructs used by the various practitioners in the field of multidatabases. We also discuss techniques for representing uncertainty but only as an aspect of the semantic similarity between objects. We shall also restrict ourselves to attempts to represent semantic similarity in the multidatabase context. We discuss related work in Section 3.8.

Attempts have been made to capture the similarity of objects by using mathematical tools, such as value mappings between domains, and abstractions, such as generalization, aggregation, etc. However, it is our belief that the RWS of an object cannot be captured using mathematical formalisms. We need to understand and represent more knowledge in order to capture the semantics of the relationships between the objects. The knowledge should be able to capture and the representation should be able to express the *context* of comparison of the objects, the *abstraction* relating the domains of the two objects, and the *uncertainty* in the relationship between the objects.

In Section 3.1, we explore these three perspectives of semantics in detail and illustrate how the various researchers have tackled these issues in their attempts to represent semantic similarity. In Section 3.2, we discuss semantic proximity proposed by [SK93]. In Section 3.3, we discuss the context building approach taken by [ON93]. The context interchange approach taken by [SSR92a] is covered in Section 3.4, and in Section 3.5, we discuss the common concepts approach of [YSDK91]. In Section 3.6, we cover the semantic abstractions approach taken by [GSCS93], and in Section 3.7, we discuss [FKN91]'s utilization of *fuzzy terminological knowledge*.

3.1
Semantics: Perspectives and Representation

We begin by showing how attempts of various researchers to represent semantic similarities relate to the perspectives on semantics—context, abstraction, and uncertainty—identified in the previous section.

3.1.1   Context: The Semantic Component

The context in which the objects are being compared provides the semantic fulcrum of capturing and representing the object similarities. Researchers in the field of heterogeneous databases have realized the importance of context. Some of the proposals are as follows:

- [SK93] propose the concept of semantic proximity (Section 3.2) to characterize semantic similarity in which the context is the primary vehicle to capture the RWS.

- [ON93] propose a dynamic context building approach (Section 3.3) for meaningful information exchange between various information systems.

- [SSR92a] propose an approach using metadata (Section 3.4) to represent context and to achieve "context mediation."

- [YSDK91] propose common concepts (Section 3.5) to characterize similarities between attributes in multiple databases. [CMG90] propose that a concept may be thought of as the image of a function mapping contexts to propositions. Thus a context may be implicitly represented in the functional definitions of the concepts.

3.1.2   Abstractions/Mappings: The Structural Component

Abstraction here refers to the relation between the domains of the two objects. Mapping between the domains of objects is the mathematical tool used to express the abstractions. However, since abstractions by themselves cannot capture the semantic similarity, they have to be associated either with the context [KS] or with extra knowledge in order to capture the RWS. Some of the proposals are as follows:

- [SK93] define abstractions in terms of value mappings between the domains of objects and associate them with the context as a part of the semantic proximity (Section 3.2).

- [ON93] define mappings between schema elements, which they term interschema correspondence assertions or ISCAs (Section 3.3). A set of ISCAs under consideration defines the context for integration of the schemas.

- [SSR92a] define mappings that they call conversion functions (Section 3.4), which are associated with the meta-attributes that define the context.

- [YSDK91] associate the attributes with "common concepts" (Section 3.5). Thus the mappings (relationship) between the attributes are determined through the extra knowledge associated with the concepts.

- [GSCS93] upgrade the semantic level of the schemas using abstractions that they call semantic abstractions (Section 3.6). This is achieved as a result of the knowledge acquisition process described in [Cas93].

- In Chapter 4 of this volume, Hammer and McLeod discuss an approach for resolving the representational differences, which involves: (1) determining as precisely as possible the relationships between sharable objects and (2) detecting possible conflicts in their structural representations.

3.1.3   Modeling Uncertainty, Inconsistency, and Incompleteness

Understanding and representing semantic similarity between objects may involve understanding and modeling uncertainty, inconsistency, and incompleteness of the information pertaining to the objects and the relationships between them as modeled in the database (both at the intensional and extensional levels). Some proposals are as follows:

- [FKN91] propose an approach that combines fuzzy terminological knowledge with schema knowledge (Section 3.7) to determine semantic similarity.

- [ON93] model uncertain information by using the degrees of likelihood of the various intermediate contexts. The Dempster-Shafer (D-S) theory of belief functions is used to model the likelihood of alternative contexts (Section 3.3).

- [SK93] use semantic proximity as a basis for representing the uncertainty of the information modeled at the database level (Section 3.2). They propose a framework in which the semantic proximity can be mapped to fuzzy strengths comprising the fuzzy terminological knowledge or to the likelihood of the assertions comprising the context discussed in Section 3.1.1.

- [YSDK91] represent each attribute as a vector depending on the concepts associated with it. A similarity measure between two attributes is defined as a function of the vectors associated with the attributes.

3.2
Semantic Proximity: A Model for Representing Semantic Similarities

We recognize three basic aspects in the representation of semantics. The first aspect concentrates on pinning down the real-world semantics of the various entities and the relationships between them. The second aspect is to represent all known knowledge about the domain to which the various entities and objects belong. The relationships between various objects can then be determined on the basis of the encoded domain knowledge. We consider this knowledge itself as an implicit context. The final aspect is when the context is represented explicitly and reasoned about as a first-class construct.

We distinguish between the real world and the *model world*, which is a representation of the real world. (See [SGN93] and [GSCS] for further discussion.) The term *object* in this chapter refers to an object in a model world (i.e., a representation or intensional definition in the model world, e.g., an object class definition in object-oriented models) as opposed to an entity or a concept in the real world. These objects may model information at any level of representation, namely, attribute level or entity level.[1]

We introduce the concept of semantic proximity to characterize semantic similarities between objects and use it to provide a classification of semantic similarities between objects. Our approach embodies the explicit context representation approach. Given two objects O_1 and O_2, the *semantic proximity* (Figure 3.1) between them is defined by the 4-tuple given by

$$\text{semPro}(O_1, O_2) = \langle \text{Context, Abstraction, } (D_1, D_2), (S_1, S_2)\rangle$$

where D_i is domain of O_i, and S_i is state of O_i.

The context of an object is the primary vehicle to capture the RWS of the object. Thus, the respective contexts of the objects, and to a lesser extent the abstraction used to map the domains of the objects, help to capture the semantic aspect of the relationship between the two objects.

---

[1]Objects at the entity level can be denoted by single-place predicates P(x), and attributes can be denoted by two-place predicates Q(x,y) [SGN93].

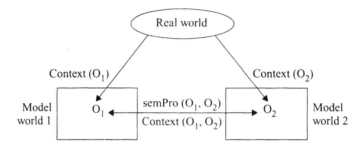

FIGURE 3.1
Semantic proximity between two objects.

3.2.1   Context(s) of the Two Objects:
The Semantic Component

Each object has its own context. The term *context* in semPro refers to the context in which a particular semantic similarity holds. This context may be related to or different from the contexts in which the objects were defined. It is possible for two objects to be semantically closer in one context than in another context. Some of the alternatives for representing a context in an interoperable database system are as follows:

- In [ON93], context is defined as the knowledge that is needed to reason about another system, for the purpose of answering a query, and is specified as a set of assertions.

- In [SSR92a], context is defined as the meaning, content, organization, and properties of data and is modeled using metadata associated with the data.

- A context may also be associated with a database or a group of databases (e.g., the object is defined in the context of DB1).

- The relationship in which an entity participates may determine the context of the entity.

- From the five-level schema architecture for a federated database system [SL90], a context can be specified in terms of an *export schema* (a context that is closer to a database) or an *external schema* (a context that is closer to an application).

- At a very elementary level, a context can be thought of as a named collection of the domains of the objects.

- When using a well-defined ontology, such as Cyc, a well-defined partition (called Microtheory) of the ontology can be provided a context [Guh90].

- Sometimes a context can be "hard-coded" into the definition of an object. For example, when we have the two entities EMPLOYEE and TELECOMM-EMPLOYEE, the TELECOMMUNICATIONS context is hard-coded in the second entity.

3.2.2   Issues of Representation and Reasoning

Various approaches have been proposed for representing semantic structures similar to context and for reasoning with the help of these representations. We now discuss some of the approaches in the context of multidatabase systems.

[KS] have used context to provide intensional descriptions of database objects. They represent contexts as a collection of contextual coordinates and values. A contextual coordinate denotes an aspect of context that models some characteristic of the subject domain and may be obtained from a domain-specific ontology. Values can be a set of symbols, objects from a database, or concepts from a domain-specific ontology. Operations to compare the specificity of two contexts and to compute the greatest lower bound of two contexts are defined. These operations are used to reason with the intensional descriptions.

A similar approach has been adopted by [SSR92a], who represent a context as a collection of meta-attributes and their values (Section 3.4). This representation of context is at the level of data values and object instances. They are not able to model constraints at an intensional level (namely, cardinality constraints). Context mediation is used for reasoning and is implemented using rules [SM91] and predicates in a relational model [SSR92a].

[KS] have illustrated how contextual descriptions may be expressed using description logic expressions. [MK] have used CLASSIC [BBMR89] to represent the intensional descriptions and subsumption reasoning to query the intensional descriptions at a semantic level.

[ON93] represent as a collection of ISCAs (interschema correspondence assertions), which are correspondences between different data elements in different databases (Section 3.3). They use assumption-based truth maintenance systems [DeK86] to reason with contexts, as multiple sets of contexts can coexist in the absence of complete knowledge.

3.2.3   The Vocabulary Problem

In constructing contexts and intensional descriptions for modeling semantics, the choice of vocabulary is very important. It is important that we choose terms that are specific to the subject domain. Traditional multidatabase approaches have utilized data dictionaries to enumerate the vocabulary used in the component databases. Researchers in multidatabases are now using ontologies for building semantic descriptions. An *ontology* may be defined as the specification of a representational vocabulary for a shared domain of discourse, which may include definitions of classes, relations, functions, and other objects [Gru93].

[KS] have illustrated how terminological relationships in ontologies enable representation of extra information in the contextual descriptions. [DG$^+$95] have used an ontology from the financial domain to construct contexts. [MK] have used ontologies belonging to the bibliographic information domain to construct description logic expressions. Concept hierarchies have also been used in the common concepts approach [YSDK91] discussed in Section 3.5. Terminological relationships have been represented across ontologies in [MK] and in [HM93] to handle cases where contexts or intensional descriptions may be constructed from different ontologies. An approach for resolving representational conflicts using terminological relationships is discussed in the next chapter.

3.2.4   The Structural Components

In this section, we discuss the three structural components of semantic proximity—abstraction, domain, and states.

Abstraction Used to Map the Objects

We use the term *abstraction* to refer to a mechanism used to map the domains of the objects to each other or to the domain of a common third object. Note that an abstraction by itself cannot capture the semantic similarity. Some of the more useful and well-defined abstractions are listed here:

- *Total 1-1 value mapping:* For every value in the domain of one object, there exists a value in the domain of the other object and vice versa.

- *Partial many-one mapping:* In this case, some values in the domain of one of the objects might remain unmapped, or a value in one domain might be associated with many values in another domain.

- *Generalization/specialization:* One domain can generalize/specialize the other, or domains of both the objects can be generalized/specialized to a third domain.

- *Aggregation:* One domain can be an aggregation, or collection, of other domains.

- *Functional dependencies:* The values of one domain might depend functionally on the other domain.

- *ANY:* This is used to denote that any abstraction such as the ones defined here may be used to define a mapping between two objects.

- *NONE:* This is used to denote that no mapping is defined between two semantically related objects.

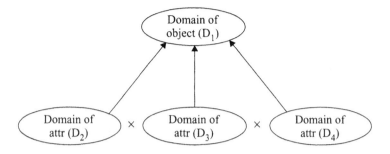

FIGURE 3.2
Domain of an object and its attributes. D_1 is a subset of $D_2 \times D_3 \times D_4$.

Domains of the Objects

Domains refer to the sets of values from which the objects can take their values. When using an object-oriented model, the domains of objects can be thought of as types, whereas the collections of objects might themselves be thought of as classes. A domain can be either *atomic* (i.e., cannot be decomposed any further) or composed of other atomic or composite domains. The domain of an object can be thought of as a subset of the cross product of the domains of the properties of the object (Figure 3.2). Analogously, we can have other combinations of domains, such as union and intersection of domains.

An important distinction between a context and a domain should be noted. One of the ways to specify a context is as a named collection of the domains of objects; i.e., it is associated with a group of objects. A domain, on the other hand, is a property of an object and is associated with the description of that object.

States (Extensions) of the Objects

The state of an object can be thought of as an extension of an object recorded in a database or databases. However, this extension must not be confused with the actual state of the entity (according to the real-world semantics) being modeled. Two objects having different extensions can have the same state real-world semantics (and hence be semantically equivalent).

3.2.5   Modeling Uncertainty: Fuzzy Strengths as a Function of Semantic Proximity

In this section, we establish the semantic proximity as a basis for the assignment of fuzzy strengths to the terminological relationships between two semantically similar objects. As noted in the previous section, when we assign fuzzy strengths to semantic similarities between schema objects, they should reflect the real-world semantics. Thus any such assignment of belief measures should depend on and reflect:

- The context(s) to which the two schema objects belong.

- The mapping(s) that may exist between the domains of the objects or the domains of the individual attributes of the objects. Here, it may be noted that the mappings between two attributes of the objects might not be independent of each other but may be dependent on each other.

- The state(s) or the extensions of the two objects.

The semantic proximity described previously is able to capture this information, which represents the semantic similarity between two objects according to the real-world semantics. Also, the interactions between any two attributes of an object can be captured using the interactions between the mappings of the two attributes, thus avoiding the need for the implicit independence assumption.

We define an uncertainty function μ between two objects O_1 and O_2 that maps the semantic proximity to the real interval $[0, 1]$. Thus

$$\mu : \text{semPro}(O_1, O_2) \rightarrow [0, 1]$$

i.e., $\mu(\text{Context, Abstraction, } (D_1, D_2), (S_1, S_2)) = X$, where $0 \leq X \leq 1$.

μ is a user-defined function such that it accurately reflects the real-world semantics and may not have specific mathematical properties. It may or may not be a computable function.

3.2.6   A Semantic Classification of Object Similarities

Our emphasis is on identifying semantic similarity independent of the representation of the objects. The concept of semantic proximity defined earlier provides a qualitative measure to classify the semantic similarities between objects.

The Role of Context in Semantic Classification

A partial context specification can be used by humans to decide whether the context for modeling of two objects is the same or different and whether the comparison of semantic similarity of objects is valid in all possible contexts or specific ones. A more detailed discussion of the nature of context, the operations on contexts, and the relationship of context to semantics is provided in [KS].

- *ALL:* The semPro between the objects is being defined with regard to all known and *coherent*[2] comparison contexts. There should be coherence between the definition contexts of the objects being compared and between the definition contexts and the context of comparison.

---

[2]Intuitively, coherent contexts are such that the constraints used to express them are not inconsistent with each other. The reader may refer to [KS] for a formal exposition.

- *SOME:* The semPro between the objects is being defined with regard to some context. This context may be constructed in the following ways:

    —*GLB:* The greatest lower bound of the contexts of the two objects. Typically, we are interested in the *glb* of the context of comparison and the definition context of the object.

    —*LUB:* The least upper bound of the contexts of the two objects. Typically, we are interested in the *lub* of the definition contexts of the two objects when no abstraction/mapping exists between their domains in the context of comparison.

- *SUBCONTEXTS:* We might be interested in the semPro between two objects in contexts that are more specific or more general with regard to the context of comparison.

- *NONE:* No context exists in which a meaningful abstraction or mapping between the domains of the objects may be defined. This is the case when the definition contexts of the objects being compared are *not coherent* with each other.

The types of semantic proximity, illustrated in Figure 3.3, are discussed next.

Semantic Equivalence

Two objects are defined to be *semantically equivalent* when they represent the same real-world entity or concept. This is the strongest measure of semantic proximity two objects can have. Expressed in our model, it means that given two objects O_1 and O_2, it should be possible to define a total 1-1 value mapping between the domains of these two objects in any known and coherent context. Thus we can write it as

$$\text{semPro}(O_1, O_2) = \langle \text{ALL, total 1-1 value mapping}, (D_1, D_2), \_\rangle^3$$

This notion of equivalence depends on the definition of the domains of the objects and can be more specifically called *domain semantic equivalence*. We can also define a stronger notion of semantic equivalence between two objects that incorporates the state of the databases to which the two objects belong. This equivalence is called *state semantic equivalence* and is defined as

$$\text{semPro}(O_1, O_2) = \langle \text{ALL, M}, (D_1, D_2), (S_1, S_2) \rangle$$

where M is a total 1-1 value mapping between (D_1, S_1) and (D_2, S_2).

---

[3]We use the "_" sign to denote don't care.

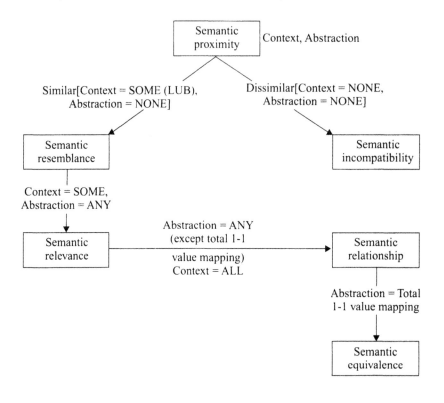

FIGURE 3.3
Semantic classification of object similarities.

Semantic Relationship

Two objects are said to be *semantically related* when there exists a partial many-one value mapping, or a generalization, or aggregation abstraction between the domains of the two objects. This type of semantic similarity is weaker than semantic equivalence. Here we relax the requirement of a 1-1 mapping in a way that given an instance O_1, we can identify an instance of O_2 but not vice versa. The requirement that the mapping be definable in all the known and coherent contexts is not relaxed. Thus we define the *semantic relationship* as

$$semPro(O_1, O_2) = \langle ALL, M, (D_1, D_2), \_ \rangle$$

where M may be a partial many-one value mapping, generalization, or aggregation.

Semantic Relevance

We consider two objects to be *semantically relevant* if they can be related to each other using some abstraction in some context. Thus the notion of semantic relevance between two objects is context dependent; i.e., two objects may be semantically relevant in one context but not so in another. Objects can be related to each other using any abstraction.

$$\text{semPro}(O_1, O_2) = \langle \text{SOME, ANY}, (D_1, D_2), \_\rangle$$

Semantic Resemblance

The weakest measure of semantic proximity, semantic resemblance, might be useful in certain cases. Here, we consider the case in which the domains of two objects cannot be related to each other by any abstraction in any context. Hence, the exact nature of semantic proximity between two objects is very difficult to specify. In this case, the user may be presented with extensions of both the objects. In order to express this type of semantic similarity, an aspect of context, called role, is introduced, and semantic resemblance is expressed with its help. A detailed discussion on roles and semantic resemblance is presented in [SK93].

$$\text{semPro}(O_1, O_2) = \langle \text{SOME(LUB), NONE}, (D_1, D_2), \_\rangle$$

where coherent$(C_{def}(O_1), C_{def}(O_2))$ and $\exists \text{Cntxt}_1, \text{Cntxt}_2$ exported by DB_1, DB_2, respectively, and SOME(LUB) denotes a context defined as follows:

$$\text{context} = \text{lub}(\text{Cntxt}_1, \text{Cntxt}_2) \text{ and } D_1 \neq D_2$$

and

$$\text{role-of}(O_1, \text{context}) = \text{role-of}(O_2, \text{context})$$

Semantic Incompatibility

While all the qualitative proximity measures defined so far describe semantic similarity, semantic incompatibility asserts semantic dissimilarity. Lack of any semantic similarity does not automatically imply that the objects are semantically incompatible. Establishing semantic incompatibility requires asserting that the definition contexts of the two objects are incoherent with regard to each other and there exist no contexts associated with these objects such that they have the same role.

$$\text{semPro}(O_1, O_2) = \langle \text{NONE, NONE}, (D_1, D_2), \_\rangle$$

where $C_{def}(O_1)$ and $C_{def}(O_2)$ are incoherent with each other, D_1 may or may not be equal to D_2, and $\not\exists$ context such that role-of$(O_1, \text{context}) = $ role-of$(O_2, \text{context})$.

3.3
Context Building Approach

The approach followed by [ON93] centers on the construction and maintenance of the context, within which meaningful information between heterogeneous information systems is proposed to be exchanged. The context is defined as a set of *interschema correspondence assertions* (ISCAs). Each ISCA consists of three dimensions: naming, abstraction, and level of heterogeneity.

The mathematical formalism used to model the structural similarity is expressed as the last two dimensions of the ISCA, abstraction and level of heterogeneity. The association between the abstraction and the context is achieved through the ISCAs that comprise the appropriate context. A classification of semantic conflicts is used as a basis for building and refining the context, by discovering the ISCAs between corresponding elements of the component systems. A truth management system is used to manage the multiple intermediate contexts. Uncertainty in modeling the information is present in the degrees of likelihood of the various intermediate contexts. The Dempster-Shafer (D-S) theory of belief functions is used to model the likelihood of alternative contexts.

Context is described here as the knowledge that is needed to reason about another system, for the purpose of answering a specific query. The context must provide an easily understood representation of how much is known and what is still needed in order to answer the query. The (partial) schemas and the subsequent query in Example 3.1 are used to elaborate on the issues of context building.

EXAMPLE 3.1
Database: A database of a cereal manufacturer
Data model: Relational
Schema: COMPETITOR(Name, Location, Mkt_Sgmt, Mkt_Shr, Qtly_Income)
Database: Financial information of companies in the European Community
Data model: Relational
Schema: COMPANY(Rank, Co-Name, Location, Industry)
Query: "What is the performance of my competitors in Europe?"

3.3.1   Context-Dependent Interpretation

Different contexts can lend different interpretations to a schematic conflict. The processes of detection of conflicts and integration help build a context dynamically. The query itself may be important in providing a context for the meaningful interpretation of schematic elements. Consider Example 3.2, based on the schemas and query shown in Example 3.1, which illustrates the above ideas.

EXAMPLE 3.2

Hypothesis: `COMPETITOR.Name` and `PRODUCT.Name` appear to be synonyms.

Context: Suppose `COMPETITOR` and `PRODUCT` are unrelated, say, homonyms.

Interpretation: We may conclude there is a high probability that `COMPETITOR.Name` and `PRODUCT.Name` are homonyms.

Hypothesis: `COMPETITOR.Name` and `COMPANY.Co-Name` appear to be related.

Context: Suppose the term "competitor" is the specialization of the term "company." The query specifies "competitor" and provides a context.

Interpretation: We may conclude that `COMPETITOR.Name` and `COMPANY.Co-Name` are synonyms.

Organization of Context by Levels of Heterogeneity

The object level is considered to be a coarser or higher level of heterogeneity than the attribute level, which is coarser than the instance level. In addition to structural schematic levels of heterogeneity, there are metadata levels of heterogeneity. These include the differences that require knowledge describing the objects and the attributes of the schema (commonly called *descriptive metadata*); knowledge of the semantics inherent, implicit, and explicit in data models; and general or domain-specific knowledge available about the database itself. Concepts at the metadata level could be objects, attributes, or instances (see Example 3.3).

EXAMPLE 3.3

The interschema correspondence assertion (ISCA) that `COMPETITOR.Name` and `COMPANY.Co-Name` are corresponding attributes triggers an attempt to place them in the context of the respective objects they describe. This may result in the inference of an ISCA that `COMPETITOR` and `COMPANY` are corresponding objects. This is called *upward propagation* through the levels of heterogeneity. If there is enough evidence to refute the synonymy of `COMPETITOR` and `COMPANY`, this would trigger a *downward propagation* to reclassify the relationship of `COMPETITOR.Name` and `COMPANY.Co-Name` as homonyms.

The semantic knowledge of another system, organized by levels of heterogeneity, provides a context for interpreting the view of the system.

Classification and Representation of Semantic Conflicts

The classification and representation of semantic conflicts is the fundamental building block of dynamic context building. Conflicts are classified along the three dimensions of naming, abstraction, and level of heterogeneity. The semantic relationship between two elements of different databases is represented as an interschema correspondence assertion as follows:

Assert[x,y](naming, abstraction, heterogeneity)

The first two dimensions (naming and abstraction) include what they view as fundamental relationships between semantic concepts. The third dimension (level of heterogeneity) is needed to place the semantic relationship in the appropriate schematic context (see Example 3.4).

- *Naming: Naming conflicts* refer to the relationship of the object, attribute, or instance names. These conflicts include synonyms and homonyms. If a conflict cannot be categorized as either a synonym or a homonym, it is classified as unrelated.

- *Abstraction:* A conflict can involve objects that refer to the same class of objects, objects that represent similar semantic concepts at different levels of abstraction (generalization/specialization), an object that maps to a group of objects in another database (aggregation/part-of), or an incompatibility that occurs when one object can be mapped to another through a computed or derived function.

- *Levels of heterogeneity:* Naming and abstraction conflicts can exist at the object, attribute, and instance levels of the schema.

EXAMPLE 3.4
The conflict between COMPANY.Co-Name and COMPETITOR.Name can be classified as:

Assert[COMPANY.Co-Name, COMPETITOR.Name]
(synonyms, generalization, (attribute, attribute))

Assertions that have been inferred through upward propagation require reconciliation to fill the slots of the classification.

Assert[COMPANY, COMPETITOR](?, ?, (object, object))

3.3.2   Context Management Using a Truth Maintenance System

Let us compare the attributes COMPETITOR.Location and COMPANY. Location. It can be reasonably proposed that the attributes are synonyms or that they are homonyms. These two assertions are contradictory to each other, yet they are temporarily both compatible with the evidence (or the lack of it). A truth maintenance system is used for

- Handling the effect of retracting assumptions when they are invalidated by the evidence and keeping track of the multiple plausible sets of assertions that can coexist in the absence of complete knowledge. The assumption-based truth maintenance system (ATMS) [DeK86] is used.

- Providing a symbolic mechanism for identifying the set of assumptions needed to assemble the desired proofs, so when probabilities are assigned to these assumptions, the system can be used as a symbolic engine for computing the degrees of belief sought by the D-S theory [Dem68, Sha76].

Multiple Context Management

At any given moment, in systems based on this approach, an assertion is either believed to be true (*Confirmed*), believed to be false (*Retracted*), or not believed to be either (*Undetermined*). A value *Undetermined* is assigned when, based on the current evidence, A and not A coexist in the set of assertions.

A context is a set of consistent assertions. Therefore, these assertions must all be *Confirmed*. An *Undetermined* may be part of a context so long as its contradiction is not. Several contexts may coexist at any given point in time. The sets of assertions in the various contexts may be mutually exclusive or overlapping.

Each set of assertions is managed by an ATMS, which provides a mechanism for keeping track of a context of noncontradictory plausible assertions and the evidence developed during an inference session. An ATMS can retract some of the plausible assumptions in light of new information. All conclusions that were derived from these assumptions have to be retracted as well. The degrees of belief of the assertions associated with a context determine whether the context is chosen for further refinement.

Assigning Degrees of Belief to Assertions

The D-S approach considers a set of assertions and assigns to each of them an interval [B, Pl] in which the degree of belief must lie. B measures the strength of evidence in favor of a set of assertions. Plausibility measures the probability that an assertion is compatible with the evidence; i.e., the probability that it cannot be disproved and is therefore possible. Initially, the exhaustive universe of initially exclusive assertions Ω is considered. This is referred to as the *frame of discernment*. However, not all evidence is directly supportive of individual elements. Generally, the evidence supports subsets of the frame of discernment.

The D-S theory defines a probability density function, which is denoted by d. The function d is defined for all subsets of Ω. The quantity d(q) measures the amount of belief that is currently assigned to exactly the set q of assertions. The values of d are assigned so that the sum of all degrees of belief of all subsets of Ω is 1.

Typically, the context with the highest degree of belief is selected for further refinement. A context is essentially a set of assertions, which would be some subset of Ω. Typically, in a dynamically evolving system, there would be several pieces of evidence for a set of assertions q associated with the context. The D-S theory provides a simple mechanism for computing the degrees of belief of all intersections of current frames of discernment. This can be used to combine the various pieces of evidence in support of the context.

3.3.3   Discussion

The context defined in the context building approach embodies both the semantic and the structural components. As defined earlier, the context is a set of ISCAs, which are used to direct the process of dynamic schema integration. The semantic component in the ISCA is the naming dimension that corresponds to the real-world semantics aspect of representation of semantics. The other components—abstraction and level of heterogeneity—are structural in nature. Thus the context is a partly semantic and partly structural entity. This is in contrast to the semantic proximity approach, in which the context is a purely semantic entity and has structure associated with it as abstractions.

3.4
Context Interchange Approach

[SSR92a] discuss the problem of transfer of data from one environment to another and its manipulation in another environment. They use the context to deal with the meaning, content, organization, and properties of data and to model the environment to which the data belongs. The context of the data is essentially a collection of meta-attributes that model the metadata associated with the data. The mathematical formalism used to model the structural similarity is expressed using conversion functions. These *conversion functions* are used to translate data from one context to another, thus enabling *context interchange*. The association between the mappings (conversion functions) and the context is achieved by defining a conversion function for each meta-attribute that may be a part of the definition of some context.

3.4.1   Context and Metadata

The definition of context in [SSR92a] is guided by the requirements for effective data interchange among information systems. A data source's metadata defines the *export context* and consists of stored information or rules describing the data provided by the source. A data receiver's metadata is called its *import context* and consists of predicates describing the properties of the data expected by the receiver.

EXAMPLE 3.5
A data source provides trade prices for stocks on the NYSE. The context of a trade price value might be the latest trade price in U.S. dollars. Data from this environment may be moved to the environment of a Japanese company where the context might be the latest trade price in yen.

During the data interchange in Example 3.5, the export context of the source is compared to the import context of the receiver to determine whether the data is meaningful to the receiver. Thus it is necessary to represent context using context specifications and comparing those specifications to achieve context mediation. The approach adopted in [SSR92a] is to represent all context from the data environment at the attribute level, using meta-attributes. Meta-attributes are attributes that have a special relationship to the attributes whose context they define. For the financial data source discussed in Example 3.5, `Currency` and `PriceStatus` would be meta-attributes of the `TradePrice` attribute. Consider the schema in Example 3.6 for the financial data source.

EXAMPLE 3.6
```
TRADES(InstrumentType, CompanyName, Exchange,
                        TradePrice(PriceStatus, Currency))
```
An example tuple can be given by

```
⟨'equity', 'IBM', 'NYSE',
    89.25('latestTradePrice', 'USDollars')⟩
```

3.4.2 Data Conversion (Conversion Functions)

A *conversion function* changes values of a tuple's attributes and meta-attributes in a way that leaves the "meaning" of the information unchanged. Each meta-attribute has a conversion function defined for it; by default, the conversion function for M is called cvtM. For example, suppose that a tuple in the `TRADES` relation has a `TradePrice` value of 3 and a `TradePrice.Currency` value of 'USDollars'. The conversion function call `cvtTradePrice(3,` `'USDollars, 'Yen')` returns the value 330 (assuming 1 U.S. dollar $=$ 110 yen). The function `cvtTradePrice` is an example of a total and lossless conversion function. A *total* function is one that is defined for all arguments. A *lossless* function is one for which every conversion has an inverse. Not all functions have these features.

Context Mediation

The *context mediator* component examines each incoming tuple and attempts to build a new conversion function that will produce a tuple that conforms to the receiver's assumptions. The receiver's assumptions about the incoming tuple are described by the receiver's import context—a predicate on the tuple's attribute values. The job of the context mediator is to return a conversion function that maps the input tuples to the receiver's import context. This function is used to define a relational operator called `cvtContext` (see Example 3.7).

> EXAMPLE 3.7
> Suppose the `TRADES` table contains values for the attribute `TradePrice` with `TradePrice.Currency = 'USDollars'`
> Suppose the receiver context is `TradeCurrency = 'Yen'`
> The conversion function used will be
>
> $$\text{cvtTradePrice(X, 'USDollars', 'Yen')}$$
>
> The relational operator can be defined using the above conversion function:
>
> $$\text{cvtContext(TRADES, TradePrice.Currency = 'Yen')}$$

3.4.3 Discussion

The context defined in the context interchange approach is essentially a semantic entity on the lines of the semantic proximity approach. Here, an attempt is made to give an explicit (partial) representation of context by using metadata. A context is defined as a collection of meta-attributes and values. This corresponds to the explicit context aspect of the representation of semantics. The association of the structural component (conversion functions) with the semantic component (context) is also similar to the semantic proximity approach.

3.5
Common Concepts: An Approach to Determine Attribute Similarities

[YSDK91] seek to capture the denotation or meaning of the attributes to some extent by using common concepts, concept hierarchies, and aggregate concept hierarchies. It is our opinion, based on Chierchia and McConnell-Ginet's definition of a linguistic concept [CMG90], that the context is considered to be implicitly represented in the functional definition of the concepts. The attributes are associated with the common concepts. Thus the mappings (relationships) between attributes are determined through their association with the extra knowledge or the implicit context embodied in the common concepts. Uncertainty in the relationship between two attributes is modeled using similarity values. Each attribute is defined as a vector depending on the concepts associated with it. The *similarity value* between two attributes is a function of the vectors associated with the attributes.

3.5.1   Representation of Attribute Semantics by Common Concepts

Each attribute can be characterized by a set of *common concepts*. Each concept represents a certain characteristic or a property that may be possessed by many objects (physical and/or abstract objects—see Example 3.8). These concepts are generic; i.e., they are not application dependent.[4]

EXAMPLE 3.8

The common concepts *horizontal_position* and *vertical_position* represent the horizontal and vertical position of a point, respectively.

The common concept *identification* can be associated with the attributes *sensor, mission,* and *platform* in the NASA databases, as these attributes have the property of identifying object.

Concepts may have hierarchical relationships with other concepts. Two relationships of particular significance are aggregate concept hierarchies and IS-A concept hierarchies.

Aggregate Concept Hierarchies

The example of the concept *time_interval* is considered, which specifies a duration of time. It could be modeled as an aggregate concept of the concepts *begin_time* and *end_time*:

$$time\_interval = \text{aggregate}(begin\_time, end\_time)$$

The attributes `tpstart` and `tpstop` can be characterized, respectively, by

$$time\_interval.begin\_time \text{ and } time\_interval.end\_time$$

The two attributes are recognized to be an aggregate attribute and are characterized by the aggregate concept *time_interval*.

Consider the possible attribute similarity between (`start_date`, `length`) and (`tpstart`, `tpstop`). There are two levels of possible similarity:

- *Individual similarity:* There is a similarity between `start_date` and `tpstart` as they are associated with the concept *time_interval.begin_time*.

- *Aggregate similarity:* There is a similarity between (`start_date`, `length`) and (`tpstart`, `tpstop`) as they are associated with the concept *time_interval*.

It should be noted that a similarity on the basis of aggregate attributes does not necessarily imply that a similarity exists among individual attributes involved in the aggregate attributes. The attribute `start_date` is associated with *time_interval.begin_time*, but the attribute `length` is not associated with

---

[4]The discussion in Section 3.5.3 gives our view on this assumption.

time_interval.end_time. For each aggregate concept in a hierarchy, a component concept labeled "others" illustrates the incompleteness of any preexisting hierarchy and enables the user to specify other component concepts.

IS-A Concept Hierarchies

The IS-A concept hierarchy is in fact the generalization/specialization used in most semantic data models and object-oriented data models. If objects characterized by concept X are a subset of objects characterized by concept Y, then we call Y the generalization of X (equivalently, X is the specialization of Y). X is also called a *subconcept* of Y, and Y is called the *superconcept* of X. For example, the concept *square* is a subconcept of *rectangle*, which in turn is a subconcept of *quadrangle*.

3.5.2   Establishing Attribute Relationships

Let C be an n-component vector, where n is the total number of concepts in the system, and $C(i)$, $1 \leq i \leq n$, denote its ith component of C, namely the ith concept. The association of a set of concepts with an attribute X can be represented by an n-component vector C_X, where $C_X(i) = 0$ if concept $C(i)$ is not associated with X; otherwise $C_X = 1$.

Aggregation Between Attributes

A set of attributes forms an aggregate attribute if

1. their vectors agree on all the concepts in the hierarchy except one, and

2. in that hierarchy, they correspond to all the component concepts of an aggregate concept, with the possible exception of one component (see Example 3.9).

EXAMPLE 3.9
The attribute **tpstart** is associated with the concepts *time_interval* and *time_interval.begin_time*, and the attribute **tpstop** is associated with the concepts *time_interval* and *time_interval.end_time*. Thus, they disagree in the component concepts *time_interval.begin_time* and *time_interval. end_time*, while these two component concepts are all the components of the aggregate concept *time_interval*.

Attribute Similarities

Given two vectors, C_X and C_Y, of two (aggregate or individual) attributes X and Y, a similarity function can be defined as follows,

$$\text{sim}(C_X, C_Y) = \frac{C_X \cdot C_Y}{\sqrt{|C_X| \times |C_Y|}}$$

where · is the dot product of two vectors and |Z| is the number of 1 components in the vector Z. This similarity function between two vectors is similar to that used in information retrieval [Sal89]. The intuition of the dot product is that if more components of the two vectors agree, then the more similar the two attributes are. Clearly, if the two vectors are identical (sim = 1.0), then the attributes are said to be equivalent.

An advantage of using a similarity function is that some attributes that are related but not equivalent—i.e., "similar"—may also be revealed. Suppose the attributes *income* and *salary* are not equivalent but closely related. It can be expected that the similarity between these two vectors would be very high.

3.5.3   Discussion

The common concepts defined in the approach of [YSDK91] may be application independent to some extent but cannot be context independent. In some cases, applications might belong to the same domain, and hence it might be possible to define concept hierarchies in an application-independent manner. However, we believe that in the case where the concepts span more than one domain of discourse, the concepts encode some form of the domain context in their functional definitions. This illustrates the implicit context aspect of representations of semantics in contrast to the explicit context aspect adopted in the semantic proximity approach.

3.6
Semantic Abstractions Approach

The integration of database schemas into a federated one involves identifying similarities between the classes of different databases in order to determine their semantic relationships. [GSCS93] adopt an approach of upgrading the semantic level of the local schemas. The abstractions (called *semantic abstractions*) used to model the structural similarities play a key role in this approach. Context is not represented or used explicitly in this approach. However, these abstractions are the result of the knowledge acquisition process described in [Cas93] and have extra knowledge associated with them. The search of the comparison process is guided by the structure of the generalization/specialization semi-lattices and aggregation graphs of the resulting rich schemas.

3.6.1   The Semantic Enrichment Phase

The canonical model chosen must be rich enough to model the semantics already expressed in the local schemas, as well as the semantics obtained from a semantic enrichment process to upgrade the semantic level of the schemas. This would help to detect easily the similarities between classes and specify interdatabase semantic relationships. The canonical model chosen is BLOOM

[CSGS91]. It can represent the following abstractions, allowing it to capture a rich set of semantic relationships:

- Classification/instantiation

- Generalization/specialization

    —*Disjoint specialization:* Each object of the superclass belongs to at most one subclass.

    —*Complementary specialization:* Each object of the superclass belongs to at least one subclass.

    —*Alternative specialization:* Each object belongs to exactly one subclass.

    —*General specialization:* No restrictions.

- Aggregation

    —*Simple aggregation:* The attributes are used to express the properties of the object.

    —*Collection aggregation:* The collection of a given class of objects gives rise to a new complex object.

    —*Association aggregation:* The component objects are not simply properties of the aggregate, but it is their association that gives rise to it.

- Existence and interest dependencies

The Knowledge Acquisition Phase

In the knowledge acquisition phase, the relational databases are analyzed both in extension and intension in order to discover hidden semantics in the form of restrictions, such as keys and different types of dependencies. This is the extra knowledge associated with and used to define the abstractions discussed later in this section. This is done through a series of steps explained in [Cas93]:

1. Key inference

2. Functional dependency inference

3. Normalization

4. Determination of identifier type

5. Inclusion dependency inference

6. Inference of exclusion and complementariness dependencies

The Schema Conversion Phase

Once the relational models have been augmented with the knowledge extracted in the previous stage, they are converted to rich BLOOM schemas through a series of steps enumerated in [GSCS93, Cas93]:

1. Analysis of inclusion dependencies

   a. Detection of missing entities

   b. Identification of semantic abstractions

2. Processing of remaining attributes

3. Creation of classes

3.6.2   The Detection Phase

The similarities that exist among the classes of the component schemas are discovered in order to determine their semantic relationships. The strategy proposed to find resemblance between classes has two components:

- which pairs of classes to compare at each moment and

- criteria to determine how similar the classes are.

The authors take advantage of the fact that the canonical model clearly distinguishes not only the generalization and the aggregation dimensions but also different kinds of abstractions in each dimension.

The strategy is guided, at a coarse level, by the generalization/specialization semi-lattices of the BLOOM schemas. Specialization is analyzed from the more restrictive to the more permissive. If no similar classes are found, restrictions can be relaxed to alternative, disjoint, complementary, and general, in that order.

At a finer level, the aggregation dimension makes it possible to establish an order of comparison of classes according to their aggregation abstractions. Thus, the comparison of the classes of two groups begins with those that involve the same kind of relevant abstraction (first, collections and then associations). Only if no similarities are found, or if there is no class with the same relevant abstraction in the other group, then relaxation is applied on the kind of aggregation to continue the search for a similar class. With this approach, the more promising comparisons are identified first.

The criteria for similarity between a pair of classes are provided by the aggregation dimension. On one side it indicates at every moment which aspects of the classes are to be compared, and on the other side it indicates how similar the classes are.

The process of detection cannot be completely automated. Even when a strong similarity is found, the human integrator has to confirm it, as it is based on structural similarity. This approach is based on classes and not on attributes because classes have a clearer meaning than attributes, and there are many fewer classes than attributes.

3.6.3   Discussion

The critical component in enriching the local schema is the knowledge acquisition phase. In this phase, the local schema is analyzed to infer knowledge about the database, namely, keys, functional dependencies, inclusion and exclusion dependencies, etc. This may be viewed as an attempt to infer and represent the knowledge about the domain to which the entities in the local database belong. This knowledge can be considered as the implicit context with regard to which the semantic abstractions are defined in the enriched schema. This is in contrast to the explicit context aspect adopted in the semantic proximity approach.

3.7
Semantic Similarity Based on Fuzzy Knowledge

The approach adopted by [FKN91] to determine the similarity of classes utilizes fuzzy and incomplete terminological knowledge together with schema knowledge. There is a clear distinction between *semantic* similarity determining the degree of resemblance according to real-world semantics, and *structural* correspondence explaining how classes can actually be interrelated. The authors do not represent or use context explicitly in this approach. However, the structural schema knowledge is combined with fuzzy terminological knowledge to determine semantic similarity. The notion of semantic relevance is introduced, and fuzzy set theory is applied to reason both about terminological knowledge and schema knowledge.

3.7.1   Terminological Knowledge

This approach to determining semantic similarity assumes that some classes or some of their attributes and/or relationships are assigned meaningful names in a preintegration phase. Thus the knowledge about the terminological relationship between the names can indicate the real-world correspondence between the classes. The terms are related by three kinds of binary relationships, which are represented in an associative network.

- *Generalization/specialization:* A term a is related by generalization to term b if a comprises b in a taxonomic sense (e.g., *Person, Employee*) or partitive sense (e.g., *Name, FirstName*).

- *Negative association:* Terms are related by negative association if they are complementary (e.g., *Man, Woman*), incompatible (e.g., *isEmployed, counsel*) or antonyms (e.g., *small, big*).

- *Positive association:* This is the most general relationship. It relates terms that are synonyms in some context (e.g., *Title, Heading*) and terms that are typically used in the same context (e.g., *Letter, Address*).

Since the real-world semantics of terms can vary, the relationships are *fuzzy* [Zad78]; i.e., they have a strength out of [0, 1] assigned. It is not possible to associate all terms with each other. Relationships that are not explicitly specified are inferred by traversing the associative networks. The paths traversed in the network are investigated in the order of their strength.

The *kind* of a path depends on the component relationships in the path. Positive association, generalization, and specialization are *transitive*; thus, their composition forms the same kind of relationship again. *Anti-transitive* negative associations are not composed at all. Specialization composed with (its inverse) generalization results in a (least specific) positive association. The kind of a positive (negative) association composed with a generalization (specialization) depends on the existence of other (possibly weaker) paths between two terms (see Example 3.10).

EXAMPLE 3.10
Consider the two paths in an associative network:

1. *Instructor* p *Student* g *Person*

2. *Instructor* g *Employee* g *Person*

The weaker of the two paths is chosen (2), and hence the relationship between *Instructor* and *Person* is that of generalization.

The *strength* of a path depends on the degree of dependence between its relationships. The strengths of the relationships are combined using different triangular norms (t-norms). The authors restrict themselves to the following t-norms,

$$\tau_1(\alpha, \beta) = \max(0, \alpha + \beta - 1)$$
$$\tau_2(\alpha, \beta) = \alpha\beta$$
$$\tau_3(\alpha, \beta) = \min(\alpha, \beta)$$

where $\tau_1(\alpha, \beta) \leq \tau_2(\alpha, \beta) \leq \tau_3(\alpha, \beta)$ for all $0 \leq \alpha, \beta \leq 1$.

The most pessimistic t-norm τ_1 is used to compose specialization with generalization or vice versa. The neutral t-norm τ_2 is used to compose positive (negative) associations with specialization and generalization. The optimistic τ_3 norm is used to compose the transitive relationships' generalization and specialization, respectively, with themselves.

3.7.2 Semantic Similarity of Classes

The authors propose to consider semantic knowledge to achieve a more intuitive notion of similarity. The main consideration for this purpose is the semantic relevance of an attribute to a class. The attribute of an object may not be semantically relevant to the object. The semantic relevance can be expressed by a positive association or by a generalization. The semantically relevant parts of the structure of classes also has to be considered. This can be achieved by matching classes only via attributes that are relevant to at least one of the classes. We consider an example discussed in [FKN91] and the strategy to determine semantic similarity (Example 3.11).

> EXAMPLE 3.11
> Consider the following schema:
> CarOwner: [Name: string, Address: string, Cars: string]
> Letter: [From: Person, To: Person, Text: string]
> Person: [Name: string, Address: string, Send: Letter, Receive: Letter]
>
> Consider the following terminological knowledge base:
> Send g Communicate, strength = 0.8
> Receive g Communicate, strength = 0.6
> Communicate p Person, strength = 0.6
> Address p Letter, strength = 0.8

The strategy consists of the following three steps:

1. *Collect the semantic aspects:* An attribute is relevant to C, either if there exists a (derived) terminological relationship between the attribute and C directly, or if the attribute is semantically relevant to a class C′, which can be reached via a (schema) relationship that is relevant to C. In the latter case, the relevance of the attribute to C′ is composed with the relevance of the (schema) relationship between C and C′ by the neutral t-norm τ_2.

   CarOwner$_{sem}$ = {}
   Person$_{sem}$ = {(0.48, Send), (0.48, Receive), (0.38, Address)}
   Send g Communicate g Person, Strength = 0.6*0.8 = 0.48
   Receive g Communicate g Person, Strength = 0.6*0.8 = 0.48
   Address p Letter, Letter is related to Person via Send and Receive
   Strength = max(0.48, 0.48)*0.8 = 0.38

2. *Collect the structural aspects:* C$_{struct}$ is defined as the set of the immediate, but not semantically relevant, attributes of a class:

   CarOwner$_{struct}$ = {Name, Address, Cars}
   Person$_{struct}$ = {Name}

3. *Determine semantic similarity:* For two classes A and B, the set of terminological relationships between all pairs of elements of (A$_{sem}$, B$_{sem}$), (A$_{sem}$, B$_{struct}$), and (A$_{struct}$, B$_{sem}$). The strength of each terminological relationship found in this step is multiplied with the relevance of the

attribute in C_{sem}.

The only non-null set is the set of all pairs in $Person_{sem}$ and Car-$Owner_{struct}$, which is given by $\{(0.38, Address)\}$. Thus the overall similarity of CarOwner and Person is 0.38.

3.7.3   Discussion

The fuzzy knowledge approach attempts to combine the semantic and the structural (schematic) knowledge available. The semantic knowledge employed is represented in the form of a fuzzy terminological knowledge base with relationships like synonymy and generalization associated with fuzzy strengths. This may be viewed as an attempt to capture and represent the real-world semantics aspect of representation of semantics. This is in contrast to the semantic proximity approach, in which the explicit context aspect is modeled and used as a framework for assigning the fuzzy strengths.

3.8
Related Work

[CHS91] discuss an approach in which resource integration is performed by mapping the individual schemas to concepts in the Cyc knowledge base using a set of articulation axioms. In addition to the structural description of the local schema, schema knowledge, resource knowledge, and organization knowledge are used. [SGN93] discuss an approach in which the attributes are mapped to an attribute hierarchy based on the RWS, which is then used in schema integration. [She91c] lays a framework for semantic relationships between objects. [Ken91a] discusses how multidatabases violate implicit assumptions about how databases model reality, giving rise to semantic conflicts and uncertainty. [DeM89b] has used partial values and maybe tuples, using the framework of 3-valued logic to model uncertainty. [TCY93] have used discrete probability distributions to model uncertainty in relational databases.

Bibliography

[BBMR89]   A. Borgida, R. Brachman, D. McGuinness, and L. Resnick. Classic: A structural data model for objects. In *Proceedings of the ACM SIGMOD*, 1989.

[BOT86]   Y. Breitbart, P. Olson, and G. Thompson. Database integration in a distributed heterogeneous database system. In *Proceedings of the Second IEEE Conference on Data Engineering*, February 1986.

[Cas93]   M. Castellanos. Semantic enrichment of interoperable databases. In *Proceedings of the RIDE-IMS*, April 1993.

[CHS91]   C. Collet, M. Huhns, and W. Shen. Resource integration using a large knowledge base in carnot. *IEEE Computer*, December 1991.

[CMG90]   G. Chierchia and S. McConnell-Ginet. Meaning and grammar: An introduction to semantics. chapter 6. Cambridge, MA: MIT Press, 1990.

[CRE87]   B. Czejdo, M. Rusinkiewicz, and D. Embley. An approach to schema integration and query formulation in federated database systems. In *Proceedings of the Third IEEE Conference on Data Engineering*, February 1987.

[CSGS91]   M. Castellanos, F. Saltor, and M. Garcia-Solaco. *The Development of Semantic Concepts in the BLOOM Model Using an Object Metamodel.* Technical report LSI-91-22. UPC, 1991.

[DeK86]   J. DeKleer. An assumption-based truth maintenance system. *Artificial Intelligence* 28, 1986.

[Dem68]   A. Dempster. A generalization of the bayesian inference. *Journal of the Royal Statistical Society, Series B* 30, 1968.

[DeM89b]   L. DeMichiel. Resolving database incompatibility: An approach to performing relational operations over mismatched domains. *IEEE Transactions on Knowledge and Data Engineering* 1(4):484–493, 1989.

[DG+95]   A. Daruwala, C. Goh, et al. The context interchange network. In *Proceedings of the IFIP WG2.6 Conference on Database Semantics, DS-6*, May 1995.

[DH84]   U. Dayal and H. Hwang. View definition and generalization for database integration in a multidatabase system. *IEEE Transactions on Software Engineering* 10(6):628–644, 1984.

[FKN91]   P. Fankhauser, M. Kracker, and E. Neuhold. Semantic vs. structural resemblance of classes. *SIGMOD Record, Special Issue on Semantic Issues in Multidatabases* 20(4), December 1991.

[Gru93]   T. Gruber. A translation approach to portable ontology spec-
            ifications. *Knowledge Acquisition, An International Journal of
            Knowledge Acquisition for Knowledge-Based Systems* 5(2), June
            1993.

[GSCS]   M. Garcia-Solaco, M. Castellanos, and F. Saltor. Semantic
            heterogeneity in multidatabase systems.

[GSCS93]   M. Garcia-Solaco, M. Castellanos, and F. Saltor. Discovering
            interdatabase resemblance of classes for interoperable databases.
            In *Proceedings of the RIDE-IMS*, April 1993.

[Guh90]   R. V. Guha. *Micro-Theories and Contexts in Cyc Part I: Ba-
            sic Issues.* Technical report ACT-CYC-129-90. Austin, TX:
            Microelectronics and Computer Technology Corporation, June
            1990.

[HM85]   D. Heimbigner and D. McLeod. A federated architecture for
            information systems. *ACM Transactions on Office Information
            Systems* 3(3):253–278, July 1985.

[HM93]   J. Hammer and D. McLeod. An approach to resolving seman-
            tic heterogeneity in a federation of autonomous, heterogeneous
            database systems. *International Journal of Intelligent and
            Cooperative Information Systems* 2(1):51–83, March 1993.

[Ken91a]   W. Kent. The breakdown of the information model in multi-
            database systems. *SIGMOD Record, Special Issue on Semantic
            Issues in Multidatabases* 20(4), December 1991.

[KLK91]   R. Krishnamurthy, W. Litwin, and W. Kent. Language features
            for interoperability of databases with schematic discrepancies.
            In J. Clifford and R. King, editors, *Proceedings of the ACM
            SIGMOD*, pages 40–49. New York: ACM, May 1991.

[KS]   V. Kashyap and A. Sheth. Semantic and schematic similarities
            between database objects: A context-based approach. *The VLDB
            Journal.* To appear; *http://www.cs.uga.edu/LSDIS/~amit/66b-
            VLDB.ps.*

[KS91]   W. Kim and J. Seo. Classifying schematic and data hetero-
            geneity in multidatabase systems. *IEEE Computer* 24(12):12–18,
            December 1991.

[LA86]   W. Litwin and A. Abdellatif. Multidatabase interoperability. *IEEE Computer* 19(12):10–18, December 1986.

[MK]   E. Mena and V. Kashyap. Observer: An approach for query processing in global information systems based on interoperation across pre-existing ontologies. Working paper; *http://www.cs.uga.edu/LSDIS/infoquilt.*

[ON93]   A. Ouksel and C. Naiman. Coordinating context building in heterogeneous information systems. *Journal of Intelligent Information Systems,* 1993.

[Sal89]   G. Salton. *Automatic Text Processing.* Reading, MA: Addison-Wesley, 1989.

[SG89]   A. Sheth and S. Gala. Attribute relationships: An impediment in automating schema integration. In *Proceedings of the NSF Workshop on Heterogeneous Databases,* December 1989.

[SGN93]   A. Sheth, S. Gala, and S. Navathe. On automatic reasoning for schema integration. *International Journal on Intelligent and Cooperative Information Systems* 2(1), March 1993.

[Sha76]   G. Shafer. *A Mathematical Theory of Evidence.* Princeton, NJ: Princeton University Press, 1976.

[She91a]   A. Sheth. Federated database systems for managing distributed, heterogeneous, and autonomous databases. In *Tutorial Notes— the 17th VLDB Conference,* September 1991.

[She91c]   A. Sheth. Semantic issues in multidatabase systems. *SIGMOD Record, Special Issue on Semantic Issues in Multidatabases* 20(4), December 1991.

[SK93]   A. Sheth and V. Kashyap. So far (schematically), yet so near (semantically). In *Proceedings of the IFIP TC2/WG2.6 Conference on Semantics of Interoperable Database Systems, DS-5.* Amsterdam: North-Holland, November 1993.

[SL90]   A. Sheth and J. Larson. Federated database systems for managing distributed, heterogeneous, and autonomous databases. *ACM Computing Surveys* 22(3):183–236, September 1990.

[SM91]   M. Siegel and S. Madnick. A metadata approach to resolving
              semantic conflicts. In *Proceedings of the 17th VLDB Conference*,
              September 1991.

[SSR92a]   E. Sciore, M. Siegel, and A. Rosenthal. Context interchange using
              meta-attributes. In *Proceedings of the CIKM*, 1992.

[TCY93]   F. Tseng, A. Chen, and W. Yang. Answering heterogeneous data-
              base queries with degrees of uncertainty. *Distributed and Parallel
              Databases, An International Journal* 1(3), July 1993.

[Woo85]   W. J. Wood. What's in a link?: Foundations for semantic net-
              works. In R. Brachman and H. Levesque, editors, *Readings in
              Knowledge Representation*. Los Altos, CA: Morgan Kaufmann,
              1985.

[YSDK91]   C. Yu, W. Sun, S. Dao, and D. Keirsey. Determining rela-
              tionships among attributes for interoperability of multidatabase
              systems. In *Proceedings of the First International Workshop on
              Interoperability in Multidatabase Systems*, April 1991.

[Zad78]   Lotfi Zadeh. Fuzzy sets as a basis for a theory of possibility. *Fuzzy
              Sets and Systems* 1(1), 1978.

4

Resolution of Representational Diversity in Multidatabase Systems

Joachim Hammer
Dennis McLeod

Introduction

A major problem that arises frequently when attempting to support information sharing among autonomous heterogeneous database systems is the occurrence of representational differences that exist among related data objects in different component systems. A collection of cooperating but heterogeneous, autonomous component database systems is known as a multidatabase system (MDBS) [LMR90] or a loosely coupled federated database system [SL90]. Such cooperating systems attempt to support operations for partial and controlled sharing of data with minimal effect on existing applications.

In this context, a key to supporting sharing involves folding of nonlocal data into the schema of an importing (local) component as gracefully as possible. Essential to achieving this is to support the resolution of semantic and representational (modeling) differences between the local and nonlocal perspectives. By resolving representational differences we mean two things: (1) determine as precisely as possible the relationships between sharable objects in different components, and (2) detect possible conflicts in their structural representations that pose problems when folding the nonlocal data into the local schema later on. In this chapter, we present an approach for resolving representational differences that preserves the autonomy of the participating databases.

4.1
Related Research

Research in the area of collaboration among heterogeneous database systems (HDBSs) began only a decade ago [FS83, SBD+81]. The term *heterogeneous databases* was originally used to distinguish work that included database model and conceptual schema heterogeneity from work in distributed databases,[1] which addressed issues solely related to distribution [CP84]. Recently, there has been a resurgence in the area of heterogeneous database systems. This work can be characterized by the different levels of integration of the component database systems and by different levels of global (federation) services. In Mermaid [TBD+87], for example, which is considered a tightly coupled HDBS, component database schemas are integrated into one centralized global schema with the option of defining different user views on the unified schema. While this approach supports preexisting component databases, it falls short in terms of flexible sharing patterns. Due to the tight integration of conceptual schemas, no mechanism for dynamically resolving representational differences is needed.

---

[1]The term *distributed database* is used here as it has been mainly used in the literature, denoting a relatively tightly coupled, homogeneous system of logically centralized, but physically distributed, component databases.

The federated architecture proposed in [HM85], which is similar to the multidatabase architecture of [LA86], involves a loosely coupled collection of database systems, stressing autonomy and flexible sharing patterns through intercomponent negotiation. Rather than using a single, static global schema, the loosely coupled architecture allows multiple import schemas, enabling data retrieval directly from the exporter and not indirectly through some central node, as in the tightly coupled architecture. Examples of loosely coupled federated databases are MRSDM [Lit85b], OMNIBASE [REMC+89], and Calida [JPSL+88]. Resolution of representational differences is performed manually.

Most of the early work on methodologies and mechanisms for integrating individual, user-oriented schemas focused on relational and semantic database models, and (partial) unification of multiple heterogeneous object-based databases is still in its infancy. In their 1986 survey paper, Batini et al. [BLN86] investigated twelve integration methodologies and compared them on the basis of five commonly accepted integration activities. However, most of the approaches examined in their survey do not directly address the problem of resolving representational differences. Kim et al. [KCGS93] provide the most up-to-date enumeration and classification of techniques for resolving representational conflicts arising within the context of multidatabase schema integration.

One common approach to conflict resolution is to reason about the meaning and resemblance of heterogeneous objects in terms of their structural representation [LNEM89]. However, one can argue that any set of structural characteristics does not sufficiently describe the real-world meaning of an object, and thus their comparison can lead to unintended correspondences or fail to detect important ones. Other promising methodologies that were developed include heuristics to determine the similarity of objects based on the percentage of occurrences of common attributes [HR90, NEML86, SLCN88]. More accurate techniques use classification for choosing a possible relationship between classes [SSG+91]. Whereas most of these methods primarily utilize schema knowledge, techniques utilizing semantic knowledge (based on real-world experience) have also been investigated. Sheth et al. [SK93] introduce the concept of semantic proximity in order to formally specify various degrees of semantic similarities among related objects in different application domains based on the real-world context in which these objects are used. Fankhauser and Neuhold [FN92] present an approach that utilizes fuzzy and possibly incomplete real-world knowledge for resolving semantic and representational discrepancies. In their methodology, class definitions, or more generally schemas, are disambiguated by matching unknown terms with concepts in an interconnected knowledge base. A similar methodology is suggested by Ventrone and Heiler [VH93] that uses so-called enterprise models to provide an application context for describing unknown terms in the schemas of the participating components.

A different approach uses behavior to solve domain and schema mismatch problems [Ken91b]. Domain and schema mismatches are two important semantic integration problems for interoperating heterogeneous databases. The domain mismatch problem generally arises when some commonly understood concept, such as money, is represented differently in different databases (i.e., U.S. dollars vs. English pounds). Schema mismatches arise when similar concepts are expressed differently in the schema (i.e., a relationship that is being modeled as one-to-one in one schema and one-to-many in another). Kent [Ken91b] proposes an object-oriented database programming language to express mappings between these common concepts, which would allow a user to view them in some integrated way. It remains to be seen whether a language that is sophisticated enough to meet all of the requirements given by Kent in his solution can be developed in the near future.

4.2
Heterogeneity in a Collaborative Sharing Environment

In order to support the sharing of information among a collection of autonomous, heterogeneous databases, we must overcome many types of heterogeneity that exist at various levels of abstraction (e.g., hardware heterogeneity, operating system heterogeneity), making it difficult for components to cooperate. Heterogeneity is a natural consequence of the independent creation and evolution of autonomous databases that are tailored to the requirements of the application system they serve, and there is not always agreement regarding the clear definition of the problem. In this section, we will focus on a specific kind of heterogeneity that occurs at the database system level, called *representational heterogeneity*. By this we mean variations in the meaning in which data is specified and structured in different components.

Before we can present a solution to resolving representational heterogeneity, it is useful to examine the different kinds of heterogeneities that may occur. In order to clarify the concepts we employ in this work, we use several sample database schemas taken from the scientific community. Specifically, our example scenario depicted in Figure 4.1 draws from several existing gene banks (e.g., Brookhaven Protein Databank [BKW+77], the human genome repository [NRC88]) that store information about structure and sequence of macromolecules in humans as part of a large-scale genomic decoding initiative by the National Science Foundation [Fre91].

4.2.1   A Spectrum of Representational Heterogeneities

Within the context of a multidatabase system with heterogeneous, autonomous components, we can identify a spectrum of representational heterogeneity based on the following five levels of abstraction.

1. *Metadata language (conceptual database model):* The components may use different collections of and techniques for combining the structures,

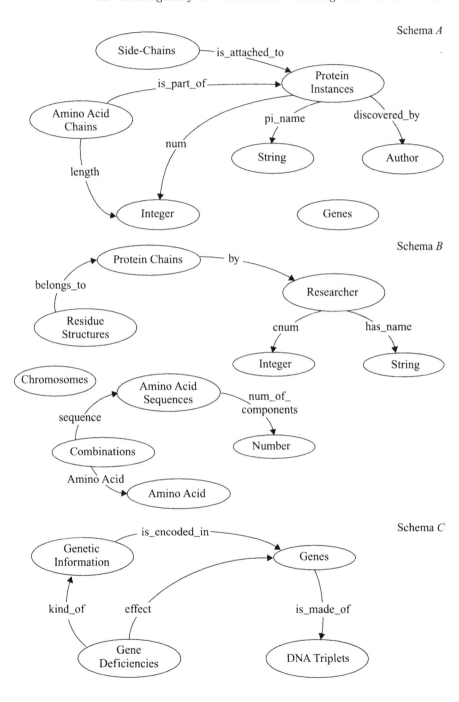

FIGURE 4.1
Example 1, semantic heterogeneity: partial conceptual schemas representing similar genomic data.

constraints, and operations used to describe data. Different data models provide different structural primitives (e.g., records in the relational data model vs. objects in the functional data model) and operations for accessing and manipulating data (e.g., QUEL vs. OSQL^2). Note, even when two database systems support the same data model, differences in their data definition languages may still contribute to semantic heterogeneity.

2. *Metadata specification (conceptual schema):* While the components share a common metadata language (conceptual database model), they may have independent specifications of their data (varied conceptual schemas). For example, this refers to the different schemas in Figure 4.1 modeling similar information on genomic data in four different ways.

3. *Object comparability:* The components may agree on a conceptual schema or more generally agree on common subparts of their schemas; however, there may be differences in the way information facts are represented [Ken89]. This variety of heterogeneity also relates to how information objects are identified and to the interpretation of atomic data values as denotations of information modeled in a database (e.g., naming, missing information). In Figure 4.2, the types `Amino Acid Chains` in Schema A and `Amino Acid Sequences` in Schema B probably represent the same kind of information despite a difference in their type names. Both types have associated with them information regarding the length of an amino acid chain or sequence as well as information on who processed a particular sample. However, Schema A does not contain information on the exact structure of a chain, whereas Schema B does (missing information).

4. *Low-level data format:* Although the components agree at the model, schema, and object comparability levels, they may use different low-level representation techniques for atomic data values (e.g., units of measure). In terms of our example, this refers to the problem that arises when values such as molecular weight or electrical charge of an atom are represented in different units (ounce vs. gram) or different precisions (16-bit float vs. 8-bit integer), respectively (see Figure 4.3).

5. *Tool (database management system):* The components may use different tools to manage and provide an interface to their data. This kind of heterogeneity may exist with or without the varieties described immediately above. This kind of heterogeneity is due to the fact that components may use a different DBMS.

We assume that the components utilize a common model (see Section 4.3.1), thus ruling out the occurrence of heterogeneities of type 1, conceptual

---

^{2}Object flavored dialect of SQL. used as a DDL/DML in function-based database systems such as IRIS [FBC$^+$87].

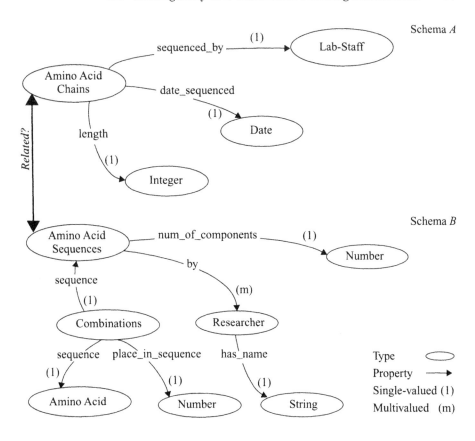

FIGURE 4.2
Example 2, semantic heterogeneity: object comparability. Semantic heterogeneities include naming problems, missing information, and mapping constraints.

database model. Furthermore, tool heterogeneity, which is type 5 in the above spectrum, is treated as somewhat orthogonal to our concern in this discussion. As a result, for the remainder of this work we will focus on resolving heterogeneities of types 2, 3, and 4.

4.2.2   Causes of Representational Diversities

According to Batini et al. [BLN86], there are three major causes for representational heterogeneity:

- *Different perspectives and needs:* This is a modeling problem that finds its roots mostly during the design phase of a database schema. Different user groups or designers adopt their own viewpoints when modeling the same information. For instance, in Example 1 in Figure 4.1, different naming conventions were used when modeling similar genomic information. By

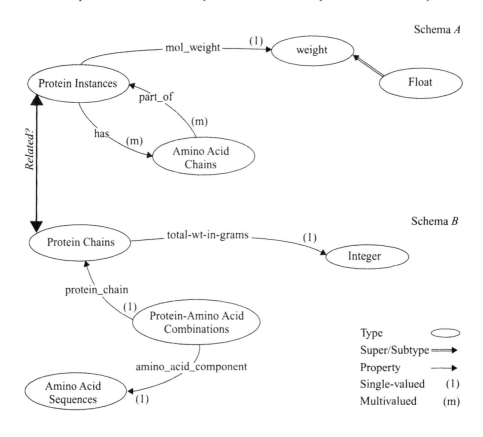

FIGURE 4.3
Example 3, semantic heterogeneity: different low-level data formats. Semantic heterogeneities include naming problems, missing information/overloading, type relativism, and mapping constraints.

the same token, Schema *B* in Figure 4.2 contains information on the structure of an amino acid chain, whereas Schema *A* does not.

- *Equivalent constructs:* The rich set of constructs in data models allows for a large number of modeling possibilities, which results in variations in the conceptual database structure [Ken89]. Typically, in conceptual models, several combinations of constructs can model the same real-world domain equivalently. For example, a many-to-many relationship between two types such as the one depicted between Protein Instances and Amino Acid Chains in Schema *A* in Figure 4.3 can be modeled as several one-to-one relationships, as shown between Protein–Amino Acid Combinations and Protein Chains and Protein–Amino Acid Combinations and Amino Acid Sequences in Schema *B* in the same figure. A ternary relationship such as this one is the preferred design choice in systems in which the DBMS does not support multivalued properties.

- *Incompatible design specifications:* Different design specifications result in different schemas. In Example 3 in Figure 4.3, the relationship between Amino Acid Chains and Lab-Staff in Schema A indicates that each new amino acid chain can only be sequenced by one lab worker, since the cardinality constraint (1) (single- valued property) has been specified. The more realistic situation (that an amino acid sequence may be processed by several researchers at once) is depicted in Schema B.

Thus far, we have discussed the nature of semantic heterogeneity and identified the causes and implications of such diversities. In the following sections, we present the details of our mechanism for resolving semantic heterogeneity. We will illustrate our mechanism using examples from a federation of macromolecular biologists such as the one introduced in Figures 4.1, 4.2, and 4.3.

4.3
Remote-Exchange Architecture

Remote-Exchange [FHMS91] is an architecture that supports the controlled sharing of information among a collection of autonomous, heterogeneous database systems. In Remote-Exchange, unification of remote objects with local objects plays a vital role, as does the ability to resolve representational conflicts stemming from reasons listed in Section 4.2.1.

The four major components of Remote-Exchange are the core object data model (CODM), the remote sharing language (RSL), the local lexicon, and the semantic dictionary. Figure 4.4 provides a schematic overview of Remote-Exchange, and in the following sections, we will introduce each component separately. A detailed description of the role each component plays in our resolution mechanism follows in Section 4.4.

4.3.1   Core Object Data Model

Before any collaboration can take place among the heterogeneous components of a federation, a common model for describing the sharable data must be established. This model must be semantically expressive enough to capture the intended meanings of conceptual schemas that may reflect several or all of the kinds of heterogeneity enumerated above. Further, this model must be simple enough so that it can be readily understood and implemented. To this end, we have chosen to use the core object data model (CODM), which is a refinement of an earlier version called MODM (see, e.g., [HM93]), as the common data model for describing the structure, constraints, and operations for sharable data.

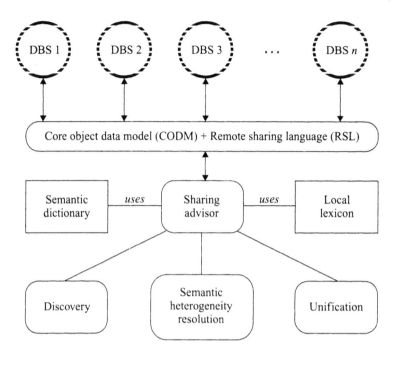

FIGURE 4.4
The Remote-Exchange architecture and its major components.

CODM is a generic functional object data model that supports the usual
object-based constructs. In particular, it draws upon the essentials of functional
database models, such as those proposed in DAPLEX [Shi81], Iris [FBC+87],
and Omega [G+91]. CODM contains the basic features common to most semantic [AM89, HK87] and object-oriented models [A+89], such as GemStone
[MSOP86], O2 [LRV88], and Orion [KBC+87]. The model supports complex
objects (aggregation), type membership (classification), subtype to supertype
relationships (generalization), inheritance of stored functions (attributes) from
supertype to subtypes, and user-definable functions (methods). Not supported
at this point are run-time binding of functions (method override), overloading
of operations, constraints (semantic integrity rules) on types and functions,
and remote transparency. We expect that CODM will eventually incorporate
some of the concepts from [LM88, LM84] for additional support in the sharing
process.

    Some advantages of using an object-based common data model include
the ability to encapsulate the functionality of shared objects [BPS89], its extensible nature [L+88], and object uniformity [CL88]. This last item is especially
important for the unification phase in which one can ask about the equiva-

TABLE 4.1
An overview of the RSL syntax.

RSL Command	Description
ShowMeta(d:DB)	Returns a list of all sharable types in database d
HasProperties(d:DB, t:Type)	Returns a list of all functions defined on type t in d
HasInstances (d:DB, t:Type)	Returns a list of all instances of user-defined type t in d
HasValue(d:DB, i:Inst, f:Func)	Returns the value of function f on instance i in d
HasValueType(d:DB, f:Func)	Returns the value type for a function f in d
HasDirectSubtypes(d:DB, t:Type)	Returns a list of all direct subtypes of type t in d
HasDirectSuperType(d:DB, t:Type)	Returns the direct supertype of type t in d
ImportMeta(d1:DB, t1:Type, d2:DB, t2:Type, r:Rel)	Integrates type $t1$ from database $d1$ into $d2$ at position $t2$ using relationship r
ImportInstances(d1:DB, t1:Type, d2:DB, t2:Type)	Copies all instances of type $t1$ into a local type $t2$

lence of actual data values, types, and operations. Note, the use of a common data model that is object based does not rule out the participation of components with record-based data models, such as the relational or hierarchical model. However, at this point we will limit our discussion to object-based multidatabase systems.

4.3.2 Remote Sharing Language

The remote sharing language (RSL) is part of CODM and provides a standardized interface to the conceptual schemas of the participating components. RSL provides the capabilities to (1) query the metadata of selected databases in order to obtain structural information about type objects (resolution) and (2) augment selected database schemas with remote objects (unification). Table 4.1 presents a preliminary list of RSL commands.

Note that we cannot depend on examining supertypes of an object because the supertype might not be available for sharing; however, we always assume that subtypes are available. Since a subtype is a specialization of a type, it makes sense to allow all subtypes of a sharable type to be sharable as well. Also remember that the term *function* in our data model refers to an attribute denoting an intertype relationship. Components that wish to share and exchange information must agree on a common interface (CODM) that can provide the functionality described above.

TABLE 4.2
Preliminary list of relationship descriptors.

R-Descriptor	Meaning
Identical	Two types are the same
Equal	Two types are equivalent
Compatible	Two types are transformable
KindOf	Specialization of a type
Assoc	Positive association between two types
CollectionOf	Collection of related types
InstanceOf	Instance of a type
Common	Common characteristic of a collection
Feature	Descriptive feature of a type
Has	Property belonging to all instances of a type

4.3.3   Local Lexicon

A foundation of our approach is the ability to maintain semantic information about all the sharable objects in each component beyond the information that is already provided by the underlying schema. For this purpose, each component database system is augmented by a *local lexicon* where it defines all type objects it is willing to share with the other components. The common vocabulary in which shared knowledge is represented in a lexicon draws some ideas from declarative knowledge representation forms such as the Knowledge Representation Language (KRL) [BW77], semantic networks [Rap68], and the Cyc knowledge base [HJK+92]. In our approach, knowledge is represented in a local lexicon as a static collection of facts of the simple form:

```
<term> relationship-descriptor <term>
```

A term on the left side of a relationship descriptor represents the unknown concept that is described by the term on the right side of a relationship descriptor. The set of descriptors is extensible and specifies the relationships that exist between the two terms. Table 4.2 shows a preliminary list of conceptual relationship descriptors used in our mechanism.

The terms used to describe the unknown concepts are taken from a dynamic list that characterizes commonalities in an MDBS. This list of commonly understood terms is called an *ontology* and varies from application domain to application domain. For example, the ontology for a multidatabase system consisting of cooperating biologists is different from the ontology used by collaborating travel agencies. Part of each multidatabase system is an initial "ontology package" that consists of a general-purpose ontology (GPO) and several special-purpose ontologies (SPOs). The GPO is application independent and constitutes a minimal working set for each multidatabase system. SPOs are application dependent and contain terms that cover specific topics. Both the

TABLE 4.3
An incomplete snapshot of A's local lexicon.

Term	Relationship Descriptor	Key Concept	Textual Description (not part of lexicon)
Protein Instances	KindOf	Protein	A protein instance is a specialization of the class of proteins.
pi_name	Equal	Name	Pi_name is used in the same way as name.
discovered_by	Equal	Researcher	Discovered_by refers to a person, which is used in the same way as researcher.
AA Chains	CollectionOf	Amino Acid	An amino acid chain is a collection of many different amino acids.
is_part_of	Equal	Component	Is_part_of is used in the same way as component.
...	...	...	...

GPO and SPOs are highly dynamic, meaning that the number of terms in them grows depending on the usage of vocabulary by the participating components. The complete package is stored in the semantic dictionary. We will have more to say on ontologies in the next section when we talk about the semantic dictionary. Since interoperability only makes sense among components that model similar or related information, it is reasonable to expect a common understanding of a minimal set of concepts taken from the application domain among all the participants. Going back to the example of collaborating macromolecular biologists, a snapshot of an ontology package could be as follows:

$$\mathcal{GPO} = \{\text{Component, Person, Name, Number, Thing, } \dots \}$$

$$\mathcal{SPO}_{Sci} = \{\text{Force, Mass, Researcher, Weight, } \dots \}$$

$$\mathcal{SPO}_{Bio} = \{\text{Amino Acid, Atom, Chain, Chromosome, DNA, Gene,}$$
$$\text{Genome, Protein, Mol-Weight, Molecule, RNA, Sequence, } \dots \}$$

The GPO includes all those terms that form the basis for any kind of communication among English-speaking components. SPO_{Sci} is a special-purpose ontology containing terms taken from the general scientific world. SPO_{Bio} contains terms used specifically in the biological community. Using this package, some possible terms in Schema A's local lexicon are given in Table 4.3.

The underlying idea of the lexicon is to define new, nontrivial terms so that they can be understood by other components in the collection; thus, local lexicons represent the real-world meaning of sharable objects in order to complement the structural representation given in the conceptual schema. In most cases, it is not possible to resolve representational discrepancies only by looking at the different type hierarchies. For example, Protein Instances in Schema

A and `Researcher` in Schema *B* have similar properties, such as *pi_name* and *has_name* of type `STRING` and *cnum* and *num* of type `INTEGER`, but the two types are not related.

4.3.4 Semantic Dictionary

Whereas local lexicons contain semantic descriptions about local, sharable objects, they do not contain any knowledge about relationships among entries in different lexicons. This information is collected in a global repository, called a *semantic dictionary*. Like the local lexicon, the semantic dictionary is dynamic, meaning that its content is updated whenever new or additional information becomes available (e.g., after a relationship between two similar remote types has been established).

Specifically, related types from different components that have been identified are grouped into a collection called a *concept*, within which subcollections called *subconcepts* can be further identified. This generates a *concept hierarchy* much like the one shown later in the bottom of Figure 4.7. In a sense, the semantic dictionary represents a dynamic federated knowledge base about the different relationships that exist among the sharable objects in a federation.

In addition to the concept hierarchy of sharable objects, the semantic dictionary also contains the ontology package described earlier as well as a list of relationship descriptors that are used in the local lexicons to describe relationships between unknown objects and terms from the ontologies (see Figure 4.5). The ontology package consists of a GPO, which is static, and several SPOs, which are dynamic and can be updated over the lifetime of the federation. The GPO and SPOs taken together provide the components with a vocabulary that describes the application areas of the database systems involved. As a result, our resolution mechanism works best if all the components have a similar background, thus reducing the need for many additional SPOs or SPOs with a lot of terms.

4.4
Resolving Representational Heterogeneity in Remote-Exchange

One reason for the relatively slow progress in the area of resolution is that heterogeneous databases provide a wide spectrum of vocabulary and name usage that is inherently difficult for computers to "understand." The narrower the domain—i.e., the higher the degree of redundancy in the vocabularies and the closer the relationships among objects—the higher the chances of successful resolution. Currently, the process of resolution (which consists of disambiguating representational differences) is still only partially automated and requires human interaction along the way.

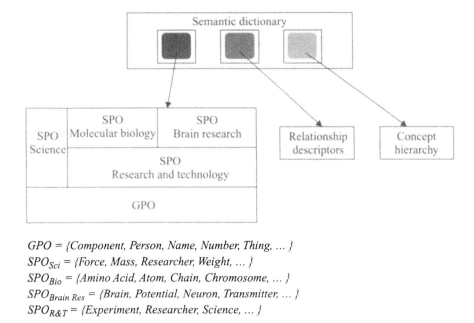

$GPO = \{Component, Person, Name, Number, Thing, ... \}$

$SPO_{Sci} = \{Force, Mass, Researcher, Weight, ... \}$

$SPO_{Bio} = \{Amino Acid, Atom, Chain, Chromosome, ... \}$

$SPO_{Brain Res} = \{Brain, Potential, Neuron, Transmitter, ... \}$

$SPO_{R\&T} = \{Experiment, Researcher, Science, ... \}$

FIGURE 4.5
The semantic dictionary and its contents.

To determine the relationship between objects within a broader context, we realize that not one single method (e.g., schema resolution based on structural knowledge—see [DH84]) but a combination of several different approaches taken together is highly promising. When studying the different types of semantic heterogeneities (see Figures 4.1, 4.2, and 4.3), it becomes evident that structural information alone will not be sufficient to resolve interobject relationships. Instead, we have decided to augment the conceptual schemas of participating components with additional semantic information describing the usage of sharable objects in their application environment. While it is nearly impossible to completely automate the resolution of interobject relationships, the following mechanism provides substantially useful functionality. We now describe our approach for resolving semantic heterogeneity, namely, determining relative object equivalence.

Using the RSL, a local dictionary or lexicon, as well as the semantic dictionary mentioned earlier, the meanings of concepts unknown to another component are "derived." RSL commands return structural information about an object (supertype, subtype(s), properties, etc.). The local lexicon, which is created and updated by each component separately, contains a semantic description of every sharable type object in the database. In order to make the

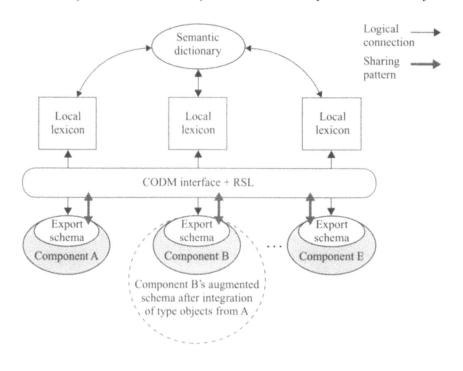

FIGURE 4.6
Sharing architecture and the various interactions among its components.

local lexicons usable throughout the entire federation, a common knowledge representation is used. Terms in question can be located and compared with each other. The semantic dictionary describes the relationships between terms in the local lexicons. See Figure 4.6 for a pictorial description of the interactions among these components. To provide components with a way to protect their private data from the rest of the federation, sharable objects must be placed in a special section of the conceptual schema termed *export schema*. Everything that is not part of the export schema is invisible to the rest of the federation.

4.4.1   Relationships among Objects

Before we present the details of our approach to resolving representational heterogeneity, we first present an overview of the various relationships that can exist among objects that model the same or similar real-world concepts in different components of a multidatabase system [BLN86].

4.4.2   Common Concepts

As a direct result of the different causes for schema diversity described above, it may happen that the same concept of an application domain is modeled by different representations R_1 and R_2 in different schemas. Returning to the example in Figure 4.1, we can see that the concept of an "amino acid chain" as it can be found in Schema A is also represented by the type Amino Acid Sequence in Schema B. In addition to the obvious naming differences, both abstract objects mirror closely related real-world information but use different modeling constructs in their representations. Several types of semantic relationships can exist between two representations R_1 and R_2: they may be identical, equivalent, compatible, or incompatible.

1. *Identical:* R_1 and R_2 are the same. This happens when the same modeling constructs are used, the same perceptions are applied, and no extraneous information enters into the specification. For example, Protein Instances in Schema A and Protein Chains in Schema B are equal representations for the same real-world concept, namely, collections of proteins. Both types have similar properties, such as structural information (e.g., Side Chains and Residue Structures) and the person who discovered each protein (e.g., Author and Researcher). This type of relationship between two representations R_1 and R_2 is expressed using the Identical relationship descriptor.

2. *Equivalent:* R_1 and R_2 are not the same because different modeling constructs have been applied. For example, in Figure 4.3, the property *mol_weight* with value type weight in schema A and *total-weight-in-grams* with value type Integer model the same information (the weight of a protein molecule), but the representation is different. In A's schema, no information is kept about the units of measure, whereas in B's schema, the unit information is already part of the property name. This kind of relationship between two representations R_1 and R_2 is expressed using the Equal relationship descriptor.

3. *Compatible:* R_1 and R_2 are neither identical nor equivalent. However, their representation is not contradictory. For example, in Figure 4.2, the two partial schemas displaying Amino Acid Chains and Lab-Staff (Schema A) and Amino Acid Sequences and Researcher (Schema B) both model the same information about certain chemical structures and the researchers who process them, but they differ in the cardinalities of their relationships. In Schema A, the property *sequenced_by* between Amino Acid Chain and Lab-Staff is single-valued, meaning that each chain can only be processed by one lab staff member. In Schema B, a multivalued relationship (*by*) exists, allowing one or more researchers to work on each amino acid sequence. The relationship between these two

representations R_1 and R_2 is expressed using the Compatible relationship descriptor.

4. *Incompatible:* R_1 and R_2 are contradictory because of inconsistent design specifications or fundamental differences in the underlying information. For example, in Figure 4.3, the relationship between Protein Instances and Amino Acid Chains is represented using a multivalued property *part_of* (and its inverse *has*). In Schema *B*, however, an additional type Protein-Amino Acid Combinations is introduced in order to store the information about which protein has which kind of amino acid sequences. This kind of information is lost in Schema *A*. The two representations R_1 and R_2 are incompatible.

4.4.3   Related Concepts

In addition to common concepts, related concepts arise frequently; we can enumerate the following most commonly used types of interschema (binary) relationships of this kind:

1. *Generalization/specialization:* Generalization is the result of taking the union of two or more types to produce a higher level type. In our example, Genetic Information in Schema *C* is the generalization of Genes (Schema *A*) and Chromosomes (Schema *B*). Specialization is the opposite of generalization. The relationship descriptor that represents generalization/specialization is called KindOf.

2. *Positive association:* It is impossible to accurately classify all kinds of relationships that can exist between objects. This category includes concepts that are "synonyms" in some context, for example, Genes and Chromosomes, and those that are typically used in the same context, for example, DNA and Nucleotides. The relationship descriptor that represents positive association is called Assoc.

This list is by no means exhaustive but rather indicative of useful interrelationships vis-à-vis semantic heterogeneity resolution.

4.4.4   Strategy for Resolving Object Relationships

The basic problem addressed by the resolution mechanism may be expressed, without loss of generality, as given two objects, a local and a foreign one, return the relationship that exists between the two. Specifically, our strategy is based on structural knowledge (conceptual schema) and the (known) relationships that exist between keywords and the two objects in question (local lexicon, semantic dictionary). One characteristic of our approach is that the majority of user input occurs before, rather than during, performance of the resolution step (i.e., when selecting the set of keywords and creating the local lexicon). In Figure 4.7, we can see a pictorial description of parts of two

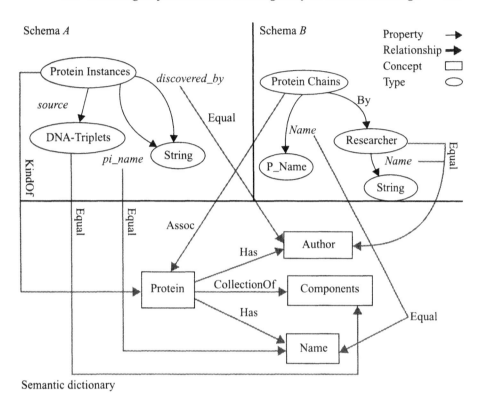

FIGURE 4.7
Resolution of representational heterogeneity between Schema A and Schema B.

local lexicons belonging to Schema A and Schema B, respectively. In the same picture, we can also see a subpart of the concept hierarchy in the semantic dictionary. Looking at A's lexicon, we can see that the property *discovered_by* is equivalent to the concept **Author** from the ontology package. We also see that schema B's **Researcher** and *Name* combination is equivalent to the concept **Author**. Therefore, *discovered_by* and the type property combination of **Researcher** and *Name* must be equivalent.

As a final note, we can make the following observation on the use of RSL commands with respect to resolution of representational heterogeneity. All information about the structure of a type object is provided through selected RSL commands: an approach that can be viewed as a variation to the usual paradigm of behavior encapsulation in object-oriented programming languages. Rather than encapsulating behavior, these commands "encapsulate" the structure of a type object. The advantage of this approach is that RSL commands that are essentially computed or foreign functions in our data model can be part of each component's schema without modifications to the underlying architecture.

4.5
Sharing in Remote-Exchange

The approach to resolving representational heterogeneity presented in this chapter is couched in the framework of Remote-Exchange, a research project at the University of Southern California. The Remote-Exchange architecture provides three "services" to its multidatabase components: an intelligent sharing advisor, resolution of representational heterogeneity, and sharing. When a new component initially joins the collection, it must first register, by invoking the sharing advisor. The sharing advisor enters the data that the component is willing to share into the semantic dictionary so that it can be used by other components. Assuming that the new component has met the two basic conditions above, namely register with the sharing advisor and define its sharable type objects using the common terminology in the semantic dictionary, it is then ready to participate in the exchange of information. Sharing takes place on a component-pairwise basis when the sharing advisor has located the sources of relevant information. The importing component selects those relevant foreign objects that it wants to integrate into its local framework. Given a foreign object, a related local object, and the relationship between the two, the sharing tool places the foreign object (including its instances and stored functions) into the appropriate place in the local metadata framework (type hierarchy). At this point, the unification is complete, and the newly imported object can be used by the remote component.

An experimental prototype of our mechanism is currently under development. This initial prototype, which we are using to demonstrate, evaluate, and refine our approach, is based on a test bed consisting of Omega [G+91] DBMS components. Omega was chosen for two reasons. First, by using an existing DBMS, we were able to focus our attention on implementing the resolution and sharing mechanism. Second, the Omega database model contains most of the modeling constructs needed to implement CODM.

4.6
Summary

We have presented an approach and mechanism for resolving representational heterogeneity in the context of a multidatabase system. While our mechanism is general enough to apply to schemas in most data models, we claim successful resolution only within the context of object-based databases. For this mechanism to operate effectively, each participating component must agree to meet two principal conditions: First, the CODM data model must be supported at the federation interface, including the RSL functionality as presented in Section 4.3.2. Second, a local lexicon must be provided, wherein a component describes the meaning of the (type) objects it is willing to share with other components in federation. These objects must be described using the conceptual relationship descriptors supported by our mechanism.

We note that it is not at present possible to completely automate the tasks of the sharing advisor, particularly in supporting the resolution of representational heterogeneity. Consequently, in practice one or more humans will likely be required to assist. In order to facilitate the establishment of a multidatabase system, we employ so-called ontologies, which contain an initial set of terms that can be used to describe unknown concepts in the local lexicon of each component. A complete ontology package describes general as well as specific information from the application domain and will evolve and grow over time to accommodate additional, more complex concepts within a given federation. Such packages can be provided for particular domains, e.g., the travel industry or genetic information.

The result of this research may have both a direct and practical impact on information sharing among heterogeneous databases, specifically in the following areas:

- *Framework:* We have presented a framework for accommodating representational heterogeneity in interoperable object-based database systems. We specifically use a functional object-based data model (extended with a sharing language) for describing the sharable data as well as their relationships to the real-world concepts they represent.

- *Architecture:* We have introduced an architecture and experimental system for resolving representational heterogeneity. Our system is based on the interaction between RSLs that provide structural information, local lexicons that provide semantic information, and the semantic dictionary that provides partial or incomplete knowledge about the relationships between the concepts in the local lexicons. Relationships are described using a set of fundamental descriptors, which is extensible.

- *Existing components and autonomy:* Throughout this work, we have paid careful attention to limiting required modifications to existing DBMS software and conceptual schemas. As a result, our approach requires no modification to the query processor or any other aspect of the local architecture. Other than the basic requirements of a CODM interface and support of a local lexicon, each component retains autonomy over its database. Furthermore, through the export schema, it can specify at any given time which objects are sharable and which objects should remain private.

Our approach to resolving representational heterogeneity can be utilized by a variety of intelligent and cooperative information systems (ICISs) [McL93, PLS92], such as Services and Information Management for Decision Systems (SIMS) [ACHK93] or Microsoft's Open Database Connectivity (ODBC), for example.

Acknowledgments

This research was sponsored in part by the Integrated Media Systems Center, a National Science Foundation Engineering Research Center, with additional support from the Annenberg Center for Communication at the University of Southern California and the California Trade and Commerce Agency. The authors would like to acknowledge the very useful insights of Brian Harp and Matthias Klusch, as well as other researchers involved in Remote-Exchange, including K. J. Byeon and Antonio Si.

Bibliography

[A+89]   M. Atkinson et al. The object-oriented database system manifesto. In *Proceedings of the First International Conference on Deductive and Object-Oriented Databases*, December 1989.

[ACHK93]   Y. Arens, C. Y. Chee, C. Hsu, and C. Knoblock. Retrieving and integrating data from multiple information sources. *International Journal of Intelligent and Cooperative Information Systems* 2(2):127–158, June 1993.

[AM89]   H. Afsarmanesh and D. McLeod. The 3DIS: An extensible, object-oriented information management environment. *ACM Transactions on Office Information Systems* 7:339–377, October 1989.

[BKW+77]   F. C. Bernstein, T. F. Kötzle, G. B. Williams, E. F. Mayer, M. D. Bryce, J. R. Rodgers, O. Kennard, T. Himanouchi, and M. Tasumi. The protein databank: A computer-based archival file for macromolecular structures. *Journal of Molecular Biology* 112:535–542, 1977.

[BLN86]   C. Batini, M. Lenzerini, and S. B. Navathe. A comparative analysis of methodologies for database schema integration. *ACM Computing Surveys* 18(4):324–364, December 1986.

[BPS89]   E. Bertino, G. Pelagatti, and L. Sbattella. An object-oriented approach to the interconnection of heterogenous databases. In *Proceedings of the Workshop on Heterogenous Databases*, December 1989.

[BW77]   D. G. Bobrow and T. Winograd. An overview of KRL, a knowledge representation language. *Cognitive Science* 1(1):10–29, 1977.

[CL88]   T. Connors and P. Lyngbaek. Providing uniform access to heterogeneous information bases. In *Proceedings of the Second International Conference on Object-Oriented Database Systems*, September 1988.

[CP84]   Stefano Ceri and Giuseppe Pelagatti. *Distributed Databases: Principles and Systems.* New York: McGraw-Hill, 1984.

[DH84]   U. Dayal and H. Hwang. View definition and generalization for database integration in a multidatabase system. *IEEE Transactions on Software Engineering* 10(6):628–644, 1984.

[FBC$^+$87] D. Fishman, D. Beech, H. Cate, E. Chow, T. Connors, T. Davis, N. Derrett, C. Hoch, W. Kent, P. Lyngbaek, B. Mahbod, M. Neimat, T. Ryan, and M. Shan. Iris: An object-oriented database management system. *ACM Transactions on Office Information Systems* 5(1):48–69, January 1987.

[FHMS91]   D. Fang, J. Hammer, D. McLeod, and A. Si. Remote-Exchange: An approach to controlled sharing among autonomous, heterogenous database systems. In *Proceedings of the IEEE Spring Compcon.* Los Alamitos, CA: IEEE Computer Society Press, February 1991.

[FN92]   P. Fankhauser and E. Neuhold. *Knowledge based integration of heterogeneous databases.* Technical report. Technische Hochschule Darmstadt, 1992.

[Fre91]   K. Frenkel. The human genome project and informatics. *Communications of the ACM* 34(11):41–51, 1991.

[FS83]   A. Ferrier and C. Stangret. Heterogeneity in the Distributed Database Mangagement System SIRIUS-DELTA. In *Proceedings of the International Conference on Very Large Databases*, 1983.

[G⁺91]   S. Ghandeharizadeh et al. *Design and Implementation of OMEGA Object-Based System.* Technical report USC-CS. Los Angeles: Computer Science Department, University of Southern California, September 1991.

[HJK⁺92]   M. Huhns, N. Jacobs, T. Ksiezyk, W. Shen, M. Singh, and P. Cannata. *Enterprise information modeling and model integration in carnot.* Technical report Carnot-128-92. MCC, 1992.

[HK87]   R. Hull and R. King. Semantic database modeling: Survey, applications, and research issues. *ACM Computing Surveys* 19(3):201–260, September 1987.

[HM85]   D. Heimbigner and D. McLeod. A federated architecture for information systems. *ACM Transactions on Office Information Systems* 3(3):253–278, July 1985.

[HM93]   J. Hammer and D. McLeod. An approach to resolving semantic heterogeneity in a federation of autonomous, heterogeneous database systems. *International Journal of Intelligent and Cooperative Information Systems* 2(1):51–83, March 1993.

[HR90]   S. Hayne and S. Ram. Multi-user view integration system (MU-VIS): An expert system for view integration. In *Proceedings of the Sixth International Conference on Data Engineering.* Los Alamitos, CA: IEEE Computer Society Press, February 1990.

[JPSL⁺88] G. Jacobsen, G. Piatetsky-Shapiro, C. Lafond, M. Rajinikanth, and J. Hernandez. CALIDA: A knowledge-based system for integrating multiple heterogeneous databases. In *Proceedings of the Third International Conference on Data and Knowledge Bases,* pages 3–18, June 1988.

[KBC⁺87]   W. Kim, J. Banerjee, H. T. Chou, J. F. Garza, and D. Woelk. Composite object support in an object-oriented database system. In *Proceedings of the Conference on Object-Oriented Programming Systems, Languages, and Applications,* pages 118–125, 1987.

[KCGS93]   W. Kim, I. Choi, S. Gala, and M. Scheevel. On resolving schematic heterogeneity in multidatabase systems. *Distributed and Parallel Databases* 1(3):251–279, July 1993.

[Ken89]   W. Kent. The many forms of a single fact. In *Proceedings of the IEEE Spring Compcon*. Los Alamitos, CA: IEEE Computer Society Press, February 1989.

[Ken91b]   W. Kent. Solving domain mismatch problems with an object-oriented database programming language. In *Proceedings of the International Conference on Very Large Databases*, pages 147–160. Los Alamitos, CA: IEEE Computer Society Press, September 1991.

[L⁺88]   V. Linnemann et al. Design and implementation of an extensible database management system supporting user defined data types and functions. In *Proceedings of the International Conference on Very Large Databases*, pages 294–305, 1988.

[LA86]   W. Litwin and A. Abdellatif. Multidatabase interoperability. *IEEE Computer* 19(12):10–18, December 1986.

[Lit85b]   W. Litwin. An overview of the multidatabase system MRSDM. In *Proceedings of the ACM National Conference*, pages 495–504. New York: ACM, October 1985.

[LM84]   P. Lyngbaek and D. McLeod. Object management in distributed information systems. *ACM Transactions on Office Information Systems* 2(2):96–122, April 1984.

[LM88]   Q. Li and D. McLeod. Object flavor evolution in an object-oriented database system. In *Proceedings of the Conference on Office Information System*. New York: ACM, March 1988.

[LMR90]   W. Litwin, L. Mark, and N. Roussopoulos. Interoperability of multiple autonomous databases. *ACM Computing Surveys* 22(3):267–293, September 1990.

[LNEM89]   J. Larson, S. B. Navathe, and R. El-Masri. A theory of attribute equivalence and its applications to schema integration. *IEEE Transactions on Software Engineering* 15(4):449–463, April 1989.

[LRV88]   C. Lecluse, P. Richard, and F. Velez. O_2, an object-oriented data model. In *Proceedings of the ACM SIGMOD International Conference on Management of Data*. New York: ACM, June 1988.

[McL93]   D. McLeod. Beyond object databases. In *Datenbanksysteme in Büro, Technik, und Wissenschaft*. New York: Springer-Verlag, 1993.

[MSOP86]   D. Maier, J. Stein, A. Otis, and A. Purdy. Development of an object-oriented DBMS. In *Proceedings of the Conference on Object-Oriented Programming Systems, Languages, and Applications*, pages 472–482. New York: ACM, 1986.

[NEML86]   S. Navathe, R. El-Masri, and J. Larson. Integrating user views in database design. *IEEE Computer* 19(1):50–62, 1986.

[NRC88]   National Research Council. *Mapping and Sequencing the Human Genome*. National Academy Press, April 1988.

[PLS92]   M. Papazoglou, S. Laufmann, and T. Sellis. An organizational framework for cooperating intelligent information systems. *International Journal of Intelligent and Cooperative Information Systems* 1(1):169–202, 1992.

[Rap68]   B. Raphael. A computer program for semantic information retrieval. In M. Minsky, editor, *Semantic Information Processing*. Cambridge, MA: MIT Press, 1968.

[REMC+89]   M. Rusinkiewicz, R. El-Masri, B. Czejdo, D. Georgakopoulos, G. Karabatis, A. Jamoussi, K. Loa, and Y. Li. Query processing in a heterogeneous multidatabase environment. In *Proceedings of the First Annual Symposium on Parallel and Distributed Processing*, 1989.

[SBD+81]   J. Smith, P. Bernstein, U. Dayal, N. Goodman, T. Landers, K. Lin, and E. Wong. Multibase: Integrating heterogeneous distributed database systems. In *Proceedings of the National Computer Conference*, pages 487–499. AFIPS, June 1981.

[Shi81]   D. Shipman. The functional data model and the data language DAPLEX. *ACM Transactions on Database Systems* 2(3):140–173, March 1981.

[SK93]   A. Sheth and V. Kashyap. So far (schematically), yet so near (semantically). In *Proceedings of the IFIP TC2/WG2.6 Conference on Semantics of Interoperable Database Systems, DS-5*. Amsterdam: North-Holland, November 1993.

[SL90]   A. Sheth and J. Larson. Federated database systems for managing
              distributed, heterogeneous, and autonomous databases. *ACM
              Computing Surveys* 22(3):183–236, September 1990.

[SLCN88]   A. Sheth, J. Larson, A. Cornelio, and S. B. Navathe. A tool
              for integrating conceptual schemata and user views. In *Proceed-
              ings of the Fourth International Conference on Data Engineering*,
              pages 176–183. Los Alamitos, CA: IEEE Computer Society Press,
              February 1988.

[SSG+91]   A. Savasere, A. Sheth, S. Gala, S. Navathe, and H. Marcus. On
              applying classification to schema integration. In *Proceedings of
              IMS'91—The First International Workshop on Interoperability in
              Multidatabase System*, pages 258–261, 1991.

[TBD+87]   M. Templeton, D. Brill, S. K. Dao, E. Lund, P. Ward, A. L. P.
              Chen, and R. MacGregor. Mermaid: A front-end to distributed
              heterogeneous databases. *Proceedings of the IEEE* 75(5):695–708,
              May 1987.

[VH93]   V. Ventrone and S. Heiler. *A practical approach for dealing with
              semantic heterogeneity in federated database systems*. Technical
              report. The MITRE Corporation, October 1993.

5

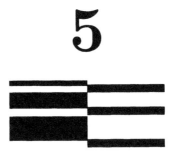

Schema Integration:
Past, Present, and Future

Sudha Ram
V. Ramesh

Introduction

Modern organizations use many diverse databases to accomplish their day-to-day data management functions. Typically, these databases are heterogeneous in that they store different types of data, represent data differently, use different software to manage the data, and run on different computer hardware. Each organizational unit can have many of these databases accomplishing a portion of its data management functions. In such a scenario, effective decision making often requires access to data from multiple databases. Research on heterogeneous database management has emphasized the development of mechanisms to provide access to data from multiple databases while preserving the local autonomy of the databases, i.e., without making changes to the existing databases.

Two popular approaches to heterogeneous database integration are the global schema approach and the federated schema approach [SL90, BHP92]. In the global schema approach, schemas corresponding to each local database are combined into a single integrated schema. In the federated approach, each local database provides an export schema, i.e., a portion of its schema that it is willing to share with other databases. Local database administrators can then use these schemas to define an import schema—a partial global schema— representing information from remote databases that is accessible locally.

Schema integration is at the core of methodologies that use either of these approaches to provide heterogeneous database interoperability. Schema integration is the process of generating one or more integrated schemas from existing schemas. These schemas represent the semantics of the databases being integrated and are used as inputs to the integration process. The output of the process is one or more integrated schemas representing the semantics of the underlying databases. The output schemas are represented using a common data model, and they hide any heterogeneities resulting from schematic differences in the underlying databases or differences in the data models upon which they are based. These schemas are used to formulate queries that may possibly need to span multiple databases. With the global schema approach, users need not be aware of the existence of the multiple underlying databases or the location of data relevant to the query. Hence, such an approach provides location, distribution, and replication transparencies in addition to providing data model and schematic transparencies.

The term *schema integration* has been loosely used in the literature to refer to methodologies that facilitate integration of schemas as defined above, as well as methodologies for view integration. This is because many of the techniques applicable in a schema integration context can be used in view integration and vice versa. However, the two processes differ in important ways [SL90, SPD92]:

1. *View integration* is the process of generating a single integrated schema
from multiple user views and is typically used in the design of a new
database schema. Hence, view integration is used in top-down database
design. We start with multiple user views, generate the integrated schema
corresponding to these views, and then design the database corresponding
to that schema. *Schema integration*, on the other hand, is a bottom-up
process because it attempts to integrate existing databases.

2. In view integration, users define views using a single data model. In
schema integration, since the underlying databases can be heterogeneous,
the schemas to be integrated may be represented using multiple data
models.

3. At the time view integration is performed, user views do not reflect existing data in a database. However, in schema integration, we integrate
schemas that represent existing databases. This is an important distinction, because the schema generated by the schema integration process
cannot violate the semantics of the existing databases. However, in view
integration, because the views represent abstract objects, there is more
flexibility in the interpretation of their semantics.

Schema integration is a complex and time-consuming problem, primarily
because most schematic representations cannot capture the intended semantics
of the databases completely. Hence, the process of integration requires extensive interaction with database designers and administrators to understand the
semantics of the databases and ensure that the semantics of the integrated
schema do not violate the semantics of the underlying databases. This also
means that the process of schema integration cannot be completely automated
[SG89, RB91]. However, tools that can reduce the amount of human interaction
can be developed and are elaborated upon later in this chapter.

It should also be noted that schema integration is not a one-time process.
Since the integrated schema represents the underlying databases, changes to it
may be needed due to

- changes in the database structure that result in changes to the underlying
schemas,

- changes in the constraints specified on the underlying databases, and

- changes to data values due to additions, modifications, or deletions in the
underlying databases.

As a result, a desirable property of any schema integration approach is that it
should be able to dynamically handle changes to the underlying databases.

The rest of this chapter is organized as follows. Section 5.1 presents a
framework for schema integration and the different dimensions on which schema

integration methodologies can be classified. Section 5.2 describes the various steps in schema integration in detail. In Section 5.3, we discuss how the schema integration process can be automated and present several automated software tools. Section 5.4 covers some directions for future research, and Section 5.5 summarizes the chapter.

5.1
Framework for Schema Integration

To provide a framework for schema integration, we first outline the steps in a typical methodology and then present a classification of the various integration strategies that have been used.

5.1.1 Steps in Schema Integration

A typical schema integration methodology can be divided into four phases [RR95b]. The steps, shown in Figure 5.1, are as follows:

1. *Schema translation:* In this phase, schemas that correspond to the individual databases being integrated are translated into schemas using a common model. Traditionally, a semantic model, such as the entity-relationship model [Che76], has been used for this purpose. Figure 5.2 shows an example of a relational and a network database. The schemas are examples of databases that may exist in a bank such as Bank One or your local credit union. The first database contains information about customers and their accounts in the bank. The second database keeps track of loans issued to borrowers. The translation of these schemas may be performed manually or with the aid of a translation tool. However, even with the use of a translation tool, it is more than likely that some form of manual interaction with the tool will be needed. Any schema translation technique should have the following characteristics:

   a. the schema using the common model should completely represent the semantics of the underlying database, and

   b. it should be possible to translate a command on the translated schema into commands on the local schema. Figure 5.3 shows the translated ER representations of the schemas in Figure 5.2.

2. *Schematic interschema relationship generation:* The objective of this phase is to identify objects in the underlying schemas that may be related—i.e., entities, attributes, and relationships—and to categorize the relationships among them. This is done by examining the semantics of the objects in the different databases and identifying relationships based on their semantics. The semantics of an object can be ascertained by analyzing schematic properties of entity classes, attributes, and relationships

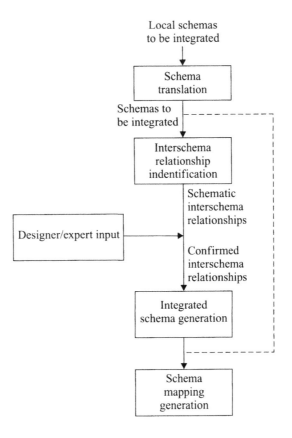

FIGURE 5.1
Steps in a schema integration methodology.

in the schema as well as by interacting with designers and exploiting their knowledge and understanding of the application domain. For example, integrity constraints, cardinality, and domains are properties of attributes that convey their partial semantics.

The ultimate objective of this step is the generation of a reliable set of relationships among database objects. It is important that these relationships be accurate because they are used as input to the integrated schema generation phase. For example, in Figure 5.3, we would identify the two entities CUSTOMER in part (a) and BORROWER in part (b) as related to each other. In addition, we can classify the relationship as being a subsumption relationship; i.e., the set of borrowers in the second database is a subset of the set of customers identified in the first database.

(a)

CUSTOMER (SSNo, FName, LName, Address, PhNo, NYears, CR)

ACCOUNTS (AcctNo, Balance, Type, CustNo)

(b)

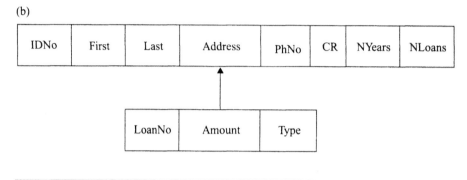

FIGURE 5.2
Local schemas: (a) database 1 (relational) and (b) database 2 (CODASYL network).

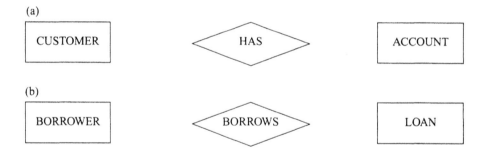

FIGURE 5.3
ER representation of translated schemas: (a) database 1 (translated relational schema) and (b) database 2 (translated CODASYL schema).

Finally, we would identify attributes in the two entity classes that may be related.

3. *Integrated schema generation:* In this phase, the interschema relationships generated previously are used to generate an integrated representation of the underlying schemas. Generating such a representation involves resolving various forms of heterogeneity that may exist between related objects. Sheth and Kashyap [SK93] classify these heterogeneities into

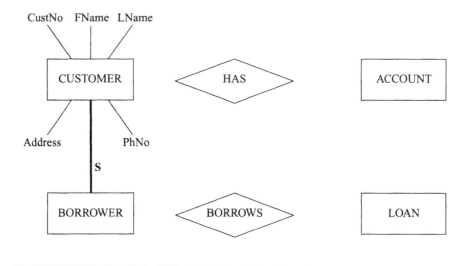

FIGURE 5.4
Integrated schema.

five major categories: domain definition, entity definition, data value, abstraction level, and schematic incompatibilities.

The integrated schema generation process resolves these different forms of heterogeneity and generates an integrated schema that hides the heterogeneity from the user. In our example, in the integrated schema (Figure 5.4), a subsumption relationship between CUSTOMER and BORROWER is generated to reflect the nature of the relationship among these entity classes. Note that the attributes SSNo and IDNo have been integrated into a single attribute (CustNo) in the superclass. This type of integration assumes that these attributes have been identified as being equivalent to each other in the interschema relationship generation step.

4. *Schema mapping generation:* This step accompanies the integrated schema generation step and involves storing information about mappings between objects in the transformed (integrated) schemas and objects in the local schemas. Such mappings are important for query transformation. For example, we would need to note that the attribute CustNo in the integrated schema (Figure 5.4) maps back to SSNo in database 1 and IDNo in database 2.

It should be noted that these steps may need to be performed iteratively to resolve the heterogeneity and arrive at an integrated representation(s) of the underlying schemas.

5.1.2   Classification of Schema Integration Strategies

Two primary properties distinguish integration strategies in the literature: (1) the abstraction level at which integration is attempted, which in turn dictates the types of heterogeneity that need to be considered by a methodology, and (2) the semantics conveyed by the input schemas. The semantic richness of the input schemas depends partly on the data model used. Hence, we classify schema integration strategies based on the abstraction level at which they operate and on the data model used to represent input schemas. A third classification based on the degree to which the integration methodologies can deal with changes to the underlying databases can also be generated. However, as we discuss later, this classification parallels the classification based on abstraction level.

Classification Based on Abstraction Level

Integration methodologies presented in the literature can be classified as operating at one of three levels: the user view level, conceptual schema level, or data level. We begin our discussion with the most common level—user views.

Most view integration methodologies fall in the category of *user views*. The objective of view integration methodologies is to integrate several user schemas (representing users' views of a database) into a single integrated schema. Hence, view integration is part of the top-down database design process [SL90]. Most users' views are represented using a common data model. As a result, it is unlikely that these methodologies require the schema translation step. Moreover, since the views do not represent an existing database, much of the intended semantics is conveyed by the schema itself. If we assume the schemas shown in Figure 5.3 represent user views of the banking database, then the integrated schema generated in Figure 5.4 would represent the result of applying view integration strategies on those views.

It should be noted that in the example, we considered the case where user views were created statically. User views can also be created dynamically using a multidatabase language. A description of this strategy can be found in Chapter 7, Multidatabase Languages. The integrated schema could then be used as the starting point for designing a new database. Many of the integration methodologies reported in Batini et al. [BLN86] are view integration methodologies. Navathe and Gadgil [NG82], Batini and Lenzerini [BL84], Biskup and Convent [BC86], Navathe et al. [NEML86], Shoval and Zohn [SZ91], and Gotthard et al. [GLN92] are examples of view integration methodologies.

Methodologies that operate at the *conceptual schema* level generate one or more integrated schemas from schemas of the local databases being integrated. To achieve this objective, it is necessary for the methodologies to cope with both structural and semantic heterogeneity in the underlying databases. Methodologies at this level can be divided into two classes:

1. *Schema restructuring methodologies:* Those that generate integrated schemas by applying schema restructuring operators to the underlying databases.

2. *View generation methodologies:* Those that generate an integrated representation by developing views or defining queries on the local databases of interest.

The difference between these strategies is explained in the next few paragraphs.

Prominent examples of schema restructuring methodologies include El-Masri et al. [EMLN86], Larson et al. [LNEM89], and Spaccapietra et al. [SPD92]. Application of any of these methodologies to the schemas in Figure 5.3 (representing local schemas after translation) would result in an integrated schema similar to that shown in Figure 5.4. Thus, the primary difference between schema restructuring strategies and view integration strategies lies in the fact that in schema restructuring methodologies, the schemas being integrated are derived from heterogeneous data models and represent one or more underlying databases.

Examples of approaches using the view generation methodology can be found in Kaul et al. [KDN90], Ahmed et al. [ASD⁺91], Bertino [Ber91], and Kim and Seo [KS91]. In our example, assume that we relax the restriction that all borrowers have an account with the bank. To generate an entity class representing the set of all customers who are associated with the bank, we would define a query on the CUSTOMER and BORROWER entity classes from the underlying databases and create a supertype entity class called ALL_CUSTOMER. Figure 5.5 shows the view and the query that can result in such a view being generated.

It should be noted that if the SSNo and IDNo fields in the CUSTOMER and BORROWER entity classes are different, we may have to define a new attribute called CustNo and define a function that maps CustNo to IDNo and SSNo. The same argument holds for other attributes that may differ. It is interesting to note that although early methodologies, such as Motro and Buneman [MB81], Casanova and Vidal [CV83], Mannino and Effelsberg [ME84], and Templeton et al. [TBD⁺87], seem to adopt the view generation paradigm, the process of developing the integrated view in these methodologies is much closer to the schema restructuring paradigm.

The primary difference between the schema restructuring and view generation approaches lies in the static nature of the former and dynamic nature of the latter. An integrated schema generated using schema restructuring is a representation that reflects schema definitions at the time integration was performed. Any changes to the underlying databases that affect the schemas will require that the process be repeated. The view generation approach is more dynamic because the integrated representation is generated by defining a view on the local schemas. As a result, if the schemas change, only a new view needs to be defined and that, too, only if the change can affect the existing view. For

View Creation Query

CREATE TYPE ALL_CUSTOMER

SUPERTYPE OF CUSTOMER, BORROWER

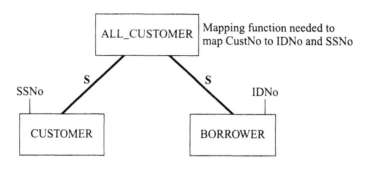

FIGURE 5.5
View generation using a query.

example, if the bank wanted to merge information about its money market account customers (maintained separately) with the rest of the databases, we would define a new view to include customers with regular, loan, and money market accounts, as shown in Figure 5.6.

The third class of integration methodologies operates at the *data level*. Methodologies at this level rely on actual data values to accomplish integration. Much of the work at this level has focused on integrating relational databases. Instance-level integration strategies presented in DeMichiel [DeM89b], Chatterjee and Segev [CS91], and Prabhakar et al. [PRSL93] fall into this category. Data-level methodologies address two main problems:

1. *Entity identification:* How does one identify representations of the same real-world entity in different databases?

2. *Attribute-value conflicts:* How does one deal with differences in data values among attributes that represent the same real-world entity?

Such differences can arise due to differing attribute domains as well as differences in the actual data values stored in the databases.

For example, let us assume we are trying to generate a relation that represents the list of customers with outstanding loans. This could be generated by defining an intersection of the two databases shown in Figure 5.7. The process of intersection is relatively easy if the two relations share a common key. Generating an integrated relation requires that we identify, for instance, that two tuples represent the same person. However, consider the tuples shown

View Creation Query

CREATE TYPE ALL_CUSTOMER

SUPERTYPE OF CUSTOMER, BORROWER, MM_CUSTOMER

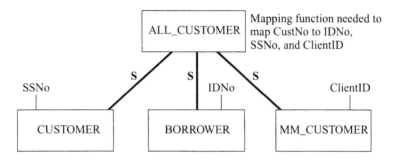

FIGURE 5.6
New view generation using a query.

SSNo	FName	LName	Address	PhNo
123456005	John	Doe	111, E. Mocking Bird Lane	555-3333
123456007	Bob	Smith	2, W. Broadway	555-2347
132695008	John	Doe	1, E. Speedway	555-9898

IDNo	First	Last	Address	PhNo
5008	John	Doe	1, E. Speedway	9898
6005	John	Doe	111, E. Mocking Bird Lane	3333
1010	Jane	Smith	5000, Melrose Avenue	3535
5007	Bob	Smith	2, W. Broadway	2347

FIGURE 5.7
Instance-level integration problems with the CUSTOMER relation (top) and the BORROWER relation (bottom).

in Figure 5.7. It is clear that tuple 1 in the CUSTOMER relation and tuple 2 in the BORROWER relation refer to the same entity. However, because the SSNo and IDNo do not match, they cannot be used as the sole source of identification for matching tuples. The combination of last and first names also cannot be used because there may exist more than one customer with the same combination. Thus, differences in data and the lack of a key can make identifying related tuples and performing a join difficult. Instance-level integration deals with resolving such incompatibilities. It should be noted that changes to the data values may void any integration performed previously. Thus, instance-level integration strategies are inherently dynamic in nature.

Another technique that falls into the data-level category deals with semantic integrity constraints and their use in schema integration. Ramesh and Ram [RR95b] present a methodology that describes how integrity constraints from multiple databases can be combined to develop constraints at the global/federated schema level and the use of these integrated constraints in semantic query processing. For example, consider the following constraints defined on the CUSTOMER relation. For relational database 1:

```
CUSTOMER(SSNo, FName, LName, Address, PhNo, NYears, CR)
1C1:  CR >= 10 ⟨- CUSTOMER(SSNo, FName, LName, Address, PhNo,
   NYears, CR), NYears⟩
```

For network database 2:

```
BORROWER(IDNo, First, Last, Address, PhNo, CR, NYears, NLoans)
```

The constraint on the customer database states that if a customer has been with the bank for more than five years, the customer's credit rating is at least 10. Now assume that it can be determined that the constraint on the CUSTOMER relation is valid in the BORROWER relation. If integration results in the schema shown in Figure 5.4, we can associate a new constraint with the integrated entity class BORROWER:

```
CUSTOMER(SSNo, FName, LName, Address, PhNo, NYears, CR)
1C1:  CR >= 10 ⟨- CUSTOMER(SSNo, FName, LName, Address, PhNo,
   NYears, CR), NYears⟩
```

For network database 2:

```
BORROWER(IDNo, First, Last, Address, PhNo, CR, NYears, NLoans)
1C2:  CR >= 10 ⟨- BORROWER(IDNo, First, Last, Address, PhNo,
   CR, NYears, NLoans), NYears⟩
```

This new constraint can then be utilized to semantically transform a query on the BORROWER entity class. For example, consider the query

```
Select BORROWERS where NYears > 5 and CR < 8
```

which asks for a list of borrowers who have been banking for more than five years and have a credit rating less than 8. This can be answered without accessing the database because we have been able to associate a new constraint with the BORROWER entityclass guaranteeing that all borrowers who have been with the bank for more than five years have a minimum credit rating greater than 10. Hence, no tuple will satisfy this query.

Classification Based on Data Model of Input Schemas

Strategies for schema integration are highly dependent on the semantics conveyed by the local schemas. Since this is directly related to the type of model used, one can classify methodologies based on the data model used to represent the local schemas. Four models have been used: relational models, semantic models, object-oriented models, and logic-based models.

1. *Approaches based relational models:* The earliest schema integration methodologies used relational models to represent the local schemas [AFS81, CV83]. The drawback of using a relational model is the limited expressive power of the model, which results in inadequate semantics being captured by the schemas. However, the widespread existence of relational databases, the simplicity of the relational model, as well as the existence of a powerful query formulation language seem to make the relational model and relational databases ideal starting points for new research domains. As a result, the relational model is the choice of researchers developing prototypes of heterogeneous database systems. For example, the prototypes and methodologies described in Deen et al. [DAT87b], Templeton et al. [TBD+87], Chung [Chu90], and Kim and Seo [KS91] all use relational models. Relational models and databases are also the choice of researchers attempting to solve heterogeneity problems at the data level [DeM89b, CS91, PRSL93].

2. *Approaches based on semantic models:* Approaches based on semantic models use variants of the entity-relationship model to represent local schemas as well as the integrated schemas. Larson et al. [LNEM89], Shoval and Zohn [SZ91], Spaccapietra et al. [SPD92], and Sheth et al. [SGN93] are examples of methodologies that belong to this category. The primary reason for using semantic models is that they can express richer semantics than the relational model, which can then be exploited during schema integration. Since semantic models are most commonly used to represent views and conceptual schemas, most of these methodologies fall into the user view/conceptual schema-level categories of the previous classification.

3. *Approaches based on object-oriented models:* We classify approaches based on object-oriented models separately because unlike approaches based on semantic models, some of the methodologies in this category attempt to integrate methods along with schemas. They also deal with integration of complex attributes and object hierarchies. Most of these methodologies fall into the view integration/conceptual schema integration category presented above. Examples of research belonging to this category include Bertino [Ber91], Czejdo and Taylor [CT91], Kaul et al. [KDN90], Geller et al. [GMP+92], Gotthard et al. [GLN92], and Thieme and Siebes [TS93].

TABLE 5.1
Methodologies for schema integration.

Methodology	Abstraction Level	Data Model	Output Data Model/ Representation Type
Templeton et al. [TBD$^+$87]	Conceptual	Relational	Relational/View
Spaccapietra et al. [SPD92]	Conceptual	Semantic	Semantic/Schema
Whang et al. [WNC91]	Conceptual	Logic	Logic/View
Larson et al. [LNEM89]	Conceptual	Semantic	Semantic/Schema
Gotthard et al. [GLN92]	View	Object-oriented	Object-oriented/View
Shoval and Zohn [SZ91]	View	Semantic	Semantic/View
Prabhakar et al. [PRSL93]	Data	Relational	–
Chatterjee and Segev [CS91]	Data	Relational	–
DeMichiel [DeM89b]	Data	Relational	–
Ahmed et al. [ASD$^+$91]	Conceptual	Object-oriented	Object-oriented/View
Kaul et al. [KDN90]	Conceptual	Object-oriented	Object-oriented/View
Bertino [Ber91]	Conceptual	Object-oriented	Object-oriented/View
Czejdo and Taylor [CT91]	Conceptual	Object-oriented	Object-oriented/View
Kim and Seo [KS91]	Conceptual	Object-oriented/ Relational	Object-oriented/View
Ramesh and Ram [RR95b, RR97]	Conceptual/ Data	Semantic/Logic	Semantic/Schema
Johannesson [Joh93]	Conceptual	Logic	Logic/Schema

4. *Approaches based on logic:* The final category, logic-based approaches, have recently begun to appear in the literature. This represents a natural step in the development of schema integration methodologies, because first-order logic has been shown to be capable of representing the semantics of relational databases in a formal manner. Using a logic-based approach also provides the capability to capture more semantics than is possible using semantic models. For example, logic-based models allow us to express semantic integrity constraints. Semantic integrity constraints are explicit user-defined integrity constraints that have been found useful in query transformations [SHKC93]. Ramesh and Ram [RR97] describe how semantic integrity constraints can be used to facilitate schema integration. Whang et al. [WNC91] also note that it is easier to translate relational schemas to logic-based schemas than to semantic models. Whang et al. [WNC91] and Johannesson [Joh93] present logic-based approaches to schema integration.

Table 5.1 presents a classification of the methodologies in tabular format. Each row in the table identifies a methodology and provides details about the methodology. The final column indicates the type of model used to represent the output of the integration process and whether this output is an integrated schema or a view.

5.2
Techniques for Interschema Relationship Identification and Integrated Schema Generation

In this section, we summarize the key research efforts that have contributed to the interschema relationship identification (IRI), integrated schema generation (ISG), and schema mapping generation steps of the schema integration process.

It is most appropriate to classify IRI techniques based on the abstraction level at which they operate because the abstraction level defines the nature of semantic knowledge (about the databases and applications) available. Hence, our discussion of IRI techniques focuses on methodologies belonging to conceptual schema– and data-based approaches. On the other hand, ISG techniques are dependent on the model-level classification. This is logical because the characteristics of the data model used, its semantics, and the heterogeneity in the representation of the underlying databases using these models are the primary factors affecting the ISG process. Hence, the discussion on integrated schema generation centers around the data model used. Finally, schema mapping generation is relevant only in the context of approaches based on conceptual models. Thus, the discussion on schema mapping generation focuses on the differences in schema restructuring and view generation approaches.

5.2.1   Interschema Relationship Identification

The objective of the IRI phase is to identify objects in the underlying schemas that may be related and to classify the relationships among them.

Approaches Based on Conceptual Schemas

IRI techniques based on conceptual schemas use a two-phase process consisting of

1. identifying objects that are related and

2. classifying the relationships among these objects.

The first phase requires that the intended semantics of objects in databases be extracted and objects that are semantically related be identified. Once a potential set of related objects has been identified, the second phase involves classifying these relationships into various categories. The inability of existing data models to convey the true semantics of the databases causes this phase to require extensive interaction with a designer or expert who has an understanding of the applications and domains served by the database.

Approaches based on conceptual schemas use the knowledge conveyed by the various schematic constructs to deduce relationships among objects. Entity classes, attributes, and relationships represent the primary schematic constructs that can be analyzed to arrive at these relationships. Larson et al. [LNEM89] use various properties of an attribute to establish relationships among attributes of two different entities belonging to different schemas. Properties include uniqueness property, lower and upper cardinality constraints, the domain of the attribute, static and dynamic integrity constraints, security constraints, set of allowable operations on the attribute, and the scale (interpretation) of the attribute. The authors suggest that attributes be compared on these properties, and they provide definitions for assessing the degree of equivalence of the attributes. Ramesh and Ram [RR95b] suggest that properties of all schematic constructs be used to determine relationships among database objects. For example, entity classes could be compared on their names and the description of their roles in the database. Relationships can be compared on their names, cardinality, and the similarity of other participating entity classes. To support the comparison on names, roles, etc., sophisticated dictionary and thesauri mechanisms could be used. The process itself can be done manually, or it can be partially automated. Toolkits that perform automated interschema relationship identification are described in Section 5.3.

The objective of analyzing these schemas is to identify objects that are semantically related. However, it is necessary not only to identify but also to classify the relationships among these objects. The classification generated is dependent on the methodology used.

1. Larson et al. [LNEM89] generate four types of equivalences between attributes. These are a EQUAL b, a CONTAINS b, a CONTAINED-IN b, and a OVERLAP b. They go on to define five types of relationships among entities and relationships, each of which can be derived based on attribute equivalences of key attributes. These relationships include A EQUAL B, A CONTAINS B, A CONTAINED-IN B, A OVERLAP B, and A DISJOINT B. Users are asked to specify one of these types of relationships for every entity/relationship whose attributes have equivalence relationships specified on them.

2. DeSouza [DeS86], Hayne and Ram [HR90], and Ramesh and Ram [RR95b] describe relationships among objects in terms of degrees of similarity and dissimilarity. Such a classification is amenable to automating the process of determining the interschema relationship. It is assumed that the objects and their degrees of similarity will be presented to the schema integrator for generation of relationships described in step 1.

3. Song et al. [SJB92] suggest classifying semantic relationships among database objects into four types: weak semantic relation, compatible semantic relation, equivalent semantic relation, and mergeable semantic relation. These relations are defined in terms of property sets and key property sets (i.e., attributes and key attributes). A weak semantic relation implies overlap in property sets, compatible semantic relation implies overlap in

key property sets, equivalent relation implies identical key property sets, and a mergeable relation implies identical property sets.

4. Kashyap and Sheth [KS94] describe how a measure of semantic proximity among database objects can be derived based on the context, abstraction, domain, and database state. See Chapter 3 for details.

Approaches Based on Data

The objective of most IRI techniques using the data-based approach is to determine instances of entity classes in different databases that refer to the same real-world entity. The simplest approach assumes that relations from different databases possess a common key. Hence, tuples that have a common key value [DeM89b] identify the same real-world entity. However, as noted in Prabhakar et al. [PRSL93], a common key may not always be available. This is referred to as the key equivalence problem. Pu [Pu91] presents a probabilistic key equivalence technique that in essence evaluates the probability that two tuples refer to the same real-world entity. Chatterjee and Segev [CS91] suggest that one compare not only keys but all attribute values in tuples to compute the probability that two tuples refer to the same real-world entity. Li and Clifton [LC94] present an automated technique for determining attribute equivalence that combines schematic and data-level knowledge. Their method uses discriminators from the schema level, such as data type of the attributes, and from the data level, such as patterns in numeric and character fields, to determine equivalence among attributes. Finally, Prabhakar et al. [PRSL93] present an extended definition of key equivalence based on the concept of instance-level functional dependencies to identify tuples that may be equivalent. All of these techniques are intended to solve the problem of referencing tuples from heterogeneous database relations.

Ramesh and Ram [RR97] present a technique for determining relationships among database objects using the integrity constraints specified against the database. Consider an integrity constraint of the form,

$$S1 \leftarrow R1$$

where $S1$ utilizes an attribute $x1$ and $R1$ utilizes an attribute $y1$. This constraint describes restrictions placed by certain values of $y1$ on the values that $x1$ takes. Hence, the integrity constraint can be thought of as describing a property of the attribute $y1$ as well as describing characteristics of the entity class E to which $y1$ belongs. If the same constraint is valid in another database for an attribute $y'1$ belonging to an entity class E', then it is likely that $y1$, $y'1$ and E, E' are related.

This is the premise underlying the generation of constraint-based relationships among objects (entities and attributes) in heterogeneous databases. The details of this technique are presented in Section 5.4.1. It should be noted that this technique is classified as a data-level technique because these relationships are generated based on examining the actual data values in the databases. However, this technique is different from other techniques presented in this section, in that it attempts to identify relationships among entity classes rather than identify equivalent entities (instances). Thus the nature of IRI using this technique is closer to the approaches based on conceptual schemas than to those based on data.

5.2.2   Integrated Schema Generation

The ISG phase is affected by the data model used; thus our discussion deals separately with semantic model approaches, object-oriented approaches, and logic-based approaches.

Semantic Model Approaches

The following discussion focuses on ISG techniques used in schema restructuring methodologies. This is because in view generation methodologies, the techniques are driven by the capabilities of the data language used.

The main issue addressed by the methodologies is that of generating an integrated representation that reflects the semantics of the underlying databases. The primary technique adopted is the creation of generalization/specialization relationships in the integrated schema. The schema in Figure 5.4 is an example. Larson et al. [LNEM89] present an approach to schema integration that is based on the premise that any pair of objects whose identifying attributes can be integrated can themselves be integrated. The work presented in their paper extends Mannino and Effelsberg's work [ME84]. As discussed in the previous section, Larson et al. define four types of relationships between attributes. Entity class and relationship equivalence are then defined in terms of relationships between identifier attributes. Rules for integrating entity classes and relationships belonging to each category are presented along with rules for integrating attributes. Categorizing the relationships among attributes, entity classes, and relationships is the primary contribution of this research, and most methodologies that have appeared since rely on these categories to a certain extent.

Larson et al. [LNEM89] present general guidelines for transforming related objects into objects in the integrated schema. However, since an object is typically linked with other objects in the schema, such a transformation may require that changes be made to the links between objects in order to generate a correct integrated schema. El-Masri and Navathe [EMN84] and Navathe et al. [NEML86] present techniques for integrating entity class and relationship pairs that may have one of the five possible relationship pairs identified by Larson et al. They present their work in the context of an Entity-Category-Relationship model. It should be noted that these rules implicitly require that naming conflicts be handled by the methodologies. Naming conflicts manifest themselves in two forms: (1) when two unrelated objects share the same name, one of the objects needs to be renamed; and (2) two equivalent objects have the same name. In this case, a decision has to be made as to which name should be used in the integrated schema. The work presented by El-Masri and Navathe and Navathe et al. can only deal with relationships among objects represented using the same schematic construct.

Structural conflicts arise when two related objects are defined using different data model constructs or using the same construct with different properties. For example, in Figure 5.4, IDNo and SSNo represent related attributes, but they may have different properties. Most methodologies for schema integration address the structural conflict problem. Spaccapietra et al. [SPD92] and Spaccapietra and Parent [SP94] present a methodology for integration of any two types of objects. They view a schema as a graph with edges and nodes. Relationships between objects in the schema are specified using correspondence assertions. The correspondence assertions presented in the work by Spaccapietra et al. can be regarded as extensions of the concepts of object and relationships equivalence presented in Larson et al. [LNEM89].

The ability to specify relationships between objects of different types is a unique contribution of Spaccapietra et al. [SPD92]. The authors provide a comprehensive set of rules for integrating objects, specifying in detail the actions to be taken to integrate objects related through assertions. For example, one of the issues dealt with is the resolution of differences in domains and cardinalities of attributes that need to be integrated. Another contribution of Spaccapietra et al.'s methodology is the specification of rules to integrate paths. A path between two objects can be visualized as a set of links in a schema. Hence, such a path may include one or more entity classes, their attributes, and relationships. The rules for integration of paths in two schemas thus involve the simultaneous integration of multiple schema objects (objects in the path). This is different from most other methodologies, which typically specify integration rules for a pair of objects.

A methodology for resolving structural conflicts is also presented in Bouzeghoub and Comyn-Wattiau [BCW90]. Comyn-Wattiau and Bouzeghoub [CWB93] deal with another problem, that of integrating differing constraints, such as cardinality constraints and key and functional dependencies, during schema integration. Many of the early methodologies summarized in Batini et al. [BLN86] also presented guidelines for resolving structural conflicts in a variety of models. For example, El-Masri and Wiederhold [EMW79] address the problem of integration for structural models; Motro and Buneman [MB81], Yao et al. [YWH82], and Dayal and Hwang [DH84] present methodologies for functional models; Batini and Lenzerini [BL84] focus on the entity-relationship model.

Object-Oriented Approaches

Object-oriented approaches deal with all the issues relevant to approaches based on semantic models as well as some additional ones. Gotthard et al. [GLN92] describe a methodology that uses object-oriented schemas as the input schemas to a view integration algorithm. The details of their methodology and toolkit are presented in Section 5.3.1.

Additional issues dealt with by object-oriented techniques are twofold:

1. They develop mechanisms for integrating class hierarchies. A class hierarchy represents a set of classes participating in generalization/specialization relationships, such as *Borrower ISA Customer*. Such a class hierarchy can be complicated by the fact that an attribute in one of the classes may have another entity class as its domain, leading to recursive hierarchies. Thieme and Siebes [TS93] present techniques for integrating class hierarchies on the basis of semantic and structural equivalence of classes in the hierarchy. They define structural equivalence of classes based on type equivalence. Semantic equivalence is defined in terms of functional equivalence as determined by the methods specified in the classes being compared. The key contribution of this work is in recognizing the additional complexity introduced by object-oriented constructs (in the form of potentially recursive class hierarchies) and in presenting a technique for integrating them. Geller et al. [GMP+92] also present algorithms for integrating object-oriented schemas that are structurally related to each other.

   Sull and Kashyap [SK92] describe a schema integration methodology that also integrates object-oriented schemas. The aim of Sull and Kashyap's paper, however, is to present a methodology that is self-organizing; i.e., updates to local schemas can be propagated unambiguously to the integrated schema. The authors present strategies to map from relational schemas and rule bases to object-oriented schemas. They then present strategies to integrate these object-oriented schemas. As was the case with the other object-oriented schema integration methodologies, the primary emphasis is on integrating class hierarchies.

2. The methodologies have to deal with integration of methods. Two cases arise here:

   a. new methods may need to be defined for the integrated view, and

   b. preexisting methods in the entity classes being integrated may need to be integrated.

   Because existing methods may differ in name and parameters, techniques for resolving these differences need to be developed. The methodology in Bertino [Ber91] presents some techniques for incorporating method integration during structural integration. Kaul et al. [KDN90] present techniques for inheriting constraints (in the integrated class) from the classes being integrated, without making changes to the existing method definitions.

Logic-Based Approaches

Work on using logic-based approaches for schema integration is still in its early stages. Thus, unlike the previous two sections, no specific thread of research can be identified. However, as mentioned previously, the desirability of the logic-based approaches stems from the type of semantics that can be conveyed by a logic-based representation as well as the formal nature of such a representation.

Whang et al. [WNC91] describe a rule-based approach to schema integration. Each of the local schemas being integrated is represented as a schema using first-order logic. These databases constitute the extensional databases (EDBs). The integrated schema is then defined by a set of first-order logic rules applicable to the EDBs. In other words, the integrated schema is a set of intentional database (IDB) relations. Whang et al. show that the use of a logic-based representation for the integrated schema makes it conducive to query processing because most SQL-based languages can be translated easily into logic-based queries. Also, since the integrated schema is generated using horn clauses, a query issued against an integrated schema relation can be broken down using resolution until the query is expressed in terms of the base relations. The authors also mention that the semantics inherent in a logic-based schema can be exploited to facilitate semantic query optimization.

Johannesson [Joh93] describes the importance of schema transformations in view integration. The basic problem addressed here is that of merging semantically equivalent yet structurally different concepts. He suggests standardizing the schemas to be integrated by applying schema transformations prior to integration. Johannesson presents his work in a logic-based modeling context. The paper presents transformation algorithms for partial attributes, m-m attributes, lexical attributes, and attributes with fixed ranges. In addition, transformation algorithms for lattice structures and stable subtypes are presented. Again, it is interesting to note that a logic-based model is used to define these transformations, although the underlying schemas being transformed may be relational or object-oriented in nature. The primary reason seems to be that a logic-based representation allows for formal definitions of the transformations mentioned above.

5.2.3   Schema Mapping Generation

Schema mapping generation is performed concurrently with both the schema translation and integrated schema generation steps of a schema integration methodology. Developing mappings during schema translation is necessary for issuing correct queries to the local databases. This mapping may be stored as a dictionary at each local database. The mapping generated during the integrated schema generation process maps an object in the integrated schema to objects in the local schemas being integrated. If the schema restructuring approach is used, this mapping is generated as the integrated schema is being generated and is stored in a global directory/dictionary. If the view generation approach is used, this mapping is usually defined as part of the query/statement used to create the new view. Once again, the mapping information is usually stored in a global catalog [ASD+91].

5.3
Automating Schema Integration

The methodologies presented in the previous sections describe the general principles that can be used to achieve schema integration. It is clear from this discussion that schema integration is a complex and time-consuming process, and automation is desirable. However, automation of the process presents a number of challenges. Sheth and Gala [SG89] note that the schema integration process cannot be completely automated. In fact, substantial interaction with designers is required during all phases of the process. This is primarily because schema integration attempts to understand the semantics of existing databases using knowledge representations that cannot completely capture the intended semantics of the data. Furthermore, the same two schemas can be integrated differently based on their intended use [She91b]. However, it is possible to automate schema integration to the extent that tools take over mundane tasks, thus reducing the amount of user interaction. This section presents a description of tools that automate portions of the schema integration process.

5.3.1   Schema Integration Toolkits

One of the first efforts to automate any phase of the schema integration process was DeSouza's [DeS86]. This work focuses on interschema relationship identification. The author presents an expert system designed to integrate conceptual schemas defined using the Abstract Conceptual Schema (ACS) [SC83]. A set of functions (called *resemblance functions*) that can be used to compare objects in the schemas are defined. These functions use both names and structure to estimate the resemblance between constructs. Each resemblance function also has a weight associated with it, indicating the relative importance that the user would like it to have. For example, if having similar attributes is the most important criterion, the weight associated with that function would be high. Objects whose computed values of similarity fall above a certain threshold are presented to the user as being possibly similar. The significant contributions of DeSouza's paper to interschema relationship identification are

- it uses multiple properties of a database object in analyzing schema objects for similarity, and

- it associates variable weights with each of these properties.

The drawback is that this methodology is specific to ACS schemas. Also, this paper does not deal with the integrated schema generation step.

Sheth et al. [SLCN88] present a tool that leads users/designers through a five-step schema integration process: Schema Information Collection, Equivalence Class Creation and Deletion (Entities and Categories), Equivalence Class Creation and Deletion (Relationships), User Assertions (Entities and Categories), and User Assertions (Relationships). In the schema information collection step, the schemas to be integrated are input to the tool in the form of Entity-Category-Relationship schemas. The user is asked to specify relations among attributes for entities and relationships that the user thinks may be related. Once these equivalences have been specified, they are used to generate an ordered list of object (entity and relationship) pairs. The ordering indicates the likelihood that an object pair may need to be integrated. Users are then required to analyze this ordered list and specify one of five types of relationships between the objects. These relationships are based on El-Masri et al. [EMLN86] and include *equal, contained_in, contains, disjoint but integratable,* and *disjoint and nonintegratable*. The toolkit presented in the paper by Sheth et al. requires a large amount of interaction with users/designers. Users can only specify equivalence assertions among attributes, limiting the amount of semantic information that can be captured.

This deficiency is addressed in the next-generation toolkit BERDI [SM92]. BERDI allows users to define relationships among objects that belong to a potentially related set of entities, called *entity clusters*. The system allows users to assert three types of relationships among attributes: *equivalence, inclusion,* and *disjoint*. The system then provides mechanisms for generating attribute hierarchies based on these relationship assertions among attribute pairs. However, even with all these modifications, the user still bears the burden of identifying entity clusters that may be related. BERDI contains several tools, such as access to dictionary information and graphical query and display facilities, to assist users in this process.

Hayne and Ram [HR90] present some techniques for automated inter-schema relationship identification during schema integration. In their methodology, schemas are represented using a variant of the Semantic Data Model (SDM) [HM81]. They compute similarities of entity classes based on names and the properties of the associated attributes. However, they do not use the relationship information available in the schemas in their similarity computations. Moreover, they attempt to generate only equivalence relationships among database objects.

The toolkit presented in Ramesh and Ram [RR95b] addresses this deficiency. The authors utilize knowledge about entity classes, attributes, and relationships to generate similarity values among entity class, attribute, and relationship pairs, as well as among related objects represented using different constructs. Their approach to identifying interschema relationships measures the similarity or dissimilarity between entity classes, attributes, and relationships in the schemas to be integrated. They use two distinct measures: an *index_of_similarity* (IS) and an *index_of_dissimilarity* (ID) for this purpose. The IS can take on values between 0 and 1, and ID can take on values between 0 and -1. A high IS between objects indicates a high probability of a relationship between the objects. A high ID suggests that the objects in question may not be related. Heuristics are used to reduce the search space of comparisons. The primary heuristics involve termination of computation if it is clear that the resulting value will not cross a certain threshold. Once the similarity values have been determined, an attempt is made to establish the type of relationship (as classified by Larson et al. [LNEM89]) that could exist among the various database objects. This is done partially using system heuristics and then confirmed by human integrators. The rules laid out in Larson et al. [LNEM89] are followed during the integrated schema generation phase.

A key characteristic of the methodology in Ramesh and Ram [RR95b] is that it utilizes a blackboard architecture to provide explicit support for the human interaction needed during schema integration. This is achieved by viewing human interaction as an additional knowledge source needed during schema integration. The system, described in Ram and Ramesh [RR95a], utilizes three types of knowledge sources: an interschema identification engine, an integrated schema generation engine, and the human integrators. It uses a four-level blackboard architecture (Figure 5.8) to support the schema integration process. The levels are organized such that the higher the level, the closer the information at the level is to a goal state. The goal state in schema integration is the generation of an integrated schema. Each knowledge engine utilizes information available at a lower level and outputs information to higher levels.

The data level of the blackboard stores a representation of each schema (using the common data model) that needs to be integrated. This information represents the raw data that is going to be utilized by an interschema relationship identification engine. The interschema identification engine analyzes the schemas from the data level of the blackboard and generates transient assertions about the similarity or dissimilarity between entity classes, attributes, and relationships in the schemas to be integrated. These assertions are posted on the assertion level of the blackboard. The interschema identification engine consists of three distinct knowledge sources: entity class definition similarity, attribute similarity, and relationship similarity computation engines. These different knowledge sources are activated by information becoming available on the blackboard. The interschema relationship identification scheduler (IRS) is responsible for monitoring the blackboard and triggering the appropriate knowledge sources as necessary. The output of IRI engines is best classified

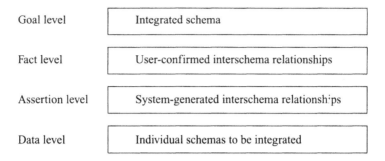

Goal level	Integrated schema
Fact level	User-confirmed interschema relationships
Assertion level	System-generated interschema relationships
Data level	Individual schemas to be integrated

FIGURE 5.8
Four-level blackboard architecture.

as *transient assertions* because these relationships may not always be accurate and need confirmation from the user.

Human integrators operate on information available at the assertion level of the blackboard. Their role is to transform the transient assertions generated by the interschema relationship identification process into facts by modifying or confirming them. These facts appear at the fact level of the blackboard. The human integrators interact with the blackboard through a graphical environment. This environment allows a group of designers to work simultaneously on modifying/confirming assertions placed on the blackboard. It also provides users with (computer) communication channels for resolving differing viewpoints among users during this process. Users can also use this environment to view other objects on the blackboard, such as individual schemas, the (partially) integrated schema, facts, and other assertions [RR98].

The integrated schema generation process operates on information available at the fact level. It consists of three components: the integrated schema generation scheduler (SGS), the preprocessor, and the integrator. The preprocessor inputs facts about similarity between entity classes (from the fact level) and attempts to generate possible equivalence relationships between them. As pointed out before, these relationships may be overlapping, subsumption, or equivalence relationships [SSG+91]. The results of the computation are output to the assertion level of the blackboard for confirmation by the human integrators. The integrator utilizes information from the various areas of the fact level of the blackboard to integrate the individual schemas. Output from the integrator is posted to the goal level of the blackboard. The SGS monitors the fact level of the blackboard and triggers the preprocessor and integrator components when appropriate.

Shoval and Zohn [SZ91] present a methodology and toolkit for integrating schemas represented using the binary-relationship model. A binary integration strategy is used. The methodology and toolkit reported in Shoval and Zohn

[SZ91] provide the bare minimum of support for automatic interschema relationship identification in the form of detecting homonym conflicts (based on name matches) automatically. The authors present techniques for resolving naming and structural conflicts. Naming conflicts dealt with in the methodology include homonym or synonym conflicts. Although the methodology presented in this paper is comprehensive for the binary-relationship model, this is primarily because the number of possible cases in the binary-relationship model is limited. Hence, there isn't much generalizability of the methodology to more common models that have been derived from the ER model.

Gotthard et al. [GLN92] present a view integration methodology for schemas specified using an object-oriented model. Their methodology presents some techniques for automated interschema relationship identification. The schemas in this methodology are represented using CERM (Complex Entity-Relationship model), an object-oriented model. Gotthard et al. introduce the concept of *assumption predicates*, which specify possible similarities between structures in the schemas to be integrated. The functions for computing assumption predicates use names and intentions as the primary means of arriving at these assumption predicates. For example, attributes are compared on their names and domains. These assumption predicates are then presented to the user for confirmation. The input to the integrated schema generation step is a set of factual predicates. Each factual predicate specifies relationships among similar object types and relationships. For example, to specify relationships between two object types a and b, designers can use one of the following four predicates: $equal_{obj}(a, b)$, $subset_{obj}(a, b)$, $arbitrary_{obj}(a, b)$, and $disjoint_{obj}(a, b)$. These specify equal, subset, overlap, and disjoint relationships, respectively. A similar set of predicates is available for specifying relationships among relationship types. For each of these predicates, the authors define integration primitives that when applied will generate an integrated object of the appropriate type. The authors deal with structural conflicts by defining a set of transformation primitives that will make the objects in question integration compatible.

The primary contribution of the work by Gotthard et al. is that it defines a methodology applicable to integrating object-oriented schemas. The methodology suffers from two drawbacks. First, it is specific to the (CERM) object-oriented model. Second, the assumption predicates that are generated specify only equivalence relationships among the various types of objects.

All the techniques described above fall into the category of schema restructuring mechanisms operating at the conceptual schema level.

Ahmed et al. [ASD+91] describe the Pegasus system, a system that utilizes a view generation mechanism and operates at the conceptual schema level. Integration is achieved by defining new objects using a Heterogeneous Object Structured Query Language (HOSQL) query. The language is used for generating object-oriented classes from existing database relations. Users can also use the language to create supertypes of classes defined on the underlying databases. Differences in domains and schematic representations of similar objects are resolved through the definition of mapping functions using HOSQL.

Kaul et al. [KDN90] describe the architecture of ViewSystem, an object-oriented environment that facilitates integration of heterogeneous information bases using a view generation technique. The intermediate schemas in ViewSystem are represented using VODAK, an object-oriented language. The system provides class constructors, e.g., specialization and generalization, which can be used to derive new classes from existing classes. Techniques for inheriting methods (in the new class) from existing classes are also described. An object-oriented and set-oriented query language is also provided as part of the environment.

Table 5.2 presents a summary of the tools discussed in this section. The table shows the phases of the schema integration process addressed by each of the toolkits, the degree to which each of these phases is automated, the data model used by each toolkit, and the key feature of each toolkit.

Note that a majority of the toolkits described here are prototype systems that have been developed as *proof of concept* for techniques presented in papers. The systems presented in Ahmed et al. [ASD+91] and Sheth and Marcus [SM92], however, have been used in commercial environments. The toolkits cover a broad spectrum of the classification presented in Section 5.1, including view integration approaches, schema restructuring, and view generation approaches to schema integration.

5.4
Future Directions in Schema Integration

Despite the fact that researchers have been studying issues in schema integration since the early 1980s, the complex nature of the problem has left several issues still unresolved. In this section, we present some directions for future research. We classify these ideas as being applicable to improving the interschema relationship identification process or integrated schema generation process.

5.4.1 Improving Interschema Relationship Identification

One of the key areas for research is the development of improved approaches to automated IRI. The problem with current approaches is that they utilize schematic information as their sole source of knowledge for determining relationships. As pointed out by Sheth and Gala [SG89], such approaches can lead to incorrect inferences. The authors point out that such relationships should be derived based on an understanding of the semantics of the objects represented in the database. We believe that approaches combining information from multiple knowledge sources to arrive at interschema relationships can

TABLE 5.2
Summary of toolkits for schema integration.

Methodology	Abstraction Level	Data Model Type/Name	Interschema Relationship Identification	Integrated Schema Generation
SIS (DeSouza, [DeS86])	Conceptual	Semantic/Abstract Conceptual Schema	Automated	Not applicable
Sheth et al. [SLCN88]	Conceptual	Semantic/Entity-Category-Relationship model	System assistance for manual input	Automated
BERDI (Sheth and Marcus, [SM92])	Conceptual	Semantic/Entity-Category-Relationship model	Partially automated with extensive manual input	Automated
Ram and Ramesh [RR95a]	Conceptual	Semantic/Unifying Semantic Model	Automated with user input	Automated/blackboard architecture to facilitate human interaction
MUVIS [HR90]	View	Semantic/Semantic Data Model	Automated	Automated/based on Navathe et al. [NEML86]
Shoval and Zohn [SZ91]	View	Semantic/Binary-Relationship model	Partially automated with extensive manual input	Automated/focus on resolution of conflicts in schemas
Gotthard et al. [GLN92]	View	Object-oriented/Complex Entity-Relationship model	Partially automated with user input	Automated/uses integration primitives
Kaul et al. [KDN90]	Conceptual	Object-oriented/VODAK	Manual	Integration achieved by defining views using specialized class constructors
Ahmed et al. [ASD+91]	Conceptual	Object-oriented/HOSQL	Manual	Integration achieved by defining views in HOSQL

generate real-world relationships that are more likely to reflect the relationships among database objects based on their real-world semantics.

Ramesh and Ram [RR97] present an approach that describes how the semantics conveyed by integrity constraints can be used in IRI. They introduce the concept of constraint-based relationships among database objects and present a methodology for generating such relationships. Integrity constraints in the schemas to be integrated are analyzed to generate interschema relationships among objects involved in the constraints. These relationships are generated based on the degree to which integrity constraints involving an object a in database D_1 are valid (after appropriate transformation) in database D_2, and constraints involving an object b in database D_2 are valid in database D_1, where a and b are related objects. Two objects can have four types of constraint-based relationships between them: equivalence, overlap, subsumption, and disjoint. See Ramesh and Ram [RR97] for details on the definitions of the four types of relationships as well as techniques for evaluating them. Once these constraint-based relationships have been generated, they can be used in conjunction with schematic interschema relationships (generated using one of the methods described in the previous section) to generate real-world relationships among database objects.

The semantics conveyed by data values can also be used to derive real-world semantics of database objects. Techniques in data mining [HS94] can be extended for use in a heterogeneous database context. Combining the results of this process with the constraint-based and schematic interschema relationships generation should facilitate the generation of interschema relationships among database objects that closely reflect their real-world semantics. The work done by Shekhar et al. [SHKC93] on discovering semantic integrity constraints from data values represents a first step in this direction.

Bright and Hurson [BH91] describe a system that incorporates concepts from linguistics and information retrieval theory to aid in object identification. The system builds a taxonomy for terms in the schemas based on existing classification schemes such as those in Roget's thesaurus and Webster's dictionary. This taxonomy is then used to resolve ambiguities in queries in which users may have specified data using their own terminology. Although the approach described in the paper is intended for use as an adjunct to a multidatabase system, we believe the appropriate use of concepts from the field of information retrieval, such as sophisticated dictionary and thesaurus mechanisms, can be used effectively in the context of interschema relationship identification.

5.4.2   Improving Integrated Schema Generation

Integrated schema generation techniques that focus on resolving structural differences among database schemas have reached a mature stage. However, several other areas are open to research.

Ramesh and Ram [RR97] describe how the schema integration process can be augmented to generate an integrated set of integrity constraints (from constraints specified on the local databases) applicable to an integrated schema. They also describe how the generation of such a set of constraints enables the use of semantic query processing (SQP) techniques [Kin81, CFM90, SSS92] in a heterogeneous database environment.

Geller et al. [GMP+92] present a methodology for schema integration that supplements the traditional schema integration methodologies (integration by generalization) in situations where there is structural similarity between semantically different objects. This paper describes situations where it might be necessary to integrate objects in schemas because of structural correspondence, even though semantically the objects may not be similar. The procedure of structural integration is presented in the context of an object-oriented database model: the DUAL model.

One of the most challenging problems that is yet to be resolved is that of managing schema evolution. Over time, the schemas of local databases change in response to changes in user requirements. This implies that the integrated schema has to evolve (or change) in response to the underlying schemas. The problem of developing techniques for efficiently updating the integrated schema(s) when local schemas are changed is an important area of research. Sull and Kashyap [SK92] present some techniques that address this problem. However, the majority of current schema integration techniques assume that local schemas are primarily static and changes to them are infrequent.

5.5
Summary

Interoperability among heterogeneous databases is becoming increasingly important for effective decision making in organizations. Schema integration, although it is a complex, time-consuming problem requiring extensive human interaction, is a key technique for providing interoperability among heterogeneous databases. In this chapter, we have described a four-step process for schema integration. We also present a classification of existing schema integration methodologies based on the abstraction level and data model they use.

Key problems in schema integration are identified, and a summary of existing techniques to address these problems is presented. We also present a framework for developing automated schema integration tools using blackboard architectures and describe prototype toolkits that implement one or more phases of the schema integration process. Finally, we discuss several directions for future research on schema integration.

Bibliography

[AFS81]   S. Al-Fedaghi and P. Scheuermann. Mapping considerations in the design of schemas for the relational model. *IEEE Transactions on Software Engineering* Se-7(1):99–111, 1981.

[ASD⁺91]   Rafi Ahmed, Phillipe De Smedt, Weimin Du, William Kent, Mohammad A. Ketabchi, Witold A. Litwin, Abbas Rafii, and Ming-Chien Shan. The Pegasus heterogeneous multidatabase system. *IEEE Computer* 24(12):19–27, December 1991.

[BC86]   J. Biskup and B. Convent. A formal view integration method. In *Proceedings of the ACM SIGMOD*, pages 398–407, 1986.

[BCW90]   M. Bouzeghoub and I. Comyn-Wattiau. View integration by semantic unification and transformation of data structures. In *Proceedings of the Ninth International Conference on Entity-Relationship Approach*, pages 381–398, 1990.

[Ber91]   E. Bertino. Integration of heterogeneous data repositories by using object-oriented views. In *Proceedings of IMS'91—The First International Workshop on Interoperability in Multidatabase Systems*, pages 22–39, 1991.

[BH91]   M. W. Bright and A. R. Hurson. Linguistic support for semantic identification and interpretation in multidatabases. In *Proceedings of IMS'91—The First International Workshop on Interoperability in Multidatabase Systems*, pages 306–313, 1991.

[BHP92]   M. W. Bright, A. R. Hurson, and Simin H. Pakzad. A taxonomy and current issues in multidatabase systems. *IEEE Computer* 25(3):50–60, March 1992.

[BL84]   C. Batini and M. Lenzerini. A methodology for data schema integration in the entity-relationship model. *IEEE Transactions on Software Engineering* Se-10(6):650–664, 1984.

[BLN86]   C. Batini, M. Lenzerini, and S. B. Navathe. A comparative analysis of methodologies for database schema integration. *ACM Computing Surveys* 18(4):324–364, December 1986.

[CFM90]   U. S. Chakravarthy, D. Fishman, and J. Minker. Logic-based approach to semantic query optimization. *ACM Transactions on Database Systems* 15(2):162–207, 1990.

[Che76]   P. P. Chen. The entity-relationship model: Toward a unified view of data. *ACM Transactions on Database Systems* 1(1):9–36, 1976.

[Chu90]   C. W. Chung. Dataplex: An access to heterogeneous distributed databases. *Communications of the ACM* 33(1):70–80, 1990.

[CS91]   A. Chatterjee and A. Segev. A probabilistic approach to information retrieval in heterogeneous databases. In *Proceedings of the First Workshop on Information Technology Systems*, pages 107–124, 1991.

[CT91]   B. Czejdo and M. Taylor. Integration of database systems using an object-oriented approach. In *Proceedings of IMS'91—The First International Workshop on Interoperability in Multidatabase Systems*, pages 30–37, 1991.

[CV83]   M. A. Casanova and M. V. P. Vidal. Towards a sound view integration methodology. In *Proceedings of the ACM SIGACT/SIGMOD*, pages 36–47. New York: ACM, 1983.

[CWB93]   I. Comyn-Wattiau and M. Bouzeghoub. Constraint confrontation: An important step in view integration. In *Proceedings of the Fifth International Symposium on Advanced Information Systems Engineering, CAiSE'93*, pages 507–523, 1993.

[DAT87b]   S. M. Deen, R. R. Amin, and M. C. Taylor. Implementation of a prototype for Preci*. *Computer Journal* 30(2):157–162, 1987.

[DeM89b]   L. DeMichiel. Resolving database incompatibility: An approach to performing relational operations over mismatched domains. *IEEE Transactions on Knowledge and Data Engineering* 1(4):484–493, 1989.

[DeS86]   J. M. DeSouza. Sis—a schema integration system. In *Proceedings of the Fifth British National Conference on Databases*, pages 167–185, 1986.

[DH84]   U. Dayal and H. Hwang. View definition and generalization for database integration in a multidatabase system. *IEEE Transactions on Software Engineering* 10(6):628–644, 1984.

[EMLN86]   R. El-Masri, J. Larson, and S. B. Navathe. *Schema Integration Algorithms for Federated Databases and Logical Database Design.* Technical report. Honeywell Systems Development Division, 1986.

[EMN84]   R. El-Masri and S. Navathe. Object integration in logical database design. *IEEE Transactions on Data Engineering*, pages 426–433, 1984.

[EMW79]   R. El-Masri and G. Wiederhold. Data model integration using the structural model. In *Proceedings of the 1979 ACM SIGMOD*, pages 191–202, 1979.

[GLN92]   W. Gotthard, P. C. Lockemann, and A. Neufeld. System-guided view integration for object-oriented databases. *IEEE Transactions on Knowledge and Data Engineering* 4(1):1–22, 1992.

[GMP+92]   J. Geller, A. Mehta, Y. Perl, E. Neuhold, and A. P. Sheth. Algorithms for structural schema integration. In *Proceedings of the Second International Conference on Systems Integration*, pages 604–614, 1992.

[HM81]   M. Hammer and D. McLeod. Database description with sdm: A semantic database model. *ACM Transactions on Database Systems* 6(1):351–386, 1981.

[HR90]   S. Hayne and S. Ram. Multi-user view integration system (MU-VIS): An expert system for view integration. In *Proceedings of the Sixth International Conference on Data Engineering.* Los Alamitos, CA: IEEE Computer Society Press, February 1990.

[HS94]   M. Holsheimer and A. Siebes. *Data Mining: The Search for Knowledge in Databases.* Technical report CS-R9406. Amsterdam: CWI, 1994.

[Joh93]   P. Johannesson. Schema transformation as an aid in view integration. In *Proceedings of the Fifth International Symposium on Advanced Information Systems Engineering, CAiSE'93*, pages 71–92, 1993.

[KDN90]   M. Kaul, K. Drosten, and E. J. Nuehold. Viewsystem: Integrating heterogeneous information bases by object-oriented views. In *Proceedings of the Sixth International Conference on Data Engineering*, pages 2–10, 1990.

152   Chapter 5. Schema Integration: Past, Present, and Future

[Kin81]   J. J. King. Quist: A system for semantic query optimization in relational databases. In *Proceedings of the Seventh VLDB Conference*, pages 510–517, 1981.

[KS91]   W. Kim and J. Seo. Classifying schematic and data heterogeneity in multidatabase systems. *IEEE Computer* 24(12):12–18, December 1991.

[KS94]   V. Kashyap and A. Sheth. *Semantics-Based Information Brokering: A Step Towards Realizing the Infocosm*. Technical report DCS-TR-307. New Brunswick, NJ: Rutgers University, March 1994.

[LC94]   W. S. Li and C. Clifton. Semantic integration in heterogeneous databases using neural networks. In *Proceedings of the 20th Conference on Very Large Data Bases*, pages 1–12, 1994.

[LNEM89]   J. Larson, S. B. Navathe, and R. El-Masri. A theory of attribute equivalence and its applications to schema integration. *IEEE Transactions on Software Engineering* 15(4):449–463, April 1989.

[MB81]   Amihai Motro and Peter Buneman. Constructing superviews. *ACM SIGMOD Record*, pages 56–64, 1981.

[ME84]   M. V. Mannino and W. Effelsberg. Matching techniques in global schema design. In *Proceedings of the First International Conference on Data Engineering*, pages 418–425, 1984.

[NEML86]   S. Navathe, R. El-Masri, and J. Larson. Integrating user views in database design. *IEEE Computer* 19(1):50–62, 1986.

[NG82]   S. B. Navathe and S. G. Gadgil. A methodology for view integration in logical database design. In *Proceedings of the Eighth VLDB Conference*, pages 142–162, 1982.

[PRSL93]   S. Prabhakar, J. Richardson, J. Srivastava, and E. P. Lim. Instance-level integration in federated autonomous databases. In *Proceedings of the 26th Annual Hawaii International Conference on System Sciences*, volume III, pages 62–69, 1993.

[Pu91]   C. Pu. Key equivalence in heterogeneous databases. In *Proceedings of IMS'91—The First International Workshop on Interoperability in Multidatabase Systems*, pages 314–317, 1991.

[RB91]   S. Ram and E. Barkmeyer. The unifying semantic model for accessing multiple heterogeneous databases in a manufacturing environment. In *Proceedings of IMS'91—The First International Workshop on Interoperability in Multidatabase Systems*, pages 212–216, 1991.

[RR95a]   S. Ram and V. Ramesh. A blackboard based cooperative system for schema integration. *IEEE Expert* 10(3):56–62, 1995.

[RR95b]   V. Ramesh and S. Ram. A methodology for interschema relationship identification in heterogeneous databases. In *Proceedings of the Hawaii International Conference on Systems and Sciences*, pages 263–272, 1995.

[RR97]   V. Ramesh and S. Ram. Integrity constraint integration in heterogeneous databases: An enhanced methodology for schema integration. *Information Systems* 22(8):423–446, 1997.

[RR98]   S. Ram and V. Ramesh. Collaborative database design: A process model and system. Forthcoming ACM Transactions on Information Systems, 1998.

[SC83]   P. M. Stocker and R. Cantie. A target logical schema: The acs. In *Proceedings of the Ninth VLDB Conference*, 1983.

[SG89]   A. Sheth and S. Gala. Attribute relationships: An impediment in automating schema integration. In *Proceedings of the NSF Workshop on Heterogeneous Databases*, December 1989.

[SGN93]   A. Sheth, S. Gala, and S. Navathe. On automatic reasoning for schema integration. *International Journal on Intelligent and Cooperative Information Systems* 2(1), March 1993.

[She91b]   A. P. Sheth. Issues in schema integration: Perspective of an industrial researcher. *ARO Workshop on Heterogeneous Databases*, 1991.

[SHKC93]   S. Shekhar, B. Hamidzadeh, A. Kohli, and M. Coyle. Learning transformation rules for semantic query optimization: A data-driven approach. *IEEE Transactions on Knowledge and Data Engineering* 5(6):950–964, 1993.

[SJB92]   W. W. Song, P. Johannesson, and J. A. Bubenko. Semantic similarity relations in schema integration. In *Proceedings of the 11th International Conference on the Entity-Relationship Approach*, pages 97–120, 1992.

[SK92]   W. Sull and R. L. Kashyap. A self-organizing knowledge representation scheme for extensible heterogeneous information environment. *IEEE Transactions on Knowledge and Data Engineering* 4(2):185–191, 1992.

[SK93]   A. Sheth and V. Kashyap. So far (schematically), yet so near (semantically). In *Proceedings of the IFIP TC2/WG2.6 Conference on Semantics of Interoperable Database Systems, DS-5*. Amsterdam: North-Holland, November 1993.

[SL90]   A. Sheth and J. Larson. Federated database systems for managing distributed, heterogeneous, and autonomous databases. *ACM Computing Surveys* 22(3):183–236, September 1990.

[SLCN88]   A. Sheth, J. Larson, A. Cornelio, and S. B. Navathe. A tool for integrating conceptual schemata and user views. In *Proceedings of the Fourth International Conference on Data Engineering*, pages 176–183. Los Alamitos, CA: IEEE Computer Society Press, February 1988.

[SM92]   A. P. Sheth and H. Marcus. *Schema Analysis and Integration: Methodology, Techniques and Prototype Toolkit*. Technical report TM-STS-019981/1. Bellcore, 1992.

[SP94]   S. Spaccapietra and C. Parent. View integration: A step forward in solving structural conflicts. *IEEE Transactions on Knowledge and Data Engineering* 6(2), April 1994.

[SPD92]   S. Spaccapietra, C. Parent, and Y. Dupont. Independent assertions for integration of heterogeneous schemas. *Very Large Database Journal* 1(1), 1992.

[SSG$^+$91]   A. Savasere, A. Sheth, S. Gala, S. Navathe, and H. Marcus. On applying classification to schema integration. In *Proceedings of IMS'91—The First International Workshop on Interoperability in Multidatabase System*, pages 258–261, 1991.

[SSS92]   M. Seigel, E. Sciore, and S. Salveter. A method for automatic rule derivation to support semantic query optimization. *ACM Transactions on Database Systems* 17(4):563–600, 1992.

[SZ91]   P. Shoval and S. Zohn.   Binary-relationship integration
            methodology. *Data and Knowledge Engineering* 6:225–250, 1991.

[TBD+87]   M. Templeton, D. Brill, S. K. Dao, E. Lund, P. Ward, A. L. P.
            Chen, and R. MacGregor. Mermaid: A front-end to distributed
            heterogeneous databases. *Proceedings of the IEEE* 75(5):695–708,
            May 1987.

[TS93]   C. Thieme and A. Siebes. Schema integration in object-oriented
            databases. In *Proceedings of the Fifth International Symposium
            on Advanced Information Systems Engineering, CAiSE'93*, pages
            54–70, 1993.

[WNC91]   W. K. Whang, S. B. Navathe, and S. Chakravarthy.   Logic-
            based approach for realizing a federated information system. In
            *Proceedings of IMS'91—The First International Workshop on
            Interoperability in Multidatabase Systems*, pages 92–100, 1991.

[YWH82]   S. B. Yao, V. E. Waddle, and B. C. Housel. View modeling and
            integration using the functional data model. *IEEE Transactions
            on Software Engineering* Se-8(6):544–553, 1982.

6

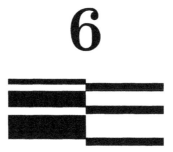

Schema and Language Translation

Bogdan Czejdo
Le Gruenwald

Introduction

In order to obtain schema(s) in a common global data model, a process called *schema translation* must be performed. The export schemas expressed in local data models (source schemas) should be translated into export schemas expressed in a global data model (target schemas) and then integrated into the global schema if feasible. Note that the translation may not be explicitly identified if the schema integration process is done in a single phase [OV91]. As discussed in [SL90], when performing schema translation, additional semantic information might be needed. But at the same time, this additional information must be treated with care because a source schema should represent the same database that is represented by its corresponding target schema [SL90]. The schema translation issues will be discussed in the first six sections of this chapter.

The multidatabase systems that use a common global data model also use a common data manipulation language to specify global queries. Global queries are decomposed into subqueries, and then subqueries are translated into respective local data manipulation languages before they can be executed by local DBMSs. Note again that the translation may not be explicitly identified if the decomposition process produces subqueries in the local data manipulation languages [RCE91]. The techniques for efficient translation of subqueries into local data manipulation languages will be discussed in Sections 6.5–6.10.

6.1
Schema Translations into the Relational Model

Many multidatabase systems have used the relational model as the common model for defining export schemas [BT85, DAT87a, Lit86, REMC+89, TBD+87]. The relational model as a common model has been advocated for distributed systems because of the ease of decomposing and recomposing relations, and because of the existence of high-level set-oriented operations that avoid the need for navigation via internodal pointers. Another advantage of using the relational model for a multidatabase system lies in the fact that the mappings for defining the integration can be expressed in a query language, thereby rendering query decomposition quite straightforward [DAT87a, CRE87]. On the other hand, the relational model does not possess the necessary semantics for defining all the integration mappings that might be desired for integrating databases. Therefore, the current tendency is to use semantic data models such as an ER model, functional model, or object-oriented models as a common data model.

6.2
Schema Translations into an ER Model

One of the most popular global data models is the entity-relationship (ER) model [Che76], due to its semantic expressiveness. A multidatabase system designed by Cardenas [CP86] has used ER to describe its global conceptual model, which is the union of the local conceptual models at participating DBMSs. His global conceptual model is used for query interpretation and decomposition. The system DDTS [DL87] uses a modified version of the ER model called an Entity-Category-Relationship model as its global data model.

Local data models can be network, hierarchical, relational, or object-oriented. The translations from these models to an ER model have been extensively studied in the literature. A CODASYL network model can be translated into ER by simply mapping each record type in a CODASYL schema to an entity and each DBTG set to a relationship. However, a special treatment must be made to those dummy records that are used to describe many-to-many relationships. A detailed correspondence between CODASYL and ER has been presented in [Che76].

A translation between a hierarchical model such as IMS to an ER model must recognize those IMS virtual pointers stored in child segments of IMS physical databases that are used to establish many-to-many relationships. A translation algorithm described in [CP86] essentially performs the following: For each parent segment in physical databases, it identifies an entity, keys, types of relationships with its child segments, attributes of relationships, and integrity constraints. Then it establishes the relationships between physical databases by determining types, attributes, and integrity constraints for relationships. A decomposition of composite entities and relationships is also performed to ensure that all equivalent ER local schemas are compatible.

A translation of the relational model into an ER model requires conversion of tables into entities and relationships. One must distinguish data tables from relationship tables, or in other words, one must recognize the role of each table. In many cases, there are no clean separations between data tables and relationship tables. For example, a data table might contain a foreign key. References to foreign keys are then translated into relationships. Types of relationships (one-to-one, one-to-many, many-to-one, many-to-many) and constraints of relationships are generally difficult to determine directly from tables themselves. Additional information might need to be obtained for these purposes.

6.3
Schema Translations into a Functional Model

Some systems do not use ER in their global models. For example, in MULTIBASE [LR86], a global schema is defined in a data language called

DAPLEX, which is based on a functional data model, the basic constructs of which are entities and functions corresponding to conceptual objects and their properties. Entity sets result from grouping entities of similar properties. An entity's properties can be derived by applying functions to it.

Besides a global schema, there are two so-called lower-level schemas in MULTIBASE: DAPLEX local schema and local host schema for each local DBMS. The DAPLEX local schema is an equivalent DAPLEX representation of the local host schema. A global DAPLEX query on the global schema is decomposed into several DAPLEX subqueries corresponding to DAPLEX local schemas before being submitted to local DBMSs. The differences among local systems are managed at the DAPLEX local schema level. The translation between a local host schema and a DAPLEX local schema is done as follows: Each relation and each domain in the relational model are equivalent to an entity and a single-valued function, respectively, in DAPLEX. Each record type and each set in the network model are translated to an entity and a multivalued function, respectively, in DAPLEX.

6.4
Schema Translations into an Object-Oriented Model

Recent proposals concentrate on using an object-oriented model as a global model [BPS89, UW91, CT91]. The translation process between local schemas and an object-oriented global schema can be facilitated by an extended metamodel [UW91]. The metadata includes local and global schema information and mapping information between local and global schemas. The structural differences between global and local models are explicitly described in such metamodels. For example, in the case of relational local schemas, the metamodels describe mappings between relations in the local schema and the classes in the object-oriented global view. In [UW91], metadata is described using the semantic data models and self-describing data models.

Similar translations are performed in KOPERNIK* [CT92a]. The local schemas are translated into an object-oriented export schema in two phases. In the first phase (assuming the relational model as a local data model), the binary relational views are constructed. In the second phase, the object-oriented classes are created for all attributes, and appropriate messages are generated for each of the binary relational views. The additional information about the attribute domains might be necessary to identify subclass/superclass hierarchies.

6.5
Example of a Schema Translation

As an example, let us consider a simple multidatabase system for a university, involving two nodes. One node contains the database system for the central administration, and the other node holds the database system for the computer science department.

Let us assume that the database for the central administration is described by an object-oriented model [CT92b] and provides the export schema that contains the class PERSON with the subclass EMPLOYEE. Each attribute of PERSON also has its own class, such as SSN, NAME, and ADDRESS. Similarly, each attribute of EMPLOYEE has its own class, such as SALARY, DEPARTMENT, and OFFICE. Additionally, messages allow the identification of related objects. For each subset of PERSON, we can identify the corresponding subset within the class SSN, NAME, and ADDRESS by invoking the message has_ssn, has_name, and has_address, respectively. Similarly, for each subset of EMPLOYEE, we can identify the corresponding subset within the class SALARY, DEPARTMENT, and OFFICE by invoking the message has_salary, has_department, and has_office, respectively.

Let us also assume that the database for the computer science department is described by the relational model and provides the following schema (for each relation the first attribute is the primary key):

```
INSTRUCTOR(SSN, Name, Rank, Email)
EXTERNAL_INSTRUCTOR(SSN, Company)
TEACHES(SSN, Course_No)
COURSE(Course_No, Course_Name)
```

In a typical approach, the export schemas are translated into schemas in a common model. Let us use the object-oriented model as a common model. In this case, it is only necessary to translate the computer science department schema into the object-oriented model.

The result could be the schema that contains the class INSTRUCTOR with the subclass EXTERNAL_INSTRUCTOR. Note that the additional information about the domain of attributes is necessary to generate this part of the object-oriented schema. There is also a class COURSE. Each attribute in the relational schema corresponds to a separate class, such as SSN, NAME, RANK, and EMAIL, for PERSON. For each subset of PERSON, we can identify the corresponding subset within the class SSN, NAME, RANK, and EMAIL by invoking the message has_ssn, has_name, has_rank, and has_email, respectively. Similarly, for each subset of EXTERNAL_INSTRUCTOR, we can identify the corresponding subset within the class COMPANY by invoking the message has_company.

Assuming an object-oriented model discussed in [CT92a], the relation TEACHES is converted into a message, teaches. This message, when applied to a subset of INSTRUCTOR, returns the corresponding subset within the subclass COURSE. Note that to generate this part of the object-oriented schema, the additional information about the role of the table TEACHES is necessary.

During this translation process, several issues need to be resolved, for example, how to determine subclass/superclass hierarchy and how to identify the relations playing the role of relationship sets. One way to resolve these problems is to assume existence of the metamodel that would contain this additional information about schemas (e.g., about the computer science department schema) [UW91].

Once all local schemas are translated into a common global object-oriented model, it is necessary to specify several integrating messages [CT92a] to construct the global queries. This is valid with the assumption that the construction of the global schema is not feasible.

6.6
Language Translation

The multidatabase systems that use a common global data model as discussed above also use a common data manipulation language (DML) for information exchanges among different local databases. Global queries written in this common language are then translated into respective local DMLs before they can be executed by local DBMSs. For example, as noted earlier, global user queries in MULTIBASE are written in the DAPLEX language [CP84]. The global data manager (GDM) of this system accepts the DAPLEX user queries and decomposes each of them into several DAPLEX queries for the local schemas. The GDM passes these decomposed queries to the Local Data Interfaces (LDIs), which in turn translate these queries into their respective local languages, request for query execution, assemble results, and send them to the GDM. The GDM then performs final processing on the results received from LDIs and returns the final answer to the user.

In order to better describe the heterogeneous environment of the multidatabase systems, several new languages have been proposed as global languages. In addition to DAPLEX, the language GSQL (Generalized Structured Query Language), similar to SQL, has been used to form a global query for heterogeneous databases [Jac85]. The processing of global queries in GSQL is similar to processing global queries in the other languages. After the global query goes through a GSQL translation processor, an expression tree is derived, and subqueries are constructed and submitted to the local resident DBMS for execution. Similarly, DDTS [CP84] and MRDSM [LA87] use GORDAS [EMW81] and MDSL, respectively, as their global data manipulation languages.

A translation from a global language to local DMLs is one of the important phases of processing for multidatabase (global) queries. Two queries written in two different DMLs are said to be equivalent if with the same inputs and the same initial database states, they produce the same outputs and final database states. To facilitate the translation process, syntax and semantic information about the global and local DMLs can be maintained in a directory or in an auxiliary database, as is done in MULTIBASE [CP84]. This auxiliary database also stores mapping/conversion information; for example, temperature in a global schema is represented as Fahrenheit degrees while in a local schema, as Celsius degrees. Conversion formulas and procedures must be available in this database.

A major problem in language translation is that the source and target languages might not have the same functionality (expressive power). Mermaid [TBD⁺87] provides a simple solution by defining a minimum set of functions to be supported. If a local DBMS cannot perform all functions in this minimum set, it cannot participate in the multidatabase system.

6.7
Translations Using an Intermediate Language

The translation from a global language to a local one very often is done through an intermediate language. In [HFG87], the process of query language translation for the relational query language (RQL) family is automated. A metatranslation system implemented in PROLOG accepts specifications of one relational query language as input and produces those of another relational query language as output. This translation is done via an intermediate stage: an internal tree representation of relational algebra. To translate a language RQLi to another language RQLj, the metatranslator module has access to a destination database schema and a number of translation schemes (RQLi→tree) and (tree→RQLj). The tree is represented in a linear internal intermediate language form that corresponds to a preorder traversal of the tree. Each node of the tree has several arguments: the first one is an input relation, and the last one is a schemalike specification of the relation that is produced if the relational algebra function of the node is applied. Tree nodes can thus be translated without consulting the associated schema.

The translation from relational query languages to trees (or vice versa) can be facilitated by a metalanguage [HFG87]. The syntax of an input query language is entered in a PROLOG-compatible BNF form. To translate from an internal tree form to a relational query language, sets of prompts are generated that list all relational algebra nodes. At a prompt, the system asks the user to identify whether a node exists in the output query language. If it does, an equivalent statement in this language is then constructed.

An intermediate language can also contain the primitives describing communication between processes. Such primitives and languages are described in detail in other chapters. An example of a system using such primitives is AIDA (Architecture for Integrated Data Access) [T[+]86, TBD[+]87]. In this system, a global query is first written in a nonprocedural language, such as ARIEL or SQL, and is then validated through syntactic and semantic checking done by a translator called QUEST (Query and Schema Translator). If the query is valid, it is translated into DIL (Distributed Intermediate Language), a highly structured language used for communication between processes. The DIL query is then sent to a component called Mermaid, which optimizes the query and passes its DIL subqueries to local sites. Each local site subsequently calls the translator QUEST to translate a DIL subquery into its respective local language and sends the translated subquery to its local DBMS for processing.

6.8
Translations Involving Rule-Based Languages

Problems of translation to and from rule-based languages have also been extensively studied. The translation from relational languages into PROLOG [RC91] is relatively straightforward because expressiveness of PROLOG is sufficient to represent all relational operators. Such translators allow incorporation of knowledge bases having both extensional and intensional components into a multidatabase environment. In this case, an export schema from the PROLOG node can be viewed as a relational system manipulated by relational operators, even though some of the underlying "relations" are, in fact, logical predicates (possibly defined recursively).

The translations from PROLOG into relational languages are much harder because the expressive power of relational languages is not sufficient to express the complex PROLOG statements. One way to deal with this problem is to design a local front end (interpreter) to a relational database system [JCV84] instead of the language translator.

However, the interoperability between local sites supporting rule-based languages and local sites supporting the languages with comparable expressiveness can be accomplished to a larger extent. For example, the translations between a rule-based language called RL and an object-oriented language called SOL is discussed in [ZCT91]. A portion of the schema and data specified in one language can be made visible to the other language as an export schema. Translations between RL and SOL are achieved by using two language primitives: export and import. RL consists of classes and predicates, while SOL consists of classes and methods. The two primitives allow exporting and importing static elements (classes) as well as dynamic elements (predicates and methods) in the two languages.

6.9
Using a Metamodel in the Language Translation Process

The metamodel (or an extended metamodel) [UW91] discussed in Section 6.5 not only can help for the schema translation but also can be very useful for the language translation. Structural differences between a global and local data model can be represented explicitly in metadata. The global-to-local mappings can facilitate the translation of a query expressed in a global language to queries expressed in local languages [UW91]. Additional specifications are required to improve the mappings when semantic differences between global and local views involve computational differences. This can be done by means of import and export procedures.

Another method of using metamodels to translate object-oriented queries into relational expressions is discussed in [CT92b]. The technique is based on syntax-directed translation. First, the BNF notation is used to describe an object-oriented query. Then, some semantic actions are attached to each BNF statement. Those actions are responsible for constructing the components of the resulting relational expression, and they are expressed in terms of queries for the metamodel.

6.10
General Query Transformation Systems

Some proposals stress the generality of their transformation approaches. In such systems, addition of a new language (or a new node with the new language) does not require that the new translators to and from the language be developed; rather, it is sufficient to provide the syntax descriptions of the new language and the necessary translation rules.

For example, let us discuss the approach based on general symbolic transformation techniques [RC85]. Such transformation techniques could be used for both query decomposition [CR84] and query translation [CR91b]. We will concentrate here on problems of language translation. The universal symbolic transformation system allows for translation of expressions belonging to a wide class of relational data sublanguages based on either relational algebra or relational calculus. The description of syntax rules for source and target languages constitutes an input to the system rather than being reflected in the translation algorithm.

The translation process using a universal symbolic transformation system is based on a language transformation module. This module accepts the following inputs:

- query expressed in a source language,

- syntax description of a source language,

- syntax description of a target language, and

- transformation definition (rules).

It then produces as its output the transformed query expressed in the target language.

The syntax of source and target languages is given in the form of BNF statements. A transformation definition *(transformation* for short) is an ordered collection of transformation rules that are executed according to the if-then-else structure, i.e., the first applicable rule is applied.

Each rule contains a source part, specifying when the rule can be applied, and a target part. In general, the source part of each transformation rule (and the input query) should be parsed according to the grammar of the source language, while the target part of each transformation rule should be parsed according to the grammar of the target language. However, when a transformation rule is applied to a query, an intermediate result that conforms neither to the source nor to the target grammar specification may be obtained. For this reason, the syntax specifications should be extended to allow expressions of one language to be embedded in the other languages. This is equivalent to defining a "superlanguage," which specifies all legal syntactical structures for source, intermediate, and target expressions.

Using the BNF definitions, a syntax-directed parser converts the input query and transformation rules into tree expressions. The transformation process is then performed based on subtree matching and replacement techniques. This process can be done in several modes. The simplest one is the mode called "explicit transformation." In this mode, the tree expressions are compared once, and if they match, the replacement is performed. Recursive calls in the target part are allowed. Another mode is called "traversal with multiple replacement." In this mode, the expression tree corresponding to the argument expression is traversed, and every occurrence of the subtree matching the source part of the transformation rule is replaced by the tree expression corresponding to the target part of the transformation rule. Therefore, in this mode several replacements are possible. For transformation modes that could result in several replacements, the order of traversal can be selected (top down or bottom up).

For every transformation rule, its source part specifies a condition that must be satisfied in order to perform a transformation. However, sometimes it is desirable to impose additional conditions for the rule invocation. These additional conditions are called *quantifiers*. The quantifiers describe more precisely the components of the query that can be transformed, e.g., a component needs to be a simple symbol (not a subtree), a component needs to include or exclude some substructure, etc.

6.11
Example of Language Translations

Let us assume the simple multidatabase [RC85] with the following global schema,

```
SUPPLIERS(Snumber, Sname, City)
PARTS(Pnumber, Pname, Color)
PROJECTS(Jnumber, Jname)
SHIPMENTS(Sno, Pno, Jno, Qty)
```

with Pnumber and Pno, Snumber and Sno, Jnumber and Jno being defined over common domains, respectively. Let us also assume the three nodes A, B, and C described as follows:

Node A
    Language: SQL
    Relations: SUPPLIERS
Node B
    Language: QUEL
    Relations: PARTS
Node C
    Language: Relational Algebra
    Relations: PROJECTS, SHIPMENTS

As an example, let us consider the following global query originating from node A: "Get names of suppliers, part names, and quantities of shipments for all shipments of GRAY parts for the project DDB." Such a query can be expressed in the common language (SQL) as

```
SELECT Sname, Pname, Qty
    FROM SUPPLIERS, PARTS, SHIPMENTS
    WHERE Snumber = Sno
        AND Pnumber = Pno
        AND Color='GRAY'
        AND Jno IN (SELECT Jnumber
                        FROM PROJECTS
                        WHERE Jname = 'DDB')
```

The global query decomposition might result in the following nodal subqueries.
    Subquery-1 for node B:

```
SELECT Pnumber, Pname
    INTO T1
    FROM PARTS
    WHERE Color = 'GRAY'
```

Subquery-2 for node C:

```
SELECT Sno, Pno, Qty
    INTO T2
    FROM SHIPMENTS
    WHERE Jno IN (SELECT Jnumber
                    FROM PROJECTS
                    WHERE Jname = 'DDB')
```

Subquery-3 for node A:

```
SELECT Sname, Pname, Qty
    FROM SUPPLIERS, T1, T2
    WHERE Snumber = Sno
        AND Pnumber = Pno
```

Here we assume that the query execution plan is designed in such a way that the results of Subquery-1 (T1) and Subquery-2 (T2) will be sent to site A for further processing.

Subquery-1 needs to be translated to an equivalent query in QUEL. One of the techniques described in this chapter would need to be used to perform this goal. Assuming the transformation rules approach, several transformation rules must be designed and invoked. Part of one such rule is given below.

```
TRANSFORMATION-1
RULE-11:
Qualifiers: attribute-1 is simple-symbol;
REL-OP in {=, >, <, <=, >=}
CONST is string;

Source: SELECT attribute-list
INTO relation-2
FROM relation-1
WHERE attribute-1 REL-OP CONST

Target:   RANGE OF ? IS relation-1
RETRIEVE INTO relation-2
(TRANSFORMATION-2 (attribute-list))
WHERE ?.attribute-1 REL-OP CONST
```

In the above rule, the qualifiers block is used to identify the type of SQL structures that can fire the rule. The qualifiers in this example restrict the attribute-1 to a simple symbol. Also, REL-OP can be only one of the simple relational operators. The question mark "?" denotes the name of the tuple variable that will be generated during the transformation. The TRANSFORMATION-2 is called to insert the generated name of the tuple variable as a prefix for each attribute. This transformation can be defined as follows:

```
TRANSFORMATION-2
RULE-21:
Qualifiers: attribute-2 is simple-symbol;
Source: attribute-2
Target:  ?.attribute-2
```

This rule simply inserts a tuple variable for each attribute. The special mode called "traversal with multiple replacements" needs to be declared for this rule in order to apply it to any component of the attribute list.

When the rule system is applied to Subquery-1, the rule RULE-11 will be fired (followed by an invocation of RULE-21), and as a result, the following QUEL expression will be generated:

```
Target:  RANGE OF p IS PARTS
RETRIEVE INTO T1
    (Pnumber = p.Pnumber, Pname = p.Pname)
    WHERE p.Color = 'GRAY'
```

To translate an SQL statement into an equivalent relational algebra expression, we can define and invoke the transformation rules, similar to those used to perform SQL into QUEL transformation. In order to obtain the query in relational algebra equivalent to Subquery-2, it is sufficient to consider TRANSFORMATION-3:

```
TRANSFORMATION-3
RULE-31:
Qualifiers: relation-1 is simple-symbol;
condition exclude
(SELECT a FROM b WHERE c)

Source: SELECT attribute-1
    FROM relation-1
    WHERE condition
    Target:  Projection
    ((attribute-1),
    Selection
        (condition,
        relation-1));

RULE-32:
Qualifiers: relation-1 is simple-symbol;
Source: SELECT attribute-1
    INTO relation-2
    FROM relation-1
    WHERE attribute-2 IN
        (Projection
```

```
     ((attribute-3),
REL_EXPR))
Target: relation-2 <=
Projection
((attribute-1),
   Join
   (attribute-2 = attribute-3,
   relation-1,
   Projection
   ((attribute-3),
REL_EXPR)))
```

The above transformation is performed in the bottom-up direction and may involve several replacements during the traversal. The qualifiers define the type of SQL expressions that can be transformed as SQL blocks containing a single relation at each level of nesting. In the first phase of transformation, RULE-31 is applied to replace the innermost SELECT block, resulting in a relational algebra subexpression being embedded in the SQL. For this reason, RULE-32, which will be applied in the second phase, contains a relational algebra expression embedded in the SQL block of its source part.

When the rule system is applied to Subquery-2, the rules RULE-31 and RULE-32 will be activated, and as a result, the following relational algebra expression will be generated:

```
T2 <=
Projection
((Sno, Pno, Qty),
   Join
   (Jnumber = Jno,
   SHIPMENTS,
   Projection
   ((Jnumber),
   Selection
      (Jname = 'DDB',
      PROJECT))))
```

6.12
Summary

Most multidatabase systems use a common global data model to describe the entire database either by a single global schema or by several export schemas. In order to obtain schema(s) in a common global data model, a process called schema translation must be performed. The export schemas expressed in local data models (source schemas) should be translated into export schemas expressed in a global data model (target schemas) and then integrated into the global schema if feasible. When performing schema translation, additional semantic information might be needed. But at the same time, this additional information must be treated with care because a source schema should represent the same database that is represented by its corresponding target schema. In this chapter, several major schema translation techniques are described, and an example of translation from a relational schema into an object-oriented schema is presented. Several specific issues are discussed, such as how to determine a subclass/superclass hierarchy and how to identify the relations playing the role of relationship sets in case of translation from relational model into a semantic data model (e.g., an object-oriented model).

The multidatabase systems that use a common global data model also use a common data manipulation language to specify global queries. Global queries are decomposed into subqueries, and then subqueries are translated into respective local data manipulation languages before they can be executed by local DBMSs. The techniques for efficient translation of subqueries into local data manipulation languages are surveyed, and some are discussed extensively in this chapter. Also, several solutions are discussed to resolve the major problem in language translation: the source and target languages might not have the same functionality.

Bibliography

[BPS89]   E. Bertino, G. Pelagatti, and L. Sbattella. An object-oriented approach to the interconnection of heterogenous databases. In *Proceedings of the Workshop on Heterogenous Databases*, December 1989.

[BT85]   Y. Breibart and L. R. Tieman. Adds—heterogeneous distributed database system. In F. Schreiber and W. Litwin, editors, *Distributed Data Sharing Systems*. Amsterdam: North-Holland, 1985.

[Che76]   P. P. Chen. The entity-relationship model: Toward a unified view of data. *ACM Transactions on Database Systems* 1(1):9–36, 1976.

[CP84]   Stefano Ceri and Giuseppe Pelagatti. *Distributed Databases: Principles and Systems*. New York: McGraw-Hill, 1984.

[CP86]   Alfonso Cardenas and Mir Pirahesh. Data base communication in a heterogeneous data base management system network. *Distributed Systems* 2:386–390, 1986.

[CR84]   B. Czejdo and M. Rusinkiewicz. Query transformation in an in-
            structional database management system. In *Proceedings of the
            ACM SIGCSE Conference*, 1984.

[CR91b]   B. Czejdo and M. Rusinkiewicz. Generation and translation
            of database queries in an instructional DBMS. *The Journal of
            Computer Information Systems* 31(4), 1991.

[CRE87]   B. Czejdo, M. Rusinkiewicz, and D. Embley. An approach to
            schema integration and query formulation in federated database
            systems. In *Proceedings of the Third IEEE Conference on Data
            Engineering*, February 1987.

[CT91]   B. Czejdo and M. Taylor. Integration of database systems us-
            ing an object-oriented approach. In *Proceedings of IMS'91—The
            First International Workshop on Interoperability in Multidatabase
            Systems*, pages 30–37, 1991.

[CT92a]   B. Czejdo and M. Taylor. Integration of information systems
            using an object-oriented approach. *The Computer Journal* 35(5),
            1992.

[CT92b]   B. Czejdo and M. Taylor. Integration of object-oriented program-
            ming languages and database systems in kopernik. *The Data and
            Knowledge Engineering Journal* 7, 1992.

[DAT87a]   S. M. Deen, R. R. Amin, and M. C. Taylor. Data integration in
            distributed databases. *IEEE TSE* 13(7), 1987.

[DL87]   P. Dwyer and J. Larson. Some experiences with a distributed
            database testbed system. In *Proceedings of the IEEE*, volume 75,
            May 1987.

[EMW81]   R. El-Masri and G. Wiederhold. Gordas: A formal high-level
            query language for the entity-relationship model. In *Proceedings
            of the International Conference on Entity-Relationship Approach*,
            1981.

[HFG87]   D. I. Howells, N. J. Fiddian, and W. A. Gray. A source-to-
            source meta-translation system for relational query languages. In
            Proceedings of the 13th VLDB Conference, pages 227–234, 1987.

[Jac85]   D. Jacobs. *Applied Database Logic*, volume 1. Englewood Cliffs,
            NJ: Prentice Hall, 1985.

[JCV84]   M. Jarke, J. Clifford, and Y. Vassiliou. An optimizing prolog front end to a relational query system. In *Proceedings of the SIGMOD Conference*, June 1984.

[LA87]   W. Litwin and A. Abbellatif. An overview of the multi-database manipulation language MDSL. *Proceedings of the IEEE*, May 1987.

[Lit86]   W. Litwin. A multidatabase interoperability. *IEEE Computer* 19(12):10–18, December 1986.

[LR86]   Terry Landers and Ronni Rosenberg. An overview of multibase. *Distributed Systems* 2:391–421, 1986.

[OV91]   M. Tamer Özsu and Patrick Valduriez. *Principles of Distributed Database Systems*. Englewood Cliffs, NJ: Prentice Hall, 1991.

[RC85]   M. Rusinkiewicz and B. Czejdo. Query transformation in heterogeneous distributed database systems. In *Proceedings of the Fifth International Conference on Distributed Computer Systems*, 1985.

[RC91]   M. Rusinkiewicz and B. Czejdo. Processing of queries involving data and knowledge base systems. In *Proceedings of the Third International Conference on Software Engineering and Knowledge Engineering*, 1991.

[RCE91]   M. Rusinkiewicz, B. Czejdo, and D. Embley. An implementation model for multidatabase queries. In *Proceedings of the International Conference DEXA '91*. New York: Springer-Verlag, 1991.

[REMC+89]   M. Rusinkiewicz, R. El-Masri, B. Czejdo, D. Georgakopoulos, G. Karabatis, A. Jamoussi, K. Loa, and Y. Li. Query processing in a heterogeneous multidatabase environment. In *Proceedings of the First Annual Symposium on Parallel and Distributed Processing*, 1989.

[SL90]   A. Sheth and J. Larson. Federated database systems for managing distributed, heterogeneous, and autonomous databases. *ACM Computing Surveys* 22(3):183–236, September 1990.

[T+86]   Marjorie Templeton et al. An introduction to aida—a front-end to heterogeneous databases. *Distributed Systems* 2:483–490, 1986.

[TBD⁺87] M. Templeton, D. Brill, S. K. Dao, E. Lund, P. Ward, A. L. P. Chen, and R. MacGregor. Mermaid: A front-end to distributed heterogeneous databases. *Proceedings of the IEEE* 75(5):695–708, May 1987.

[UW91] Susan Urban and Jian Wu. Resolving semantic heterogeneity through the explicit representation of data model semantics. *SIGMOD Record* 20(4):55–58, December 1991.

[ZCT91] Roberto Zicari, Stefano Ceri, and Letizia Tanca. Interoperability between a rule-based database language and an object-oriented database language. In *First International Workshop on Interoperability in Multidatabase Systems*, pages 125–134, April 1991.

7

Multidatabase Languages

Paolo Missier
Marek Rusinkiewicz
W. Jin

Introduction

Database systems based on SQL are well suited for homogeneous data-bases—either centralized or distributed. Most traditional database architectures, however, seem inadequate to handle different types of heterogeneity. Interoperability at the system level can be achieved to some degree by interposing an additional interface layer between a database system and the application, as in the ODBC solution [Mic94] and, more recently, in the analogous, Java-based JDBC proposal [HC96]. Other vendor-specific solutions provide network and protocol transparency by standardizing their SQL interface.

The problem of data, or semantic, heterogeneity, however, remains. Different systems that own different pieces of data may come into conflict when they need to agree, at least in part, on the meaning of each other's data. This situation is common in loosely coupled database federations, where private data from a common domain of discourse is shared, and yet each local system insists on maintaining its ownership, autonomy, and local views over its own portion.

In this chapter, we focus on the multidatabase access and manipulation language aspect of semantic interoperability. The proposed solutions we present are interesting in their common attempt to provide an expressive access language that can be used to describe and resolve semantic heterogeneity conflicts. Their common approach is to extend standard access languages, such as SQL, with features to describe some of the semantics of the data being accessed (metadata)—the design of SQL3, still an ongoing process [Mel96], does not seem to address semantic conflict resolution.

One of the first attempts in this direction is described in [L+90]. MSQL introduced multiple identifiers and semantic variables to facilitate writing multidatabase queries; however, its ability to resolve semantic heterogeneity conflicts is limited. MSQL was later extended to MSQL+, with features to define "multidatabase objects" and their mapping to the local database objects [MR95]. Both MSQL and MSQL+ are discussed in detail in this chapter.

The area of multidatabase access with conflict resolution has been receiving increasing attention, and many more projects are under way than we can cover in this chapter. Among them are the InfoSleuth project at MCC, InfoHarness/InfoQuilt [SSKT95, SSKS95, KSS95], TSIMMIS [PGMU96], and Garlic [C+]. Most of these systems use extensions of SQL as their information access language, in an attempt to preserve the declarative nature of the query language.

The rest of this chapter is organized as follows. In Section 7.1, we present a classification of semantic heterogeneity and proposed techniques for conflict resolution. Section 7.2 covers some history and basic design issues for multidatabase access languages. In Section 7.3, we discuss MSQL and its extensions. We conclude the chapter in Section 7.4, with an introduction to updates in multidatabase systems and in MSQL+ in particular.

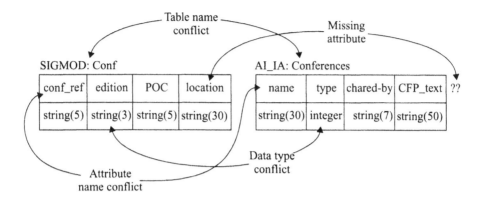

FIGURE 7.1
Semantic heterogeneity example.

7.1
Classification of Semantic Heterogeneity

Heterogeneity in multidatabase systems refers either to *system* differences, e.g., different DBMSs, operating system architectures, or networking protocols, or *semantic* differences, which refer to the different ways similar real-world entities are modeled. In this section, we concentrate exclusively on the latter. We offer a definition and classification of semantic heterogeneity and give an overview of heterogeneity resolution methodologies described in the literature.

7.1.1 Semantic Heterogeneity

Semantics can be broadly defined as "the scientific study of the relations between signs and symbols and what they denote or mean" [Woo85]. *Semantic heterogeneity*, in particular, refers to differences in the meaning and use of data that make it difficult to identify the various relationships that exist between similar or related objects in different components [HM93].

For instance, consider the two example databases, SIGMOD and AI_IA, which we will use throughout this chapter to illustrate semantic differences among schemas (Figure 7.1). (AI_IA represents the database used by the AI*IA Association to keep track of its conferences and publications.) Tables `SIGMOD.Conf` and `.AI_IA.Conferences` are intended to model similar information in different ways. Conflicts are generated when using different table names, different attribute names (`conf_ref` vs. `name`), and type definitions (`integer` vs. `string(3)`), as well as modeling different fragments of the real-world entities (the conference venue is not modeled at all in AI_IA).

Hammer and McLeod [HM93] introduce the following levels of abstraction to define the spectrum of possible semantic heterogeneity:

1. *Metadata language:* Each local DBMS may use different data models and, consequently, different data definition sublanguages. For instance, one such alternative consists of describing an ER model using the SQL DDL, rather than adopting a functional DB language to describe a functional model.

2. *Ontology/terminology:* When discrepancies occur at the ontological level.

3. *Metadata specification:* When conflicts exist in the conceptual schemas.

4. *Object comparability:* When equivalent/related objects cannot be easily identified.

5. *Low-level data format:* When mismatching data types occur at the attribute level in corresponding database objects.

6. *Tools:* When each site uses a different DBMS, offering different system features.

The problem of semantic heterogeneity can thus be described as one of integrating "structurally dissimilar but semantically equivalent" objects and of determining semantic equivalence of heterogeneous schemas. Although no widely accepted, fully automated techniques exist to accomplish this, we believe database languages can and should be provided with the additional expressivity required to assist in the systematic analysis and resolution of semantic heterogeneity.

7.1.2   Summary of Semantic Heterogeneity Conflicts

A classification of the most common heterogeneity conflicts is a good starting point for understanding the expressive power required in a federationwide access language.

In [SK93],[1] the authors describe a measure of distance between entities in different schemas, called *semantic proximity*, and apply it to the analysis of the relationship between semantic and structural heterogeneity. In this section, we present an overview of the kinds of structural conflicts identified in [SK93].

These conflicts can be broadly divided into the two classes of domain definition and entity definition incompatibility. Domain definition conflicts include naming (synonyms and homonyms), data type, data scaling, data precision, default value, and attribute integrity constraint problems. Entity definition conflicts include key equivalence, union compatibility, schema isomorphism, and missing data item problems. Outside of these two classes are abstraction-level incompatibility and schematic discrepancy conflicts.

---

[1] A different classification is offered in [KS91].

We briefly describe some of these conflicts here. *Synonyms* occur when a set of semantically equivalent objects carry different names. Conversely, *homonyms* are semantically unrelated objects that incidentally carry the same name. *Data type* conflicts occur when equivalent objects have different types. Using different units of measure to describe similar objects, as when prices are expressed in different currencies, results in a *data scaling* conflict. Similarly, *data precision* conflicts refer to the use of different granularity for equivalent entities in different schemas.

Key equivalence problems result from two or more relations modeling the same entity by means of semantically different keys. Since a common key is not available, this conflict makes it difficult to retrieve data from the different entities using a single (multiple) query. Reconciliation, when possible, may be achieved through some forms of structural abstraction.

A *union compatibility* problem between two relations is generated when the number or the domains of their attributes do not match or, alternatively, when a one-to-one mapping among the respective sets of attributes does not exist. In [RC87], a generalized outer union operator is defined to deal with this problem.

Schema isomorphism conflicts refer to the different *number* of attributes used to describe entities that are schematically similar. A typical example is represented by a *name* attribute in one entity, which is split into *lastname* and *firstname* in the other.

Missing data item conflicts arise when objects described by a set of attributes in one schema are represented by only a subset of those attributes in another. However, sometimes the values of missing attributes can be deduced through an inference mechanism or assumed as a default. For instance, the value of a *type* attribute for table Grad-Student can be assumed to be "Graduate" and thus matched with an explicit corresponding attribute for a Student table.[2]

Abstraction-level incompatibility refers to generalization and aggregation conflicts. As an example of generalization, consider the entity *publication*, which can be represented in two databases by the table Publ(publ#, author, title, ...) and the two tables Book(isbn, author, title, ...) and Journal(issn, author, title, ...), respectively. The first schema defines the same entity at a more general level of abstraction.

As an instance of aggregation conflict, consider the case of a database that lists summary characteristics of a collection of books versus one of the two publication databases mentioned above. Data in the two databases cannot be easily related because, from the first, it is not possible to map values onto the second by de-aggregating the data.

Schematic discrepancy conflicts arise when data in one schema corresponds to metadata in another. Resolution of schematic discrepancies generally

---

[2]This example is taken from [SK93].

requires a language, such as the one described in [KLK91], that allows references to data and metadata to be mixed in one specification.

7.1.3   Semantic Heterogeneity Resolution Methodologies

Recent work in heterogeneity reconciliation covers a wide spectrum of techniques. Uncertainty modeling and "instance-level" conflict resolution have been addressed [LS93, LS$^+$93, DeM89a]. The use of semantic values and arbitrary conversion functions is proposed in [SSR92b]. Techniques for "schema-level" resolutions address specific incongruities. For instance, a query language influenced by the Datalog paradigm is adopted in [KLK91] to resolve schematic discrepancy conflicts.

Common to most of these proposals is the acknowledged need for some form of meta-information whose purpose is to describe how data integration is to be performed. The general term *mediators* has been used [Wie92] to encompass the wide variety of tools used for entity and object description that incorporate forms of meta-information.

In this section, we consider four broad approaches to the resolution of semantic heterogeneity in multidatabase systems: translation, integrated, fully decentralized, and broker based.

Translation Approach

The translation approach is commonly used in a workflow scenario, where the flow of data among tasks involves access to several LDBSs (see Figure 7.2a), and the data paths are known in advance. In addition, the schemas of the LDBSs should be stable and well known. These requirements apply well to corporate environments where some data-intensive business processes are being automated using workflow technology. In this situation, it is possible to include, as part of the workflow design, ad hoc semantic translators on each segment of a data path between two LDBSs.

Using highly specialized translation modules has two advantages: (1) specific knowledge about the pairwise translation rules is localized in each module, and (2) the architecture can be extended incrementally as needed. Although in theory the number of translators required grows exponentially in the number of nodes in the workflow, in practice the number of useful combinations is usually quite manageable.

Integrated Approach

In the fully integrated architecture (Figure 7.2b), all the information about local and global semantics and schema integration is stored and managed in one central site. The main modules in this architecture are a schema manager, a multiquery processor, a global transaction manager, and a collection of local translators, one for each LDBS in the federation. LDBSs are required to join the federation by registering their schema with the schema manager.

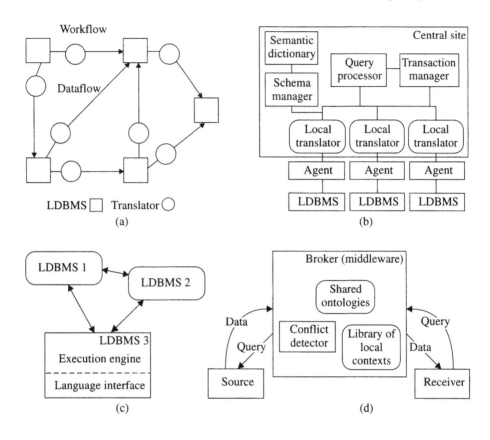

FIGURE 7.2
Semantic heterogeneity resolution methodologies: (a) translation approach,
(b) integrated approach, (c) fully decentralized approach, and (d) broker-based
approach.

One example of this architecture is the Pegasus MDBMS [ASD+91]. In
Pegasus, integration can be performed by the users, and it is partially visible by
other users through the central site. Semantic heterogeneity is resolved by the
schema manager, using a semantic dictionary. This method allows the central
site to maintain a single repository for the semantics of the MDBS. Centralization also simplifies global concurrency control but at the cost of increased
complexity in the management of multiple semantic translations.

Fully Decentralized Approach

Opposite in nature to full integration is full decentralization (Figure 7.2c),
where in the absence of central control, each LDBS contains a multidatabase
language execution engine and a communication module. Semantic conflict

resolution is performed at query formulation time by the multidatabase application developers. The multidatabase language is typically an extension of a standard access language such as SQL, enhanced with features to define multidatabase objects and their correspondence to the local objects. Although integration is normally performed autonomously for each LDBS, local sites are free, but not constrained, to define common ontologies to express common database semantics for similar local schemas.

This distributed architecture affords great flexibility in the definition of different schemas, at the expense of a more complex local execution module and more difficult global concurrency control. Examples of this approach are UniSQL/M and MSQL+ [MR95]. The latter is presented in detail in Section 7.3.

Broker-Based Approach

The general architecture of a broker for the resolution of semantic conflicts [DGH+95] includes a conflict detector module that uses shared ontologies and libraries of local contexts (see Figure 7.2d). When the receiver submits a query, the broker generates a conflicts table for the query using shared ontologies and the local context libraries, resolves the conflicts, and then converts the receiver's query into the source context. The source processes the query and sends the result to the broker, which converts the result back to the receiver's context and sends it to the receiver.

The major advantage of this approach is that semantic heterogeneity resolution becomes totally transparent to the user. However, the process of building shared ontologies and libraries of local contexts has not been completely automated. Furthermore, if the broker is connected to many sites, and each site has a large number of schemas, then the local context library can grow considerably in size. Finally, some components of the local schema, such as integrity constraints, may be difficult to capture using ontologies.

7.1.4 Summary

We have described the definition and the spectrum of semantic heterogeneity in MDBMSs and discussed the comprehensive classification of semantic heterogeneity. We introduce semantic heterogeneity resolution methodologies developed so far under MDBMSs—a simple translation approach, integrated approach, fully decentralized approach, and broker-based approach—along with some of the advantages and disadvantages of each method. We believe that a fully decentralized approach with a rich multidatabase language may prove to be a practical way to handle semantic heterogeneity.

7.2
Functionalities of Multidatabase Query Languages

In this section, we outline some historical notes on multidatabase languages, list some basic requirements and design principles, and recall some basic notions of multirelational algebra that will be used in the rest of the chapter.

7.2.1 Historical Perspective

One early proposal for a relational multidatabase system is MRDSM, a prototype developed at INRIA as an extension to the MRDS DBMS, based on the Multics Relational Data Store [Lit85a]. The main goals of the system were to allow for the retrieval of data from multiple relational sources in a mostly transparent way. The assumption underlying the development of MRDSM and its successors, mainly MSQL, was to overcome the lack of integration among local schemas by providing an expressive, user-level language that could be used to pose queries to those schemas directly, rather than to a unified global schema. The language, called MML and designed as an extension to SQL, would support the specification of multidatabase queries that include interdatabase joins. A multiquery processor implements the execution model of MML by decomposing an MML multiquery into a collection of monodatabase SQL queries that can be sent independently to each local SQL processor.[3] The results returned by each query would then be recomposed to form one final relation for the multiquery.

Following the same paradigm, the immediate successor of MRDMS, Multidatabase SQL (MSQL), was designed to provide a rich language for both schema (MultiDDL) and data (MultiDML) manipulation. MSQL is presented in detail in Section 7.3. The MDDL includes constructs for creating "virtual" multidatabases, copying schema objects' definitions from one schema to another, and in general, accessing and manipulating multiple data dictionaries. The MDML includes such advanced features as dynamic attributes, semantic variables, and multidatabase triggers.

The scope of an MSQL query is a collection of local relational schemas. A *multiquery* is a synthetic expression for a set of queries, one for each schema in the scope. Collective names, called *semantic variables*, can be used to refer to different identifiers in different schemas, thereby allowing the factorization of a single abstract multiquery into a set of elementary queries. By considering the bindings between semantic variables and the corresponding real data items, the multiquery processor can map each variable onto the schemas, yielding a set of elementary queries. The results of these queries can be joined. *Interdatabase joins* actually represent a rudimentary form of data fusion, through which data retrieved from different sources can be explicitly recombined to yield new information.

---

[3]In particular, a standard SQL query is an MML query directed to a single database.

A first implementation of MSQL is available as part of the OMNIBASE project at the University of Houston, Department of Computer Science [SRL93]. The prototype, built on top of the Narada multiapplication environment [HAB+92], demonstrates the execution of an MSQL SELECT multiquery against several databases residing on heterogeneous platforms and served by different SQL engines. The evaluation plan, compiled into DOL, the scripting language of Narada, includes full handling of distributed, interdatabase joins. That version of the language was later augmented to include notions of multidatabase transactions. Based on the assumptions of local execution autonomy and transaction model heterogeneity, the proposal included using compensating transactions [KLS90] to deal with committed transactions that need to be "semantically rolled back" at sites that do not support the two-phase commit protocol. Databases were also partitioned into the two classes of "vital" and "nonvital" information within the scope of a transaction, depending on the relative importance of a successful commit and the probability of failure at each local site. Transaction semantics were defined to ensure execution correctness with respect to the vital set. These notions, along with support for update multiqueries, were implemented as a second prototype [Mis93b, Bre93].

The experience accumulated from these experiments on the advantages and limitations of MSQL highlighted the need for new features that would address the resolution of schema conflicts, a fundamental aspect of multidatabase processing that the language did not seem to handle adequately. Semantic variables represent a first step in the direction of structural abstraction, but their use is limited to the resolution of synonym conflicts on isomorphic schemas. Interdatabase joins are limited to domain-compatible attributes, on which standard relational operators can be applied without transformation of the operands. Furthermore, the language offers little help in the case of data type discrepancies and union incompatibility. In general, the expressivity of the language appears to be limited by the lack of external knowledge available to the query processor.

New extensions were proposed and discussed in [Mis93a]. Among these were the explicit inclusion of a context surrounding a multiquery and the use of higher level attributes for conflict resolution. So augmented, MSQL has become an experiment in dynamic integration, with increased flexibility being the main benefit over traditional, static integration. Rather than designing a global schema and corresponding translating processors [HM85], a number of global views can be dynamically created and manipulated to reflect the needs of specific multidatabase applications. This version of MSQL and the corresponding extensions to the query processor are described in [MR95] and have been partially implemented as part of the OMNIBASE project mentioned above.

Finally, we mention the approach to schema integration and query formulation with limited integration visibility, described in [ECR87]. The notions of connectors among relations and of extended abstract data types, which are comprehensive representations of knowledge about a domain of data values, are used to resolve a few well-defined structural incompatibilities. Additional information is represented by the domain knowledge base, together with some heuristics based on the interpretation of object identifiers, which help disambiguate implicit (i.e., undeclared and not explicitly described) relationships among given data items. The language features a generalized outer union operator to deal with union incompatibility conflicts. Connectors are used to resolve key equivalence conflicts and domain mismatch in joining attributes.

7.2.2   Design Principles

Common to the various experiments in multidatabase access outlined in the previous section is a collection of basic requirements that multidatabase languages (MDBLs) should satisfy:

- *Multitable manipulation:* Minimally, an MDBL should support simultaneous manipulation of tables in different schemas. The MSQL notion of *multitables* extends individual relational tables to sets of tables that can be referred to using a single identifier.

- *Subsumption:* A monodatabase query is a particular case of a multidatabase query. The language should extend a standard DB language so that standard queries are executed according to their usual semantics.

- *Local schema accessibility:* As a consequence of the subsumption requirements, the language should allow direct reference to local database objects, as well as to export schema objects that may have been defined for the sake of joining the federation.

- *Location:* Location transparency is not enforced; i.e., a global naming scheme may be used (as is the case for commercial distributed DBMSs) to refer to distributed objects.[4]

- *Metadata accessibility:* The multiquery processor should have access to relevant data dictionary information from each LDBMS, either directly through queries or by keeping private views of the LDBMS schemas.

- *Query contextualization:* A multiquery is interpreted with respect to a *context*, which defines the semantics of the multiquery, much the same way as the customary LDBMS schema constitutes a context for a regular query. In addition, a context should extend the LDBMS object's name space by providing new names for multidatabase objects. Section 7.3 provides examples of multidatabase objects. In MSQL+, the context definition is explicit and available to the user, and contexts can be switched, altered, and otherwise adapted to represent different multiquery semantics.

---

[4]However, an alias mechanism can be used to hide location information in the query.

- *Conflict resolution:* The language should provide enough expressivity to allow for semantic conflict resolution at query definition time.

7.2.3   Multirelational Algebra

Multirelational algebra [GLRS91] is an extension of relational algebra. A *multirelation* is a set of relations. Multirelational operators apply to multirelations, extending relational operators in a natural way; i.e., for each multirelational operator op, there is a corresponding relational algebra expression Exp_{op} such that $op(R) = Exp_{op}(R)$.

The following basic multirelational operators will be useful in the examples presented in the rest of this section. Let $\mathcal{R} = \{R_1, \ldots, R_n\}$, $\mathcal{S} = \{S_1, \ldots, S_m\}$ be two multirelations, let $Attr(R) = \{R.A_1, \ldots, R.A_k\}$ identify the set of attributes of a relation R, and let p be a predicate on the set of attributes $\bigcup_i Attrs(R_i)$.

Projection

$$\pi_{A_1,\ldots,A_n}(\mathcal{R}) = \{\pi_{A_1,\ldots,A_n}(R_1), \ldots, \pi_{A_1,\ldots,A_n}(R_n)\},$$

where $\{A_1, \ldots, A_n\} \subseteq \bigcup_i Attrs(R_i)$. Notice that some of the attributes $A_1, \ldots, A_n$ may not be defined for a particular R_i. In this case, $\pi_{A_1,\ldots,A_n}(R_i)$ is the null relation.

Selection

$$\sigma_p(\mathcal{R}) = \{\sigma_p(R_1), \ldots, \sigma_p(R_n)\};$$

if $A_j \notin Attrs(R_i)$ for some A_j appearing in p, then $\sigma_p(R_i)$ is the null relation.

Join

$$\mathcal{R} \bowtie_p \mathcal{S} = \{R_i \bowtie_p S_j \mid i : 1 \ldots n, j : 1 \ldots m\};$$

again, element $R_i \bowtie_p S_j$ is null if p predicates over attributes not in $Attrs(R_i) \cup Attrs(S_j)$.

Union

$$\mathcal{R} \cup \mathcal{S} = \{R_i \cup S_j \mid i : 1 \ldots n, j : 1 \ldots m\}$$

Difference

$$\mathcal{R}/\mathcal{S} = \{R_i \setminus S_j \mid i : 1 \ldots n, j : 1 \ldots m\}$$

Interdatabase joins, a common operation in multidatabase SQL, are expressed as regular semijoins on the relations returned by elementary queries. An example is presented in the next section.

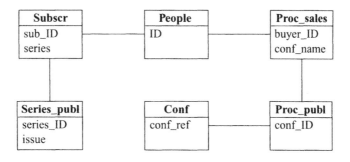

FIGURE 7.3
Schema for the SIGMOD database.

7.3
MSQL+ Approach

In this section, we present the part of the MSQL language that deals with read-only queries. We introduce three schemas for our examples and describe the data definition (Section 7.3.2) and the data manipulation (7.3.3) sublanguages, giving the semantics of multiquery execution and outlining some implementation issues.

7.3.1 Example Database Schemas

The three schemas we will use to support our running example deal with professional computer associations, SIGMOD, AI*IA, and IFIP, that need to keep track of conferences, memberships, paper submissions, etc. The need for targeted advertisement about some new publication, for instance, may motivate the grouping of those databases into a loose federation. By being able to formulate multiqueries that reveal correlations among heterogeneous data (e.g., the same researcher having attended different types of conferences), advertisers can narrow down their marketing target.

The database schema for SIGMOD is defined as follows:[5]

```
People(ID, institution, e_mail, status)
Subscr(sub_ID, series, sub_start_date)
Proc_sales(buyer_ID, conf_name, n_copies, tot_cost)
Conf(conf_ref, edition, POC, location)
Proc_publ(conf_ID, publisher, editor, procs_cost)
Series_publ(series_ID, issue, publisher, editor, spec_topic)
```

Figure 7.3 illustrates this schema. Association members are recorded in the

---

[5]Here and below, underlined attributes are part of the primary key.

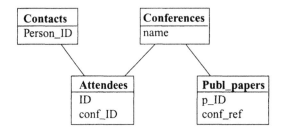

FIGURE 7.4
Schema for the AI*IA database.

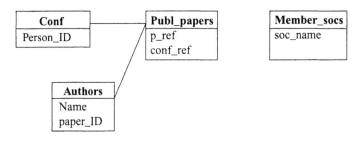

FIGURE 7.5
Schema for the IFIP database.

People table, together with their membership status. Each member may subscribe to any number of series. For each conference, we record the number of copies of the proceedings bought by each member in the Proceedings table.

Here is the database for AI*IA, illustrated in Figure 7.4:

```
Contacts(Person_ID, name, member_status, institution, e_mail)
Conferences(name, type, chaired_by, CFP_text, procs_price)
Attendees(ID, conf_ID, speaker, reg_total, procs_copies)
Publ_papers(p_ID, title, first_author, other_authors,
            keywords, conf_ref)
```

Here, members are referred to as Contacts, and their attributes are similar, but not the same, as those in SIGMOD. We have conference attendees, rather than general members, who purchase proceedings. Table Publ_papers records the papers published at each conference.

The third database is for IFIP. Being an association of associations, it keeps a table of member societies. Here, we have a very simple relationship linking Authors to Publ_papers and, indirectly, to the Conferences table (Figure 7.5).

```
Member_socs(soc_name, mailbox, start_date, status)
Conf(conf_ID, organized_by, location, procs_publisher,
           publ_date)
Publ_papers(p_ref, title, conf_ref, abstract, full_text_ref)
Authors(Name, e_mail, paper_ID, reviews)
```

7.3.2   Data Definition Language

The extensions to the SQL DDL, proposed in the original MSQL paper [Lit88], reflect a number of assumptions that are crucial to the design of the language itself. First, the federated databases have access to each other's data dictionaries, and each of them may copy fragments of others' schemas into their own. Each schema object creation construct is augmented with a FROM clause to reference corresponding remote schema objects, as in statements for database and table creation:

```
CREATE DATABASE ⟨new database name⟩
[ ... ]
FROM ⟨source database id⟩
```

Here the schema defined for ⟨*source database id*⟩ is copied into an identical schema for ⟨*new database name*⟩.

Similarly, but at a finer level of granularity, it is possible to create and alter tables by copying only the definition of single columns:

```
CREATE TABLE ⟨new table name⟩
           (⟨column definition⟩ [⟨column definition⟩])
FROM ⟨source table id⟩
```

The usual syntax for ⟨*column definition*⟩ is also augmented to allow for copying from an existing remote column definition:

```
⟨column definition⟩ ::= [(usual SQL syntax) ... ]
FROM ⟨source column definition⟩
```

This syntax suggests a strongly cooperative environment, whereby each local schema results from a variation of a basic, common definition that is agreed upon by all members. In this scenario, essentially different from that of totally independent schemas evolving in complete autonomy, potential definition conflicts are largely absent, and there is little need for extensive knowledge about local domains. As a consequence, schema reconciliation is hardly ever needed. In our example databases, on the other hand, we can assume that schemas were designed and continue to evolve independently of each other, yielding a potential for conflicts.[6]

---

[6]In fact, very few of the MSQL import and copy features for object definition can be used to construct those examples.

The second assumption is that the scope of each statement potentially involving multiple schemas is always made explicit. The scope of a multidatabase statement, be it a query or a DDL command, is defined through the USE clause. In particular, fragments of one schema can be imported into a number of other schemas using a single statement, like the following:

```
USE            DB_A, DB_B
CREATE TABLE   T_common
FROM           DB_Source.original_t;
```

This statement creates two identical copies of table Original_t from database DB_Source, in schemas DB_A and DB_B. Also, each schema object can be fully qualified with the schema name, e.g., DB_A.T_COMMON.X, to disambiguate. Finally, the Create multidatabase statement lets a user define a single name for a set of databases, as in

```
CREATE MULTIDATABASE FED_1 (DB_A, DB_B);
```

Likewise, the Alter multidatabase statement allows deletion or insertion from the set of member databases. Using a single identifier offers more than just a shorthand notation for the USE clause. The multidatabase data dictionary, defined as the collection of all schema objects in the scope, can be used to refer to sets of schema objects; e.g., FED_1.T_COMMON now represents the set {DB_A.T_COMMON, DB_B.T_COMMON}.

7.3.3 Data Manipulation Language

We now present some novel database manipulation features that make MSQL suitable for schema and data interoperability. First, we exemplify the use of multiple identifiers and semantic variables and give the semantics of a multiquery in terms of multirelational algebra (see Section 7.2.3). Semantic variables are collective names defined to refer to collections of local schema objects, and they represent a first step toward the definition of an explicit multiquery context. By providing the means to achieve some schema abstraction, they help in the resolution of some types of schema conflicts. The use of dynamic attributes, outer join, and outer union is also intended to help in cases where schemas present some limited form of conflict. However, as we have pointed out when describing the DDL, one original assumption in MSQL was that these conflicts would rarely occur. Consequently, the ability to handle schema conflicts using these mechanisms alone is naturally limited. In the subsection "Explicit Multiquery Context and User-Defined Operators," we relax the assumption of nonconflicting schemas. We describe a more general framework that, although requiring the context to be declared explicitly and more exhaustively, allows a better definition of the abstract schema that multiqueries operate on. Together with a generalization of semantic variables, we introduce a few additional mechanisms to help in schema conflict resolution, mainly type coercion, user-defined operators, and implicit joins completion.

Multiple Identifiers and Semantic Variables

To begin, Example 7.1 introduces an elementary multidatabase query that operates on our example databases.

EXAMPLE 7.1

The following multiquery retrieves the names and e-mail addresses of authors who have published a paper both in some IFIP and AI*IA conference, together with the title of the paper.

```
USE        AI_IA, IFIP
SELECT     name, e_mail, title
FROM       Authors, IFIP.Publ_papers IFIP_paper, Contacts,
           Attendees, AI_IA.Publ_papers
WHERE      Authors.Name = Contacts.Name
AND        Contacts.Person_ID = Attendees.ID
AND        Attendees.speaker = 'Y'
AND        Authors.paper_ID = IFIP_paper.p_ref;
```

The intended purpose of the query is to retrieve *name*, *e_mail*, and *title* from both schemas in the scope by computing some local joins (between Contacts and Attendees in AI_IA and between Authors and Publ_papers in IFIP) and one interdatabase join on the author's name. Identifiers in the SELECT clause are multiple: they refer to different attributes in different schemas. The result of this multiquery is the following set of two relations known as a *multirelation*

[Authors.name, Authors.e_mail, Publ_papers.title]

for AI_IA, and

[Contacts.name, Contacts.e_mail, Publ_papers.title]

for IFIP. The semantics of this multiquery can be expressed using multirelational algebra, as follows,

$$\pi_{name,e\_mail,title}(R_1', R_2')$$

where

$$R_1 = \text{Authors} \bowtie_{paper\_ID=p\_ref} \text{Publ\_papers},$$
$$R_2 = \sigma_{attendees.speaker='Y'}(\text{Contacts} \bowtie_{person\_ID=ID} \text{Attendees})$$

and

$$R_1' = R_1 \ltimes_{name} R_2,$$
$$R_2' = R_2 \ltimes_{name} R_1$$

Notice that the two semijoins actually express the interdatabase join across the relations produced by each elementary query. In particular, when the resulting multirelations are *union compatible*, the result can be expressed as a single relation whose content is the union of the contents of the relations in the set.

Multiqueries like the one in the example above can only be expressed as long as attribute names are the same (or very similar if wildcards are allowed in identifiers) across several schemas. This is not the case in general, especially when the federation includes schemas that have been evolving autonomously from each other. Semantic variables provide a more general naming mechanism whereby different object identifiers can be referred to using a common name. Example 7.2 illustrates the idea.

EXAMPLE 7.2

We are interested in advertising a new book on Datalog, and we identify our potential target as people who have an interest both in databases and logic programming. We want to retrieve the addresses of researchers who have in the past bought copies both of SIGMOD and AI*IA proceedings. The following multiquery uses semantic variables to refer to identifiers in the two schemas:

```
USE         AI_IA, SIGMOD
LET         person.membership BE people.status,
            contacts.member_status
LET         conf.name BE proc_sales.conf_name, attendees.conf_ID
SELECT      person.e_mail, person.membership, conf.name
FROM        person, conf, attendees
WHERE       people.ID = proc_sales.buyer_ID
AND         conf.n_copies > 0
AND         contacts.person_ID = attendees.ID
AND         attendees.procs_copies > 0
AND         people.ID = attendees.ID;
```

In this query, the semantic variables *person* and *membership*, introduced by the LET clauses, are common names for the identifiers on the right-hand side of the "BE" keyword. The general syntax for the LET clause is

LET ⟨variable⟩[.⟨variable⟩] ... BE ⟨object group⟩ [⟨object group⟩] ...
⟨object group⟩ ::= ⟨object name⟩[.⟨object name⟩] ...

where the number of elements in each ⟨object group⟩ equals the number of variables on the left-hand side. ⟨object name⟩ can be the name of either a local attribute or a table. In general, variables range over the domains of table names and attribute names, respectively. We represent a LET clause L using the notation:

$$L = (x_1, \ldots, x_n) \rightarrow \{(A_{11}, \ldots, A_{1n}), \ldots, (A_{m1}, \ldots, A_{mn})\}$$

Upon query evaluation, these variables are lexically replaced pairwise by their respective object identifiers,

$$(\text{person}, \text{membership}) \rightarrow \{(\text{people}, \text{status}), (\text{contacts}, \text{member\_status})\}$$

and

$$(\text{conf}, \text{name}) \rightarrow \{(\text{proc\_sales}, \text{conf\_name}), (\text{attendees}, \text{conf\_ID})\}$$

The process of lexical substitution yields the following equivalent set of four multiqueries, without LET clauses.

```
1.   USE      AI_IA, SIGMOD
     SELECT   people.e_mail, people.status, proc_sales.conf_name
     FROM     people, proc_sales, attendees
     WHERE    people.ID = proc_sales.buyer_ID
     AND      proc_sales.n_copies > 0
     AND      contacts.person_ID = attendees.ID
     AND      attendees.procs_copies > 0
     AND      people.ID = attendees.ID;
```

This multiquery is then equivalent to the set of two elementary queries, with no interdatabase joins, obtained by resolving the multiple identifiers. The result is relation R_1 from AI_IA,

$$R_1 = [\text{people.e\_mail}, \text{people.status}, \text{proc\_sales.conf\_name}]$$

containing the tuples for which the people.ID also meets the conditions in SIGMOD.

```
2.   USE      AI_IA, SIGMOD
     SELECT   people.e_mail, people.status, attendees.conf_ID
     FROM     people, attendees
     WHERE    people.ID = proc_sales.buyer_ID
     AND      attendees.n_copies > 0
     AND      contacts.person_ID = attendees.ID
     AND      attendees.procs_copies > 0
     AND      people.ID = attendees.ID;
```

In this query, the object *attendees.n_copies* resulting from the substitution does not belong to any of the schema in the scope. Therefore, the query is discarded as nonpertinent and does not contribute to the final relation.

```
3.   USE      AI_IA, SIGMOD
     SELECT   contacts.e_mail, contacts.member_status,
              proc_sales.conf_name
     FROM     contacts, proc_sales, attendees
     WHERE    people.ID = proc_sales.buyer_ID
```

```
AND        proc_sales.n_copies > 0
AND        contacts.person_ID = attendees.ID
AND        attendees.procs_copies > 0
AND        people.ID = attendees.ID;
```

This multiquery results in relation R_2, with attributes from both schemas, namely,

$$R_2 = [\text{contacts.e\_mail, contacts.member\_status,proc\_sales.conf\_name}]$$

where again the tuples satisfy the stated conditions on both schemas.

```
4.  USE        AI_IA, SIGMOD
    SELECT     contacts.e_mail, contacts.member_status,
               attendees.conf_ID
    FROM       contacts, attendees
    WHERE      people.ID = proc_sales.buyer_ID
    AND        attendees.n_copies > 0
    AND        contacts.person_ID = attendees.ID
    AND        attendees.procs_copies > 0
    AND        people.ID = attendees.ID;
```

As in query 2, this multiquery is also discarded because *attendees.procs_copies* is not defined in the scope.

The final result of the original multiquery is multirelation $\{R_1, R_2\}$. If R_1 and R_2 happen to be union compatible, then the multirelation reduces to the union of the component relations, i.e., $R_1 \cup R_2$. The semantics of the LET clause can be formalized by introducing a set of operators that capture the decomposition process, as shown in the following example.

Given a query Q and a LET clause L, operator

$$Let_{base}(Q, (x_1, \ldots, x_n) \to \{(A_{11}, \ldots, A_{1n}), \ldots, (A_{m1}, \ldots, A_{mn})\}) = \{Q_1, \ldots, Q_k\}$$

for $k \leq n$ represents the basic decomposition process, producing queries Q_j by lexically replacing each occurrence of x_i in Q with A_{ij}. Notice that, as we have seen in the previous example, $k < n$ because some of the resulting queries may not be pertinent; that is, the substitution may yield combinations of table and attribute identifiers that may be inconsistent for some of the queries.

Next, we define decomposition over a set of queries:

$$Let_1(\{Q_1, \ldots, Q_n\}, L) = \bigcup_{i:1}^{n} Let_{base}(Q_i, L)$$

Decomposition of a set $\mathcal{Q} = \{Q_1, \ldots, Q_n\}$ of queries against a set of LET clauses is defined recursively,

$$Let_{rec}(\mathcal{Q}, \{L_1, \ldots, L_k\}) = Let_{rec}(Let_1(\mathcal{Q}, L_k), \{L_1, \ldots, L_{k-1}\}) \text{ for } k > 0$$

and

$$Let_{rec}(\mathcal{Q}, \emptyset) = \mathcal{Q}$$

Finally, the entire substitution process for multiquery Q and LET clauses $\{L_1, \ldots, L_k\}$ is represented by $Let_{rec}(\{Q\}, \{L_1, \ldots, L_k\})$.

In this example, the use of semantic variables helped create a compact multiquery by overcoming lexical differences. However, some of the limitations in this approach make it difficult to use:

- The LET-substitution process exhaustively replaces all semantic variables with each legal combination of corresponding local variables. This process yields a number of elementary queries equal to the product of the number of list elements in the right-hand side of each LET clause. Unfortunately, some of the combinations are not meaningful; i.e., a number of spurious queries are potentially generated. Discovering the subset of meaningful, or pertinent, queries requires looking up each identifier in a local data dictionary. Apart from the computational inefficiency, this process makes it hard for the user to figure out the meaning of the multiquery without a careful scrutiny of the database schemas.

- While it seems convenient to "factorize" identifiers in the SELECT clause, figuring out common identifiers for the joining attributes that, once replaced, correctly represent all the intended joins can become a real puzzle. Having to list explicitly the local and interdatabase joins may defeat the whole purpose of using LET.

- The local identifiers represented by a semantic variable belong to different domains and are not necessarily union compatible. The LET construct is not expressive enough to account for these differences, as well as to specify how they should be reconciled.

- Semantic variables have an implicit type, since they may range over different object name domains, e.g., table name and attribute names. Making the type explicit would help in understanding their intended meaning.

Explicit Multiquery Context and User-Defined Operators

We have presented semantic variables as a first step toward an explicit representation of the context surrounding the evaluation of a multiquery. The main limitation of this approach, which is based on the introduction of new identifiers in the name space of database objects, is that these identifiers are simply aliases and are only defined to the extent that they refer to existing database objects. To solve this problem, [MR95] proposed to introduce a new set of virtual database objects, as opposed to just names, and to supply a mechanism to relate those virtual objects to existing local objects. In the current proposal, these objects are defined in particular as attributes of a new "global" entity—a type of degenerate schema composed of only one entity—that can be referred to in multiqueries. These attributes are typed the same way regular attributes are. The virtual attributes are used to represent collections of type-compatible expressions on local attributes. The expressions can include operators that are available at local database sites, either as built-in database functions (e.g., aggregation functions) or as user-defined applications with a well-defined interface to the database.[7] A *mapping descriptor* maps an expression, which has local attributes as operands and uses the defined operators, onto a type-compatible virtual attribute.

The main shift from the viewpoint of semantic variables is that virtual attributes now exist independently of the local schemas. They are generally used to describe a particular database domain at a higher level of abstraction than local objects. Virtual objects and local operators are defined in a special declarations section. A multiquery is now evaluated within the context defined by the declarations,[8] complemented with the definition of the mapping descriptors required to use the virtual objects. Virtual objects used in a multiquery are really a particular case of semantic variables where variables are restricted to range only on local attributes, rather than on tables. This is a consequence of grouping the virtual objects as attributes of a new, higher level table; since the mappings preserve the type, virtual attributes can only represent type-compatible expressions on local attributes.[9] The trade-off for introducing this restriction is that the resulting context definition is better structured and easier to understand, customize, and reuse.

Example 7.3 introduces a simple notation for the declaration of virtual objects and illustrates a formulation of the multiquery shown in Example 7.2 that uses the new features.

EXAMPLE 7.3
Declare
    virtual

```
            ID: string(50);
            membership:  string(3);
            e_mail:  string(25);
            conference:  string(50);
            copies_sold:  integer;
            amount_for_procs:  real;
```

---

[7]This whole design could be rephrased in terms of an object model: the virtual objects become data members of a virtual class, each local schema can be mapped into one class, and functions that are available at local sites become public methods of those classes.

[8]Notice that we now have two notions of scope: the semantic scope, in the MSQL sense, defined as the collection of databases addressed by the query, and the syntactic scope of a declaration with respect to a multiquery. The scope of a declaration may include a whole transaction unit or, it is hoped, a whole multidatabase application.

[9]There is no notion, in the current version of the language, of a "higher level table" that can be mapped onto a local table.

operators
```
            string(3) status_to_membership(string(1)) @ SIGMOD;
            string(1) membership_to_status(string(3)) @ SIGMOD;
            string(50) to_standard(string25) @ SIGMOD;
            string(3) std_status(short) @ AI_IA;
            string(50) export_format(varchar(30)) @ AI_IA;
```
begin
```
        USE    SIGMOD, AI_IA
        LET    membership BE
               status_to_membership(people.status),
               std_status(contacts.member_status);
        LET    e_mail BE people.e_mail, contacts.e_mail;
        LET    conference BE proc_sales.conf_name,
               attendees.conf_ID;
        LET    copies_sold BE proc_sales.n_copies,
               attendees.procs_copies;
        SELECT e_mail, membership, conference
        WHERE  people.ID = proc_sales.buyer_ID
        AND    contact_person_ID = attendees.ID
        AND    to_standard(people.ID) =
               export_format(attendees.ID)
        AND    copies_sold > 0;
```
end;

The example contains three parts. The first part is the declaration of virtual objects and operators. Objects have a type and a domain. To be useful, the type system for virtual objects must contain the type system assumed for the local schemas, and the type of virtual objects should be more general than that of any local object that can be made to correspond to them through the mapping descriptors. In the current syntax, the domain of a virtual object is not expressed explicitly.[10] In this example, we assume the domain of *Membership* is the set {ST, JR, SR, HO}.[11] Operators are declared through their signature. The local schema where the operator is available is also given, together with additional information, not shown here, on system-dependent details such as the invocation mechanism and the communication protocol. These declarations can be thought of as a collection of export interfaces made available by each local system to the federation. They suggest that the local administrators are responsible for their maintenance.

In Example 7.3, the SIGMOD site has two functions, one inverse of the other, to translate between the local format for association membership

---

[10]In some database systems, domains are expressed separately as constraints on the attributes. In the current version of MSQL, the constraint mechanism and its corresponding sublanguage are not yet available.

[11]For STudent, JunioR, SenioR, and HOnorary, respectively.

status and the "standard" one. For instance, SIGMOD may use codes such as "S" for "student," "R" for "regular," and "H" for "honorary." Function *status_to_membership* then maps "S" into "ST," "R" into "JR," and so forth. ALIA only defines one function for its numeric codes for the status, to the "standard" one. In addition, the two functions *to_standard* and *export_format* change the format of subscriber identifiers in the respective schemas. These functions are used to reconcile mismatched ID attributes in the query interdatabase join.

In the second part of Example 7.3, LET clauses introduce the mappings. The new syntax for the LET clause is simply,

LET (⟨virtual object⟩ [,⟨virtual object⟩, ...]) BE
(⟨local expression⟩ [, ⟨local expression⟩], ...) [,
(⟨local expression⟩ [, ⟨local expression⟩], ...)]
] ...

where each ⟨local expression⟩ is an expression on local, fully qualified attributes that may involve local operators declared as above, as well as local built-in database functions.[12] Notice that all virtual objects now range over the same domain (expressions on local attributes), and unlike the regular LET, it is now possible to perform type checking on the mappings. The notion of mapping descriptors has been formalized to some extent in [MR95] by introducing a functional MD as follows: Let S be the multiquery scope and $\mathcal{VO}$ the set of virtual objects. For each schema $s \in S$, let $\mathcal{A}_s$ be the set of all local (table qualified) attributes for database s. Also, let $\mathcal{F} = \{f_i : \tau_1, \ldots, \tau_{n_i} \to \tau\}$ represent the collection of signatures for the declared operators. For a given pair $s \in S$, $vo \in \mathcal{VO}$ the mapping descriptor

$$MD_{vo}^s = \langle A, f, f' \rangle$$

is defined, where $A = \{A_1, \ldots, A_k\} \subseteq \mathcal{A}_s$, $f : type(A_1), \ldots, type(A_k) \to type(vo) \in \mathcal{F}$ and $f' = f^{-1}$ if f is unary and invertible and undefined otherwise. Notice that MD is a partial function; i.e., it may not be defined for some vo and s. Using this notation, the MDs for the example can be written as follows (I indicates the identity function, S is short for SIGMOD, and A for ALIA):

---

[12]The requirement that each operator in the expression be local can actually be relaxed, if the implementation supports the execution of remote functions on local arguments.

$$MD^S_{\text{membership}} = \langle\{\text{people.status}\}, \text{status\_to\_membership},$$
$$\text{membership\_to\_status}\rangle$$
$$MD^A_{\text{membership}} = \langle\{\text{contacts.member\_status}\}, \text{std\_status}, \perp\rangle$$
$$MD^S_{\text{ID}} = \langle\{\text{people.ID}\}, \text{to\_standard}, \perp\rangle$$
$$MD^A_{\text{ID}} = \langle\{\text{contacts.person\_ID}\}, \text{export\_format}, \perp\rangle$$
$$MD^S_{\text{e\_mail}} = \langle\{\text{people.e\_mail}\}, I, I\rangle$$
$$MD^A_{\text{e\_mail}} = \langle\{\text{contacts.e\_mail}\}, I, I\rangle$$
$$MD^S_{\text{conference}} = \langle\{\text{proc\_sales.conference\_name}\}, I, I\rangle$$
$$MD^A_{\text{conference}} = \langle\{\text{attendees.conf\_ID}\}, I, I\rangle$$
$$MD^S_{\text{copies\_sold}} = \langle\{\text{proc\_sales.n\_copies}\}, I, I\rangle$$
$$MD^A_{\text{copies\_sold}} = \langle\{\text{attendees.proc\_copies}\}, I, I\rangle$$

In the third part of Example 7.3, the multiquery refers to the declared virtual objects and operators, both in the SELECT clause and in the inter-database join. The new LET-substitution process is based on the observation that the mappings are now defined separately between each local schema and the virtual objects, making it possible to carry out the substitutions by considering one schema at a time. The resulting algorithm is somewhat orthogonal to the one outlined on page 192, where the semantic variables are exhaustively and blindly replaced in the multiquery with each legal combination of local identifiers. For each database in the scope, the virtual objects are replaced by the corresponding expressions in the mappings defined for that database. This allows, for example, the detection of a missing attribute (the mappings are partial) in the SELECT clause and the appropriate insertion of a NULL placeholder. In the process, the set of joins and selections in the WHERE clause is partitioned, yielding one query for each schema, plus one query for the interdatabase joins. The result is a set of elementary queries, one for each database, each with all of, and only, its own joins.

In each query, the SELECT clause is augmented to include the attributes required to perform the final interdatabase join.[13] Notice also that the FROM clause can be omitted because it can be inferred from the use of the local attributes after substitution of the virtual objects. The new substitution process yields the following two elementary queries (each still containing one interdatabase join):

```
Elementary Query EQ1 for database SIGMOD:
SELECT      people.e_mail, status_to_membership(people.status),
            proc_sales.conf_name, to_standard(people_ID)
```

---

[13]See [Sua92] for the derivation of a basic evaluation plan and execution of MSQL.

```
FROM       people, proc_sales
WHERE      people.ID = proc_sales.buyer_ID
AND        proc_sales.n_copies > 0;
```

```
Elementary Query EQ2 for database AI_IA:
SELECT     contacts.e_mail, std_status(contacts.member_status),
           attendees.conf_ID, export_format(attendees.ID)
FROM       contacts, attendees
WHERE      contacts.person_ID = attendees.ID
AND        attendees.procs_copies > 0;
```

This version of the example highlights some important differences as compared to the original version of MSQL. First, this controlled use of LET ensures that the relations resulting from each elementary query are all type compatible. As a result, relational algebra is sufficient to define the semantics of the language; i.e., multirelational algebra need not be used. Then, some schema and data conflicts among mismatched attributes can be resolved using the mapping descriptors involving ad hoc operators in the expressions [MR95]. In Section 7.3.4, we present an extension to the basic evaluation plan for MSQL [Sua92], which takes into account the invocation of the remote functions that implement the external user-defined operators. The multidatabase system architecture must be redesigned accordingly.

To conclude this overview of the MSQL data manipulation language, we mention two additional features, namely, type coercion and implicit joins completion, which help solve union compatibility, schema isomorphism, and key mismatch problems.

Type Compatibility

Type compatibility among equivalent, or corresponding, attributes is a necessary step to achieve union compatibility among relations. Since each local DBMS has its own type system and virtual database objects are meant to represent local database objects, the type system defined for the multidatabase should include all the types defined by the local DBMS and introduce new, more general types for the virtual objects. The resulting type lattice allows the processor to perform type coercion automatically when needed; this is done by checking type compatibility at the multidatabase level. In Example 7.3, if local attributes *proc_sales.n_copies* and *attendees.procs_copies* have different types, say SHORT and NUMBER, respectively, then the type of *copies_sold* should be more general than both of them. Upon decomposition, the processor should insert type conversion routines in the evaluation plan, either to transform one of the two types into the other or to transform each into their join type.

Implicit Joins Completion

In the multiquery of Example 7.3, local as well as interdatabase joins are listed explicitly. In some cases, given enough information to the (multi)query processor, some or all of the local joins can be left implicit; i.e., they can be omitted from the query. The notion of *implicit joins* was first introduced and formalized in the study of Universal Relation Databases [MU83]: Given a set of joins, or "natural dependencies" on a set of relations, defined independently of a specific query and involving a set A of attributes—the set of attributes in a query projection—there exists an algorithm to determine, for each subset of A, a subset of the given joins that connect those attributes and is minimal with respect to some metric.[14] A query in which some of the local joins are left implicit is called *incomplete*. In practice, referential integrity constraints, often defined with the schema, represent the basic natural dependencies.

The idea of using the implicit joins completion algorithm has been applied by Litwin [Lit85a] to the multidatabase environment. If, in fact, natural dependency information is available for each schema, then an incomplete multiquery can be first decomposed into a set of elementary, incomplete queries (using the algorithm described on page 196), and then the completion algorithm can be applied separately to each such query. The key here is on the separation of contexts during completion. If the navigation required to connect corresponding attributes through joins differs from schema to schema, then by omitting the local joins altogether, we gain in expressivity when formulating the initial multiquery, because we can now design a more abstract query that hides all those local navigation details. Furthermore, since the decomposition algorithm allows each elementary query to be evaluated within its own context independently of each other, those joins can be completed independently. The trade-off for this convenience is the extra information about the dependencies in each local schema that is required by the completion algorithm.

This technique, although potentially very powerful, presents the well-known, substantial limitation that the set of minimal completions may not be unique. Dependency information may not be sufficient to determine a unique meaning for each subset of the attributes and for arbitrary selections. In [MU83], the notion of maximal objects was introduced to deal with this potential ambiguity. The completion algorithm defined in [Lit85a] takes the union of the completed queries resulting from each completion for a given schema. Since none of these approaches is entirely satisfactory with respect to the way the original, intended meaning of a query is reconstructed, in the current version of MSQL, no predefined strategy is enforced to resolve the ambiguities. Rather, if

---

[14]Formally, join completion relies on the notion of *join dependency*: given n sets of attributes $R_1, \ldots R_n$, the join dependency $\bowtie (R_1, \ldots, R_n)$ is satisfied by a relation r over $R = \bigcup_{i=1}^{n} R_i$ if and only if: $r = \bowtie_{i=1}^{n} \pi_{R_i}(r)$. An *object* is defined as a minimal set of attributes $R_i = \{A_{j_1}, \ldots, A_{j_i}\}$ such that the join dependency $\bowtie (R_1, \ldots R_n)$ holds. A join dependency is represented as a hypergraph, with one node for each attribute appearing in one or more of the R_is, and one edge for each R_i, consisting of all its member attributes. The algorithm presented in [MU83] finds the minimal lossless joins connecting a subset of attributes in the universal relation, when and only when the hypergraph is acyclic.

the query admits more than one completion, the available choices are reported to the user.

The input to the completion algorithm is composed of two parts: the Database Graph (DBG), which includes the natural dependencies and forms part of the context (independent of query instances), and the Query Graph (QG), which represents the local joins that are explicitly included in a specific query. In our running example, the context would include a section for the declaration of the dependencies, as follows:[15]

```
For SIGMOD:
    people.ID = proc_sales.buyer_ID
    people.ID = subscr(sub_ID)
    conf.conf_ref = proc_sales.conf_name
    proc_publ.conf_ID, conf.conf_ref
    series_publ.series_ID = subscr.series

For AI_IA:
    contact_person_ID = attendees.ID
    conferences.name = attendees.conf_ID
    publ_papers.conf_ref = conferences.name
```

DBG nodes represent database relations, while arcs represent relational operators. In our simple example, only equality operators are used. In the general definition, an arc $\{\langle R.A_i, op_i, S.B_i \rangle\}$ for $1 \le i \le n$ represents the predicate $\bigwedge_{i=1}^{n}(R.A_i \langle op_i \rangle S.B_i)$, while an arc of the form $r(R.A_1, \ldots, R.A_k, S.B_1, \ldots, S.B_h)$, where r is an external $k + h$-ary predicate, represents a θ-join between relations R and S. Using these declarations, local joins can be omitted from the multiquery in Example 7.3, yielding the following, simpler query:

```
USE     SIGMOD, AI_IA
LET     membership BE
            status_to_membership(people.status),
            std_status(contacts.member_status);
LET     e_mail BE
            people.e_mail, contacts.e_mail;
LET     conference BE
            proc_sales.conf_name, attendees.conf_ID;
LET     copies_sold BE
            proc_sales.n_copies, attendees.procs_copies;
SELECT  e_mail, membership, conference
WHERE   to_standard(people.ID) = export_format(attendees.ID)
```

The QG is constructed by the processor from the local joins in the query, as follows. (In our example, the QG is empty for both elementary queries derived from the simplified multiquery above.)

---

[15] In this case, we actually list some of the referential integrity constraints.

- The QG has one node for each relation used (in the FROM clause) in the query; thus, the set of QG nodes is a subset of the DBG nodes.

- The QG has an arc labeled $\langle A, B, relop \rangle$ between nodes R and S, for each join $R.A \ relop \ S.B$ in the query, and for each θ-join:

$$r(R.A_1, \dots, R.A_k, S.B_1, \dots, S.B_h)$$

The completion algorithm, described in more detail in [Lit85a] and implemented as described in [Mis93b], finds the set of minimal-depth spanning trees for the union of the DBG and the QG, giving priority to the QG and adding arcs as necessary to generate a connected component. Note that if, in particular, the QG is already connected (enough local joins were explicit), the query is considered complete. In our example, the nodes to be connected are *people, proc_sales* and *contacts, attendees* for SIGMOD and ALIA, respectively (see Figures 7.3 and 7.4). In both these very simple cases, the algorithm finds a direct arc to connect the two tables and terminates by returning the two complete queries (with inclusion of the interdatabase joins that did not take part in the completion process) without ambiguities; the simplified multiquery has been decomposed and successfully reconstructed for the local schema.

Outer Joins and Outer Union

We conclude our discussion on the language features by observing that user-defined operators, introduced in Section 7.3.3, effectively generalize both the outer join and the outer union operators. In fact, outer joins are a particular case of θ-joins, where the θ operators may be user defined. However, sometimes the full power of external operators may not be needed, and outer joins, available in several commercial versions of SQL, can be particularly useful in the multidatabase context. A common situation occurs when trying to join on sets of columns that would logically have a primary-foreign key relationship. In the monodatabase case, referential constraints can often be enforced so that these joins are guaranteed to return all relevant tuples. In the multidatabase case, however, these constraints are generally not available, leading to the case of "children" in one table without corresponding "parents" in another schema. Outer joins resolve this problem.

The outer union operator can be used to compute the union of partially compatible relations by simply returning the union of the two sets of attributes in the two relations. Of course, this operator does not consider the semantics of the attributes involved. Since by keeping all attributes, we only look at their name, this operation may result in sets of differently named attributes with similar meaning in the resulting relation. In our example schemas SIGMOD and ALIA, suppose we want to retrieve the union of [*people.ID, people.status*] and [*contacts.person_ID, member_status*]. Using an outer union operator, we would have

```
SELECT        ID, status
FROM          people
OUTER_UNION
SELECT        person, member_status
FROM          contacts
```

This results in relation

[people.ID, people.status, contacts.person_ID, member_status]

If the pairs of attributes *people.ID*, *contacts.person_ID* and *people.status*, *member_status* are not union compatible, a user-defined operator that looks at each instance of the attributes may be more appropriate than outer union.

7.3.4   Multiquery Evaluation

The first available implementation of MSQL, described in [Sua92], followed the decomposition process outlined in Section 7.3.3, page 192, and does not include external operators. A later implementation [MR95] followed the semantics described on page 197, including steps to evaluate external operators. The evaluation strategy for MSQL presented in this section is concerned only with coordination of the execution of the elementary queries produced by the decomposition phase, regardless of which form of decomposition semantics is adopted. Thus, we first present a common basic evaluation plan and then detail the additional steps required to invoke user-defined operators that are available as local services or applications.

In the available prototype, the evaluation plan is executed in the Narada multisystem application execution environment [HAB+92]. Narada provides basic multiplatform communication services and specialized connectivity to local services, in particular to local DBMSs. The scripting language DOL (Distributed Operation Language) is available to program the control and data flow for a Narada multisystem application. DOL provides constructs for defining elementary tasks to be executed on the remote systems, for expressing control and data dependencies among said tasks, for specifying their parallel execution and synchronization points, and for evaluating conditions based on the status information the tasks return upon completion.

Basic Evaluation for SELECT

The basic MSQL processor consists of a query analyzer and a decomposer, which produce the evaluation plan, and a back-end code generator that compiles the plan into a DOL script. The design of the interface between these two modules allows the processor to be targeted to a different object language by replacing the back end. The basic plan illustrated in Figure 7.6 refers to the

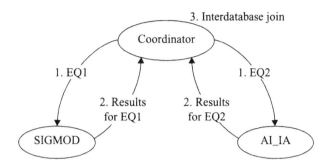

FIGURE 7.6
Basic steps in multiquery evaluation.

elementary queries EQ1 and EQ2 in Section 7.3.3. It assumes that local systems do not provide facilities to execute interdatabase joins.[16]

The multiquery is issued and decomposed at the coordinator site, where we want the final answer to be delivered. SQL queries EQ1 and EQ2 are sent in parallel to the sites of the SIGMOD and ALIA DBMSs, respectively.[17] In the actual architecture, a request for query execution is sent to the two Local Access Manager (LAM) modules that act as proxy users of the local DBMSs on behalf of the coordinator and handle the local database access. Each LAM submits the query, receives the results, and returns both the results and the status condition to the coordinator. The coordinator waits until both results are returned. If both queries are executed successfully, their results are used to perform the final interdatabase join, and the final result is produced.

The actual evaluation plan must take into account the different resources available at each local site. For instance, if the coordinator does not itself have access to a local DBMS, the final join can either be carried out locally at the shell level (operating on files), or the join can be performed at one of the local sites. In the latter case, temporary tables must be set up on the designated database, and individual query results must be rerouted appropriately. Multiquery optimization, investigated for instance in [Mon93], is still largely an open issue, complicated by the diversity of local resources that must be taken into account.

---

[16]If they do, the problem reduces to executing a distributed query using a distributed database system.

[17]Remember that these queries return the additional attributes required to carry out the final interdatabase join.

Extended Evaluation with External Operators

We now concentrate on the evaluation of a multiquery in the presence of external operators. Two basic types of operators are allowed in a multiquery—*filters* that appear in joins of the form

$$f(R.A_{i_1}, \ldots, R.A_{i_n})\langle op \rangle g(S.B_{i_1}, \ldots, S.B_{i_m})$$

and *predicates* that appear in selections of the form

$$\ldots \text{WHERE} \ldots p(R.A_{i_1}, \ldots, R.A_{i_n})$$

Both filters and predicates can be evaluated in a tuple-at-a-time fashion on an input relation. Filters transform relations into new relations, preserving their cardinality but altering their structure; whereas predicates return a subset of the input relation (the tuples that satisfy the predicate), unaltered.

Awk scripts and greplike commands provide good intuitive examples for shell-level filters and predicates, respectively. To illustrate this concept, and for simplicity's sake, we assume that filters and functions can be invoked by a system shell and that relations obtained as a result of queries are available as text files, one line for each tuple. In a more general distributed architecture scenario, local applications would be made available through some registration and brokerage environment, such as DCE, in some uniform way. We further assume, without loss of generality, that operators and the operands are available at the same site.[18] We indicate the conversion to and from the textual representation by the functions $db\_to\_file(SQL\_query, file)$ and $file\_to\_db(file, DB\_table)$.

Figure 7.7 illustrates the main problem with the application of filters and predicates—namely, that the input relations must be "broken down" to accommodate the input format accepted by the application and the output relations recomposed upon completion to be reinserted into the database. A filter $f(A,B)$ applied to table $R(ABC)$ requires first the conversion of columns A,B from table R into a file. The filtered output is placed in the resulting relation S into column $S.F$, along with the corresponding values of C. Notice that we cannot assume column C is carried through f. Similarly, a predicate $p(A,B)$ applied to relation $R(ABC)$ requires exporting $R.A$, $R.B$ columns into the file used to evaluate the predicate. The rows corresponding to the qualifying tuples are then inserted in the resulting table S.

Consider the evaluation of predicate $p(S)$, where

$$S = \pi_{A_1,\ldots,A_k}(R(A_1, \ldots, A_m))$$

Because, in general, S does not include the primary key for R, after applying p, the qualifying tuples must be joined with the original relation R:

$$R' = (p(S) \bowtie_{A_1,\ldots,A_k} R)$$

---

[18]If this is not the case, additional steps must be inserted in the evaluation plan to migrate the operands, which are usually files containing the relations.

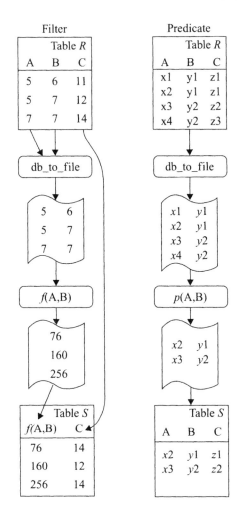

FIGURE 7.7
Effect of filter and predicate evaluation.

Operationally, this expression translates into the following sequence of elementary tasks: apply $db\_to\_file(SQL\_query, f\_in)$, where SQL_query retrieves S; apply p to f_in resulting in f_out; invoke $file\_to\_db(f\_out, TMP)$; join R with temporary relation TMP. In a DOL implementation, the first task would issue the SQL query and pass the resulting relation to the second task, which would call p as a shell script and pass its results to the third task for the final join. The generalization to the case of multiple tables involved in p is straightforward. In this case, however, there are more opportunities for optimization of the resulting task sequence.

7.4
Updates in Multidatabase Languages

In this section, we consider updates in the context of multidatabase languages. We introduce the extensions to MSQL proposed in [SRL93] for multidatabase transactions, outline the basic evaluation plan for MSQL updates, and describe the UniSQL approach to handling updates.

7.4.1 Updates in MSQL and Multitransactions

In Section 7.3.4, we presented MSQL language constructs for read-only multiqueries, which extend the SQL SELECT query construct to address a number of databases, possibly heterogeneous. Likewise, MSQL extends write operations (UPDATE, INSERT, DELETE) to modify the state of multiple databases simultaneously. When the subqueries in a multiple update operation are related to each other, it should be possible to execute them as if they were part of a single transaction (Example 7.4).

EXAMPLE 7.4
We would like to increase the cost of the proceedings book for a given conference by 10 percent, both in the SIGMOD and AI_IA databases.

```
USE SIGMOD, AI_IA
LET (conf, price) BE (proc_publ.conf_ID, proc_publ.procs_cost),
                     (conferences.name, conferences.procs_price)
UPDATE    proc_publ, conf
SET       price = price * 1.1
WHERE     conf = :conf_name
```

where the notation :⟨variable⟩ indicates an input value for the user. Notice also that, unlike in SQL, here the UPDATE keyword can be followed by a list of all the tables that are to be updated. However, each table must belong to a different database, so that upon decomposition, each resulting monodatabase update contains exactly one table in its UPDATE clause.

Decomposing this multiquery yields two elementary monodatabase queries that could be submitted independently. However, we would like to enforce a transactional semantics on their execution, so that either they both succeed or neither has any effect. At the system level, however, encapsulating the two queries in a single transaction may not be feasible, due to the difference in local transaction protocols and the local autonomy requirements. Suppose, for instance, that the DBMS for AI_IA does not support the 2PC protocol; i.e., it works only in autocommit mode. After the two updates have been submitted, at the global level, we are left with very little control on the local AI_IA transaction. In fact, if SIGMOD unilaterally aborts its transaction after AI_IA has already committed, we cannot simply roll back the AI_IA transaction, and the global state for the book price is inconsistent. In this case, at the global level, failure atomicity cannot be enforced.

The ability to control global execution while respecting local autonomy requires both a nontraditional notion of global consistency and the use of extended transaction models [GMS87, KR88, Elm92].

In this section, we present the language features that have been proposed [SRL93] to incorporate some elements of flexible transactions [Elm92, SANR92], notably vital databases and compensating transactions.

Vital databases allow the user to specify the desired level of consistency for the execution of a particular multiple update. Because global atomicity cannot always be attained due to the different types of transaction control available at the local systems, users may specify a subset of vital queries that must be executed together (i.e., they must be either committed or aborted atomically) in order for the global update to be consistent. Let us assume, in our previous example, that the SIGMOD database can be updated using 2PC, while ALIA works in autocommit mode. Then we can express the fact that SIGMOD is a vital database by extending the USE clause as follows:

```
USE SIGMOD VITAL, AI_IA
```

Assuming, in general, that a multiple query is decomposed in such a way that, at most, one local query is generated for each database, then the VITAL designators attached to the databases are effectively related to the local queries. In this case, the execution of a multiple query is successful when all vital queries are committed; it aborts when all vital queries are rolled back and is considered incorrect when some of the vital queries are committed and others are rolled back. The final state of all nonvital queries is immaterial to the final state of the global query. In other words, failure atomicity of the global query is enforced only with respect to the vital set.

The vital set for a multiquery should be defined in accordance with the different transaction protocols available locally. If all vital databases support 2PC, the commit point of all corresponding subtransactions can be synchronized, and failure atomicity can be enforced. Notice that the same property holds true in other particular cases. For instance, the example above is a special instance of a Saga [GMS87] where there is only one non-2PC transaction, the one for AI_IA. In this case, the SIGMOD transaction can be held in prepare-to-commit state until the final state for the AI_IA is known and then be committed or rolled back according to that state.

The semantics of vital designators is not applicable when databases that do not support 2PC are included in the vital set because, in general, failure atomicity cannot be enforced if the prepare-to-commit state is not visible. The notion of *compensation* [KLS90, GMS87] has been adopted in MSQL to deal with this problem. Compensating actions are queries that attempt to return a database to a consistent state following an unwanted commit by "semantically undoing" the effect of a transaction. Notice that a semantic undo is not the same as a transaction rollback. In fact, since the original transaction is already committed, the isolation property does not hold because the database state between the commit and the compensation is visible to other transactions. As a consequence, the state after compensation is not, in general, the same as the state that existed prior to the offending transaction.

The complete notation for an MSQL multidatabase transaction with compensating action is best illustrated using our familiar example:

```
BEGIN MULTITRANSACTION
USE SIGMOD, AI_IA
LET (conf, price) BE (proc_publ.conf_ID, proc_publ.procs_cost),
                     (conferences.name, conferences.procs_price)
UPDATE    proc_publ, conferences
SET       price = price * 1.1
WHERE conf = :conf_name

COMP AI_IA
UPDATE    conferences
SET       procs_price = procs_price   1.1
WHERE     name = :conf_name
END MULTITRANSACTION
```

The COMP clause introduces the compensating action for the AI_IA database, which amounts to revoking the 10 percent price increase produced by the initial transaction. As noted above, since the state of the AI_IA database is exposed between the transaction commit and its compensation, the effect of the compensation is not guaranteed to return the conference price to its original value—it simply divides whatever the *current* price value is by 10 percent.

Execution Model for UPDATE

In Section 7.3.4, we presented the basic execution plans for a read-only multiquery. A similar procedure is applied for updates, with the main difference being the coordination of local transactions and the execution of compensating actions when necessary.

The global update in the previous example yields the following three monodatabase update queries:

For SIGMOD (EQ1):

```
UPDATE    proc_publ
SET       procs_cost = procs_cost * 1.1
WHERE proc_publ.conf_ID = :conf_name
```

For AI_IA (EQ2):

```
UPDATE    conferences
```

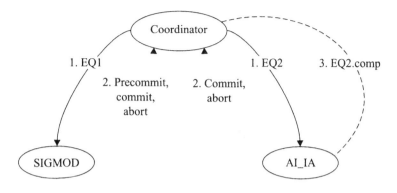

FIGURE 7.8
Transactions with compensation for MSQL updates.

```
SET       procs_price = procs_price* 1.1
WHERE conferences.name = :conf_name
```

Compensation for AI_IA (EQ2.comp):
```
UPDATE    conferences
SET       procs_price = procs_price  1.1
WHERE name = :conf_name
```

The basic evaluation plan is illustrated in Figure 7.8. First, queries EQ1 and EQ2 are generated through decomposition at the coordinator site and submitted to the local systems. Similar to the procedure for SELECT, the request for query execution is actually sent to the two Local Access Manager (LAM) modules that act as proxy users of the local DBMSs on behalf of the coordinator and handle the local database access. For SIGMOD, the 2PC protocol is followed. SIGMOD is expected to return a notification of its precommit state if the query is successful. AI_IA, on the other hand, will only notify of its commit or abort condition. This information is then evaluated by the coordinator. If SIGMOD is in precommit, then if AI_IA has committed, a request for commit is sent to SIGMOD; otherwise SIGMOD is rolled back. In either case, no compensation is necessary. However, if SIGMOD has aborted its transaction while AI_IA has committed, then the compensating action *EQ2.comp* is submitted to AI_IA.

An extension of the MSQL processor to produce this simple evaluation plan, together with a DOL implementation of the plan, are described in [Bre93] and [Mis93b]. The implementation also handles interdatabase joins in multiple updates. Similarly to the case of SELECT, to perform interdatabase joins, a number of temporary tables must be created, populated, and finally, dropped at some local sites or the coordinator site. These housekeeping operations must be part of the global transaction for the multiquery.

Multiple UPDATEs with User-Defined Operators

To conclude this section, we notice that multiple updates using expressions in their LET clauses (see Section 7.3.3) are subject to some restriction. In particular, the operators that appear in the expressions on local database objects must be invertible for the decomposition to work. To illustrate this point, consider the following example, where we would like to change the membership status for some members in SIGMOD and AI_IA:

```
BEGIN MULTITRANSACTION
USE SIGMOD, AI_IA
LET (ms) BE (status_to_membership(people.status),
             std_status(contacts.member_status));
UPDATE    people, contacts
SET       ms = :new_status
WHERE ...
END MULTITRANSACTION
```

The elementary update for SIGMOD is

```
UPDATE    people
SET       status = membership_to_status(:new_status)
WHERE ...
```

where *membership_to_status* is the inverse function of *status_to_membership*, as defined in the mapping descriptor introduced in Section 7.3.3, page 198. However, we can see from the mapping descriptor for *contacts.member_status* that operator *std_status* has no inverse. Therefore, in this case the elementary update for AI_IA cannot be defined.

The only way LET substitution can be used in these cases is by supplying inverse operators whenever update operations on the corresponding local database objects are envisioned.

Bibliography

[ASD+91]   Rafi Ahmed, Phillipe De Smedt, Weimin Du, William Kent, Mohammad A. Ketabchi, Witold A. Litwin, Abbas Rafii, and Ming-Chien Shan. The Pegasus heterogeneous multidatabase system. *IEEE Computer* 24(12):19–27, December 1991.

[Bre93]   M. Bregolin. *Extensions of MSQL: Notes on an Implementa-tion.* Technical report. Houston, TX: University of Houston, Department of Computer Science, March 1993.

[C⁺]   M. J. Carey et al. *Towards heterogeneous multimedia information systems: The garlic approach.* Technical report RJ9911.

[DeM89a]   L. DeMichiel. Performing operations over mismatched do-mains. In *Proceedings of the Fifth IEEE International Conference on Data Engineering*, pages 36–45. Los Alamitos, CA: IEEE Computer Society Press, February 1989.

[DGH⁺95]   A. Daruwala, C. Goh, S. Hofmeister, K. Hussein, S. Madnick, and M. Siegel. Context interchange network prototype. In *Pro-ceedings of the Sixth IFIP International Conference on Database Semantics*, 1995.

[ECR87]   D. Embley, B. Czejdo, and M. Rusinkiewicz. An approach to schema integration and query formulation in federated database systems. In *Proceedings of the Third International Conference on Data Engineering*, February 1987.

[Elm92]   A. Elmagarmid, editor. *Database Transaction Models for Ad-vanced Applications.* San Mateo, CA: Morgan Kaufmann, 1992.

[GLRS91]   J. Grant, W. Litwin, N. Roussopoulos, and T. Sellis. An algebra and calculus for relational multidatabase systems. April 1991.

[GMS87]   H. Garcia-Molina and K. Salem. SAGAs. In *Proceedings of the ACM Conference on Management of Data (SIGMOD)*, pages 249–259, 1987.

[HAB⁺92]   Y. Halabi, M. Ansari, R. Batra, W. Jin, G. Karabatis, P. Krych-niak, M. Rusinkiewicz, and L. Suardi. Narada: An environment for specification and execution of multi-system applications. In *Proceedings of the Second International Conference on Systems Integration*, June 1992.

[HC96]   G. Hammilton and R. Cattell. *JDBC: A Java SQL API.* 1996.

[HM85]   D. Heimbigner and D. McLeod. A federated architecture for information systems. *ACM Transactions on Office Information Systems* 3(3):253–278, July 1985.

[HM93]   J. Hammer and D. McLeod. An approach to resolving seman-
            tic heterogeneity in a federation of autonomous, heterogeneous
            database systems. *International Journal of Intelligent and
            Cooperative Information Systems* 2(1):51–83, March 1993.

[KLK91]   R. Krishnamurthy, W. Litwin, and W. Kent. Language features
            for interoperability of databases with schematic discrepancies.
            In J. Clifford and R. King, editors, *Proceedings of the ACM
            SIGMOD*, pages 40–49. New York: ACM, May 1991.

[KLS90]   H. F. Korth, E. Levy, and A. Silberschatz. A formal approach
            to recovery by compensating transactions. In *Proceedings of the
            16th International Conference on VLDB*, pages 95–106, August
            1990.

[KR88]   J. Klein and A. Reuter. Migrating transactions. In *Future Trends
            in Distributed Computing Systems in the 90's*, 1988.

[KS91]   W. Kim and J. Seo. Classifying schematic and data hetero-
            geneity in multidatabase systems. *IEEE Computer* 24(12):12–18,
            December 1991.

[KSS95]   V. Kashyap, K. Shah, and A. Sheth. Metadata for building the
            multimedia patch quilt. In *Multimedia Database Systems: Issues
            and Research Directions*. New York: Springer-Verlag, 1995.

[L⁺90]   W. Litwin et al. MSQL: A multidatabase language. *Information
            Sciences* 49(1-3):59–101, October–December 1990.

[Lit85a]   W. Litwin. Implicit joins in the multidatabase system MRDSM.
            In *Proceedings of the IEEE-COMPSAC*, October 1985.

[Lit88]   W. Litwin. From database systems to multidatabase: Why and
            how. In *Proceedings of the British Conference on Databases*, pages
            161–188. Cambridge: Cambridge University Press, 1988.

[LS93]   E.-P. Lim and J. Srivastava. *Attribute value conflict in database
            integration: An evidential reasoning approach*. Technical report
            TR 93-14. Minneapolis: University of Minnesota, Department of
            Computer Science, February 1993.

[LS⁺93]   E.-P. Lim, J. Srivastava, et al. Entity identification in database
            integration. In *Proceedings of the Ninth IEEE International Con-*

ference on Data Engineering, pages 294–301. New York: Austrian Computer Society, IEEE Computer Society Press, April 1993.

[Mel96]   J. Melton. An SQL snapshot. In *IEEE 12th International Conference on Data Engineering*, February 1996.

[Mic94]   Microsoft. *ODBC 2.0 Programmer's Reference and SDK Guide*. Redmond, WA: Microsoft Press, 1994.

[Mis93a]   P. Missier. *Extending a Multidatabase Language to Resolve Schema and Data Conflicts* (Master's thesis). Houston, TX: Department of Computer Science, University of Houston, September 1993.

[Mis93b]   P. Missier. *Extensions of MSQL: Notes on an Implementation*. Technical report. Houston, TX: University of Houston, Department of Computer Science, March 1993.

[Mon93]   S. Monti. *Query Optimization in Multidatabase Systems* (Master's thesis). Houston, TX: University of Houston, December 1993.

[MR95]   P. Missier and M. Rusinkiewicz. Extending a multidatabase manipulation language to resolve schema and data conflicts. In *Proceedings of the Sixth IFIP International Conference on Database Semantics*, 1995.

[MU83]   D. Maier and J. Ullman. Maximal objects and the semantics of universal relation databases. *ACM Transactions on Database Systems* 8(1):1–14, March 1983.

[PGMU96]   Y. Papakonstantinou, H. Garcia-Molina, and J. Ullman. Medmaker: A mediation system based on declarative specification. In *12th International Conference on Data Engineering*, February 1996.

[RC87]   M. Rusinkiewicz and B. Czejdo. An approach to query processing in federated database systems. In *Proceedings of the 20th Hawaii International Conference on System Sciences*, 1987.

[SANR92]   A. Sheth, M. Ansari, L. Ness, and M. Rusinkiewicz. Using flexible transactions to support multidatabase applications. In *US West–NSF–DARPA Workshop on Heterogeneous Databases and Semantic Interoperability*, February 1992.

[SK93]   A. Sheth and V. Kashyap. So far (schematically), yet so near (semantically). In *Proceedings of the IFIP TC2/WG2.6 Conference on Semantics of Interoperable Database Systems, DS-5*. Amsterdam: North-Holland, November 1993.

[SRL93]   L. Suardi, M. Rusinkiewicz, and W. Litwin. Execution of extended multidatabase SQL. In *Proceedings of the Ninth IEEE International Conference on Data Engineering*, 1993.

[SSKS95]   L. Shklar, A. Sheth, V. Kashyap, and K. Shah. Infoharness: Use of automatically generated metadata for search and retrieval of heterogeneous information. In *Proceedings of CAiSE-95*, 1995.

[SSKT95]   L. Shklar, A. Sheth, V. Kashyap, and S. Thatte. Infoharness: the system for search and retrieval of heterogeneous information. In *Database Application Semantics, Proceedings of the Sixth IFIP Working Conference on Data Semantics*, 1995. Extended version in *Proceedings of the ACM SIGMOD*, 1995.

[SSR92b]   E. Sciore, M. Siegel, and A. Rosenthal. Using semantic values to facilitate interoperability among heterogeneous information systems. *Transactions on Database Systems* 17(12), 1992.

[Sua92]   L. Suardi. *Execution of Extended MSQL* (Master's thesis). Houston, TX: Department of Computer Science, University of Houston, June 1992.

[Wie92]   G. Wiederhold. Mediators in the architecture of future information systems. *Computer* 25(3):38–49, March 1992.

[Woo85]   W. J. Wood. What's in a link?: Foundations for semantic networks. In R. Brachman and H. Levesque, editors, *Readings in Knowledge Representation*. Los Altos, CA: Morgan Kaufmann, 1985.

8

Interdependent
Database Systems

George Karabatis
Marek Rusinkiewicz
Amit Sheth

Introduction

Recent improvements in information technologies and research efforts in multidatabase systems allow access of data stored in multiple information repositories. These data objects located in multiple databases may form dependencies between them, which must be preserved automatically by a transaction management mechanism. However, traditional multidatabase transaction management techniques are shown to be inadequate for such environments; thus we must resort to "relaxed" techniques, suitable for interdependent data.

Multidatabase systems (MDBSs) provide access to multiple preexisting databases that support their own applications and end users. The MDBS should be able to identify data stored in different databases and support multidatabase queries and updates by resolving data incompatibilities, performing query (update) decomposition, and forming and executing multidatabase transactions. This process can be wholly or partially transparent to the end user. However, at all times the local systems should exercise full control over their data, thus preserving their own autonomy.

There are several reasons for the recent demand for MDBSs. In many organizations, various operational databases are already in service. However, new applications may need to be developed that require access to information stored in several of these databases. The sizable investment in the design of databases and the development of existing applications prohibit designing a new system that integrates all these databases. Moreover, one must consider important issues that arise in a multidatabase environment:

- *Autonomy:* A user of a local database that participates in an MDBS should be able to make decisions about the organization of the data that resides in the local database (choice of a particular DBMS, design of schemas, etc.).

- *Ownership and security:* In a large organization, many subsets of data naturally belong to a particular division or group within the organization. Although other groups may need occasional access to this data, the particular group that uses the data most of the time should control it.

- *Availability and fault tolerance:* The loose coupling of participating databases in a multidatabase system should not hinder a user who is accessing data if another participating database becomes unavailable, thus increasing availability of data as well as the overall system reliability.

Advances in network technology have provided an infrastructure to build distributed homogeneous databases. In addition, the ever increasing need to access and manage data located in heterogeneous and distributed databases has given rise to the area of multidatabases. Many industrial environments can be easily mapped into a multidatabase environment. For example, a typical

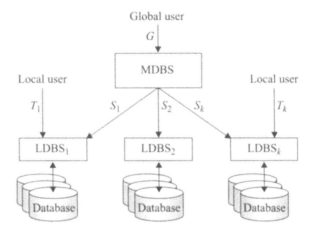

FIGURE 8.1
Architecture of a multidatabase system.

company profile consists of multiple data processing systems developed along functional or organizational divisions. A multidatabase system built on top of such an organizational structure facilitates management of data in a transparent manner, hiding semantic heterogeneities and preserving autonomy of the local database systems.

An MDBS is a system for the management of several databases without a global schema to integrate them [Lit88]. It is also referred to as a loosely coupled federated database system [SL90]. Access to these databases is controlled by autonomous database systems, called local database systems (LDBSs).

Figure 8.1 illustrates the conceptual architecture of an MDBS, where global users access data stored in various LDBSs and local users access data stored in a single LDBS.

A significant reason for a local database to participate in a multidatabase system is to provide access of its local data to global users, thus contributing to the global pool of information. In such environments, data managed by an LDBS may form semantic relationships with data stored at another LDBS. Let us assume that $LDBS_1$ maintains a database with detailed information about employees of an organization (employee name, address, salary, etc.), while $LDBS_2$ manages a database containing statistical information about the employees (such as salary averages per department). When employees in $LDBS_1$ receive a salary raise, the average salary for their department may need to be updated in $LDBS_2$ to maintain interdatabase consistency. This scenario identifies the need to access multiple databases and update related data. An increasing number of applications access data stored in information repositories that are related with each other.

We are mostly interested in data objects that form semantic relationships between them and also convey consistency requirements. We refer to these objects as *interdependent data objects*. We demonstrate the importance of interdependent data with Example 8.1, taken from the telephone industry.

EXAMPLE 8.1

Consider two divisions of a telephone company, the Network Division, which keeps detailed information for every single network switch, and the Planning Division, which maintains in its systems summary information regarding the capacity of network switches. These two divisions maintain a collection of telecommunication databases used by applications for planning and establishing new telephone services. The Network Division owns databases DB_1 through DB_3, and the Planning Division operates the DB_4 database. Here is a short description of each database:

- DB_1 contains detailed information about each switch. Switches establish circuits and route telephone calls. This is done with the help of the *slots* in each switch. DB_1 is a switch database that contains information about the contents of every slot in each switch.

- DB_2 is a statistical database that contains summary information about various pieces of equipment installed in different switches, for use by a statistical application.

- DB_3 is a database containing the status information about each switch.

- DB_4 is a planning database that contains planning information about the switches, whose capacities are close to being exhausted.

We can easily identify interdependent data objects in these databases that belong to different repository systems; they are not integrated and are manipulated possibly by inherently heterogeneous and autonomous database systems (see Figure 8.2). The consistency of the interdependent data is crucial to the company, and automatic cost-effective consistency enforcement is highly desirable. For example, the Planning Division needs to know the current capacity of the switches maintained by the Network Division, to plan ahead for possible additions of equipment. However, an approximate estimate, instead of an accurate up-to-date count, would be satisfactory for the Planning Division.

Interdependent data plays an important role in data warehouse environments [Rad95, Rin95, Inm95]. *Data warehousing* identifies a combination of technologies that are designed to serve the information needs of organizations. The data warehouse approach emerged from the realization that legacy systems do not address the decision support concerns of an organization [Rin95]. A data warehouse stores large amounts of data in several granularities, ranging from detailed information to aggregate data. This data is actually metadata that represents summary information from legacy or operation systems (i.e., source

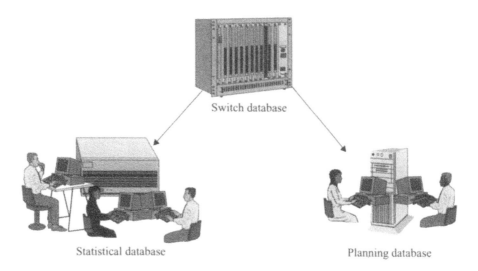

Switch database

Statistical database

Planning database

FIGURE 8.2
An example of interdependent data.

systems) of a corporation. The data is extracted from the source systems and stored in the data warehouse, a separate and autonomous database.

Data in a data warehouse forms a structure that consists of three layers, as illustrated in Figure 8.3: The lowest layer contains the most-recently acquired data from the source systems. At this level, the data warehouse supports decision making for day-to-day operations. The middle layer of a data warehouse is populated with lightly summarized data from the lowest layer. The data in the middle layer provides information suited for departmental decision making. Finally, the top layer of the data warehouse contains highly summarized data derived from either the middle or the lowest layer. This data is designed for executive decision making and is much less in volume than the data stored in the other two layers.

Decision making is a continuous process at an organization, based on the data stored in the data warehouse. However, the source systems constantly produce new data that must be incorporated into the data warehouse. When data in the warehouse becomes "old," it is moved to other repositories. During this process, a summary of this data may be kept in the warehouse, indicating the evolution of data within the organization.

The presence of interdependent data is prevalent in data warehousing, since the three layers represent different views and summary information from source systems. We may consider a data warehouse environment to be a special case of an interdependent data environment that contains derived data.

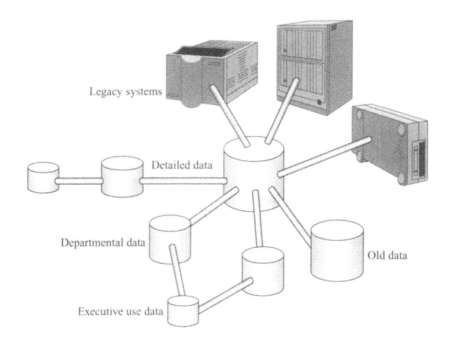

FIGURE 8.3
Conceptual design of a data warehouse.

The data stored in the warehouse is related to the data kept in the source systems, since it represents summary information created by filtering source data through manipulation and integration techniques.

In an environment of interdependent data, we assume that we can tolerate limited inconsistencies between interdependent data. This assumption is imposed by today's applications and complex data managing systems. Approximate consistency would suffice for many applications. Some other applications might not require consistency at all for a limited amount of time, e.g., two weeks. However, these inconsistencies can be tolerated only up to a specified limit. Whenever this limit is exceeded, actions are taken to restore consistency between the interdependent data objects.

An update on a data item i_1, which is dependent on another item i_2, may introduce an inconsistency between i_1 and i_2 beyond the tolerated limit. In this case, we want the system to execute a transaction to propagate the initial update of item i_1 to item i_2, without user intervention, that will eventually bring both items back into a consistent status. Due to the tolerated inconsistency between both items, there will be some delay between the original update on i_1 and the restoring transaction on i_2. Thus, we may have different degrees of coupling between the original update and the restoring transaction (*coupled*, if the initial update must wait until the restoring transaction completes, or *decoupled*, if the initial update will complete without waiting for the completion of the restoring transaction).

8.1
Current Approaches to the Management of Interdependent Data

In most existing applications, the mutual consistency requirements among multiple databases are either ignored, or the consistency of data is maintained by the application programs that perform related updates to all relevant databases. This can be accomplished using various techniques. For example, a message may be sent to another database system managing related data so that a complementary transaction will be submitted there, or a replica of the data may be sent to another system, either electronically or physically (e.g., a tape). However, these approaches have several disadvantages. First, they rely on the application programmer to enforce integrity constraints and to maintain mutual consistency of data, which is not acceptable if the programmer has incomplete knowledge of the constraints to be enforced. Second, modification of one part of an application may require changing other parts of the same or another application to maintain integrity and consistency. Since integrity requirements are specified within an application, they are not written in a declarative way. If we need to identify these requirements, we must extract them from the code, which is a tedious and error-prone task.

Alternative approaches to this problem are based on system-supported maintenance of mutual consistency. A possible solution is to enhance techniques of preserving integrity that have been proposed for distributed databases [SV86]. The main limitation of these techniques is that they assume the consistency between the related data must be restored immediately. However, in loosely coupled environments, we may need to tolerate temporary inconsistencies among related data. *Active databases* [MD89] address this problem by allowing evaluation of time constraints, in addition to data-value constraints. They use object-oriented techniques to encapsulate the maintenance of consistency inside the methods.

With the current emphasis on data as a corporate asset, the integrity of which is of basic importance [Mil89], the management of interdatabase consistency is receiving more attention. Distributed transaction technologies can be used to address some of these problems. Transaction management systems based on the traditional transaction concept [Gra81, HR83] or its extensions (nested transactions [Mos85], Sagas [GMS87], migrating transactions [KR88], multidatabase transactions [Geo90, GRS91, Reu89, LERL90]) can be used to preserve database consistency. An overview of extended transaction models can be found in [Elm92]. Transaction technology can ensure that all actions needed to preserve the interdatabase dependencies are executed in an atomic way. However, the specification of these actions and, hence, the correctness of the multidatabase updates still rest with the application programmer, who is responsible for the design of the transaction. Also, distributed concurrency control and commitment present serious problems when long-lived transactions span systems with vastly different capabilities. For example, it is not practical to enforce a two-phase-commit protocol in a multidatabase environment when the participating local databases do not have comparable processing speeds or, even worse, they need not be on-line at the same time.

8.2
Research Problems

We look at the management of interdependent data as a problem that can be divided into two smaller problems whose solutions offer the necessary foundation to design a system that automatically manages interdependent data. Briefly, the problems addressed in this research are as follows:

- Creation of a framework for specifying the relationships and consistency requirements between interdependent data objects. Correctness of the specifications and verification of correct relationships between interdependent data objects.

- Design of an execution model for transactions that can be used to maintain mutual consistency between interdependent data.

These problems are specified in the following subsections. A more detailed description and solution to these and other related problems in the area of interdependent data can be found in [Kar95].

8.2.1   The Problem of Specifying Interdependent Data

We must have a unified framework not only to identify the interdependent data objects but also to provide additional information that specifies the exact dependency that holds between them. Whenever a data manipulation command (such as an update) or some other event of interest occurs to a data object, it may affect another interdependent data object. The mutual consistency between the related objects must be specified, preferably by a predicate.

We believe that the dependency and mutual consistency specification between two interdependent data objects must incorporate trends that reflect the real world. One example of this is to allow some inconsistency to exist temporarily between interdependent data, which will eventually be eliminated. For example, if we have two replicas, and the primary copy is updated, we do not have to update the secondary copy immediately. We can postpone the update for another time when the system will be less loaded or until an operation needs to access the secondary copy. Conditions of this type imply various levels of tolerated inconsistency between the two objects. Inconsistencies may be specified in terms of difference in data values between the related objects, in terms of some temporal specification (e.g., after one week no more inconsistency is tolerated), or according to some other external event (e.g., execute the *Calculate-Interest* transaction before running the *Get-Balance* transaction in a bank).

One way to solve the specification problem is to use the *data dependency descriptors* (D^3s) introduced in [RSK91]. They provide a framework for specifying not only the relationships between interdependent data objects but also the consistency requirements and the ways to restore consistency. D^3s provide a uniform way to express these requirements. The dependency predicate of a D^3 that specifies the relationship between the interdependent objects may be expressed in relational algebra, SQL, or any other database relational language. The consistency predicate of a D^3 can be specified in a language that must be rich enough to encompass many different aspects of inconsistency mentioned above. The restoration procedures resemble the structure of guarded commands taken from CSP or Ada-like languages. The collection of all D^3s identifies all interdependent data objects together with their consistency requirements and is called the *interdatabase dependency schema* (IDS).

8.2.2   An Execution Model for Consistency-Restoring Procedures

Data objects described in the IDS are being updated by various transactions. Hence, we need to propose an execution model for the management of transactions that access interdependent data. The purpose of the execution model is threefold:

- Maintain mutual consistency between interdependent data objects; i.e., provide a mechanism to dynamically execute consistency restoration procedures, as specified in the D^3s.

- Monitor all the changes and events specified in the D^3s that may affect interdependent data objects.

- Store and maintain all D^3s in the IDS; i.e., provide a mechanism to insert, delete, update, activate, deactivate, etc., D^3s in the system.

To provide an execution model, we propose to use the concept of polytransactions introduced in [RS91] and discussed in [SRK92, GK93, KRS93]. To describe briefly the notion of a polytransaction, let us suppose that a user transaction updated a data object (source object) related through a D^3 to another data object (target object). According to a predefined D^3, the system may need to propagate this update from the source to the target object.

The propagation will be performed as a transaction which itself updates the target object. This second update on the target object may trigger another transaction as required by some other D^3. This process may continue for some time, triggering transactions before the entire transaction activity ceases. Informally, the group of transactions created by an initial update on a data object constitutes a *polytransaction*.

Problems to be solved within the execution model are identified by exploring the various modes of transaction execution, properties of polytransactions (such as ACID, etc.), and the coupling between the transactions of a single polytransaction. For example, it may not be practical to have a transaction wait for its child transaction to complete if the child transaction is long-lived, i.e., it is active for a long period of time.

Another problem of the execution model is the detection of events that occur in the IDS. We must be able to automatically execute transactions triggered from all the events that violate mutual consistency. To achieve this, there must be a facility to monitor all consistency predicates of every descriptor D^3 that may trigger a transaction of a polytransaction. The monitor approach seems to be the most appropriate for such tasks. Monitors [Ris89, SR91] have been used in many areas, including operating systems, software engineering, and active databases. The monitor will observe the status of all consistency predicates in the IDS and, according to their values, will trigger transactions to maintain consistency between interdependent data objects. Finally, a facility to manage the IDS must be present to complete the functionality of the execution model. This facility will allow execution of data manipulation commands to the various D^3s in the IDS. These commands are of the form *insert, delete, modify, activate, deactivate*, etc., a D^3.

In the remainder of this chapter, we investigate the problems we have identified and propose our solutions. In Section 8.3, we present a framework for the specification of interdependent data. We use D^3s to specify their semantic relationships, the limits of tolerated inconsistency between interdependent data objects, and the restoration procedures that restore consistency. Section 8.4 presents Aeolos, a system for the management of interdependent data. We describe all the software components of Aeolos along with their functionality. In Section 8.5, we identify differences between active databases and systems that manage interdependent data, and in Section 8.6, we show how to detect events in Aeolos. Finally, Section 8.7 presents a summary of the chapter.

8.3
Specification of Interdependent Data

In this section, we review our framework for the specification of interdependent data. A more detailed discussion can be found in [RSK91, SRK92].

We then discuss a conceptual architecture that could support maintenance and enforcement of specifications.

Our framework for specifying interdatabase dependencies consists of three components: dependency information, mutual consistency requirements, and consistency restoration procedures. While these components have been addressed in the literature separately, in our opinion they represent facets of a single problem that should be considered together. Data dependency conditions are similar to integrity constraints in distributed DBMSs [SV86]; full integrity between interdependent data in different databases may be necessary at all times or not possible in many environments. As described earlier, we use data dependency descriptors (D^3s) to specify the interdatabase dependencies. Each D^3 consists of an identification of related objects and a directional relationship defined in terms of the three components just mentioned. A D^3 is a 5-tuple,

$$D^3 = \langle \mathcal{S}, U, P, C, \mathcal{A} \rangle$$

where

- $\mathcal{S}$ is the set of *source data objects.*

- U is the *target data object.*

- P is a boolean-valued predicate called *interdatabase dependency predicate* (dependency component). It specifies a relationship between the source and target data objects and evaluates to true if this relationship is satisfied.

- C is a boolean-valued predicate called *mutual consistency predicate* (consistency component). It specifies consistency requirements and defines when P must be satisfied.

- $\mathcal{A}$ is called *action* component and contains information about how the consistency between the source and the target data object may be restored.

The objects specified in $\mathcal{S}$ and U may reside either in the same or in different centralized or distributed databases, located in the same or different sites. We are particularly interested in those dependencies in which the objects are stored in different databases managed by a local database management system (LDBMS).

The dependency predicate P is a boolean-valued expression specifying the relationship that should hold between the source and target data objects.

The consistency predicate C contains mutual consistency requirements specified along two dimensions—the data state dimension s and the temporal dimension t. The specification of the consistency predicate can involve multiple boolean-valued conditions, referred to as *consistency terms* and denoted by c_i.

Each consistency term refers to a mutual consistency requirement involving either time or the state of a data object.

The action component $\mathcal{A}$ is a collection of *consistency restoration procedures*, which specify actions that may be taken to maintain or restore consistency. There can be multiple restoration procedures, and the one to be invoked may depend on which conditions lead to the inconsistency between interdependent data. The execution mode can be defined for each restoration procedure to specify the degree of coupling between the action procedure and its parent transaction (i.e., the transaction that invokes it).

The set of all D^3s together constitutes the IDS [SRK92]. It is conceptually related to the dependency schema presented in [LBE+82].

Alternative ways to specify consistency requirements among related data have been also discussed. *Identity connections* [WQ87] introduced a time-based relaxation of mutual consistency requirements among similarly structured data items. Relaxed criteria based on numerical relationships between data items have been proposed in [BGM92]. Quasi-copies support relaxed consistency between primary copies and quasi-copies, based on several parameters [ABGM90]. E-C-A rules can be used to specify the C and A components of D^3s [DBB+88, DHL90]. In [CW90, CW92], interdatabase constraints are translated to production rules in a semiautomatic way, using a language based on SQL, to specify consistency between interrelated data objects. The derived production rules enforce consistency by generating operations automatically. However, tolerated inconsistencies are not allowed in that approach.

In the following example, we illustrate the use of D^3s for the specification of consistency requirements between a primary and a secondary copy, as a special case of replicated data. We assume that copies of data are stored in two or more databases. The dependency between all copies requires that changes performed to any copy are reflected in other copies, possibly within some predefined time. Let us consider the relation $D1.EMP$ (i.e., relation EMP stored in database $D1$) and its replica $D3.EMP\_COPY$. We assume that EMP must always be up-to-date, but we can tolerate inconsistencies in the EMP_COPY relation for no more than one day. The following pair of dependency descriptors represents this special type of replication:

$\mathcal{S}$:	$D1.EMP$	$\mathcal{S}$:	$D3.EMP\_COPY$
U:	$D3.EMP\_COPY$	U:	$D1.EMP$
P:	$EMP = EMP\_COPY$	P:	$EMP = EMP\_COPY$
C:	$\varepsilon(day)$	C:	1 *update on* $\mathcal{S}$
$\mathcal{A}$:	$Duplicate\_EMP$	$\mathcal{A}$:	$Propagate\_Update\_To\_EMP$
	(EMP is copied to		as coupled & vital
	EMP_COPY.)		(The update on EMP_COPY
			is repeated on EMP.)

The two descriptors above represent a case of a bidirectional dependency between two database objects. The target object in one descriptor is the source object in the other descriptor. The consistency predicate P is exactly the same in both D^3s. The consistency between the two objects is specified as follows: Whenever an update is performed on EMP_COPY, it must be reflected immediately in the EMP relation. On the other hand, consistency will be restored in the EMP_COPY with respect to the updates on EMP only at the end of the day (although there may be a number of updates performed to the EMP during that day).

8.4
Aeolos: A System for the Management of Interdependent Data

In this section, we introduce interdependent database systems (IDBSs), and we present *Aeolos*,[1] a system that manages interdependent data. As previously mentioned, we are interested in the automatic enforcement of dependencies that describe a "weak" or "relaxed" consistency constraint between interdependent data objects. We present a conceptual design of a generic interdependent database system and its major components. We then concentrate our discussion on specific approaches we have taken in Aeolos. We describe its various architectural components and how Aeolos maintains consistency of interdependent data.

8.4.1   Interdependent Database Systems (IDBSs)

It is the responsibility of the *interdependent database system* to monitor changes that affect interdependent data and automatically to maintain their relaxed consistency. Hence, we define such a system as follows:

DEFINITION 8.1

An interdependent database system (IDBS) is a system that contains a collection of interdependent data objects and automatically enforces the dependencies specified among them.

The data objects in an IDBS may already exist and reside in various sites, managed by different local systems. In the following discussion, we use a broader definition of the term *site* to denote either a specific node or a collection of nodes in a distributed computing environment, since this definition is more applicable to an environment of interdependent data. The term local systems refers to the software systems that manage interdependent objects stored at a given site. In an environment of interdependent data, we may have

---

[1]In ancient Greek mythology, Aeolos ($A\iota o\lambda o\varsigma$, pronounced $'e\hat{o}l\hat{o}s$) is the master and keeper of all the winds. He keeps them in a sack and selectively frees them to dominate the journeys of sea travelers.

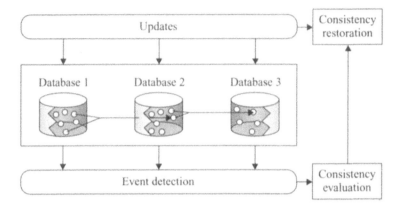

FIGURE 8.4
Conceptual representation of an IDBS.

several LDBSs called *participating* or *member* LDBSs that store and manage interdependent data objects on behalf of the IDBS.

Therefore, the architecture of an IDBS is distributed, and it resides on top of possibly heterogeneous database systems. We observe a similarity between an IDBS and an MDBS, both in the layered component structure and in the heterogeneity of the member LDBSs. The main difference is that an MDBS is designed to support multidatabase queries and transactions, while the main objective of an IDBS is to maintain consistency of data stored in multiple databases.

Figure 8.4 illustrates the conceptual representation of an IDBS. The interdependent data objects are depicted by ovals and the dependencies formed between them by arrows. These objects, in general, are under the control of separate databases, thus forming interdatabase dependencies. Updates on some data objects must be detected by a monitoring mechanism; therefore, an IDBS must provide an event detection mechanism to detect all events of interest that may affect the consistency of interdependent data. Following the event detection, the consistency evaluation module performs a consistency predicate validation with respect to the tolerated inconsistency between related data objects. If the consistency between them is violated beyond the tolerated limits, the IDBS executes consistency restoration procedures to bring the consistency of interdependent data back to acceptable levels.

The IDBS executes the restoration procedures, as database transactions, that perform the necessary updates to restore/maintain the mutual consistency of interdependent data. One may argue that the execution control just described (see Figure 8.4) forms a cycle that can lead to infinite execution of restoration procedures. However, the component that evaluates the consistency

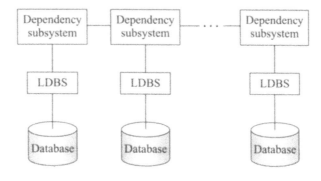

FIGURE 8.5
Conceptual architecture of an IDBS.

of interdependent data is the primary component that controls the execution cycle according to the specified limits of inconsistency; thus it constrains the cycle in accordance with the specified consistency requirements.

8.4.2   Architecture of Aeolos

In this section, we discuss a conceptual architecture of Aeolos, an IDBS. Our approach is similar to the two-level MDBS architecture. Figure 8.5 illustrates the major components of Aeolos. The lower level consists of the local databases managed by the participating LDBSs with their transaction managers, schedulers, and data managers. The higher level is dedicated to the IDBS and mainly consists of a dependency subsystem located on top of each LDBS. Each *dependency subsystem* is responsible for maintaining the consistency of the interdependent data objects that are located in the local database. Consistency is achieved by submitting transactions to the member LDBSs that update the interdependent data objects on behalf of the IDBS. All dependency subsystems are interconnected and communicate with one another to monitor, evaluate, and preserve the consistency of data.

8.4.3   Data Distribution in Aeolos

The interdependent data objects in an IDBS are distributed among various member LDBSs. In addition to the data objects themselves, we must store all the components of the IDS, namely the set of all D^3s. In general, there are two different approaches in storing and managing the D^3s: the centralized approach and the distributed approach. The advantages and disadvantages of one approach versus the other are identical to those found in data distribution in centralized and distributed databases, since the D^3s may be viewed also as data. The distributed approach provides increased availability, efficiency, and flexibility in managing D^3s at the cost of additional maintenance. For a detailed discussion on data distribution in centralized or distributed databases see [CP84]. We have decided to take the distributed approach, so we distribute the IDS over the participating sites. The most applicable distribution criterion for the D^3s is to store each D^3 either at the site that contains the source objects of the descriptor or at the site with the target object. Let us take a look at the advantages and disadvantages of one approach versus the other.

Storing D^3s at Source Object Sites

If we store a D^3 at the site of its source objects, we can take advantage of local event detection on the source objects. That is, we can detect events of interest on source objects and calculate locally the degree of inconsistency of the target object. To restore consistency of the target object, we execute a transaction remotely at the site of the target object.

However, the entire set of source objects of each D^3 may not be located at the same site. In this case, we must choose a site to store the D^3 according to some criterion. For example, we may store the D^3 at the site where the majority of the sources are located or at the site containing the source object that is expected to have a higher degree of event activity associated with it. Whenever an event occurs on a source object of a specific D^3, the various measures of consistency associated with the D^3 must be updated (especially the degree of inconsistency of the D^3). In case an event is detected on a source object located on a remote site, the site that stores and manages the associated D^3 must be notified in order to recalculate the degree of inconsistency of the target object, at the expense of some network overhead.

Storing D^3s at Target Object Sites

We may also store each D^3 at the site that contains its target object. In this case, we have a uniform way of distributing D^3s, since there is only one target object in each D^3. In addition, the transaction that will restore consistency of the target object will be a transaction in the local site.

However, this option implies that the source objects may be located at various remote sites. Whenever an event is detected on a remote site pertaining to a source object, it must be communicated over the network to the site that manages the D^3 in question, in order to recalculate the degree of inconsistency. Only events that occur on source objects that happen to be stored in the same site with the D^3 do not have to be sent over the network.

The choice of the most appropriate criterion to distribute the IDS is based on ease of implementation and frequency of event occurrences. We have chosen to adopt the second alternative; thus we store the D^3s at the site that stores their target objects.

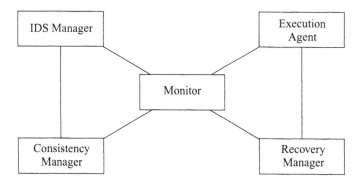

FIGURE 8.6
Components of a dependency subsystem.

8.4.4   Components of a Dependency Subsystem

Each dependency subsystem consists of a collection of software components that manage interdependent data. Figure 8.6 illustrates these components. The purpose of a dependency subsystem is to monitor the occurrence of events on source objects, calculate the degree of inconsistency of each D^3 in the IDS, and maintain the consistency of target objects within acceptable limits. In order to achieve this, the dependency subsystem must perform as follows:

- Communicate with all other dependency subsystems that contain objects that are sources of local D^3s.

- Notify other dependency subsystems of events that have occurred in the local site.

- Evaluate the degree of inconsistency of each D^3 in the local site. To accomplish this task, each c_i that appears in the consistency component C of each D^3 must be evaluated, and all the measures of consistency for the particular descriptor must be recalculated.

- Possibly schedule a transaction to restore consistency on a local target object.

Each dependency subsystem in Aeolos consists of five major components: The IDS Manager maintains the D^3s in the IDS. The Monitor detects the occurrence of specific events that happen to interdependent data. The Consistency Manager evaluates the consistency of the interdependent data objects and initiates the execution of restoration procedures when the consistency requirements specified in the D^3s are violated. The Execution Agent is responsible for the execution of restoration procedures. The Recovery Manager is the module that ensures fault tolerance of the IDBS by dealing with transaction and site failures. A more detailed discussion about each component is presented next.

8.4.5   The IDS Manager

The distribution of the IDS among the various participating sites in the IDBS leads naturally to the creation of a distributed IDS Manager. An IDS Manager is located in the dependency subsystem of each participating site responsible for the maintenance of the D^3s at that site. The IDS Manager at each dependency subsystem consists of two major components: the D^3 Administrator and the D^3 Catalog.

The D^3 Administrator

The D^3 Administrator is an internal component of the IDS Manager and is responsible for performing definition and status operations on the D^3s. The D^3 definition operations are *insert, delete,* and *modify*, whereas the status operations are *enable* and *disable*. When a new descriptor is inserted into the IDS, a name, number, or some other identifier may be given to the D^3. This identifier, along with additional system information, is internally mapped to an object identifier that uniquely identifies the new descriptor in the entire IDS over all participating sites. The Consistency Manager is informed in order to initialize the consistency measures of the new descriptor.

Several sites in Aeolos may need to exchange information when a new descriptor is created. This requires cooperation between the IDS Managers. Reliable communication between them can be implemented using the persistent pipe mechanism [HS90].

The IDS Manager must notify each Monitor at remote sites storing source objects of the new D^3, to inform the Consistency Manager at its site of any updates to the source objects. Similar notifications are sent to the Monitors at remote sites that contain data objects referenced in the consistency terms c_i of the new descriptor, to watch for events associated with these objects.

However, special precautions must be taken to ensure that the inserted D^3 does not violate the consistency of the existing IDS. That is, before the new D^3 is inserted in the IDS, it must be checked to determine whether it creates a nonstable cycle. If it does, the insert request is rejected. In addition, caution must be taken to avoid the insertion of a new D^3 with a target object that is also the target object of another preexisting D^3. As discussed in Section 8.3, we allow only one target object per D^3; thus the new descriptor must be merged with the existing one. Merging descriptors is not an easy task and in general cannot be performed automatically, due to semantic knowledge of which only humans are aware. Therefore, we suggest that a person who knows the semantic details of the interdependent data, such as a database administrator, will merge the two D^3s into one. The above precautions are also taken when a descriptor is modified, but no such checking needs to be performed if a descriptor is deleted.

The D^3 Catalog

The D^3 Catalog maintains the status of each D^3 stored in the local site. When the D^3 Administrator issues a disable or enable operation on the D^3, its status is updated in the D^3 Catalog. When a D^3 is enabled, all events pertinent to this D^3 must be observed when they occur. Therefore, all Monitors in other dependency subsystems must be notified to start watching for these events. In a similar way, the Monitors must also be notified to cease monitoring events for descriptors that have been disabled.

8.4.6   Monitors in Aeolos

Monitors are programs that observe changes in the state of the data and may optionally perform certain actions. Similar work is reported by Risch [Ris89], except that the restoration (tracking) procedures in his model are embedded in an application, whereas we keep them separate from the applications. This declarative specification of restoration procedures has the advantage of allowing the specifications to change with no modifications to the applications.

Each Monitor in Aeolos is located at a participating site and is responsible for detecting events that occur on interdependent data stored in it. An *event list* contains all primitive events that the Monitor should detect, and an *event detection mechanism* actually detects the events in the event list. Based on primitive events that are detected, the Monitor can evaluate the composite events or parts of composite events pertinent to its local site and forward the results to the local Consistency Manager for further processing.

We must emphasize that detection of events in an IDBS is more complicated when compared to an active database system. The main reasons for such complexity are

- *Data distribution:* An inherent characteristic of an IDBS is that it is distributed over several sites; thus composite events based on primitive ones that occur at distinct sites are more difficult to detect. To the best of our knowledge, there has been no research effort toward distributed active systems. Only centralized active databases have been designed and implemented.

- *Capabilities of LDBSs:* The Monitor in each dependency subsystem must use existing detection capabilities provided by the LDBS. We do not design a distributed database system from scratch; we design a system on top of existing LDBSs. Therefore, we are limited by the tools provided by the underlying LDBSs. Most commercial LDBSs do not provide event detection mechanisms; thus we must resort to additional methods to detect events under such conditions. In Section 8.4.8, we propose mechanisms to detect events in IDBSs.

To incorporate detection of events within the plethora of heterogeneous LDBSs, we must provide an *interface* between the Monitor and the underlying

LDBS at each dependency subsystem. From the Monitor's viewpoint, all interfaces are identical regardless of the capabilities of the underlying LDBS. In contrast, from the LDBS's point of view, the interface is viewed as an ordinary user with all the privileges and limitations of a proxy account. This is similar to the LAMs in the Narada environment [HAB+92]. This approach unifies design issues of Monitors and makes their implementation simpler. Particular idiosyncracies, capabilities, and limitations of each LDBS concerning event detection are captured in each interface.

8.4.7   Measures of Consistency

We are interested in the semantics of consistency requirements of interdependent data. We show how to estimate the degree of inconsistency between two objects connected by a D^3. Since the C predicate is defined along data state and time, we view each consistency predicate C of a D^3 as a pair of the two dimensions: time and data state. As an example, let us consider the following D^3:

$$
\begin{aligned}
&\mathcal{S} : a \\
&U : b \\
&P : a = b \\
&C : c_1 \vee c_2 \\
&\qquad\quad c_1 = 5 \; versions \; of \; a \\
&\qquad\quad c_2 = \varepsilon(48 \; hours) \\
&\mathcal{A} : \; Update\_Target
\end{aligned}
$$

This example identifies two interdependent data objects a and b. The target data object b is a replica of the source data object a, as specified by the dependency predicate P. If the source object is updated, the target object becomes inconsistent. We specify that we can tolerate inconsistencies between the source and the target up to 5 versions of a or until a 48-hour period ends.

DEFINITION 8.2

A state-time-pair (stp) is a pair $\langle s, t \rangle$, where s is a value in the data state dimension, and t is a value in the time dimension.

A value along the state dimension identifies the data state of a database object, and a value in the time dimension specifies time. The pair $\langle 5 \; versions, 48 \; hours \rangle$ is an example of an *stp*. In general, s and t can be logical formulas consisting of various types of consistency terms. For example, if $C = 5\%(Employee)$, then the data state dimension of the *stp* is $s = 5\%(Employee)$. A detailed presentation of the different consistency terms can be found in [RSK91, SRK92]. In our discussion, we assume that both s and t can be represented as linear functions.

DEFINITION 8.3

The limit of discrepancy along a D^3, $L(D^3)$, is an stp, $\langle l_s, l_t \rangle$, where l_s and l_t specify the maximum allowed discrepancy along the data state and temporal dimensions, between the source and the target database objects of a dependency descriptor.

For example, the limit of discrepancy between the source and the target objects of the above D^3 is either 5 versions or 48 hours specified as $L(D^3) = \langle 5 \text{ versions}, 2 \text{ days} \rangle$. The limit of discrepancy of every D^3 is constant and can be extracted from the C predicate of the D^3 itself.

DEFINITION 8.4

The consistency restoration point of a D^3, $R(D^3)$, is an stp, $\langle r_s, r_t \rangle$, where r_s and r_t specify the values along the data state and time dimension when consistency between source and target objects was restored.

R is updated every time we restore consistency between the source and the target data objects. It is the initial point of reference, used in calculation of discrepancy between source and target data objects. In the above D^3, assuming that the value of the 30th version of the source object a was propagated to the target object b, at 10 A.M. on February 26, 1992, then $R(D^3) = \langle 30, 26\text{-}02\text{-}1992@10 \rangle$.

DEFINITION 8.5

The Current Value C of discrepancy along a D^3, $C(D^3)$, is an stp, $\langle c_s, c_t \rangle$, where c_s and c_t identify the distance between current state of the source and target objects measured in terms of data state and time.

The data state dimension c_s of the current value changes every time an update is performed on the source object, and the temporal dimension c_t of the current value changes constantly with time. If an update has been performed on object a 15 hours after the last restoration of consistency, the current value of our D^3 is $C(D^3) = \langle 1 \text{ version}, 15 \text{ hours} \rangle$.

DEFINITION 8.6

The Final Value F of a D^3 is an stp, $\langle f_s, f_t \rangle$, defining when consistency between source and target objects must be restored with respect to the last restoration point of the same D^3.

The value of the final state is calculated as the sum of the consistency restoration point plus the specified limit of discrepancy, i.e., $f_s = r_s \oplus l_s$. The operator $\oplus$ denotes summation on data states and carries a broader meaning than the regular arithmetic operator $+$, since we have different types of data state terms that must be "added" together. The value f_t is calculated as the sum of the time of consistency restoration plus the specified limit of discrepancy, i.e., $f_t = r_t + l_t$. In our D^3, we have $F = \langle 35 \text{ versions}, 28\text{-}02\text{-}1992@10 \rangle$.

DEFINITION 8.7

The degree of inconsistency of a D^3, $DI(D^3)$, is an stp, $\langle s, t \rangle$, where both s and t are positive real numbers that identify the level of inconsistency between the source and target data objects with respect to the D^3 in which they participate.

For example, let us suppose that the consistency predicate of a D^3 specifies that the target can lag behind the source up to 5 versions ($C = 5\ versions$). We will calculate the value of the s element of the $\langle s, t \rangle$ pair. Calculation of the t element is similar. Initially, source and target are consistent. Then the source is updated and a new version is created. The target object is in a state of tolerated inconsistency, with a degree of inconsistency of

$$s = \frac{1\ version}{5\ versions} = 0.2$$

For this particular example, s is calculated as the number of versions that are created since source and target were consistent, divided by the number of tolerated versions specified in the D^3. In general, the formula to calculate $DI(D^3)$ is as follows:

$$DI(D^3) = \frac{C(D^3)}{L(D^3)} = \frac{\langle c_s, c_t \rangle}{\langle l_s, l_t \rangle} = \left\langle \frac{c_s}{l_s}, \frac{c_t}{l_t} \right\rangle$$

Degrees of inconsistency must be recomputed every time an event likely to affect them occurs. Hence a $DI(D^3)$ must be recomputed every time the data state and temporal consistency terms are updated in the D^3. Recomputing the degree of consistency of a D^3 may be a simple operation if the degree of consistency is measured in terms of time (i.e., minutes, days, etc.) or versions. However, if the consistency predicate is an arbitrary expression, its calculation may be nontrivial, and a specific function computing the DI must be included in the system.

THEOREM 8.1

The target data object U of a D^3 becomes inconsistent with respect to that D^3 iff $R(D^3) + C(D^3) > F(D^3)$.

Proof: Continuous updates on the source object $\mathcal{S}$, or the passage of time, are reflected on $C(D^3)$ either in terms of data state or in terms of time. When the value of $C(D^3)$ added to the value of $R(D^3)$ exceeds the value of $F(D^3)$, then using the definition of $F(D^3)$, consistency must be restored; hence the target data object becomes inconsistent. □

THEOREM 8.2

The target data object U of a D^3 is either consistent or tolerated iff $R(D^3) + C(D^3) \leq F(D^3)$.

Proof: Direct consequence of the previous theorem. $\square$

Hence, D^3 is violated (the state of the target object is inconsistent) when at least one of the following cases occurs

1. The value of the data state at restoration point r_s plus the value of the current data state c_s exceeds the value of the final state f_s, i.e., $r_s \oplus c_s > f_s$, or

2. The value of the temporal dimension at restoration point r_t plus the value of the current temporal dimension c_t exceeds the final deadline f_t, i.e., $r_t + c_t > f_t$.

8.4.8   Consistency Manager

When a D^3 is inserted by the IDS Manager, the Consistency Manager creates all the necessary structures to measure the consistency of the D^3; i.e., it initializes the $L(D^3)$, $C(D^3)$, $F(D^3)$, and $DI(D^3)$.

Every time a Monitor detects an event of interest for a particular D^3, it informs the local Consistency Manager, which in turn must find out whether the event applies to a D^3 that is local or remote. If the D^3 is stored in a remote site, it notifies the Consistency Manager of that site and communicates the events over the network. Otherwise, the event applies to a local D^3, and the Consistency Manager operates as follows:

1. Update the $C(D^3)$ and the $DI(D^3)$.

2. If $R(D^3) + C(D^3) \geq F(D^3)$, then schedule a restoration procedure to restore consistency of the target object.

3. If $R(D^3) + C(D^3) < F(D^3)$, then according to system load, optionally restore the target object to an acceptable consistency level.

When a restoration procedure is executed and the target object becomes consistent or tolerated, the Consistency Manager updates the $R(D^3)$, $C(D^3)$, and $DI(D^3)$.

Detected events are sent to the local Consistency Manager, which in turn communicates them to other remote Consistency Managers if needed to update the consistency measures of the D^3s. According to our classification of the events into data state and external type, we have the following types of event expressions that each Consistency Manager is capable of evaluating.

- Δ *expressions:* When an event to be detected contains a Δ of some attribute, then the Consistency Manager of the site responsible for detecting this event must have a pair of *old* and *new* values of the attribute to be observed. The same procedure applies to changes of an average, number of versions, etc.

- *Expressions of the form* N * primitive_event: For this type of event, a counter is specified to hold the current value of N. Every time the primitive event is detected, N is updated by the Consistency Manager and compared with the prespecified limit on N.

- *Expressions with the* before *or* after *operator:* This is the type of event such as *!calculate_payroll_checks*, meaning that before the *calculate_payroll_checks* transaction runs, consistency must be restored. However, for this type of event we must answer the question of when specifically to restore consistency, because an infinite number of instants in time that evaluate the predicate *!calculate_payroll_checks* to true. Consequently, we must provide an interval during which consistency must be restored, either immediately before the *calculate_payroll_checks* transaction runs or during some time within a prespecified interval. Similar actions are taken for events specified with the *after* operator.

- *Expressions containing external events:* We emphasize temporal events mostly, because they are easier to detect and manage within the Consistency Manager, especially when they do not need to be propagated to remote Consistency Managers. Other external events, such as user notification, must be dealt with one at a time. Therefore, we concentrate on temporal events that can be identified in a uniform manner. For example, events of the type "at a particular time" or "at a particular date" can be easily maintained at the local Consistency Manager. For temporal events of the Δ type, we take the same approach with the Δs in data state events.

8.4.9   Recovery Manager

The Recovery Manager located in each dependency subsystem is the component that adds fault tolerance to Aeolos by dealing with transaction and site failures. The topic of recovery from failures is closely related to polytransaction execution in Aeolos. However, this topic is beyond the scope of this chapter.

8.4.10   Execution Agent

The Execution Agent is a component present at each dependency subsystem. It is responsible for submitting transactions to the LDBS that restore the consistency of a target object of a descriptor D^3 stored at the local site. The Execution Agent communicates with the local Consistency Manager in two ways. First it receives the name of the procedure to run as a transaction to restore consistency of a target object. When the transaction terminates, the Execution Agent notifies the Consistency Manager of its outcome so that the measures of consistency of the D^3 are updated (if the transaction committed), or the transaction is resubmitted if needed (if the transaction is aborted).

If the target object participates as a source object in another descriptor D^3, then any update to it may affect the consistency of other interdependent data. In this case, the Execution Agent must inform the local Monitor of any changes in the value of the object.

8.5
Active Database Systems and Interdependent Data

The architecture of Aeolos, presented in the previous section, identifies a well-known cycle: event detection (*Event*), evaluation of consistency (*Condition*), and restoration of consistency (*Action*). This cycle signifies the Event-Condition-Action (E-C-A) paradigm used in active database systems (Active DBMSs). In this section, we present related work in the area of active database systems, and then we identify the differences between active DBMSs and IDBSs.

8.5.1   Active Database Systems

In traditional DBMSs, queries and transactions are submitted for execution to the DBMS explicitly by users and/or application programs. This approach characterizes traditional DBMSs as *passive*. However, many situations require timely response to events that occur and may affect data: maintenance of consistency requirements between related data, integrity constraints, enforcement of rules in production systems, and office workflow control are only a few examples where passive DBMSs cannot fulfill the requirements of the above time-constrained applications. For example, inventory control in a telephone company may require that telephone network access lines be monitored. If the current capacity falls below a specified threshold, an order for more lines should be placed in the next working day.

In response to these deficiencies of passive DBMSs, active DBMSs provide solutions. Events, conditions, and actions are declaratively specified in the system, which automatically monitors events that occur in database objects, evaluates predefined conditions when the events occur, and, according to the condition evaluation, triggers appropriate actions on the database objects.

Elements of active DBMSs appeared as early as 1973 in the CODASYL data definition language [Cod73], which introduced the ON clause. The ON clause specifies a "database procedure" (action) to be executed when a specified "triggering operation" (event) occurs. The requested procedure is executed immediately after the operation is performed.

POSTGRES

The POSTGRES database system was designed and implemented at the University of California at Berkeley [Sto86, SR86, SHP88]. POSTGRES is the

successor of the Ingres relational database system (POST inGRES). POST-
GRES incorporates user-defined rules that convey the semantics of "always,"
"never," and "one-time." The actions specified in POSTGRES rules can be
executed either in forward chaining (eager evaluation) or in backward chaining
(lazy evaluation). The trigger is executed immediately when the event occurs if
eager evaluation is specified in its definition. If lazy evaluation is specified, the
trigger is executed later, when another transaction requests a read operation
on the updated data object that caused the event. POSTGRES provides a
conflict resolution scheme based on priorities to choose a trigger for execution.
Only the one with the highest priority will be executed.

POSTGRES supports complex objects consisting of multiple attributes.
Each attribute may be not only a standard type (e.g., integer or string) but
also a query or a procedure in a high-level language. POSTGRES also supports
extendible data types, operators, and access methods to be used for new application domains. In addition, POSTGRES supports active database capabilities
through triggers that are called *rules*.

HiPAC

The HiPAC (High Performance Active DBMS) project [DBM88, DBB+88,
HLM88, CB+89, MD89] is the result of work performed at Xerox Advanced
Information Technology over a two-year period. It involved the design and
implementation of an active DBMS based on E-C-A (Event-Condition-Action)
rules. HiPAC is an object-oriented DBMS that treats rules like all other forms of
data, as objects. Every rule is an instance of the rule object class. Upon these
rules, HiPAC performs operations such as *fire, activate, deactivate, modify,
delete*, etc. A HiPAC rule is formulated [DBM88, CB+89] by specifying:

- *Rule identifier:* A unique entity identifier.

- *Event:* The event that causes HiPAC to fire the rule. Typed formal arguments may be defined for the event; these are bound to actual arguments
  when the rule fires.

- *Condition:* The coupling mode between the triggering transaction and
  the condition evaluation, and a collection of queries to be evaluated when
  the rule is fired and the condition is satisfied.

- *Action:* The coupling mode between the condition evaluation and the
  action execution, and an operation to be executed when the rule is fired
  and the condition is satisfied.

- *Timing constraints:* Deadlines, priorities/urgencies, or value functions.

- *Contingency plans:* An alternative action to be executed in case the
  timing constraints cannot be met.

- *Attributes:* Additional properties of rules.

For every rule specified in HiPAC, the Event, Condition, and Action are mandatory properties, while the rest are optional or take default values. When an event occurs, it fires the corresponding rule: it evaluates the rule's condition, and if it is satisfied, it performs the rule's action.

STARBURST

Unlike the POSTGRES and HiPAC active systems, in STARBURST (an extensible DBMS developed at IBM, Almaden) rules can respond to aggregate or cumulative changes in the database, which resembles more closely the set-oriented relational databases [LLPS91]. Two complementary components give STARBURST its "active" characteristic: a relational-oriented production rule system that monitors sets of changes to base tables, and an object-oriented system (called Alert) that monitors objects and the invocation of applications.

Rules in STARBURST are defined using an extended version of SQL [HFLP89, WF90, CW90]. These rules have an event clause (in STARBURST terminology "trigger clause"), a condition clause, and an action clause. The event is specified as one or more of the SQL operations (insert, delete, update) on a table (trigger table). The condition is an SQL query preceded by the keyword IF. When the result of the query is nonempty, the condition is satisfied and the action is executed, which is a sequence of database commands preceded by the keyword THEN. Actions can suppress changes to the database by aborting the originating transaction, or they can perform further modifications to the database, which in turn may trigger the same or other rules (forward chaining). The conditions and actions of the rules in STARBURST may reference "transition tables," which are referential tables containing changes to the rule's table that were made since the beginning of the transaction of the last time that rule was processed. STARBURST uses an explicit priority scheme to identify rule execution.

PARDES

The PARDES system is an attempt to enforce interdatabase dependencies in the frame of an active object-oriented database. The overall architecture of the system and the classification of interdatabase dependencies is found in [Etz92, Etz93]. Components include

- A database schema that includes the rules ("invariants" in PARDES terminology).

- A component that translates the schema with the rules into a dependency graph, which identifies pictorially the transitive closure of an update operation.

- A run-time controller that uses a mechanism equivalent to topological order on the dependency graph to eliminate redundancy in the update operations.

- An exception-handling component that allows inconsistencies to exist under some control identified in this component.

Dependencies are specified using the invariant-style approach to describe the relationship between source and target data objects. Invariants are abstractions, relative to rules or imperative program commands. In general, an invariant is translated into more than one rule/command. PARDES defines two types of invariants, logical invariants (predicates in first order logic) and computational invariants that represent derived data objects.

8.5.2   Differences between IDBSs and Active DBMSs

The major difference between active DBMSs and IDBSs is that IDBSs are distributed systems, whereas active DBMSs are still centralized systems. Another difference, derived from the distributed characteristic of IDBSs, is that IDBSs are heterogeneous systems that are implemented on top of conventional database systems.

In addition, the specification of the D^3s allows for a variety of tolerated inconsistencies between interdependent data objects. This property cannot be implemented with active DBMSs. Although one may argue that we can specify several E-C-A rules that correspond to each tolerated inconsistency of a given D^3, we consider this approach as impractical and incomplete.

The above differences apply to all mentioned active DBMSs except PARDES, which is an active system for interdependent data. It is interesting to note that the PARDES project is very similar to the interdependent database system we propose and can be classified as another parallel attempt. Similarities with PARDES can be found in the dependency graph, the rules that are used (common to all active and production rule systems), and the various kinds of tolerated consistencies between source and target data objects. However, the PARDES project assumes an object-oriented active environment, targets (so far) problems related to the specification of interdependent data (with no temporality involved), and does not explore issues of transaction management in such systems; i.e., the concurrent execution of rules is not in the immediate research interests of the author.

8.6
Detecting Events in Aeolos

This section discusses how the Monitors in Aeolos detect primitive events that occur at their sites. First, we present detection methods for data state events on LDBSs that provide trigger mechanisms.[2] However, not all existing

---

[2]This is a reasonable assumption, since the major database vendors support triggers in their products. There is also a provision for triggers in the future releases of standard SQL.

LDBSs support such capabilities. Therefore, we also provide detection mechanisms for LDBSs that do not have trigger capabilities. We are also limited by the type of operations that are detected by each participating LDBS. For example, if the LDBS is relational, we can detect data state events such as *insert, delete*, and *update* on local tables, since they are generated by database operations that are uniformly defined for the relational model. Heterogeneities between various models are dealt with at the interface level within each Monitor.

Detection methods for external events rely on the nature of each specific event; hence they must be customized according to the event. Temporal events are exceptions to this rule, and they can be detected using a mechanism similar to the *cron* command in Unix systems. We have implemented a system with the functionality of an IDBS Monitor that detects events in a multidatabase environment. This system is described in [Hu95].

8.6.1   Detecting Events on LDBSs That Provide Triggering Capabilities

To detect local DB access events, we assume that the LDBS supports triggers. Usually a trigger definition contains an *Event*, an optional *Constraint*, and an *Action* part. A trigger is fired by the LDBS when the triggering event occurs; then its constraint (if one exists) is evaluated, and accordingly, the action(s) are executed. Triggers on the LDBSs can be designed to notify the local Monitor when these events occur. However, further action depends on the ways the Monitor can be notified of these events. Some LDBSs allow triggering actions to be performed outside of their underlying tables. We call such triggers *unrestricted*. Triggers that do not execute actions outside of the local tables are called *restricted*. Consequently, we present two mechanisms to convey local events to the Monitor. The choice of the appropriate mechanism depends on the trigger capabilities provided by the LDBSs.

- *Using restricted triggers:* LDBSs providing restricted triggers limit their actions to local database operations; thus they cannot directly notify the Monitor. In this case, the detection of the database operation by the Monitor is performed indirectly through *active tables*: for every (passive) table we wish to monitor, we create an active table (this is a table in append-only mode), similar to the ones used in [SPAM91]. When any access is made to the passive table, the action component of the trigger appends the access information (database operations and their corresponding arguments) to the active table. These active tables are polled regularly by the Monitor to detect local events.

- *Using unrestricted triggers:* LDBSs with unrestricted triggering capabilities can directly notify the Monitor of the data access event that occurred.

8.6.2   Detecting Events on LDBSs Without Triggering Capabilities

If the LDBS does not provide any support for trigger mechanisms, we may need to modify or embed some DBMS commands if possible. However, this approach may lead to violation of the autonomy of the local system. Adjustments to the DBMS commands can be done by modification of either the DBMS software or the local applications. Related work on methods to detect events in passive databases by modification of the DBMS software appears in [SKdM92]. The approach taken in [SKdM92] applies to databases built using the client-server architecture model. The *Sql_Connect* command is modified to intercept the database operations sent to the server. This enables the analysis of each command submitted to the database server to identify the event generated by the operation. This technique can be extended to notify the Monitor of the local events when they are detected. To generalize the above mechanism to include non-client-server databases, we propose similar modifications to all the necessary communication modules, such as the *Sql_Exec*.

Sometimes it is not possible to modify the DBMS software. An alternate approach is to modify the applications instead, to detect events. In this case, the code to inform the Monitor of the occurrence of an event may be added to each application. While not providing a high degree of data independence, such a solution should be preferred to incorporating the integrity-checking code into every application.

8.7
Summary

In this chapter, we deal with issues related to the management of interdependent data. Several problems associated with the management of interdependent objects are addressed and solutions proposed.

The first problem is the specification of interdependent data. We briefly review data dependency descriptors (D^3s) for the declarative specification of interdependent data. D^3s represent a framework for specification of the relationships between interdependent data, the limits of tolerated inconsistencies between them, and ways to restore their consistency if it is violated beyond the acceptable limits. Two important features of the D^3 framework are

- Declarative specification of the relationship between interdependent data objects.

- Use of the specification to automatically generate transactions that maintain the consistency between interdependent data objects.

The set of all the D^3s together constitutes the interdatabase dependency schema (IDS). We identify metrics to measure the consistency of each D^3 in an IDS.

Data objects described in the IDS are updated by various transactions. To maintain automatically the consistency of interdependent data, we introduce the concept of an interdependent database system (IDBS). Aeolos is an IDBS that monitors interdependent data, evaluates the consistency of the data, and uses polytransactions to keep it within acceptable consistency levels. We present the conceptual design and architecture of Aeolos and discuss the similarities and differences between an IDBS and active databases. We address the problems of monitoring events in a heterogeneous distributed environment and propose our solutions for detecting events according to the capabilities provided by the participating local systems.

Bibliography

[ABGM90]   R. Alonso, D. Barbara, and H. Garcia-Molina. Data caching issues in an information retrieval system. *ACM Transactions on Database Systems* 15(3):359–384, September 1990.

[BGM92]   D. Barbara and H. Garcia-Molina. The demarcation protocol: A technique for maintaining arithmetic constraints in distributed systems. In *Proceedings of the International Conference on Extending Data Base Technology*, pages 371–397, March 1992.

[CB⁺89]   S. Chakravarthy, B. Blaustein, et al. *HiPAC: A research project in active, time-constrained database management.* Technical report. Cambridge, MA: XEROX (XAIT), July 1989.

[Cod73]   CODASYL Data Description Language Committee. *CODASYL Data Description Language Journal of Development*, June 1973. NBS Handbook 113.

[CP84]   Stefano Ceri and Giuseppe Pelagatti. *Distributed Databases: Principles and Systems.* New York: McGraw-Hill, 1984.

[CW90]   S. Ceri and J. Widom. Deriving production rules for constraint management. In *Proceedings of the 16th VLDB Conference*, pages 566–577, 1990. Also appears as Technical Report RJ 7348 (68829), IBM Almaden.

[CW92]   S. Ceri and J. Widom. Production rules in parallel and distributed database environments. In *Proceedings of the 18th VLDB Conference*, pages 339–351, 1992.

[DBB⁺88] U. Dayal, B. Blaustein, A. Buchmann, U. Chakravarthy, M. Hsu, D. McCarthy R. Ladin, A. Rosenthal, M. J. Carey S. Sarin, M. Livny, and R. Jauhari. The HiPAC project: Combining active databases and timing constraints. *SIGMOD Record* 17(1), March 1988.

[DBM88]   U. Dayal, A. Buchmann, and D. McCarthy. Rules are objects too: A knowledge model for an active, object-oriented database system. In *Proceedings of the Second International Workshop on Object-Oriented Database Systems*, September 1988.

[DHL90]   U. Dayal, M. Hsu, and R. Ladin. Organizing long-running activities with triggers and transactions. In *Proceedings of the ACM SIGMOD Conference*, pages 204–214, June 1990.

[Elm92]   A. Elmagarmid, editor. *Database Transaction Models for Advanced Applications*. San Mateo, CA: Morgan Kaufmann, 1992.

[Etz92]   O. Etzion. *Active interdatabase dependencies*. Technical report ISE-TR-92-1. Haifa, Israel: Technion, January 1992.

[Etz93]   O. Etzion. PARDES—a data driven oriented active database model. *SIGMOD Record* 22(1):7–14, March 1993.

[Geo90]   D. Georgakopoulos. *Transaction Management in Multidatabase Systems* (PhD thesis). Houston, TX: Department of Computer Science, University of Houston, December 1990.

[GK93]   S. Gantimahapatruni and G. Karabatis. Enforcing data dependencies in cooperative information systems. In *Proceedings of the International Conference on Intelligent and Cooperative Information Systems*, May 1993.

[GMS87]   H. Garcia-Molina and K. Salem. SAGAs. In *Proceedings of the ACM Conference on Management of Data (SIGMOD)*, pages 249–259, 1987.

[Gra81]   Jim Gray. The transaction concept: Virtues and limitations. In *Proceedings of the Seventh International Conference on Very Large Data Bases*, pages 144–154, September 1981.

[GRS91]   D. Georgakopoulos, M. Rusinkiewicz, and A. Sheth. On serializability of multidatabase transaction through forced local conflicts. In *Proceedings of the Seventh International Conference on Data Engineering*, pages 314–323, 1991.

[HAB+92]   Y. Halabi, M. Ansari, R. Batra, W. Jin, G. Karabatis, P. Krychniak, M. Rusinkiewicz, and L. Suardi. Narada: An environment for specification and execution of multi-system applications. In *Proceedings of the Second International Conference on Systems Integration*, June 1992.

[HFLP89]   L. Haas, J. Freytag, G. Lohman, and H. Pirahesh. Extensible query processing in Starburst. In *Proceedings of the ACM SIGMOD Conference*, pages 377–388, May 1989.

[HLM88]   M. Hsu, R. Ladin, and D. McCarthy. An execution model for active data base management systems. In *Proceedings of the Third International Conference on Data and Knowledge Bases*, June 1988.

[HR83]   Theo Haerder and Andreas Reuter. Principles of transaction-oriented database recovery. *ACM Computing Surveys* 15(4):287–317, December 1983.

[HS90]   M. Hsu and A. Silberschatz. Persistent transmission and unilateral commit—a position paper. In *Workshop on Multidatabases and Semantic Interoperability*, October 1990.

[Hu95]   X. Hu. *Making Multidatabases Active* (Master's thesis). Houston, TX: University of Houston, May 1995.

[Inm95]   W. Inmon. Data warehouse defined. *Computerworld*, March 1995.

[Kar95]   G. Karabatis. *Management of Interdependent Data in a Multidatabase Environment: A Polytransaction Approach* (PhD thesis). Houston, TX: University of Houston, May 1995.

[KR88]   J. Klein and A. Reuter. Migrating transactions. In *Future Trends in Distributed Computing Systems in the 90's*, 1988.

[KRS93]   G. Karabatis, M. Rusinkiewicz, and A. Sheth. Correctness and enforcement of multidatabase interdependencies. In N. Adam and B. Bhargava, editors, *Advanced Database Systems*. New York: Springer-Verlag, 1993.

[LBE+82]   W. Litwin, J. Boudenant, C. Esculier, A. Ferrier, A. M. Glorieux, J. La Chimia, K. Kabbaj, C. Moulinoux, P. Rolin, and C. Stangret.   SIRIUS system for distributed data management.   In *Distributed Databases*, pages 311–343. Amsterdam: North-Holland, 1982.

[LERL90]   Y. Leu, A. Elmagarmid, M. Rusinkiewicz, and W. Litwin. Extending the transaction model in a multidatabase environment. In *Proceedings of the 16th International Conference on Very Large Databases*, August 1990.

[Lit88]   W. Litwin. From database systems to multidatabase: Why and how. In *Proceedings of the British Conference on Databases*, pages 161–188. Cambridge: Cambridge University Press, 1988.

[LLPS91]   G. Lohman, B. Lindsay, H. Pirahesh, and K. Bernhard Schiefer. Extensions to Starburst: Objects, types, functions, and rules. *Communications of the ACM* 34(10):94–109, October 1991.

[MD89]   D. McCarthy and U. Dayal. The architecture of an active data base management system. In *Proceedings of the ACM SIGMOD Conference*, pages 215–224, 1989.

[Mil89]   J. Mills. *Semantic Integrity in OSCA of the Totality of Corporate Data*. Technical report TM-STS-014112. Bellcore, August 1989.

[Mos85]   J. E. B. Moss. *Nested Transactions: An Approach to Reliable Distributed Computing*. Cambridge, MA: MIT Press, 1985.

[Rad95]   A. Radding. Support decision makers with a data warehouse. *Datamation*, pages 53–58, March 1995.

[Reu89]   A. Reuter. Contract: A means for extending control beyond transaction boundaries. In *Proceedings of the Third International Workshop on High Performance Transaction Systems*, September 1989.

[Rin95]   D. Rinaldi. Matadata management separates prism from data warehouse pack. *Client/Server Computing*, March 1995.

[Ris89]   T. Risch. Monitoring database objects. In *Proceedings of the 15th International Conference on Very Large Databases*, pages 445–453, 1989.

[RS91]   M. Rusinkiewicz and A. Sheth. Polytransactions for managing interdependent data. *IEEE Data Engineering Bulletin* 14(1), March 1991.

[RSK91]   M. Rusinkiewicz, A. Sheth, and G. Karabatis. Specifying interdatabase dependencies in a multidatabase environment. *IEEE Computer* 24(12):46–53, December 1991.

[SHP88]   M. Stonebraker, E. Hanson, and S. Potamianos. The POSTGRES rule manager. *IEEE Transactions on Software Engineering* 14(7):897–907, July 1988.

[SKdM92]   E. Simon, J. Kiernan, and C. de Maindreville. Implementing high level active rules on top of a relational DBMS. In *Proceedings of the 18th VLDB Conference*, pages 315–326, 1992.

[SL90]   A. Sheth and J. Larson. Federated database systems for managing distributed, heterogeneous, and autonomous databases. *ACM Computing Surveys* 22(3):183–236, September 1990.

[SPAM91]   U. Schreier, H. Pirahesh, R. Agrawal, and C. Mohan. Alert: An architecture for transforming a passive DBMS into an active DBMS. In *17th VLDB*, September 1991.

[SR86]   M. Stonebraker and L. Rowe. The design of POSTGRES. In *Proceedings of the ACM SIGMOD Conference*, pages 340–355, June 1986.

[SR91]   Y. Shim and C. Ramamoorthy. Monitoring of distributed systems. In *Symposium on Applied Computing*, pages 248–256, 1991.

[SRK92]   A. P. Sheth, M. Rusinkiewicz, and G. Karabatis. Using polytransactions to manage interdependent data. In A. K. Elmagarmid, editor, *Database Transaction Models for Advanced Applications*, pages 555–581. San Mateo, CA: Morgan Kaufmann, 1992.

[Sto86]   M. Stonebraker. Triggers and inference in database systems. In M. Brodie and J. Mylopoulos, editors, *On Knowledge Base Management Systems*. New York: Springer-Verlag, 1986.

[SV86]   E. Simon and P. Valduriez. Integrity control in distributed data-
           base systems. In *Proceedings of the Hawaii 20th International
           Conference on System Sciences*, 1986.

[WF90]   J. Widom and S. Finkelstein. Set-oriented production rules in
           relational database systems. In *Proceedings of the ACM SIGMOD
           Conference*, pages 259–270, May 1990.

[WQ87]   G. Wiederhold and X. Qian. Modeling asynchrony in distributed
           databases. In *Proceedings of the Third International Conference
           on Data Engineering*, pages 246–250, February 1987.

9

Correctness Criteria and Concurrency Control

Panos K. Chrysanthis
Krithi Ramamritham

Introduction

Database systems have been widely incorporated in almost all aspects of the operations of large organizations. Database systems offer reliability guarantees concerning the correctness of data in spite of failures and concurrent accesses by multiple users. Similar guarantees are expected from multidatabase systems (MDBSs), which logically integrate multiple preexisting database systems, providing uniform and transparent access to data stored in these databases.

MDBSs meet the need for organizations to interoperate their databases already in service by supporting new global applications that access multiple databases. An MDBS allows each local database system to continue to operate independently. That is, an MDBS preserves the *autonomy* of the local database systems because it does not require any changes to existing databases and applications or to the local database management systems. Further, an MDBS offers flexibility in expanding database platform by adding new local database systems without concerns for compatibility with systems that already exist.

Since different database systems are suitable for different applications, MDBSs are typically heterogeneous, employing different correctness criteria and correctness-enforcing mechanisms. Correctness criteria define acceptable execution orderings of database operations, which satisfy data consistency correctness requirements. Autonomy and heterogeneity cause additional problems and tensions in satisfying traditional correctness criteria in MDBSs. Traditional correctness entails control over all data across the multiple databases, whereas autonomy implies (1) lack of any such global control and (2) lack of information regarding the execution orderings at the local database systems.

Database correctness has been traditionally studied with respect to the two sources of inconsistencies and incorrectness, namely, concurrency and failures. This chapter focuses on the former, discussing the issue of correctness in the absence of failures and the problem of concurrency control in MDBSs.

9.1
Databases, Multidatabases, and Transactions

A database integrates and stores related data in an organized manner. Each database is associated with a set of integrity constraints that captures the correctness of the data in the database. Data values are allowed to be stored in the database if they do not violate the integrity constraints of the database.

In traditional database systems, correctness of the database is ensured by means of transactions. A *transaction* is a program segment in execution that performs a task by accessing and manipulating the database. Transactions are designed so that each preserves the integrity constraints on the database at its

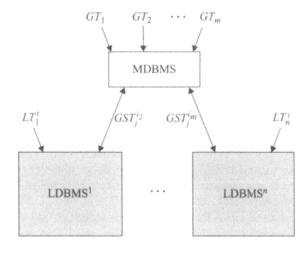

FIGURE 9.1
A multidatabase system model.

boundaries. That is, a transaction takes the database from one consistent state to another only when it executes all its statements. Thus, all the operations of a transaction are treated as a single, indivisible, *atomic* unit, and the effects of partially executed transactions are obliterated from the database. The effects of a transaction are also obliterated when the transaction invokes the *abort* transaction management primitive, informing the system that the transaction cannot successfully complete its task. A transaction informs the system that the transaction has successfully completed its task and that all its effects on the objects should be made permanent in the database by invoking the *commit* primitive.

Even if individual transactions are correct programs, transactions can interfere with each other when they are executed concurrently, thereby producing inconsistent results. By inconsistent results, we mean either the output of the transaction is not consistent with the values of the objects in the database, or the effects of the transaction on the database destroy the integrity of the database. Hence, the interleaved execution of a set of transactions is controlled, providing the necessary *isolation* between concurrent transactions to execute without any interferences in observing and operating on a consistent database.

As mentioned earlier, an MDBS is built on top of a number of existing database systems (Figure 9.1). These traditional database systems ensure the atomicity and isolation properties of their transactions. Two types of transactions execute in an MDBS:

- *local transactions* that access data from a single database and

- *global transactions* that access data from multiple databases.

In accordance with the local autonomy requirement, local transactions are submitted directly to the transaction manager (TM) of a local DBMS (LDBMS), and the global transaction manager (GTM) of the MDBS is not aware of their existence. Neither is an LDBMS aware of the existence of global transactions, which are submitted directly to the GTM.

A global transaction G is decomposed by the GTM based on the distribution of the data into several *subtransactions* g_i, each of which executes as a local transaction on some LDBMS with the available data. The GTM submits a subtransaction to an LDBMS with the help of an *agent* that resides above each local database system, serving as the interface between the GTM and the local database system.

As TMs are responsible for controlling the execution of local transactions to ensure the correctness of the local database, the GTM is responsible for controlling the execution of global transactions to ensure global consistency. This splitting of control is a manifestation of the tension that exists between autonomy and consistency requirements, complicating correctness in MDBSs and making global concurrency control difficult.

Three main approaches have emerged in addressing the issue of data consistency in MDBSs. The first approach attempts to guarantee multidatabase global serializability, since serializability is a widely used correctness criterion [EH88, WV90, BS88, Pu88, PV88, GRS91, ZE93a, ZE93b]. This approach also includes proposals for commit protocols suitable for MDBSs [BST90, Geo90, SKS91, AHC96]. The second approach replaces serializability with other correctness criteria, since serializability is considered very constraining when applied to multidatabase environments. In most cases, these correctness criteria are relaxations of serializability, such as quasi-serializability [DE89] and predicate-wise serializability [KS88]. The third approach redefines or extends the traditional transaction model to a more suitable transaction model for MDBSs with different correctness properties. These include Sagas [GMS87], S-Transactions [VEH92], flexible transactions [RELL90], and polytransactions [RSK91, SRK92]. This approach attempts to come up with correctness criteria that view database consistency requirements and transaction correctness properties independently.

We will be using ACTA [CR91a, CR94b], a first-order logic-based formalism, to precisely state correctness requirements, transaction properties, as well as the behavior of transaction processing mechanisms. In the next section, we will introduce the ACTA formalism while discussing serializability as the traditional notion of correctness for the concurrent execution.

Whereas serializability and its relaxations are, in general, independent of the application and transaction model, the other MDBS correctness criteria are specific to the application and transaction model. In Sections 9.3 and 9.4, we will examine MDBS correctness criteria from the two perspectives of independence and dependence, respectively. Section 9.5 summarizes the chapter.

9.2
Correctness of Concurrent Executions

As stated in Section 9.1, the execution of a set of transactions must be controlled so that transactions perform operations on objects in a certain manner that is considered correct. That is, correctness criteria can be defined as constraints on the ordering of concurrent operations and transaction primitives in *histories* [BHG87], which represent the concurrent execution of the set of transactions.

Intuition tells us that any correct execution of a set of transactions must be free from interferences. Assuming that individual transactions are correct, a serial execution of a set of transactions is correct, since transactions that execute serially execute in isolation and cannot interfere with each other. *Serializability* is the traditional notion of correctness for the concurrent execution of a set of transactions that satisfies isolation. The key idea is that since serial executions are correct, then any execution whose behavior or effects are the same as some serial execution must also be correct. Such concurrent executions that are equivalent to serial executions are called *serializable*.

In most concurrency control protocols, serializability is based on the notion of conflicting operations and is called *conflict serializability*. Two operations conflict when their effect is order dependent.

DEFINITION 9.1

Let s be the state of an object representing its value, return(s, p) be the output produced by operation p defined on the object, and state(s, p) be the state produced after the execution of p.

Two operations p and q conflict *in a state s, denoted by* conflict(p, q), *iff*

$$(state(state(s,p), \ q) \neq state(state(s,q), \ p))$$
$$\lor (return(s, \ q) \neq return(state(s,p), \ q))$$
$$\lor (return(s, \ p) \neq return(state(s,q), \ p))$$

Two operations that do not conflict are compatible *or* commute.

Two operations conflict if their effects on the state of an object or their return values are not independent of their execution order. Clearly, for this to be true (i.e., the two operations conflict), both should operate on the same object and one of them modifies the object; e.g., it is a write operation. On the other hand, two read operations on the same object commute and can be executed in any order.

Conflict serializability ensures that pairs of conflicting operations appear in the same order in any two equivalent executions [EGLT76, GLPT75, Gra78].

DEFINITION 9.2   *Transaction Definition*

Let $p_i[ob]$ be an object event corresponding to the invocation of the operation p on object ob by transaction T_i.

A transaction T_i is a partial order with ordering relation $\rightarrow_i$ where:

1. $T_i = \{p_i[ob] \mid p$ *is an operation on ob*$\} \cup \{\beta_i, \alpha_i, c_i\}$
   Operations in T_i can be operations on objects, begin (β), commit (c), and abort (α) primitives.
2. $\forall i \; \forall p \; \forall ob \;\; p_i[ob] \in T_i \Rightarrow (\beta_i \rightarrow_i p_i[ob])$
   All operations of a transaction follow its begin operation.
3. $\alpha_i \in T_i \Leftrightarrow c_i \notin T_i$
   A transaction can either commit or abort but not both.
4. *if ϵ is c_i or α_i, $\forall i \; \forall p \; \forall ob \;\; p_i[ob] \in T_i \Rightarrow (p_i[ob] \rightarrow_i \epsilon)$*
   All operations of a transaction precede its commit or abort.
5. $\forall i \; \forall p, q \; \forall ob \; p_i[ob] \in T_i \wedge q_i[ob] \in T_i \wedge \text{conflict}(p, q) \Rightarrow$
   $(p_i[ob] \rightarrow_i q_i[ob]) \vee (q_i[ob] \rightarrow_i p_i[ob])$
   The order of conflicting operations is defined.

In general, we use ϵ_j to denote the invocation of an event ϵ by transaction T_j. The predicate $\epsilon \rightarrow_i \epsilon'$ is true if event ϵ precedes event ϵ' in transaction T_i. Otherwise, it is false. (Thus, $\epsilon \rightarrow_i \epsilon'$ implies that $\epsilon \in T_i$ and $\epsilon' \in T_i$.) We will omit the subscript in an ordering relation $\rightarrow$ when its context is clear.

DEFINITION 9.3

Let $T = \{ T_1, T_2, \dots, T_n \}$ be a set of transactions. A (complete) history H of the concurrent execution of a set of transactions T contains all the operations and primitives invoked by the transactions in T and indicates the partial order $\rightarrow_H$ in which these operations occur.

1. $H = \cup_{i=1}^{n} T_i$
   Operations in H are exactly those in $T_1, \dots, T_n$.
2. $\forall i \; \forall p, q \; \forall ob \;\; (p_i[ob] \rightarrow_i q_i[ob]) \Rightarrow (p_i[ob] \rightarrow_H q_i[ob])$
   The order of operations within each transaction is preserved.
3. $\forall i, j \; \forall p, q \; \forall ob \; p_i[ob] \in H \wedge q_j[ob] \in H \wedge \text{conflict}(p, q) \Rightarrow$
   $(p_i[ob] \rightarrow_H q_j[ob]) \vee (q_j[ob] \rightarrow_H p_i[ob])$
   The ordering of every pair of conflicting operations is defined.

H denotes a complete history. When a transaction invokes an event, that event is appended to the current history, denoted by H_{ct}. That is, H_{ct} is a prefix of a complete history and is useful in capturing incomplete executions of transactions that contain active transactions. Incomplete executions may result from a system failure or describe a scheduler in execution. A complete history does not contain any active transactions.

The projection of a history H according to a given criterion is a subhistory that satisfies the criterion. It is constructed by eliminating any events in H that do not satisfy the given criterion while preserving the partial ordering of the events in the projection. For instance, the projection of a history with respect to committed transactions, denoted by H_{comm}, includes only those events invoked by committed transactions. The projection criterion can be formally specified as

$$\forall t \in T \ \epsilon_t \in H_{comm} \Rightarrow c_t \in H$$

H_{comm} is obtained from H by deleting all operations of noncommitted transactions in it. Note that H_{comm} is a complete history with respect to committed transactions in T. Given that in H_{comm} the effects of aborted transactions are nullified, serialization ordering requirements only consider operations invoked by committed transactions; hence, serializability criteria are expressed in terms of committed projection of histories.

As mentioned in the previous section, we need to define the notion of equivalence between two histories before being able to determine whether a history is equivalent to a serial history and hence serializable. Here we will assume that any history H is over a set of committed transactions T_{comm}; i.e., $T = T_{comm}$ and $H = H_{comm}$.

DEFINITION 9.4

Two histories H and H' are (conflict) equivalent, ($H \equiv H'$) if

1. $\forall i \ \forall p \ \forall ob, \ T_i \in T, p_i[ob] \in T_i \ \ p_i[ob] \in H \Leftrightarrow p_i[ob] \in H'$
   They are defined over the same set of transactions and have the same operations.
2. $\forall i \ \forall p, q \ \forall ob \ \text{conflict}(p, q) \wedge (p_i[ob] \to_H q_j[ob]) \Leftrightarrow (p_i[ob] \to_{H'} q_j[ob])$
   Any pair of conflicting operations p_i and q_j belonging to committed transactions T_i and T_j is ordered in the same way in both histories.

DEFINITION 9.5

A history H_{serial} is serial if for every pair of transactions T_i and T_j that appears in H_{serial}, either all operations of T_i appear before all operations of T_j or vice versa; i.e.,
$$\exists p_i[ob] \in T_i, q_j[ob] \in T_j \ (p_i \to_{H_{serial}} p_j) \Rightarrow$$
$$\forall r_i \in T_i, o_j \in T_j \ (r_i \to_{H_{serial}} o_j)$$

DEFINITION 9.6

A history H is (conflict) serializable if its committed projection H_{comm} is (conflict) equivalent to a serial history H_{serial}; i.e., $H_{comm} \equiv H_{serial}$.

Clearly, conflicting operations induce serialization ordering requirements between the invoking transactions. Specifically, if an operation $p_i[ob]$ invoked by transaction T_i precedes an operation $q_j[ob]$ invoked by T_j and with which it conflicts (*conflict*(p,q)), then T_i must precede T_j in a serializable history. We will denote this ordering dependency by $\mathcal{C}$ binary relation on transactions.

DEFINITION 9.7   *Serialization Ordering*

$\forall t_i, t_j \in T_{comm}, t_i \neq t_j$

$\quad (t_i \; \mathcal{C} \; t_j) \; \textit{iff} \; \exists ob \; \exists p, q \; (\text{conflict}(p, q) \wedge (p_i[ob] \rightarrow q_j[ob]))$

Let $\mathcal{C}^*$ be the transitive-closure of $\mathcal{C}$; i.e.,

$\quad (t_i \; \mathcal{C}^* \; t_k) \; \textit{iff} \; [(t_i \; \mathcal{C} \; t_k) \vee \exists t_j \; (t_i \; \mathcal{C} \; t_j \wedge t_j \; \mathcal{C}^* \; t_k)].$

It has been shown that serializability demands that the serialization ordering must be acyclic [BHG87]. A cycle involving transactions T_i and T_j implies that in any equivalent serial execution, T_i should precede T_j, and T_j should precede T_i, but both of these cannot hold simultaneously.

DEFINITION 9.8   *Serializability Theorem*

H_{comm} *is* (conflict) serializable *iff* $\forall t \in T_{comm} \; \neg(t \; \mathcal{C}^* \; t)$.

This means that given a history, it can be determined whether it is serializable by testing if its committed projection does not induce any ordering dependency cycles.

A simple way to recognize whether the induced ordering dependencies are acyclic is by constructing a dependency graph, called a serialization graph, and search for cycles [GLPT75, Pap86]. A *serialization graph* is a directed graph in which nodes represent transactions in H, and an edge $T_i \longrightarrow T_j, i \neq j$, means that T_i has an ordering dependency on T_j; i.e., one of T_i's operations precedes and conflicts with one of T_j's operations in H.

9.3
Application-Independent Criteria

In this section, we examine correctness criteria that apply to different applications and under different transaction models. We first define the problem of global serializability and then examine different methods for achieving it.

9.3.1   Global Serializability

To ensure global serializability in multidatabase systems, the problem of indirect conflicts must be overcome. This is illustrated in Example 9.1. Here, $r_i[x]$ $(w_i[x])$ denotes a read (write) operation performed by transaction T_i on item x, and c_i denotes the commit primitive of T_i.

EXAMPLE 9.1
Consider two local databases, one with items a and b, and another that has c and d.

Consider these transactions:

$\quad G_1 : r_1(a); r_1(c)$
$\quad G_2 : r_2(b); r_2(d)$

$$L_3 : w_3(a); w_3(b)$$
$$L_4 : w_4(c); w_4(d)$$

Here, G_1 and G_2 are global transactions, and L_3 and L_4 are local. Their concurrent execution produces the local histories H_1 and H_2:

$$H_1 : r_1(a); c_1; w_3(a); w_3(b); c_3; r_2(b); c_2 \qquad G_1 \rightarrow L_3 \rightarrow G_2$$
$$H_2 : w_4(c); r_1(c); c_1; r_2(d); c_2; w_4(d); c_4 \qquad G_2 \rightarrow L_4 \rightarrow G_1$$

Example 9.1 shows that even a serial execution of global transactions does not guarantee global serializability! This is because local transactions can create indirect conflicts between global transactions. This problem of indirect conflicts is better understood by formalizing global serializability and identifying the sources of the conflicts.

Let MDBS consist of a set of databases $\{D_1, D_2, \ldots, D_n\}$, where D_i is managed by LDBMS$_i$.

Let G be the set of global transactions and g_n^s be a (sub)transaction of a global transaction g_n ($g_n \in G$) executing all the operations of g_n on site s.

Let T_s be the set of transactions, both local transactions and global (sub)transactions, executing on site s. $T = (\cup_s T_s)$.

Let $L_s = \{l_1^s, l_2^s, \ldots, l_n^s\}$ be the set of local transactions executing on site s ($L_s \subset T_s$).

Let H be the global history of events in MDBS relating to committed transactions in T. H is a set of local histories $H = \{H_1, H_2, \ldots, H_n\}$ where H_s is the history defined over T_s.

Given the two types of transactions in MDBSs, the definition of transitive-closure of $\mathcal{C}$, which is used in the characterization of serializability (Definition 9.8), can be refined.

DEFINITION 9.9   *Local Indirect Conflicts*

Let $\mathcal{I}$ be a binary relation on a set of transactions T_s. $\forall\, t_x,\, t_y\, \in\, T_s$,
  $(t_x\, \mathcal{I}\, t_y)$ if
    $\exists k > 1, t_0 = t_x, t_k = t_y\; \forall i, 1 \leq i \leq k-1\; t_i \in T_s$
    $(t_{i-1}\, \mathcal{C}\, t_i) \wedge (t_i\, \mathcal{C}\, t_{i+1})$

where $\mathcal{C}$ is the binary relation defined in Definition 9.7 that captures direct conflicts between two transactions.

The $\mathcal{I}$ relation captures the fact that two transactions, local or global subtransactions, executing on the same site might indirectly conflict in a local history even if they do not access any shared objects. The latter is made clear when $\mathcal{C}$ is substituted with its definition.

DEFINITION 9.10

Let $\mathcal{I}$ be a binary relation on a set of transactions T_s. $\forall\, t_x,\, t_y\, \in\, T_s$,
  $(t_x\, \mathcal{I}\, t_y)$ if

$$\exists k > 1, t_0 = t_x, t_k = t_y \ \forall i, 1 \le i \le k - 1 \ t_i \in T_s$$
$$\exists ob \ \exists p, q \ ((\text{conflict}(p_{t_{i-1}}[ob], q_{t_i}[ob]) \wedge (p_{t_{i-1}}[ob] \to q_{t_i}[ob]))$$
$$\wedge \exists ob' \ \exists p', q' \ (\text{conflict}(p'_{t_i}[ob'], q'_{t_{i+1}}[ob']) \wedge (p'_{t_i}[ob'] \to q'_{t_{i+1}}[ob'])))$$

DEFINITION 9.11   *Remote Indirect Conflicts*

Let $\mathcal{R}$ be a binary relation on a set of transactions T_s. $\forall \ t_x, \ t_y \ \in \ T_s$,
$(t_x \ \mathcal{R} \ t_y)$ *if*
$$\exists k \ne s, g_i^k, g_j^k \ [(t_x \ \mathcal{C} \ g_i^s) \vee (t_x \ \mathcal{I} \ g_i^s)]$$
$$\wedge \ [(g_i^k \ \mathcal{C} \ g_j^k) \vee (g_i^k \ \mathcal{I} \ g_j^k) \vee (g_i^k \ \mathcal{R} \ g_j^k)]$$
$$\wedge \ [(g_j^s \ \mathcal{C} \ t_y) \vee (g_j^s \ \mathcal{I} \ t_y)]$$

The $\mathcal{R}$ relation captures the fact that two transactions, local or global subtransactions, executing on the same site might indirectly conflict in a global history due to conflicts between subtransactions of the same global transaction executing on different sites.

By expressing $\mathcal{C}^*$, the transitive-closure of $\mathcal{C}$, specifically for MDBSs in terms of local indirect conflicts $\mathcal{I}$ and of remote indirect conflicts $\mathcal{R}$, global serializability in MDBS can be characterized as follows:

DEFINITION 9.12

H is global serializable *iff $\forall \ t \ \in \ T \ \neg(t \ \mathcal{I} \ t) \wedge \neg(t \ \mathcal{R} \ t)$.*

Since local transactions execute under the control of individual LDBMSs and global transactions under the control of the GTM, global serializability is achieved if each $LDBMS_i$ ensures that $\forall l_i^s \in T, \neg(l_i^s \ \mathcal{C}^* l_i^s)$ and the GTM ensures that $\forall g_i^s \in T, \neg(g_i^s \ \mathcal{C}^* g_i^s)$. An LDBMS can always recognize local indirect conflicts but can never recognize remote indirect conflicts. On the other hand, the GTM can recognize both local and remote indirect conflicts as long as no local transactions are involved. Thus, with no knowledge available about the internals of LDBMSs, without any exchange of control information, or some restrictions on the executions of operations to curtail indirect conflicts, global serializability cannot be achieved in MDBS by tracing and testing for the acyclicity of ordering dependencies.

9.3.2   Achieving Global Serializability

All current schemes for achieving global serializability assume that (1) all LDBMSs ensure serializability, and (2) no control information can be exchanged between the GTM and LDBMSs. However, these schemes can be classified based on whether or not they assume an *unlabeled LDBMS*, meaning that no knowledge is available about the internals of an LDBMS—for example, whether it uses locking or time stamp–based concurrency control.

The ticket method [Geo90, GRS91] is an example of a scheme that applies to unlabeled databases. Here, conflicts are forced among global transactions using a data item called the *ticket*, maintained at each local database. Global transactions must read the ticket value, increment it, and write the incremented value into the database. By doing so, any remote indirect conflicts between two local transactions at a site are converted into local indirect conflicts (in Definition 9.11 of $\mathcal{R}$, if k = s, then $\mathcal{R}$ becomes equivalent to $\mathcal{I}$) that can be detected by the LDBMS. Hence, LDBMSs can ensure serializability of their local transactions in the presence of global subtransactions. At the same time, the GTM does not have to be concerned with indirect conflicts between global subtransactions involving local transactions, since all global subtransactions at a site conflict directly. The GTM must only be concerned with remote indirect conflicts involving only global subtransactions to ensure global serializability. In other words, the GTM has to make sure that the execution ordering of global subtransactions is consistent across all sites.

The GTM achieves consistent execution ordering of global subtransactions across sites using the values of tickets returned by each subtransaction. The idea is similar to time-stamp ordering that prevents cyclic execution orderings. The subtransactions of two global transactions execute in a consistent way in all the common sites if the ticket values of all the subtransactions of one of the transactions, say g_i, are less than the corresponding ones of the other transaction, say g_j; i.e., $\forall s \; ticket(g_i^s) < ticket(g_j^s)$. Thus, the GTM aborts a global transaction if one of its subtransactions returns a ticket that violates any previously established ticket ordering between pairs of global transactions. Ticket validation can be performed in either a pessimistic or optimistic manner.

Several solutions for achieving global serializability are available if we know something about the local concurrency control schemes and, in particular, their ordering properties. For example, a general scheme for a labeled LDBMS is based on the notion of *serialization point* (SP)—a distinguished action that determines the serialization order of the transaction in a local history. Serialization points include

- *TO (time-stamp ordering)*: Assignment of time stamp.

- *2PL (two-phase locking)*: SP at first lock release.

This notion can be used to enforce global consistency. Essentially, each site s_k is viewed as a single data object o_k, and two serialization point actions $sp_i(o_k)$ and $sp_j(o_k)$ always conflict.

Schemes can also be developed based on the recoverability properties of local schedules. A strongly recoverable DBMS restricts SPs to occur at the end of a transaction [BGRS91, Raz92]. A schedule is strongly recoverable if g_i has a direct conflict with g_j, and g_j does not commit before g_i commits. The GTM avoids cycles by making sure global transactions do not overlap—by ensuring that commit processing is done serially. That is, between the time a g_i issues its first commit at a site and its last commit at another site, no other g_j issues any commits.

If local databases produce rigorous schedules [BGRS91]—say they use the strict 2PL protocol [EGLT76, BHG87]—then our previous Example 9.1 cannot occur. Thus, if every local DBMS generates a rigorous schedule, the GTM does not perform any operation coordination, besides avoiding to commit any global subtransaction at a site before all the operations of the global transaction have been completed.

In summary, we have a hierarchy of local schedule classes, going from most general to most restrictive:

- *Serializable.*

- *Strongly serializable*: Coordinate execution of all operations of global transactions so that global transactions execute serially.

- *SP-schedules*: Coordinate transaction serialization point operations.

- *Strongly recoverable*: Coordinate commit operations to execute serially.

- *Rigorous*: No GTM coordination across global transactions. Defer commit of global subtransactions until the end of the global transaction.

As the local scheduler becomes more restrictive, the GTM can be more permissive in coordinating operations of global transactions.

9.3.3   Achieving Relaxations of Global Serializability

Rather than using serializability, alternative consistency notions are also possible. The basic idea is to consider serializability at two levels by considering two types of data, local and global, and three types of constraints:

- *Local*: Constraints involving only local items (at a single site).

- *Global*: Span more than one site, involve only global data items.

- *Global/local*: Single site constraints, but involve both local and global items.

A local transaction cannot modify global data, and the global layer is normally "added on top."

A global schedule S is *two-level serializable* (2LSR) if it is locally serializable and its projection to a set of global transactions is serializable [MRKS91]. Hence, 2LSR schedules are not always serializable, but they preserve global constraints regardless of the state of local data items. Another possibility is to constrain the access patterns of transactions such that there is no possibility of interactions between local and global transactions.

DEFINITION 9.13

H *is* two-level serializable *iff*

1. $\forall s \; \forall t \in L_s \; \neg(t \; C^* \; t)$, *and*
2. $\forall g \in G \; \neg(g \; C^* \; g)$.

Recall that G is the set of global transactions and L_s is the set of local transactions, executing on a site s.

We now examine several other relaxations, including cooperative serializability, multidatabase serializability, and quasi-serializability.

Under *cooperative serializability* (CoSR) [Chr91, RC96], transactions form cooperative transaction sets. A cooperative transaction set could be formed by the components of an extended transaction or transactions collaborating over some objects while maintaining the consistency of the objects. In such cases, consistency can be maintained if other transactions that do not belong to the set are serialized with respect to all the transactions in the set. In other words, a set of cooperative transactions becomes the unit of concurrency with respect to serializability.

Let T_c be a set of cooperative transactions, $T_c \subseteq T$.

Let $\mathcal{C}_c$ be a binary relation on transactions in T.

Let H be the history of events relating to committed transactions in T.

DEFINITION 9.14   *Cooperative Serialization Ordering*

$\forall\ t_i,\ t_j,\ t_k\ \in\ T, t_i \neq t_j, t_i \neq t_k, t_j \neq t_k\ \forall T_c \subseteq T$
$(t_i\ \mathcal{C}_c\ t_j),\ if\ \exists ob\ \exists p, q$
$\quad (((t_i \notin T_c \vee t_j \notin T_c)\ \wedge (\mathrm{conflict}(p_{t_i}[ob], q_{t_j}[ob]) \wedge (p_{t_i}[ob] \rightarrow q_{t_j}[ob])))) \vee$
$\quad (t_i \notin T_c, t_j \in T_c, t_k \in T_c\ (\mathrm{conflict}(p_{t_i}[ob], q_{t_k}[ob]) \wedge (p_{t_i}[ob] \rightarrow q_{t_k}[ob])))) \vee$
$\quad (t_i \in T_c, t_j \notin T_c, t_k \in T_c\ (\mathrm{conflict}(p_{t_k}[ob], q_{t_j}[ob]) \wedge (p_{t_k}[ob] \rightarrow q_{t_j}[ob])))))$

In Definition 9.14, the first clause expresses how a dependency between two transactions that do not belong to the same set is directly established when the transactions invoke conflicting operations on a shared object. This is similar to the clause in the classical definition of (conflict) serializability (Definition 9.7). The other two clauses reflect the fact that when a transaction establishes a dependency with another transaction, the same dependency is established between all the transactions in their corresponding cooperative transaction sets. These clauses can be viewed as expressions of the development of dependencies between transaction sets.

DEFINITION 9.15

H *is* cooperative serializable *iff* $\forall t \in T\ \neg(t\ \mathcal{C}_c^*\ t)$.

Note that if each T_c is a singleton set, then no cooperation occurs, and $\mathcal{C}_c$ is equivalent to $\mathcal{C}$. In addition, cooperative serializability does not imply that either all transactions in a cooperative set must commit or none. For example, let us consider the notion of *multidatabase serializability or m-serializability* (MSR) [MRKS91, MRB+92], which is another correctness criterion proposed for transactions in multidatabase systems.

Specifically, MSR is defined in the context of emulating two-phase commit (2PC) protocols in multidatabases using redo transactions. The idea is that the commitment of a global transaction can be decided using the 2PC protocol between the multidatabase agents that interface with the local DBMS without the participation of the local DBMS, and hence, a subtransaction is not required to enter the prepare-to-commit state during the decision phase. If the subtransaction is aborted but the final decision is to commit the global transaction, the updates of the aborted subtransaction are performed subsequently by a redo transaction. This implies that (1) the state of the database against which the redo transaction executes should be the same as the one seen by the aborted subtransaction, and (2) the redo transaction should not invalidate any other active or committed (sub)transaction. In an MSR local schedule, although a subtransaction g_i and its redo transaction $Redo(g_i)$ execute as independent transactions, they are considered as a pair. That is, database consistency is preserved by serializing all other transactions executing on the same node with respect to the pair $\{g_i, Redo(g_i)\}$. Such a pair is an instance of cooperative transactions, and the history H of interest includes events associated with all transactions, i.e., both committed and aborted transactions. MSR then corresponds to cooperative serializability if all conflicts in this history are considered with respect to two types of cooperative transaction sets: $\{g_j\}$ in case $\{g_j\}$ commits and $\{g_i, Redo(g_i)\}$ in case $\{g_i\}$ aborts.

Quasi-serializability (QSR) has been proposed in [DE89] as a correctness criterion for maintaining transaction consistency in multidatabases. As mentioned earlier, transactions in these systems are either local, i.e., execute on a single site, or global, i.e., execute on multiple sites. QSR assumes that at most one (sub)transaction of a global transaction executes on a particular site.

In QSR, the correctness of the execution of a set of global and local transactions is based on the notion of a quasi-serial history, which, unlike a serial history, specifies that only global transactions are executed serially. A history is quasi-serial if (1) all local histories are (conflict) serializable, and (2) there exists a total order of all global transactions g_m and g_n, where g_m precedes g_n in the order and all g_m's operations precede g_n's operations in all local histories in which they both appear. A quasi-serializable history is equivalent to a quasi-serial history.

Indirect conflicts between local transactions induced by conflicts of global transactions that execute on multiple sites are not captured by QSR, the reason being that QSR assumes *no* data dependency across sites. That is, remote direct conflicts captured by $\mathcal{R}$ (Definition 9.11) are not considered.

DEFINITION 9.16

H *is* quasi-serializable *iff*

1. $\forall s\ \forall t \in T_s\ \neg(t\ \mathcal{C}^*\ t)$, *and*
2. $\forall g \in G\ \neg(g\ \mathcal{R}^*\ g)$.

It is also appropriate to view QSR in terms of cooperative serializability. Specifically, transactions executing in each site s form a cooperative transaction set, with conflict relation $\mathcal{C}$ applied to them, whereas global transactions form another cooperative transaction set, with $\mathcal{C}$ again being the conflict relation applied to them.

The site-graph protocol [BS88] and altruistic locking protocol [SGMS94] are among the first methods proposed to achieve global serializability. However, it has been shown that both of them produce histories that are QSR.

- *Site-graph algorithm*: Here, each GTM maintains a bipartite graph (transactions and sites as the nodes). An arc is entered connecting T_i to each site the node will run at. T_i will run if it is not involved in any cycles. Thus, serial execution occurs if sites intersect.

- *Altruistic locking*: Here, each site has a lock maintained by the global transaction manager. If a transaction can obtain all the locks for the sites that it will visit, it proceeds; otherwise, it waits. However, transactions can release their site locks once they are done with a site even if the transaction is still in progress at the other sites. In this case, a transaction that obtains the lock executes in the *wake* of the lock-releasing transaction, as in the case of the original altruistic approach. That is, the second transaction is serialized after the first.

It should be noted that in the case of a labeled LDBS as rigorous, QSR is equivalent to global serializability, and altruistic locking and the site-graph protocols can be used to guarantee global serializability.

9.4
Application-Dependent Criteria

In this section, we discuss several criteria whose applicability is restricted to a class of applications. Consider Epsilon serializability (ESR) [PL91, WYP92], a generalization of classic serializability (SR), which explicitly allows some limited amount of inconsistency in transaction processing (TP). ESR applies mainly to numeric data. ESR enhances concurrency because some non-SR execution schedules are permitted. For example, Epsilon transactions (ETs) that only perform queries execute in spite of ongoing concurrent updates to the database. Thus, the query ETs view uncommitted, i.e., possibly inconsistent, data. Concretely, an update transaction *exports* some inconsistency when it updates a data item while query ETs are in progress. Conversely, a query ET *imports* some inconsistency when it reads a data item while uncommitted updates on that data item exist. The correctness notion in ESR is based on bounding the amount of imported and exported inconsistency for each ET [RP95]. The benefits of ESR have been discussed in the papers cited above. For instance, ESR may increase system availability and autonomy [PL91] in distributed TP systems because asynchronous execution is allowed.

Interdependent data is data stored in separate component databases that have mutual consistency requirements and whose relationship is established with the formation of the MDBS. Replicated and derived data are examples of interdependent data. Interdependent data is accessible to both global and local transactions.

So far we have approached the issue of consistency from the perspective of global transactions. Consistency, from the perspective of local transactions that access data at only a local database, is expected to be handled by the LDBMS according to the autonomy assumption. However, this assumes, in addition, that either local transactions do not access interdependent data or no interdependent data is stored in different databases. Since these are not realistic assumptions, we now consider the issue of maintaining the consistency of interdependent data accessed by local transactions.

Rusinkiewicz, Sheth, and Karabatis [RSK91] have proposed the concept of *polytransactions* by which the system, instead of reprogramming local transactions as global transactions, generates related updates to restore the consistency of interdependent data. The generation of the required updates and their execution strategy as transactions are driven by the *interdatabase dependency schema*, a declarative specification of interdatabase dependencies.

The interdatabase dependency schema is a group of *data dependency descriptors* $D^3 = \langle S, U, P, C, A \rangle$, where S is the set of source data objects, and U is the target data object. P is a predicate specified using operators of relational algebra, which captures the relationship between the source and target data objects. C is a boolean-valued mutual consistency predicate that specifies consistency requirements and defines when P is satisfied in terms of time (temporal consistency) and/or state (spatial consistency). Finally, A is a collection of consistency restoration actions that are required to restore consistency and to ensure that P is satisfied. That is, if a transaction updates a data object that is related to data objects in other databases and causes a violation of consistency requirements, a series of transactions corresponding to the restoration actions are initiated by the system.

Dependency descriptors, by means of C and A, can provide more semantic information needed for consistency maintenance than database integrity constraints. They support execution of multidatabase transactions resembling those of triggers in advanced active databases, allowing actions to perform on the basis of either the state of data or external events.

Consider two sites in a multidatabase that, respectively, maintain two versions of a data item, one that is complete and another that only contains data required at that site. The two are not required to be consistent at all times, but changes made to the complete database are required to percolate to the other within a specified delay. Clearly, this type of constraint is related to deferred consistency restoration. If the changes should be reflected within d units of time, we have the following "temporal commit dependency":

$$(t_i \in H \wedge (ts(t_i) = t)) \Rightarrow t_j \in H^{t+d}$$

This says that if t_i commits at time t, t_j should commit by time $t + d$.

Sheth and Rusinkiewicz [SR90] have proposed *eventual consistency*, similar to identity connections introduced by Wiederhold and Qian [WQ87], and *lagging consistency*, similar to asynchronously updated copies like quasi-copies [ABGM90]. Barbara and Garcia-Molina [BGM90] have proposed *controlled inconsistency*, which extends the work on quasi-copies [ABGM90]. Their demarcation protocol [BGM92], which handles linear inequality constraints, can be used for implementing ESR in distributed transaction processing systems. Recently, the demarcation protocol has been generalized in [MY98] to handle more complex constraints by observing that the key idea is to find local sufficient conditions for a global constraint.

Thus far, we have discussed correctness criteria assuming that both local and global transactions are traditional transactions associated with the ACID properties [Gra81, HR83]: atomicity, consistency, isolation, and durability. Given that serializability is a very restrictive correctness criterion, and ensuring global serializability as well as atomicity in MDBSs is a difficult task, a number of new transaction models that redefine or extend the traditional transaction model have been proposed as more suitable for MDBSs. These extended transaction models exploit the semantics of the applications and the characteristics of the individual LDBSs while considering the limitations in processing global transactions due to the autonomy requirement.

A common characteristic of these transaction models is that they exhibit a hierarchical structure in which transactions at any level of the hierarchy unilaterally release their updates in the database. These include Sagas [GMS87], Flex transactions [BEK93], S-Transactions [VEH92], DOM transactions [BOH+92], and the ConTract model [WR92] (see Chapter 10).

9.5
Summary

How to manage and guarantee consistency of semantically related data in heterogeneous and distributed computing environments is an issue that involves trade-offs between autonomy and correctness requirements. Autonomy is an issue because substantial capital investments have been made in local DBMSs, and from a practical point of view, requiring major modifications may not be an option. Thus, for legacy systems, some weakening of correctness requirements vis-á-vis serializability becomes unavoidable. Full data consistency and serializability can only be achieved with severe restrictions, in the form of proscriptions and prescriptions [CR94a], with respect to data access, transaction processing, and commit protocols. Furthermore, even if we are able to achieve global serializability, there are performance implications. Consider, for instance, the ticket method. It forces conflicts between transactions and so runs the risk of forced conflicts even when there is no potential for direct or indirect conflicts to start with.

Fortunately, emerging standards demand a 2PC protocol to be supported by transaction processing systems, which will allow for control of the commitment of global transactions, simplifying transaction management in an MDBS. Nevertheless, as long as some of the black boxes that join a multidatabase environment do not even support transactional computations, some form of support is needed either from the agents that sit above the black boxes or from the application programmers.

Bibliography

[ABGM90]   R. Alonso, D. Barbara, and H. Garcia-Molina. Data caching issues in an information retrieval system. *ACM Transactions on Database Systems* 15(3):359–384, September 1990.

[AHC96]   Y. J. Al-Houmaily and P. K. Chrysanthis. Dealing with incompatible presumptions of commit protocols in multidatabase systems. In *Proceedings of the 11th ACM Annual Symposium on Applied Computing*, pages 186–195, 1996.

[ANRS92]   M. Ansari, L. Ness, M. Rusinkiewicz, and A. Sheth. Using flexible transactions to support multi-system telecommunication applications. In *Proceedings of the 18th International Conference on Very Large Databases*, pages 65–76, 1992.

[ASSR93]   P. C. Attie, M. P. Singh, A. Sheth, and M. Rusinkiewicz. Specifying and enforcing intertask dependencies. In *Proceedings of the 19th VLDB Conference*, pages 134–143, 1993.

[BEK93]   O. Bukhres, A. Elmagarmid, and E. Kuhn. Implementation of the flex transaction model. *IEEE Data Engineering* 16(2):28–32, 1993.

[BGM90]   D. Barbara and H. Garcia-Molina. The case for controlled inconsistency in replicated data. In *Proceedings of the Workshop on the Management of Replicated Data*, pages 35–42, 1990.

[BGM92]   D. Barbara and H. Garcia-Molina. The demarcation protocol: A technique for maintaining arithmetic constraints in distributed systems. In *Proceedings of the International Conference on Extending Data Base Technology*, pages 371–397, March 1992.

[BGML+90]   Yuri Breitbart, Hector Garcia-Molina, Witold Litwin, Nick Roussopoulos, Marek Rusinkiewicz, Glenn Thompson, and Gio Wiederhold. Final report of the workshop on multidatabases and semantic interoperability. In *First Workshop on Multidatabases and Semantic Interoperability*, November 1990.

[BGMS92]   Y. Breitbart, H. Garcia-Molina, and A. Silberschatz. Overview of multidatabase transaction management. *VLDB Journal* 1(2):181–239, October 1992.

[BGRS91]   Y. Breitbart, D. Georgakopoulos, M. Rusinkiewicz, and A. Silberschatz. On rigorous transaction scheduling. *IEEE Transactions on Software Engineering* 17(9):954–960, September 1991.

[BHG87]   P. Bernstein, V. Hadzilacos, and N. Goodman. *Concurrency Control and Recovery in Database Systems*. Reading, MA: Addison-Wesley, 1987.

[BOH+92]   A. Buchmann, M. T. Özsu, M. Hornick, D. Georgakopoulos, and F. A. Manola. A transaction model for active distributed object systems. In A. K. Elmagarmid, editor, *Database Transaction Models for Advanced Applications*, pages 123–158. San Mateo, CA: Morgan Kaufmann, 1992.

[BS88]   Y. Breitbart and A. Silberschatz. Multidatabase update issues. In *Proceedings of the ACM SIGMOD International Conference on Management of Data*, pages 135–142, 1988.

[BST90]   Yuri Breibart, Avi Silberschatz, and Glenn R. Thompson. Reliable transaction management in a multidatabase system. *Proceedings of the ACM SIGMOD International Conference on Management of Data*, pages 214–224, 1990.

[Chr91]   P. K. Chrysanthis. *ACTA, A Framework for Modeling and Reasoning About Extended Transactions* (PhD thesis). Amherst, Massachusetts: Department of Computer and Information Science, University of Massachusetts, 1991.

[CR91a]   P. K. Chrysanthis and K. Ramamritham. A formalism for extended transaction models. *Proceedings of the 17th International Conference on VLDB*, pages 103–111, 1991.

[CR92]   P. K. Chrysanthis and K. Ramamritham. ACTA: The SAGA continues. In A. K. Elmagarmid, editor, *Database Transaction*

Models for Advanced Applications, pages 349–398. San Mateo, CA: Morgan Kaufmann, 1992.

[CR94a]   P. Chrysanthis and K. Ramamritham. Autonomy requirements in heterogeneous distributed database systems. In *Proceedings of the Conference on the Advances on Data Management*, pages 283–302, 1994.

[CR94b]   P. K. Chrysanthis and K. Ramamritham. Synthesis of extended transaction models using ACTA. *ACM Transactions on Database Systems* 19(3):450–491, 1994.

[DE89]   Weimin Du and Ahmed K. Elmagarmid. Quasi serializability: A correctness criterion for global concurrency control in InterBase. In *Proceedings of the 15th International VLDB Conference*, pages 347–355, 1989.

[DSW94]   A. Deacon, H. J. Schek, and G. Weikum. Semantics-based multilevel transactions management in federated systems. In *Proceedings of the 10th International Conference on Data Engineering*, pages 452–461, 1994.

[EGLT76]   K. Eswaran, J. Gray, R. Lorie, and I. Traiger. The notion of consistency and predicate locks in a database system. *Communications of the ACM* 19(11):624–633, 1976.

[EH88]   A. K. Elmagarmid and A. A. Helal. Supporting updates in heterogeneous distributed database systems. In *Proceedings of the IEEE Fourth International Conference on Data Engineering*, pages 564–569, 1988.

[ELLR90]   A. K. Elmagarmid, Y. Leu, W. Litwin, and M. Rusinkiewicz. A multidatabase transaction model for InterBase. In *Proceedings of the 16th International Conference on VLDB*, pages 507–518, 1990.

[Elm92]   A. Elmagarmid, editor. *Database Transaction Models for Advanced Applications*. San Mateo, CA: Morgan Kaufmann, 1992.

[Geo90]   D. Georgakopoulos. *Transaction Management in Multidatabase Systems* (PhD thesis). Houston, TX: Department of Computer Science, University of Houston, December 1990.

[GLPT75]   J. N. Gray, R. A. Lorie, A. R. Putzulo, and I. L. Traiger. Granularity of locks and degrees of consistency in a shared database. In *Proceedings of the First International Conference on Very Large Databases*, pages 25–33, 1975.

[GMGK⁺91]   H. Garcia-Molina, D. Gawlick, J. Klein, K. Kleissner, and K. Salem. Modeling long-running activities as nested SAGAs. *Bulletin of the IEEE Technical Committee on Data Engineering* 14(1):14–18, 1991.

[GMS87]   H. Garcia-Molina and K. Salem. SAGAs. In *Proceedings of the ACM Conference on Management of Data (SIGMOD)*, pages 249–259, 1987.

[GR93]   J. Gray and A. Reuter. *Transaction Processing: Concepts and Techniques*. San Francisco: Morgan Kaufmann, 1993.

[Gra78]   J. N. Gray. Notes on database operating systems. In R. Bayer, R. M. Graham, and G. Seegmuller, editors, *Operating Systems: An Advanced Course*, volume 60, pages 394–481. New York: Springer-Verlag, 1978.

[Gra81]   Jim Gray. The transaction concept: Virtues and limitations. In *Proceedings of the Seventh International Conference on Very Large Data Bases*, pages 144–154, September 1981.

[GRS91]   D. Georgakopoulos, M. Rusinkiewicz, and A. Sheth. On serializability of multidatabase transaction through forced local conflicts. In *Proceedings of the Seventh International Conference on Data Engineering*, pages 314–323, 1991.

[HR83]   Theo Haerder and Andreas Reuter. Principles of transaction-oriented database recovery. *ACM Computing Surveys* 15(4):287–317, December 1983.

[Kai90]   G. E. Kaiser. A flexible transaction model for software engineering. In *Proceedings of the Sixth International Conference on Data Engineering*, pages 560–567, 1990.

[KR93]   M. Kamath and K. Ramamritham. Performance characteristics of epsilon serializability with hierarchical inconsistency bounds. In *Proceedings of the Ninth International Conference on Data Engineering*, pages 587–594, 1993.

[KS88]   H. F. Korth and G. D. Speegle. Formal model of correctness
            without serializability. In *Proceedings of the ACM SIGMOD In-
            ternational Conference on Management of Data*, pages 379–386,
            June 1988.

[MRB+92]   Sharad Mehrotra, Rajeev Rastogi, Yuri Breitbart, Henry F. Ko-
            rth, and Avi Silberschatz. The concurrency control problems in
            multidatabases: Characteristics and solutions. In *Proceedings of
            the ACM SIGMOD International Conference on Management of
            Data*, pages 288–297, June 1992.

[MRKS91]   S. Mehrotra, Rajeev Rastogi, Henry F. Korth, and Avi Silber-
            schatz. Non-serializeable executions in heterogeneous distributed
            database systems. In *Proceedings of the First International
            Conference on Parallel and Distributed Systems*, December 1991.

[MY98]   S. Mazumdar and G. Yuan. Localizing global constraints: A
            geometric approach. In *Proceedings of the Ninth International
            Conference on Computing and Information*, 1998.

[Pap86]   C. Papadimitriou. *The Theory of Database Concurrency Control*.
            Rockville, MD: Computer Science Press, 1986.

[PKH88]   C. Pu, G. Kaiser, and N. Hutchinson. Split-transactions for open-
            ended activities. In *Proceedings of the 14th VLDB Conference*,
            pages 26–37, 1988.

[PL91]   C. Pu and A. Leff. Replica control in distributed systems: An
            asynchronous approach. In *Proceedings of the ACM SIGMOD
            International Conference on Management of Data*, pages 377–
            386, 1991.

[Pu88]   Calton Pu. Superdatabases for composition of heterogeneous
            databases. In *International IEEE Conference Management of
            Data*, pages 548–555, 1988.

[PV88]   J. Pons and J. Vilarem. Mixed concurrency control: Dealing with
            heterogeneity in distributed database systems. In *Proceedings of
            the 14th International Conference on Very Large Databases*, pages
            445–456, 1988.

[Raz92]   Y. Raz. The principle of commit ordering, or guaranteeing serial-
            izability in a heterogeneous environment of multiple autonomous
            resource managers using atomic commitment. In *Proceedings*

of the 18th International Conference on Very Large Databases,
August 23–27 1992.

[RC94]   K. Ramamritham and P. K. Chrysanthis. In search of acceptability criteria: Database consistency requirements and transaction correctness properties. In M. T. Özsu, U. Dayal, and P. Valduriez, editors, *Distributed Object Management*, pages 212–230. San Mateo, CA: Morgan Kaufmann, 1994.

[RC96]   K. Ramamritham and P. K. Chrysanthis. A taxonomy of correctness criteria in database applications. *Journal of Very Large Databases* 4(1):181–293, 1996.

[RELL90]   M. E. Rusinkiewicz, A. K. Elmagarmid, Y. Leu, and W. Litwin. Extending the transaction model to capture more meaning. *ACM SIGMOD Record* 19(1):3–7, March 1990.

[RP95]   K. Ramamritham and C. Pu. A formal characterization of epsilon serializability. *IEEE Transactions on Knowledge and Data Engineering* 7(6):997–107, 1995.

[RSK91]   M. Rusinkiewicz, A. Sheth, and G. Karabatis. Specifying interdatabase dependencies in a multidatabase environment. *IEEE Computer* 24(12):46–53, December 1991.

[RW91]   A. Reuter and H. Wächter. The ConTract model. *IEEE Data Engineering* 14(1):39–43, 1991.

[Sch93]   F. Schwenkreis. APRICOTS: A prototype implementation of a contract-system managing of the control-flow and the communication-system. In *Proceedings of the 12th Symposium on Reliable Distributed Systems*, pages 12–22, 1993.

[SGMS94]   K. Salem, H. Garcia-Molina, and J. Shands. Altruistic locking. *ACM Transactions on Database Systems* 19(1):117–165, 1994.

[SKS91]   Nandit Soparkar, Henry F. Korth, and Abraham Silberschatz. Failure-resilient transaction management in multidatabases. *IEEE Computer* 24(12):28–36, December 1991.

[SL90]   A. Sheth and J. Larson. Federated database systems for managing distributed, heterogeneous, and autonomous databases. *ACM Computing Surveys* 22(3):183–236, September 1990.

[SR90]   A. Sheth and M. Rusinkiewicz. Management of interdependent data: Specifying dependency and consistency requirements. In *Proceedings of the Workshop on Management of Replicated Data*, pages 133–136, 1990.

[SRK92]   A. P. Sheth, M. Rusinkiewicz, and G. Karabatis. Using polytransactions to manage interdependent data. In A. K. Elmagarmid, editor, *Database Transaction Models for Advanced Applications*, pages 555–581. San Mateo, CA: Morgan Kaufmann, 1992.

[VEH92]   J. Veijalainen, F. Eliassen, and B. Holtkamp. The S-transaction model. In A. K. Elmagarmid, editor, *Transaction Management for Advanced Database Applications*, pages 467–513. San Mateo, CA: Morgan Kaufmann, 1992.

[WQ87]   G. Wiederhold and X. Qian. Modeling asynchrony in distributed databases. In *Proceedings of the Third International Conference on Data Engineering*, pages 246–250, February 1987.

[WR92]   H. Wächter and A. Reuter. The ConTract model. In A. K. Elmagarmid, editor, *Database Transaction Models for Advanced Applications*, pages 219–264. San Mateo, CA: Morgan Kaufmann, 1992.

[WV90]   A. Wolski and J. Veijalainen. 2PC agent method: Achieving serializability in presence of failures in a heterogeneous multidatabase. In *Proceedings of the IEEE PARBASE-90 Conference*, pages 321–330, 1990.

[WYP92]   K.-L. Wu, P. S. Yu, and C. Pu. Divergence control for epsilon serializability. In *Proceedings of the Eighth International Conference on Data Engineering*, pages 506–515, February 1992.

[ZE93a]   A. Zhang and A. Elmagarmid. On global transaction scheduling in multidatabase systems. In *Proceedings of the Second International Conference on Parallel and Distributed Information Systems*, pages 117–124, 1993.

[ZE93b]   A. Zhang and A. Elmagarmid. A theory of global concurrency control in multidatabase systems. *VLDB Journal* 2(3):331–360, 1993.

10

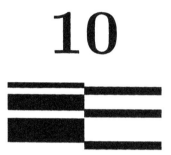

Transaction Management in Multidatabase Systems: Current Technologies and Formalisms

Ken Barker
Ahmed Elmagarmid

Introduction

Ensuring the correct execution of multiple user transactions over multidatabase management systems, the focus of research over the past decade, has proven to be a very difficult problem. The initial quantification of the problem described by Gligor and Luckenbaugh [GL84] and Gligor and Popescu-Zeltin [GPZ85] provided a series of open questions that needed to be answered before a multidatabase management system [Lit86] could be realized. Unfortunately, most of these questions still remain open today, so existing implementations of multidatabase systems (MDBSs) have been forced to make concessions with respect to the level of "correctness" used in previous database management systems. These concessions are not necessarily bad, but they typically relax one aspect of the transaction management problem in favor of another usually seen to be more important. The obvious question is which aspect of the multidatabase environment is considered most important? Most research efforts have attempted to ensure that the autonomy of the participating database management systems is maintained, because industrial-strength MDBSs must respect the proprietary nature of participants.

This chapter provides the framework necessary to understand transaction management in a multidatabase system. Initially, a transactional architectural model is described that is sufficiently generic to capture the important aspects of transactions in an MDBS. Section 10.1 provides a brief introduction to transaction management in the traditional sense, as typified by the early work of Gray [Gra78] and expanded upon by other researchers. The chapter then frames this work by discussing the most important aspect of transaction management—namely, the autonomy of the underlying systems—in Section 10.2.

Once this underlying framework is established, we turn our attention to two broad aspects of the transaction management problem: serializability and recoverability. Section 10.3 addresses transactions by describing the underlying problems associated with concurrency in a multidatabase environment and then reviewing several proposed advanced transaction models that have appeared in the literature. In Section 10.4, several of these models are examined, with specific emphasis on the effects of the multidatabase environment.

Section 10.5 concludes with some comments concerning the technical challenges presented.

10.1
Transaction Management Review

Typically, transaction models are considered using two somewhat orthogonal dimensions: serializability and reliability. *Serializability* is supported by a concurrency control mechanism that ensures each user is treated as the only one currently on the system. *Reliability* guarantees that users' queries are executed to completion, and the effects of their activities are either reflected in the database or any indication that the query existed is obliterated. Typically, these properties are supported by conformance to criteria such as those represented by the ACID acronym [GR93]:

- A*tomicity*: The transaction is executed as a single atomic unit, where all of the operations are executed or none of them affect the database.

- C*onsistency*: The transaction views are maintained so that part of the transaction sees the precise snapshot of the database at the end of the transaction's execution that it would have seen if the same access had been made earlier.

- I*solation*: Transactions should not interfere with the activities of other transactions, nor should they affect the execution of any other system activities.

- D*urability*: The system guarantees that the effects of committed transactions on the database persist after the transaction is completed or another validly executed transaction changes said values.

Generally, the atomicity and isolation properties are seen as supporting the serializability of transaction management, while the consistency and durability properties ensure reliability. Most researchers and practitioners using traditional database management systems believe that correctness can only be maintained if all four properties are supported.

Nontraditional or emerging technologies may make it impossible to support all of these properties. Therefore, the relaxation of certain aspects may be mandatory if advanced application domains are to be supported in a meaningful way. For example, a multidatabase management system may require that the atomicity property be relaxed to accommodate the temporary loss of an underlying participating database system. Before delving too deeply into how these specifications might be relaxed, it may prove useful to provide an architectural framework upon which to describe subsequent relaxations.

Figure 10.1 depicts a high-level architectural model suitable for describing transaction management issues encountered on a multidatabase system. The core component of the multidatabase is the multidatabase management system (MDBMS), which is responsible for overseeing the correct execution of transactions submitted to it. These transactions may span multiple local database management systems (LDBMSs). Transactions submitted to the MDBMS are called *global transactions* (GTs) and are posed against a schema that may represent integrated data from multiple LDBMSs.[1] Global transactions must be

---

[1]The specific issue of the need to produce a *global conceptual schema* (GCS) is ignored here because it is irrelevant to this discussion. The transaction manager only needs to be aware

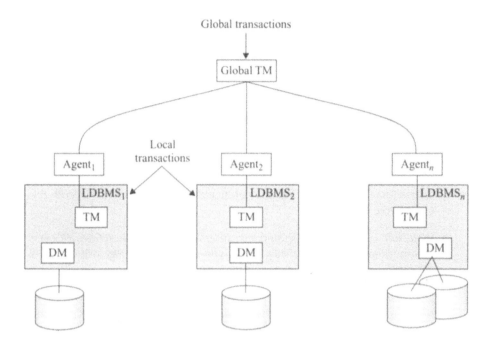

FIGURE 10.1
Architectural model for transactions in a multidatabase environment.

decomposed into *global subtransactions* (GSTs) that are directed at the specific locations where the corresponding data is located. An interface must be defined between the global level and the local DBMSs through which the GSTs must pass. Characterizing this interface is extremely important because it is central in determining the amount of autonomy the LDBMSs can retain in the MDBMS.

For example, if the only interface is a transactional one whereby a complete, self-contained transaction must be submitted, a high degree of local autonomy is maintained. However, the price paid is a significant loss in the possible concurrency. This occurs because an interface that supports only one operation submission will permit the MDBMS to exert greater control over the execution of GST operations. Further complicating the multidatabase transaction problem is the existence of local transactions (LTs) that are sub-

---

of the data that can be accessed and where it is located, so the issues that surround providing an entire, correct, and consistent universal data model can be ignored. If the data is defined in the global data directory, it can be accessed (assuming appropriate security considerations), and if the data is not defined there, it cannot be used. Therefore, managing the metadata is not central to transaction management per se, so it is ignored.

mitted without the knowledge or control of the MDBMS. An argument can be made that if local transactions are not permitted, the multidatabase transaction problem becomes trivial because there is a single point of control.

Results flow from the LDBMS to the MDBMS. The MDBMS is responsible for merging the partial results from each participating system into a single integrated result for the global user. In addition to the result flowing "up" the architecture, the interface between the MDBMS and the LDBMSs must support some form of two-phase commit protocol. Ideally, each participating system would provide a visible two-phase commit, but this is unrealistic in a "real" multidatabase environment composed of legacy information systems such as flat files. Therefore, to provide a fully functional interoperable environment, techniques must be developed that provide a two-phase commit without expecting or requiring an open systems environment. Unfortunately, the likelihood of developing such a system is quite low, so the best approach will be to develop techniques that meet specific integration needs on a case-by-case basis.

Figure 10.1 also illustrates the notation used in this chapter to describe components that exist in a multidatabase environment. An MDBS is composed of a set of local databases ($\mathcal{LDB} = \{LDB^1,\ LDB^2, \dots, LDB^n\}$), with each managed by its own corresponding local database management system ($\mathcal{LDBMS} = \{LDBMS^1,\ LDBMS^2, \dots, LDBMS^n\}$). Each of these LDBMSs is capable of servicing the set of transactions submitted by local users known as local transactions ($LT^i = \{LT^i_1,\ LT^i_2, \dots, LT^i_n\}$), where the ith LDBMS is wholly responsible for all of these local transactions. A set of global transactions ($GT = \{GT_1,\ GT_2, \dots, GT_m\}$) is submitted to the MDBMS, where each is decomposed into a set of global subtransactions ($GT_j = \{GST^{i_1}_{j_1},\ GST^{i_2}_{j_2}, \dots, GST^{i_m}_{j_p}\}$) that can be submitted to their corresponding LDBMS. Note that the superscripts (i_1, i_2, ..., i_m) are identifiers for LDBMSs. If it can be assumed that only a single GST can be submitted to any one LDBMS on behalf of each GT, this notation can be simplified to $GT_j = \{GST^{i_2}_j,\ GST^{i_2}_j, \dots, GST^{i_m}_j\}$ because the LDBMS identifier is sufficient to uniquely identify all of the global subtransactions.

This notation may appear quite complex, but the superscripts identify the LDBSs and LDBMSs, while the subscripts identify the transactions. The combination of subscripts and superscripts in the multidatabase environment uniquely identify both transactions. Unfortunately, it may not be obvious which transactions are global, global subtransactions, or local, so we have adopted the convention of "naming" local transactions with lt (or LT), global substransactions with gst (or GST), and global transactions with gt (or GT) to eliminate any ambiguity.

10.2
Unique Transaction Properties Found in Multidatabase Systems

Transaction management in a multidatabase environment is particularly challenging primarily because of the *autonomy* of the underlying local database management systems. Several researchers have attempted to describe and/or quantify the various aspects of the autonomy, but a complete description of the issues raised is beyond the scope of this chapter [Bar93]. For our purposes, the most important feature of the autonomy is the difficulty associated with modifying the components of the underlying or participating systems. Modifications may be desirable to either the database management system, the schematic description of the data in the underlying database, or the data in the underlying database. In general, modifying the underlying systems ranges from very difficult to impossible.

Ideally, no modification to parts of the participating systems should be required. This may be unrealistic, however, so certain assumptions may need to be made about the nature of these systems. For example, although a fully interoperable environment permits any type of legacy system to participate in the multidatabase, it may be impossible for this to occur because the MDBMS requires each participant to provide a visible two-phase commit protocol. Another problem with "real" interoperable system environments is the need to allow for the participation of *flat file* systems that are not managed by a management system, but contain useful data that is accessible through application programs developed in antiquity.

Several researchers argue that so-called open systems alleviate the difficulty associated with autonomy. They argue that standardization forces systems to conform to a criterion that demands a certain behavior.[2] This standardization will be supported by market forces in that, for example, a visible two-phase commit might be required of new systems or they will be impossible to sell. Although such standards may eventually develop, such a scenario does not address the fundamental question of how existing or legacy systems without a visible commit are to be incorporated into the system. Therefore, research arguing that future systems will exhibit a particular property or feature is misguided, because real interoperability problems must allow for cases where a particular behavior does not exist.

An alternative approach of interest to the research community is the one that demonstrates that a particular property of a local DBMS must exist or the system cannot be meaningfully merged into an MDBMS. Several research efforts have shown that the general problem of using global transactions to update multiple LDBMSs cannot occur correctly unless some form of visible two-phase commit exists. Great care must be taken in these "proofs," because

---

[2]It should be noted that the mechanism that supports the standard does not have to be visible.

sometimes a very minor change to the underlying model can invalidate the proof. For example, although it has been demonstrated that a visible two-phase commit is required, adding a small amount of semantic information to the transaction can change the transaction model from a traditional one to one that might permit a nonvisible subtransaction to commit without entering a "precommit" state.

10.3
Modeling Issues in Multidatabase Systems

Serializability has been well studied in other work [BHG87, Pap86], so no attempt will be made in this chapter to describe either the underlying philosophy of serializability or its correctness. Instead, a brief description of serializability is provided with pointers to a more basic introduction if required [BHG87]. The definition of correctness is based on the notion that when a set of transactions is executed so that each transaction runs in isolation from all others in the set, the execution is considered to be correct. The important feature of this definition is that the actual ordering of transactions has no bearing on the transaction's correctness (or form) or the set of transactions in the system. Therefore, any serial sequence of the transactions is correct, although executing the transactions in a different order may result in a database that is left in a different state.

Bernstein et al. [BHG87] provide a clear description of these concepts by defining a serial execution of a set of transactions, each of which exhibits ACID properties when taken in isolation, and which are also capable of moving the database from one consistent state to another. Serializability states that any execution sequence equivalent to a serial execution is correct. Thus, determining correctness requires a definition of *equivalence*. Consequently, an arbitrary history of transactions is equivalent to another execution sequence if both are defined over the same set of transactions and order all of the transaction's operations in the same way, based on some *property*. Defining the *property* is the essential element that defines the behavior of a transaction model. For example, one common property is that of *conflict*, which occurs when two operations access the same data item and at least one of them is a write operation. Advanced transaction models retain this definition of equivalence but change the property, which essentially determines legitimate orderings.

Although several different mechanisms exist for defining transactions, we will use one of the more popular approaches because of its simplicity. A transaction (T_i) is defined as a partial order $(OS_i, <)$, where OS_i is a set of operations and $<$ is an ordering relation on OS_i. The types of operations in an OS_i vary, depending on the transaction model being considered. For example, a traditional transaction model would contain the operations (r)ead, (w)rite, (c)ommit, and (a)bort.

Another common transaction model is the *nested transaction model* [Mos85], where a transaction can invoke others on its behalf. The definition of transactions provided above describes a nested transaction model by adding transactions as another operation in the OS_i. Transactions that appear as operations of another transaction are generally called *subtransactions* and are usually identified in some way as a "child" of the "parent." This forms a *transaction family*, because a hierarchy of transactions to subtransactions to subtransactions is built, based upon the invocation structure. Nested transactions can either be *closed*, meaning that partial results from a subtransaction are not visible to other transactions but their effects can be seen by other subtransactions of the same transaction family, or *open*, meaning that subtransaction results are visible to *all* other transactions in any family.

These fundamental transaction models are used in a multidatabase system, although in very different ways. LDBMSs typically use the traditional model and do not comprehend the concept of nested transactions. A nested transaction tends to have a notion of *precommit*, which is a subtransaction state entered after it has completed all of its activities but suspends the subtransaction so it cannot commit until after its parent commits. Unfortunately, the traditional transaction model does not have this notion because transactions are an atomic unit capable of deciding upon commitment or abortion as a result of their own information. The obvious implication is that we cannot assume there exists a visible commitment process that can be exploited by the MDBMS. However, it is now generally accepted that this fact makes it impossible to build a multidatabase transaction facility. Fortunately, several techniques have been developed that permit a visible commit to be retrofitted to an existing system [BO91], and it is likely that future systems will make a visible commit available as a part of being "open."

A nested transaction model is used by the MDBMS when it takes a global transaction and decomposes it into a set of global subtransactions, as depicted in Figure 10.1. Several trade-offs need to be considered when choosing the model to use (open or closed). First, consider the open model. This approach appears well suited for a multidatabase environment because partial results generated by subtransactions are visible to other transactions. This model appears to protect the local system's autonomy by quickly permitting any local locks held at the participating DBMS to be released. Unfortunately, the approach requires that the participating DBMS provide a mechanism for supporting compensating transactions if a subtransaction has committed but the global transaction submitting it must abort for some reason. If such a mechanism exists on the underlying DBMSs that does not unduly affect local transaction behaviors, the approach will provide an excellent MDBS environment. At this time, however, no commercially available DBMSs permit this form of compensation in a way that is sufficiently general to facilitate this approach. Therefore, we turn our attention to viability of the *closed nested transaction* model.

The implementation of closed nesting, as described by Moss [Mos85], will provide a correct and consistent global database environment in that the ACID properties will be supported. The key feature of this model is its need to have all subtransactions enter a *precommit* state. In this state, transaction activities are logged by recording the database state, which ensures that if a system crash occurs, the database can be correctly recovered. Two possible approaches suggest themselves. First, a visible two-phase commit protocol is provided by all participating database systems. Such an approach will solve the MDBS consistency problem, but it is unrealistic to believe such an open environment will be available in the immediate future, due to the run-time cost. Second, the problem of retrofitting a visible two-phase commit to legacy systems is both unrealistic and a significant violation of autonomy because of the need to rewrite a significant component of these older systems.

In summary, both the open and closed models provide interesting possibilities for the multidatabase environment. However, both present research challenges that must be met before they can be applied to such an environment. Therefore, research must be undertaken using both environments. The models described in the subsequent sections of this chapter use some form of nested transaction model, so all of them have had to address these questions. Each approach is unique and provides interesting but, as yet, incomplete insights.

10.4
Examples of Advanced Transaction Models

A significant number of the advanced transaction models that have appeared in the literature during the past decade have been applied to multidatabase problems with varying levels of success. This section describes several of these models, with particular attention to their suitability in an environment composed of autonomous systems that wish to exchange or share information. Recall that a pragmatic interoperable environment will probably require the sacrifice of one or more of the ACID properties, so we will state which, if any, of these are being compromised. Elmagarmid [Elm92] provides an overview of several advanced transaction models. This section is similar in approach in that it adapts the same overall structure but changes the focus to the issues surrounding the models' suitability for multidatabase systems.

The first advanced transaction model proposed was Moss's nested transaction model [Mos85]. The architectural model depicted in Figure 10.1 presents a variant of the nested transaction model, except that the depth of the transaction tree is only a single level. This nesting is used in many of the advanced models discussed here and is fundamental to research in the area. A second fundamental transaction technique often exploited in multidatabase systems is the *compensating transaction* [Mos85]. Compensation essentially "undoes" the effects of another transaction by executing a "new" transaction.

Problems with this approach include (1) ensuring the successful completion of the compensating transaction because, if it fails, the original transaction will not be compensated, and (2) correcting the effects of other transactions that have been executed based on the effects of the original transaction—essentially the cascading abort problem found in traditional transaction management systems but much more difficult to manage.

Despite these difficulties, several application environments may benefit greatly from compensating transaction environments. These environments are characterized by

- a small probability of intertransaction conflicts;

- high autonomy, so there is very little chance of discovering a system that can operate in any other way;

- a high proportion of read-only, noncritical transactions such as those found in decision support systems; and/or

- updates with a small effect on the overall characteristics of the data contained in the database (so their individual effects are relatively insignificant in the short term, thereby providing a window of opportunity to correct transient errors such as very large statistical or scientific databases).

Other environments that may be suitable for compensation include airline reservation systems, where the amount of tolerance in the system is quite high, or the banking industry, where overdrafts are often permitted on individual accounts, so small discrepancies may be acceptable, at least for short periods of time.

The remainder of this section discusses several transaction models and techniques that may be suitable for the multidatabase environment. Initially, the problem of formalizing transaction behaviors is discussed (Section 10.4.1), with particular attention paid to the most significant contribution in this area known as ACTA. Next, models that have been developed to meet the specific needs of multidatabase environments are covered. Most of these models have been based on a nested transaction model and are evolutionary steps beyond the traditional paradigms. Section 10.4.2 describes these models, with particular attention paid to the questions of how they relax the ACID properties and to what extent autonomy is violated. The systems considered include Sagas, ConTract, Split-Transactions, Flex transactions, S-Transactions, multilevel transactions, polytransactions, Epsilon transactions, and the object-oriented approaches. Other transaction models that may be suitable for the multidatabase transaction environment are described in Section 10.4.3. Most of these systems suffer from the requirement that the underlying local systems sacrifice a significant amount of their autonomy. This is not the "fault" of the models, since they were not designed for the multidatabase environment. They do, however, provide some interesting insights into the problems. Cooperative transactions are discussed as a representative sample. Finally, a brief discussion of the utility of transaction toolkits that support transaction management is provided. Although this is the most ambitious of all transaction modeling approaches because it is the most general, it is also the one that will prove the most useful if successful.

10.4.1   Formalizing Transaction Models

Consider the possible insights achieved if transactions could be formally specified using some well-understood, run-time-managed format. Such a specification would require some underlying notation that would most likely be canonical in nature. This would allow it to capture *all* of the behaviors of available transaction models but still be "executable" and trace the execution behaviors of transactions across different transaction models. Unfortunately, formally specifying transaction models so their execution is traceable has been extremely difficult and elusive. An obvious first step in achieving the goal of a run-time traceable execution would be to formally define and capture the various transaction models presented in the literature statically. This requires a classification mechanism for these transaction models and some organized mechanism for reasoning about each model. The leading candidate capable of providing such a specification is the ACTA [CR90] specification language. Although the contribution of ACTA is undeniable, its major disadvantage is that it is not executable and does not describe how nonhomogeneous data models interact. Therefore, it is primarily of value to the multidatabase researcher interested in understanding the nature of the various transaction models, but not in understanding how conflicting operations can be permitted to interoperate. The nature of ACTA is briefly described below.

ACTA

ACTA can specify how transactions affect each other and how they affect objects in the database. It has been used to formally specify atomic and nested transaction models in addition to capturing the behaviors of several nontraditional transaction environments, such as workflow models and cooperative work environments. ACTA can describe the behavior of transaction abortion and commitment, compensating transactions, and alternative and contingency transaction models. Early work with Sagas [CR90] demonstrated the utility of the ACTA classification scheme and its expressive ability.

10.4.2   MDBS-Specific Transaction Models

The transaction models reviewed in this section either were developed specifically to support multidatabases per se or have been deemed capable of supporting multidatabases even though they were not developed specifically for that purpose. Most of the models relax one or more of the ACID properties and require some specific alteration to the underlying system to ensure that it conforms to the model's behavior. Unfortunately, these ACID relaxations tend to violate traditional notions of correctness, while the conformance requirements, either implicitly or explicitly, require that autonomy be violated. The purpose of this section is not to judge the relative merit or need for a particular violation but only to indicate that it is required.

Sagas

Sagas [GMS87] were originally proposed to deal with the problems associated with *long-lived transactions*. Using the nomenclature introduced earlier, (global) transactions (GT_i) are decomposed into a set of (global) subtransactions $(GST_{i1}, GST_{i2}, \ldots, GST_{in})$ that perform some portion of the task. This permits the transactions to be executed at a smaller unit of granularity, so that once a portion of the transaction (namely, a subtransaction) is completed, its effects can be released to other waiting transactions. This can significantly increase concurrency, which is very important in a system that has long-lived transactions, particularly if the system uses a lock-based mechanism to support concurrency.

Sagas use an open nested transaction model, so a mechanism must exist to *compensate* the effects of committed subtransactions. Compensating transactions are defined for each of the subtransactions; for every GT_i composed of subtransactions $GST_{i1}, GST_{i2}, \ldots, GST_{in}$, there must exist corresponding compensating subtransactions $CGST_{i1}, CGST_{i2}, \ldots, CGST_{in}$. The subtransactions must be compensatable by invoking, at any point in the execution sequence, the corresponding compensating transaction so the transaction's entire effects can be erased by a sequence such as

$$GST_{i1}, \ GST_{i2}, \ldots, GST_{ij}. \ CGST_{ij}, \ldots, CGST_{i2}, CGST_{i1}$$

for any $j \leq n$. In the event that a transaction sequence is interrupted, the global transaction can resubmit the "failed" global subtransaction in the hope that the failure does not reoccur (called *forward recovery*) or execute the sequence of compensating transactions (*backward recovery*).

Sagas sacrifice the isolation property by revealing partial results of the global transaction before its commitment. As a consequence of revealing these partial results and another transaction possibly reading these partial results, another global transaction that read the effects may need to be subsequently compensated. Obviously, this leads to the possibility of *cascading compensation*, where all transactions that read from a now defunct transaction must be undone. Consistency may also be violated because of the interleaving of a global transaction's subtransactions, so great care must be taken to ensure that serializability is maintained.

Autonomy is not significantly violated by Sagas because each local database sees each of the subtransactions as an independent local transaction that is managed in any way chosen by the system. Consider the two types of transactions that may be submitted:

1. Global subtransactions: These are seen as local transactions, so if they execute completely and commit, the global level achieves its primary goal. If the transaction fails, the MDBMS must take some action, either forward or backward recovery, but no violation of autonomy occurs because the abortion decision is completely at the discretion of the LDBMS.

2. Compensating global subtransactions: These are seen as local transactions that execute completely and commit, thereby semantically *undo*ing a local transaction's effects or fails. In either case, the commitment decision of the compensating transaction and its execution are performed at the discretion of the LDBMS, so that no autonomy is violated.

The primary problem with Sagas is in the requirement to support compensation. Unfortunately, only transactions that can be compensated are candidates for this approach because some activities cannot be compensated (e.g., firing a missile or permitting the withdrawal of a large quantity of cash). For environments where compensation is possible, Sagas provide an interesting option for MDBSs because of the small impact they have on the LDBMSs' autonomy.

ConTract

Reuter [Reu89] described a model suitable for managing long-lived complex transactions that are not well supported by the traditional on-line transaction processing systems. A ConTract decomposes a global transaction (GT_i) into a sequence of steps (which we call global subtransactions $(\{GST_{ij}\})$) that are capable of defining how control must flow among themselves. *Forward recovery* in the model demands that if a transaction is interrupted or fails for some reason, it must be able to continue execution from the point at which the failure occurred. This recovery mechanism demands that state information be maintained during the execution of the transactions. An open nested structure is used whereby the partial results of subtransactions are made available to other transactions, so a compensating transaction mechanism is required.

As a direct result of the open nested structure, the problems described for Sagas persist in this model. Additionally, when ConTracts are applied to a multidatabase environment, a significant violation of local DBMS autonomy is required. The requirement that state information be maintained for each executing subtransaction must be met in two possible ways. First, the underlying LDBMSs could be changed to record the state information at each sequence, but this is clearly an unreasonable option given the nature of legacy systems and the need for DBMS vendors to produce efficient systems for local users. Second, a mechanism (such as that proposed by Barker and Özsu [BO91]) could be implemented to retrofit a visible two-phase commit. Unfortunately, this is also unacceptable because it requires a constant interruption of the executing systems so that state information could be saved. All of the state information would need to be communicated back to the MDBMS and logged because a site failure could lose information needed by the "global" system to facilitate "global" recovery.

The problem domains addressed by the ConTract model have some similarities with those of the MDBMS, but the autonomy consideration probably precludes its use. Two types of MDBS environments may be able to utilize ConTracts:

1. An environment in which all participating DBMSs can save state information locally.

2. An environment in which the global transactions can be decomposed into a set of global subtransactions and only a single global subtransaction is required at each participating LDBMS, and whose visible two-phase commit mechanism must communicate state information back to the MDBMS (to ensure recovery).

Both of these environments may eventually be realized, but they will not be true of all foreseeable MDBSs.

Split-Transactions

Split-Transactions have been developed to support so-called open-ended applications such as CAD/CAM, software design, or engineering type applications [KP92, PKH88]. These environments typically have long-running transactions that are dynamic and unpredictable, and may interact unpredictably with other similar transactions. This complex model supports diverse transaction environments such as computer-supported cooperative work (CSCW) or "knowbots" capable of changing their execution plans during their execution. Fortunately, the transactional aspects of the MDBS environment are not nearly as complicated to model.[3] From the viewpoint of the MDBS, the interesting contribution of this work is techniques that determine how and when to split global transactions into subtransactions. Rules are provided that describe the required behavior when a transaction (the GT) is split into two transactions (the original GT and a GST). These rules define how serialization must be enforced to ensure that database consistency is maintained. The model addresses the most difficult aspect of the problem because it attempts to determine how to serialize dynamically by inspecting the dynamically changing read and write sets of the GT and the GST. If these transaction behaviors can be determined a priori, or at compile time, it may be possible to have

---

[3] Other aspects of the MDBS environment may be very dynamic and unpredictable (e.g., consider the schema evolution problem in an MDBMS), but this problem is sufficiently complicated that most researchers make the reasonable assumption that the MDBMS and LDBMSs are static.

the MDBMS enforce a predetermined execution sequence without paying the price of the run-time serialization analysis. Unfortunately, work on compile-time transactional analysis is still in its infancy, and results have been slow to appear in the literature [GB94].

How Split-Transactions will affect autonomy has not yet been determined, because a full description of how they would be implemented on an MDBS has not yet appeared. An initial proposal [PKH88] suggests an open nested model approach be taken vis-á-vis the GST so its results would be visible to other currently executing transactions. However, the problems discussed above for other open models would also be encountered here. Finally, one of the model's claimed benefits is reduced isolation and the ability to perform adaptive recovery. Provided the user atomicity property is not considered essential, the ability to permit part of a transaction to commit without requiring other components is appealing in an MDBS. Consider the well-known travel plan GT, where the flight and hotel GSTs should be allowed to commit because they are an essential component of the GT and should not be blocked or aborted simply because the car rental GST was unsuccessful.

Flex Transactions

Elmagarmid et al. [ELLR90] and Leu [Leu91] describe a transaction model explicitly designed for managing the multidatabase environment. *Flex transactions* are transactions (GTs) that can be decomposed in a set of *functionally equivalent* subtransactions (GSTs), each with a specific task. The completion of all subtransactions is not essential for the "correct" completion of the global transaction, so GT atomicity is violated, but the GSTs remain atomic (a general requirement of the underlying LDBMSs). Fortunately, the Flex transaction model requires explicit descriptions of how atomicity will be violated. The atomicity violation must fit the dependencies defined in the model. Three dependencies have been defined:

1. Failure-dependencies: A GST_{i2} can only execute if another GST_{i1} has already executed and failed (i.e., $GST_{i1} < a_{i1} < GST_{i2}$). Although this example describes a failure dependency with respect to a single global transaction, GT_i, the full model does not restrict failure dependencies to a single "parent" Flex transaction.

2. Success-dependencies: A GST_{i2} can only execute if another GST_{i1} has already executed and succeeded (i.e., $GST_{i1} < c_{i1} < GST_{i2}$). As with failure-dependency, the full model does not restrict success-dependencies to a single GT.

3. External-dependencies: Those beyond the control of the transaction model per se. Constraints such as scheduling of transactions, system performance parameters, or cost functions are captured in the Flex model with these dependencies.

These dependencies are global integrity constraints that must be checked to ensure global consistency. The integrity constraints are implemented by the MDBMS. Transaction behavior can be specified using a type set that defines how transactions must be executed to conform to user desires. For example, a Flex transaction may be *compensatable* or *noncompensatable*.

Flex transactions are specifically designed for the MDBS environment, so they respect autonomy to the largest possible extent. Compensation enables an open nested model to be used if the application domain's consistency requirements are sufficiently relaxed. The model is implemented using Vienna Parallel Logic (VPL) language [KP91] when the correctness of a transaction mix can be shown to be consistent with the transaction specification. A complete implementation of the model illustrating how the specifications affect participating local systems is yet to appear in the literature.

S-Transactions

The primary goal of S-Transactions [VEH92] is to support the local DBMS's autonomy by ensuring the decisions made by the underlying LDBMSs are respected. An S-Transaction is a nested transaction in which the MDBMS-level transaction (GT_i) is decomposed into a set of global subtransactions $(\{GST_{i1}, GST_{i2}, \ldots, GST_{in}\})$ so that each GT_{ij} is executed in the way chosen by the LDBMSs. An interesting aspect of this model is that the precise structure and behavior of the GSTs is not known at the MDBMS level. This means that a GST can be submitted to an LDBMS, which can then execute the transaction by creating a set of other transactions to accomplish the same task. Further, it also assumes that the execution path from one invocation of GT_{ij} to the next is undefined. This means that a change to the underlying DBMS's way of implementing a GST submitted to it can occur without the knowledge of the MDBMS. Although this appears to be a fundamental requirement for autonomous interoperable MDBSs, it has been a very elusive property to capture. This approach also permits the LDBMSs to determine how reliability is implemented. Because control over the reliability rests with the LDBMS, it can determine how to recover from failures without intervention from the MDBMS.

Unfortunately, this approach means that global consistency is not "forced" on the local systems. Therefore, some technique must exist to back out of "incorrect" situations when the local system executes a GST that is globally inconsistent. This is enforced using compensating transactions, but because the execution of these is also at the discretion of the LDBMSs, it may not always be possible to force the compensation. Although S-Transactions may have the GSTs' implementation change from one invocation to another, the model assumes that the change is to a *semantically equivalent* version.

In summary, S-Transactions protect a large degree of the LDBMSs' autonomy but potentially sacrifice global consistency if compensation is unable to correct inconsistent states. The model also assumes that there is no need for a global commit procedure because the behavior of the subtransactions defines the behavior of the global transactions. In other words, if the GST commits and then the GT does, and if a GST fails, compensation is required to recover to a consistent state. An interesting result of this model is that there is no need to support a visible two-phase commit.

Multilevel Transactions

Transaction commutativity is a powerful modeling notion because whenever two transactions *commute*, their execution sequence does not have to be captured in a history's partial order. Commutativity is an extremely powerful tool in an MDBS environment because whenever two GSTs commute, they can be submitted to an LDBMS and serialized in either order without affecting global correctness. Consider the following simple example: Given are two global transactions (GT_i, GT_j) and four global subtransactions $(GST_{i1}^1, GST_{j1}^1, GST_{i2}^2, GST_{j2}^2)$. If nothing is known about the commutativity of the GSTs, it is impossible to submit GST_{i1}^1 and GST_{j1}^1 to $LDBMS^1$ at the same time that GST_{i2}^2 and GST_{j2}^2 are submitted to $LDBMS^2$ because the LDBMSs may serialize $GST_{i1}^1 < GST_{j1}^2$ at $LDBMS^1$ while $GST_{j2}^2 < GST_{i2}^2$ occurs at $LDBMS^2$. However, if all of these GSTs are known to commute, they can be submitted concurrently without concern about the autonomous decisions made by the LDBMSs.

Multilevel transactions [Wei91] explicitly capture how subtransactions commute using a hierarchy that is more general than the one needed for the MDBS environment described in Figure 10.1. A series of transaction levels are defined so that each lower level "implements" the task as a set of operations requested by higher levels. Commutativity of the lower level transactions is defined, but the higher level transactions appear to execute consistently (possibly even supporting the ACID properties).

Although the primary goal of multilevel transactions is to increase concurrency in traditional DBMS environments, the applicability of the model to MDBSs is apparent. The model is particularly attractive because it offers a high degree of autonomy to the underlying DBMS and provides a consistent global view of the MDBS. Applying the multilevel transaction model to the MDBS environment also offers some unique challenges. This model's most difficult problem is defining the commutativity of the subtransactions. If techniques can be found to define these commutativity relationships in an "automated" way, this model holds great promise as a solution to many MDBS transaction environments.

Polytransactions

One of the most important questions facing the multidatabase research community is how to define techniques that will enforce global integrity constraints. For example, if the value of a data item must be related in some specific way to another in a different database, it is extremely difficult to enforce a constraint between them without violating LDBMSs' autonomy. Polytrans-actions [SRK92] address the issue of global or distributed integrity constraints, but they were not designed to support an autonomous environment. Several types of constraints are defined using dependency predicates capable of speci-fying temporal consistency rules (e.g., a data item at one site must be updated within one day of a change at another) or data state consistency (e.g., an em-ployee's salary must be updated immediately to reflect a "title" change). The fundamental goal of the model is to make explicit how global integrity is to be managed by providing a mechanism to define the constraints and an apparently distributed system component to enforce those constraints.

The polytransaction model is particularly interesting in the MDBS envi-ronment because it explicitly attempts to support global integrity constraints using an inherent component of the MDBMS. Typically, this is supported by defining global transactions so that additional subtransactions are added to the set of global subtransactions that are executed to enforce the integrity constraints. These must be defined by the global users when they create their global transactions, and the commitment of the GT is dependent on the success-ful execution of all subtransactions. This means that if the integrity enforcing GST fails, so does the rest of the GT. Polytransactions would relieve the global user of the responsibility of writing the integrity-enforcing GST and also permit GTs that would otherwise fail to commit.

Successful application of this model to MDBS environments requires that LDBMS autonomy be preserved. Two techniques may prove useful:

- To define constraints that are relaxed to the extent that they can be enforced after the execution of the global transaction. Constraints can be defined that require the system to achieve immediate consistency, become consistent within a specified time period, or (in an extremely relaxed scenario) achieve consistency eventually.

- To develop techniques that permit the MDBS to appear to "force" new values into the LDBMS. For example, if one of the LDBMSs is considered the "home" site for a particular data item and its value is considered the correct one, then updating at the other sites containing a copy may be considered adequate for some applications.

Neither of these approaches is applicable in every situation, but they do describe many application environments being considered for MDBSs.

Epsilon Transactions

Epsilon serializability [PC93] is proposed as a solution to various problems facing multidatabase transaction management. First, it defines a mechanism for reasoning about how replicas distributed across a multidatabase system can diverge with respect to each other before their values are considered in-consistent. This addresses the global integrity constraint problem by defining "deltas." Second, Epsilon serializability can be used to commit a transaction that may need to be aborted if an underlying system is down. For example, if the delta is sufficiently large that an integrity constraint does not need to be enforced, it would be possible to permit the transaction to commit despite possible inconsistencies. Finally, Epsilon serializability can be used to define how a system recovers from failures or other inconsistencies by describing when two copies of a data value are sufficiently "close" to be acceptable.

Epsilon transaction relaxes several of the ACID properties. Atomicity may be relaxed as one part of a GT does execute because the "epsilon" definition does not require its commitment. Consistency is violated by definition because the primary goal is to define a relaxed form of consistency. Isolation may or may not be violated because partial results of an executing transaction may be made visible if one of a GT's GSTs commits before another, but this depends upon the correctness specified by the Epsilon values. Epsilon serializability does provide significant support for autonomy of local systems during their execution. It is somewhat debatable whether autonomy is being protected in general, since the LDBMSs probably do not have complete control over the consistency of all their data. However, from each DBMS's perspective, the data in its database is consistent.

Unfortunately, not all data can be described using "epsilons," so the technique may not be applicable to all MDBS application domains. Applying this model may require that it coexist with a hybrid set of other transaction models, so users that require a stronger form of consistency can be supported.

Object-Oriented Approaches

Applying object orientation to the multidatabase environment has been an active area of research since the inception of the object-oriented approach. The object model offers several interesting features that should make it an excellent technology to support interoperability. Since this chapter focuses on transaction models, we will turn our attention to one specific group's efforts, namely, the Distributed Object Management (DOM) model from GTE Laboratories [BOH+92]. The DOM transaction model was designed to exploit object orientation when integrating autonomous systems (database and nondatabase).

The model supports open and closed nesting, and compensation and contingency transactions, while also providing a notion of the vital and nonvital transactions. This provides an extremely rich environment within which to investigate MDBS transaction problems and is sufficiently verbose to address the multiple types of systems that may wish to participate in the MDBS. Although this rich set of transaction types is valuable when modeling various LDBMS environments, it permits the violation of every one of the ACID properties. Atomicity may be violated with a nonvital transaction, consistency and isolation may be violated by the open nesting, and durability may be violated by compensation. Support for LDBMS autonomy is difficult to ascertain because the model is so diverse that the integration of the underlying systems can occur in many ways, some of which may violate autonomy.

10.4.3 Adapting Other Transaction Models to the MDBS

Several other models may be of value in an MDBS environment. This section briefly reviews two other transaction models, but the reader should note that these were not developed for an MDBS environment, nor have they necessarily been suggested as a suitable approach. They are mentioned because each adds a slightly different and potentially interesting philosophy.

Cooperative Transactions

Cooperative transaction models are those that support the cooperative applications characterized by autonomous or semiautonomous units of work that either must or should work together to accomplish a common goal. Artificial intelligence (AI) applications such as Distributed AI (DAI) or multiagents are systems that benefit from such cooperation. Nodine and Zdonik [NZ84] suggest a *transaction hierarchy* that describes and captures the behavior of such environments. The particularly interesting aspect (from the viewpoint of the MDBS) is that the user, rather than the system, defines correctness. This flexibility could be a powerful feature of an MDBS transaction model because each global transaction would then be able to impose its own notion of correctness on the underlying DBMSs. The primary difficulty with this approach is that each GST in the MDBS executes under the LDBMS's control, and it is unlikely it will relinquish that control or efficiently permit communication with other subtransactions involved in the cooperative hierarchy.

MDBS Transaction Toolkits

Transaction toolkits were designed to permit subtransactions with conflicting requirements to coexist on the same system. If it were possible to develop a toolkit capable of capturing several different models with a well-understood formalism, its usefulness in the MDBS environment would be significant. Unland and Schlageter [US91] describe how subtransactions on the same transaction tree execute consistently on a single database. Their work is then extended to define how heterogeneous requirements can be supported using a set of elemental "transaction types."

Extending this work so it clearly describes transaction interleaving when each transaction has a different notion of correctness would make the work directly applicable to an MDBS environment. Unfortunately, the successful realization of such a system will require a thorough understanding of how to specify correctness and how various ideas of correctness affect one another. This work will have a tremendous impact on how to apply solutions to the general MDBS transaction environment, but how it affects the autonomy of underlying DBMSs has not been addressed.

10.5
Summary

This chapter has surveyed several transaction models, with particular attention paid to how they can be applied to a multidatabase environment. The models discussed include those specifically designed for an MDBS environment, those that have been suggested as being applicable to such an environment, and those that may have an impact at some time in the future. Unfortunately, no single model seems capable of addressing all the needs of every MDBS transaction environment. Most of the proposed models to date have sacrificed some autonomy (this is likely to be required), and most have relaxed some or all of the ACID properties (this too may be required). Determining precisely which property or properties to sacrifice and how much autonomy to relinquish will be the subject of ongoing debate for some time to come and may have to be resolved on a case-by-case basis.

Several technical challenges are raised in this chapter, and no attempt has been made to provide answers to the problems. The goal of the chapter has been to motivate thought, frame the problem, and inspire more research into these unique and challenging environments.

Bibliography

[Bar93]   K. Barker. Quantification of autonomy on multidatabase systems. *The Journal of System Integration* 1-26, 1993.

[BHG87]   P. Bernstein, V. Hadzilacos, and N. Goodman. *Concurrency Control and Recovery in Database Systems.* Reading, MA: Addison-Wesley, 1987.

[BO91]   K. Barker and M. T. Özsu. Reliable transaction execution in multidatabase systems. In *Proceedings of the First International Workshop on Interoperability in Multidatabase Systems (IMS'91)*, pages 344–347, April 1991.

[BOH+92]   A. Buchmann, M. T. Özsu, M. Hornick, D. Georgakopoulos, and F. A. Manola. A transaction model for active distributed object systems. In A. K. Elmagarmid, editor, *Database Transaction Models for Advanced Applications*, pages 123–158. San Mateo, CA: Morgan Kaufmann, 1992.

[CR90]   P. K. Chrysanthis and K. Ramamritham. ACTA: A framework for specifying and reasoning about transaction structure and behavior. In *Proceedings of the ACM-SIGMOD International Conference on Management of Data*, pages 194–203, 1990.

[ELLR90]   A. K. Elmagarmid, Y. Leu, W. Litwin, and M. Rusinkiewicz. A multidatabase transaction model for InterBase. In *Proceedings of the 16th International Conference on VLDB*, pages 507–518, 1990.

[Elm92]   A. Elmagarmid, editor. *Database Transaction Models for Advanced Applications*. San Mateo, CA: Morgan Kaufmann, 1992.

[GB94]   P. C. J. Graham and K. Barker. Effective optimistic concurrency control in multiversion object bases. In *Proceedings of the International Symposium on Object-Oriented Methodologies and Systems*, pages 313–328, September 1994.

[GL84]   V. D. Gligor and G. L. Luckenbaugh. Interconnecting heterogeneous database management systems. *Computer* 17(1):33–43, January 1984.

[GMS87]   H. Garcia-Molina and K. Salem. SAGAs. In *Proceedings of the ACM Conference on Management of Data (SIGMOD)*, pages 249–259, 1987.

[GPZ85]   V. D. Gligor and R. Popescu-Zeltin. Concurrency control issues in distributed heterogeneous database management systems. In F. Schreiber and W. Litwin, editors, *Distributed Data Sharing Systems*. New York: Elsevier Science, 1985.

[GR93]   J. Gray and A. Reuter. *Transaction Processing: Concepts and Techniques*. San Francisco: Morgan Kaufmann, 1993.

[Gra78]   J. N. Gray. Notes on database operating systems. In R. Bayer, R. M. Graham, and G. Seegmuller, editors, *Operating Systems: An Advanced Course*, volume 60, pages 394–481. New York: Springer-Verlag, 1978.

[KP91]   E. Kühn and F. Puntigam. *The VPL Vienna Parallel Logic Language*. Technical report TR-185-91-1. Vienna: University of Technology, Institute of Computer Language, January 1991.

[KP92]   G. Kaiser and C. Pu. Dynamic restructuring of transactions. In A. K. Elmagarmid, editor, *Database Transaction Models for*

Advanced Applications, pages 265–295. San Mateo, CA: Morgan Kaufmann, 1992.

[Leu91]   Y. Leu.   Composing multidatabase applications using flex transactions. *IEEE Data Engineering Bulletin* 14(1), March 1991.

[Lit86]   W. Litwin. A multidatabase interoperability. *IEEE Computer* 19(12):10–18, December 1986.

[Mos85]   J. E. B. Moss. *Nested Transactions: An Approach to Reliable Distributed Computing.* Cambridge, MA: MIT Press, 1985.

[NZ84]   M. Nodine and S. Zdonik. Cooperative transaction hierarchies: A transaction model to support design applications. In *Proceedings of the International Conference on Very Large Data Bases*, pages 83–94, 1984.

[Pap86]   C. Papadimitriou. *The Theory of Database Concurrency Control.* Rockville, MD: Computer Science Press, 1986.

[PC93]   C. Pu and S.-W. Chen. ACID properties need fast relief: Relaxing consistency using epsilon serializability. In *Proceedings of the Fifth International Workshop on High Performance Transaction Systems*, September 1993.

[PKH88]   C. Pu, G. Kaiser, and N. Hutchinson. Split-transactions for open-ended activities. In *Proceedings of the 14th VLDB Conference*, pages 26–37, 1988.

[Reu89]   A. Reuter. Contract: A means for extending control beyond transaction boundaries. In *Proceedings of the Third International Workshop on High Performance Transaction Systems*, September 1989.

[SRK92]   A. P. Sheth, M. Rusinkiewicz, and G. Karabatis. Using polytransactions to manage interdependent data. In A. K. Elmagarmid, editor, *Database Transaction Models for Advanced Applications*, pages 555–581. San Mateo, CA: Morgan Kaufmann, 1992.

[US91]   R. Unland and G. Schlageter. A flexible and adaptable tool kit approach for transaction management in non-standard database systems. *IEEE Data Engineering Bulletin*, March 1991.

[VEH92]   J. Veijalainen, F. Eliassen, and B. Holtkamp. The S-transaction model. In A. K. Elmagarmid, editor, *Transaction Management for Advanced Database Applications*, pages 467–513. San Mateo, CA: Morgan Kaufmann, 1992.

[Wei91]   G. Weikum.   Principles and realization strategies of multi-level transaction management. *ACM Transactions on Database Systems* 16(1):132–180, March 1991.

11

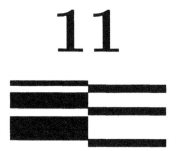

Transaction-Based Recovery

Jari Veijalainen
Antoni Wolski

Introduction

For decades, organizations have been maintaining their vital data using database systems. Because the data is a crucial information resource, it is no surprise that the failure resiliency techniques, in the form of the database recovery, have always been a major issue. The same applies to multidatabase systems (MDBSs).

The purpose of database recovery is to ensure that a database contains (and exposes) correct data, although various failures might have happened. This is achieved by guaranteeing that a transaction is either run to a successful (committed) completion and the data updated by it is made persistent, or it is run to an unsuccessful (aborted) completion and the persistent data modified by it is restored to a suitable old value, which nullifies the effects of the transaction.

From the application point of view, atomicity, isolation, and durability are provided by the database system, and the only commands needed to achieve this are the transactional ones (Begin, Commit, Abort) offered at the database interface. With them, the demarcation of each transaction (i.e., the information about where it starts and ends) can be conveyed to the database system.

An understanding of two areas, described below [HR83], is essential to an understanding of what we mean by database recovery in general.

- First, we need to know what *types of failures* a system is supposed to deal with. With respect to failure types, a multidatabase system is essentially similar to any distributed database. An important difference is that component systems of an MDBS may reflect various aspects of local autonomy. As a result, an action considered legal by a component system (e.g., aborting any locally visible transaction) may be regarded as a failure by the MDBS.

- The second area deals with *correctness criteria* for histories and data to be maintained despite the failures. In a general-purpose system, it is convenient to use transaction-based correctness criteria because transaction is an application-independent concept. A recovery approach is *transaction based* if it aims at maintaining the ACID properties [GR93] in the presence of failures. In an MDBS, some of the ACID properties (typically the atomicity and/or serializability, sometimes also consistency) may be relaxed and new correctness criteria for interleaved executions proposed. One can then speak of *generalized ACID properties* [VWP+97] that the transactions should obey.

  View serializability [BHG87, Pap86] can be seen as an ultimate correctness criterion that guarantees any semantics to be preserved in the database in spite of concurrent access to data. Therefore, it should also be maintained during recovery. Unfortunately, in this environment it is hard to achieve, as we will see.

The recovery issues in homogeneous systems are rather well understood, and they have been thoroughly discussed in the literature, e.g., [HR83, CP84, GR93]. Later in the chapter, we present a general framework for dealing with recovery in an MDBS. The new problems encountered in an MDBS are rooted in the local autonomy of participating systems. We show that it is impossible to implement an MDBS and preserve the full correctness (i.e., the overall view serializability) among fully autonomous systems, in a general case. The possible solutions must incorporate one or several of the following characteristics.

- *Restrictions on local autonomy:* The restrictions may apply to the set of local transactions running on a local system, their form, their scheduling, the degree of local concurrency, concurrent access to local data by different classes of transactions, etc. Design autonomy [Vei90] may be restricted by forcing the local system to externalize control data or internal functioning of certain mechanisms (e.g., the concurrency control mechanism) or forcing changes into the local database schemes (cf. ticket counters in [GRS91]). The communication autonomy [Vei90] may be restricted as well.

- *Restrictions on global transactions:* Global transactions may be restricted in terms of concurrency, internal dependencies, structure, etc. This way, reasonable correctness criteria may be met despite the preservation of local autonomy.

- *Relaxed correctness of histories:* When the requirement of overall view serializable executions is relaxed, the autonomy (including the local correctness criteria) may be preserved, and the global transactions need not be restricted. The bad news is that an arbitrary application semantics cannot be guaranteed anymore by the MDBS [Pap86].

We proceed as follows: Section 11.1 includes an architecture model, the basic assumptions, and the discussion of failures addressed during MDBS recovery. The proposed Multidatabase Transaction Model is presented in Section 11.2. Section 11.3 deals with known approaches to recovery in an MDBS, and the results are summarized in Section 11.4

11.1
Basic Concepts

In this section, we discuss architectural issues and basic concepts in MDBS recovery.

11.1.1 Architecture

We are assuming a generalized multidatabase transaction processing architecture shown in Figure 11.1. It is deduced from the assumption that the

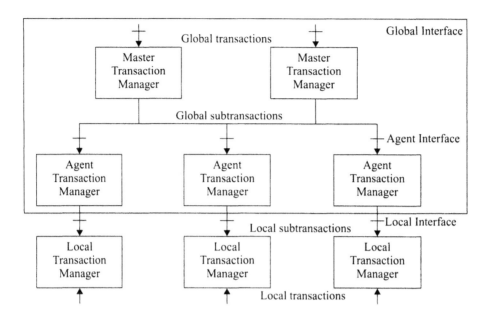

FIGURE 11.1
A generalized architecture of a Multidatabase Transaction Manager.

local systems are preexisting, autonomous, and heterogeneous. The global architecture thus is an addition on top of a set of preexisting databases. The boxes in Figure 11.1 represent program modules that are independent of each other in terms of address space and control state. Each module may execute concurrent *commands* (requests) submitted by another entity. The set of acceptable commands is called an *interface* of the module. All the interfaces in the model are synchronous in the sense that the caller regains control only after the command has been executed and a response of some kind has been returned.

A close implementation analogy of a module is a multithreaded Unix process using an interprocess communication mechanism. However, we do not assume any specific implementation of the presented architecture.

The Multidatabase Transaction Manager (MTM) comprises Master Transaction Managers (Masters for short) and Agent Transaction Managers (Agents for short). Each Agent is associated with one and only one Local Transaction Manager (LTM) participating in an MDBS. The Masters provide the applications with the global transactional service at the Global Interface (GI), having the following characteristics:

- *Standard DML:* The interface includes high-level data manipulation language commands of a given data model. Any data model is acceptable as long as the corresponding database commands (e.g., SQL commands Select, Update, Insert, and Delete, for the relational model) are transformable (by each LTM) to a sequence of Read and Write operations performed on elementary database objects.

- *Standard transactional commands:* The transaction management commands are Begin (may be implicit), Commit, and Abort. We call this interface *standard* because it conforms with the existing standards (e.g., the SQL standard [II92]) and the general practice in the database field.

- *LTM-denotation:* Each database manipulation command is explicitly related to a given LTM (i.e., we do not deal with the issues of distribution transparency).

A *global transaction* is specified, at GI, as a sequence of database commands, terminated with a Commit or an Abort.

We deal with neither model conversions nor data and command translations needed in reality, in a heterogeneous database system. We concentrate on purely transactional aspects of multidatabase system operation and assume a DML command carries the same semantics throughout the various interfaces until it becomes decomposed in an LTM.

In a general case, the global transactions are dynamic in the sense that not all the commands of a transaction are known a priori to the system. Aside from ordering, no dependencies among the commands of a global transaction are known. Note that in this model a transaction program is run outside the MTM, and the MTM cannot control it other than responding to the GI commands.

The Master decomposes global transactions into *global subtransactions* (at most one per Agent), submits the corresponding commands to the Agents, and returns the results to the application. Upon receiving the global Commit, the Master uses a commit protocol to perform the required global commit processing involving the Agents participating in the transaction.

Typical variations of the functionality of the above assumptions include "enriching" the interface by allowing an application to

- pass the Master additional information on the dependencies among the database commands,

- predefine the commands before the execution (canned transactions),

- gain control of the transaction program or part of it (e.g., to restart).

A global subtransaction is expressed as a sequence of commands performed at the Agent Interface (AI). We assume, for the moment, that there is at most one global subtransaction per global transaction at any Agent.

A global commitment protocol is used between the Master and the Agents. A special case of such a protocol is an *atomic commitment protocol* ensuring, essentially, that

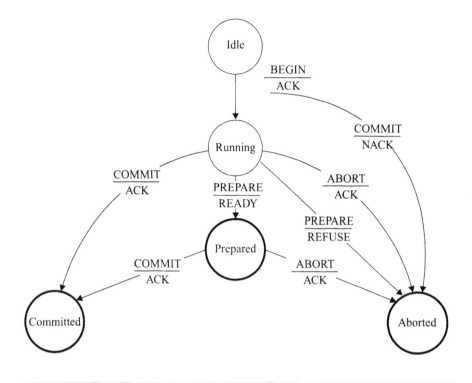

FIGURE 11.2
States of global subtransaction maintained by the Agent Manager obeying the
two-phase commit protocol.

- the completeness predicate yields true; i.e., a transaction is either committed or rolled back at all participating systems;

- the commitment decision is irreversible.

The only atomic commitment protocol considered in this chapter is the
two-phase commit protocol [II90], 2PC for short. Other applicable commitment
protocols are discussed in the literature, e.g., in [TA94].
The Agent exposes the global subtransaction states required by the commit protocol. The Agent states for the 2PC protocol are shown in Figure 11.2.
The states depicted as bold circles are *recoverable states*, meaning they should
be maintained in the presence of failures in order for the recovery protocol (e.g.,
the RESTART protocol of [II90] or the Cooperative Termination Protocol of
[BHG87]) to work. The state transitions in Figure 11.2 are annotated with the
message type causing the transition and the response message type generated
when the new state is reached.

Note that while in the *running* state, the Agent has the execution autonomy to the extent that it can accept or reject any incoming message. On the other hand, execution autonomy in the *prepared* state is restricted with respect to COMMIT and ABORT messages, as any of them has to be performed. Still, the Agent can freely decide when to issue the local Commit or Abort command. Thus, it can enforce certain commitment ordering, if necessary.

A command at the Agent Interface (AI) may be expressed by protocol message pairs. For example, the Prepare command corresponds to the PREPARE message and either READY or REFUSE message. Other assumptions about the AI are the following:

- *Standard DML:* The database manipulation commands are the same as at the GI.

- *Transaction commands with externalized prepare:* The transaction management commands are Begin, Commit and Abort, and Prepare, if 2PC is used.

Some variations are as follows:

- *No Agents:* When no atomic commitment protocol is used, or the prepared state is externalized by the LTM, there is no need for any Agent computation in terms of transaction management.

- *Transaction-Specific Agent:* In some methods, the Agent needs to have the knowledge of only one global subtransaction at a time.

An Agent interacts with the corresponding LTM. It translates global subtransactions into local subtransactions performed by the LTM. A *local subtransaction* is a series of operations performed at the Local Interface (LI) and handled as one transaction from the LTM's point of view. Here, we deal with two distinct cases [Vei93]:

- *SSS:* Single local subtransaction per global subtransaction per LTM. From the point of view of the global recovery, this situation means that whatever is needed from the LTM, it can be done within one local subtransaction. It also means that the Agent representing the global level can dictate the local subtransaction borders. A sufficient condition for this is that the LTM supports the 2PC protocol. The Agent states of Figure 11.2 are then supported within the LTM, and the global subtransaction is directly mapped to the one and only local subtransaction.

- *MSS:* Multiple local subtransactions per global subtransaction per site. This is the case if the LTM unilaterally sets the local transaction state and demarcation in a way that the Agent cannot perform global recovery within one local subtransaction. That is, the LTM either aborts the local subtransaction or commits it irrespective of the global decision. This necessitates instantiation of a new local subtransaction to perform the global recovery. From an architectural point of view, the Agent must simulate the prepared state as if the original local subtransaction would still be alive.

In a failure-free operation, there is only one local subtransaction per global subtransaction. When the LTM aborts a local subtransaction, the Agent may (1) abort the corresponding global transaction if the global subtransaction is in the running state or (2) regenerate all or part of the commands of the original local subtransaction as a new local subtransaction, to the LTM. In the latter case, the global subtransaction results in more than one local subtransaction. We assume the LTM treats each local subtransaction independently; i.e., it considers the transaction borders in a similar way as in the case of local transactions.

A *local transaction* is a transaction submitted directly to the LTM through the LI. The MTM has no direct knowledge of local transactions. All the local subtransactions and the local transactions are treated the same way by the LTM (we shall denote all the transactions seen at the LI as the local (sub)transactions).

An LTM exposes several aspects of local autonomy [EV87] with respect to a designer and user of the MDBS. The (design) D-autonomy implies that the LI interface cannot be modified nor its implementation changed to suit the needs of the MDBS. The (execution) E-autonomy forces the MDBS designer to assume the LTM may schedule the local (sub)transactions irrespectively of the desires of the MDBS, and it may unilaterally abort a local (sub)transaction at any time. In some cases, the LTM could also unilaterally commit the local subtransaction.

The main assumptions about the LI are the following:

- *No touch:* No modifications of the LTM are allowed.

- *Standard DML:* The database manipulation commands are the same as at the GI and AI. Notice that we do not exclude DML commands that can be used to invoke stored procedures or even application programs at the (server) site. We only require that the interfaces have the same DML capabilities.

- *Standard transactional commands* (as in case of GI): We call such an LTM *single phased.*

- *Rollback recovery (RR):* If a local (sub)transaction is aborted, the LTM restores the concrete before-images for all data items affected by the transaction.

- *Deterministic decomposition:* The LTM transforms the high-level database manipulation commands O^i into a sequence of elementary commands

R and W. A time-independent deterministic decomposition function (DDF) $D(O^i, S^i)$ is defined over the set of all DML commands O^i applicable at i^{th} database, and set of concrete[1] database states S^i of the ith database.

- *Trustworthiness (TW):* After a fixed number of resubmissions, any global subtransaction that should be committed can be committed; if a global subtransaction is to be aborted using a compensating local subtransaction that nullifies the effects of the global subtransaction, the compensating local subtransaction will commit after a fixed number of submissions.

The local (sub)transactions are eventually decomposed into elementary commands (Read and Write) issued at an imaginary Elementary Interface (EI) for the purpose of performing an access to the local database.

Some variations are as follows:

- The LTM externalizes the prepared state. This reduces the model to the SSS case, as the Agent does not need to simulate (and recover) the prepared state. We call such an LTM *two-phased*.

- The LTM is replaced with a transactionless data resource (such as a file system or a mail server). In this case, the Agent has to take the responsibility for preserving as much of the transactional properties of a global subtransaction as is possible in the case.

An MDBS is, typically, a distributed system. Thus, there is a notion of a (physical computer) site. We do not assume any fixed mapping of modules to sites. Whenever the issue becomes relevant, e.g., when dealing with site failures, we assume an Agent is at the same Participating Site as the corresponding LTM, and the Master is at a Master Site, which is a different site than any site participating in a transaction.

11.1.2   Failure Types

We expect the transaction properties to be preserved in the presence of various failures. For the system model assumed, we propose to discuss the following failure types:

- *UA:* Unilateral abort of a local subtransaction by an LTM. The LTM may abort the local subtransaction at any time due to a general transaction paradigm ("aborting a transaction does not harm"). Some authors deny that the failure may occur after the DML commands have been executed. However, such a behavior was observed in reality, in a commercial product [VW92b].

---

[1]For concrete/abstract states, see [MGG86] or [Vei90].

- *UC:* Unilateral commit. The LTM may commit the local subtransaction before the global commit or abort has been issued at the Master Transaction Manager.

- *LSF:* LTM software failure resulting in the termination of the LTM activity. All the uncommitted local (sub)transactions are automatically rolled back.

- *ASF:* Agent software failure. A software failure resulting in the loss of the volatile data of that component of the MTM.

- *PCF:* Participating (computer) Site failure. A total system failure (crash) at a Participating Site, resulting in the loss of all volatile data.

- *MCF:* Master (computer) Site failure. A system failure at a Master Site. A failure of the Master alone has a similar effect, because it is the only component of the transaction management system at the site.

- *COMF:* Communications failures such as message corruption or loss, loss of message sequence, or loss of connection.

We consider the failure types UA, UC, LSF, ASF, and PCF as being within the scope of this work. In case of software and site failures, we also assume the recovery may be started promptly (fail-stop) after the failure occurred.

Master Site failures and long-term failures of other components (including the network) belong to the realm of termination protocols, and we shall not discuss them here. Similarly, short-term communications failures are within the scope of protocol recovery, in general. We assume the network guarantees that the messages are not lost, corrupted, or out of order.

11.1.3 Basic Recovery Techniques for Heterogeneous Autonomous Databases

The (failure) atomicity is a primary property of typical transactions. The atomicity of global transactions is endangered by any of the failures mentioned. For example, if the Agent maintains a recoverable state of a global subtransaction, required by the commit protocol (e.g., the prepared state in the 2PC protocol), and a UA or LCF occurs, the corresponding local subtransaction is rolled back by the LTM automatically.

In transaction processing, in general, there are two main approaches to maintaining atomicity in the presence of failures:

- *Forward recovery:* The transaction is completed successfully despite the failure. In our case, this means a committed global transaction has, at every site where it has an original local subtransaction, exactly one committed local subtransaction.

- *Backward recovery:* The completion is achieved by continuing the transaction into an unsuccessful (aborted) completion. In our case, this means that the global transaction is aborted and all the local subtransactions are locally aborted (or compensated, see Section 11.3). The approach is *failure-exposing* in the sense that the application is notified about the failure.

The following remedies have been proposed for recovery of global transactions in an MDBS (mainly after [BGMS92]):

1. Redo (forward). A redo local subtransaction is executed. It consists of all the commands changing the database state. For example, in the R-W model [BHG87, VWP$^+$97], the Write commands are re-executed and the Read commands are not. The problem with this approach is that it usually contradicts the no-touch principle mentioned earlier, as the commercial database systems do not allow their internal logging mechanisms to be used in such a way that the W-operations could be resubmitted from the internal log or exposed at the LI in any way.

2. Resubmit (forward). A local subtransaction consisting of all the commands of the original subtransaction is executed [WV91]. This is in concert with the no-touch principle, as it only concerns the functionality of the agent.

3. Retry (forward). Execute a transaction program corresponding to the failed subtransaction. This approach requires that global transaction programs are decomposed into global procedures [AGMS87] executing at Participating Sites.

4. Compensate (backward). Compensating transactions are executed at sites that had not failed in order to remove the effects of a partially executed global transaction. Abort commands issued at the LI can be used to cause this effect, in case the original local subtransaction had not been committed locally. Had the local commit been issued already, a semantically meaningful compensating local subtransaction has to be generated or—if predefined—invoked by the Agent.

A recovery mechanism usually needs some input data. The data is computed during the execution of the global transactions, especially during the commit processing initialized by the global Commit. If the data is to be used after a software failure of a system component, or a site failure, it has to be in a persistent storage, usually called the *log*.

Dealing with subtransaction failures (UA and UC) does not require a persistent log because the program state of all the components of the MTM is preserved. The Agent may maintain a volatile log for recovery purposes.

In the case of the LTM failure, the LTM uses its own internal (D-autonomy) log to do local recovery, i.e., to roll back local (sub)transactions. The Agent preserves its state and it may use the volatile log. On the other hand, the Agent failures and Participating Site failures force the Agent to use a persistent log.

Recovery from subtransaction failures causes most problems because of the presence of local transactions in the system—as will be shown later in the chapter. Also, the Agent failure causes similar difficulties. The LTM failure is simpler to deal with because the local transactions cannot run. Similar to this is the Participating Site failure.

From now on, we shall concentrate on dealing with subtransaction failures (UA and UC) and Participating Site failures (PCF). The ways to deal with the other two failure types of interest (ASF and LSF) can be derived from the presented methods.

11.1.4   Dealing with Transactionless Data Servers

A variation of the architecture is possible where, in place of an LTM, a transactionless resource is used. Examples of such resources are mail servers, file and document servers, World Wide Web servers, and information retrieval systems. Such data servers are characterized by the fact that they expose a different interface than the one defined for the LTM, and they do not offer any transactional commands; consequently, they are not equipped with any internal recovery mechanism. The difficulty of the recovery problem depends on whether they are used, in the multidatabase environment, as read-only or read-write data servers.

- *Transactionless read-only data servers:* In this case, the lack of recovery capabilities does no harm because no local data recovery needs to be performed. The only requirement (from the failure-free consistency point of view) is that the server guarantees a snapshot view of data, which may be achieved by way of locking, e.g., in a file server. Because of lack of the transaction support, the Agent has to enforce the snapshot view, e.g., by reserving the resources for the time of the transaction. A typical 2PC read-only optimization [SBCM95] may be used, whereby the Agent releases the resources at the receipt of the PREPARE message.

- *Read-write data servers:* Such servers are not intended to support transactions; therefore, in order to guarantee the global recovery, some other part of the system (e.g., the Agent) has to take the responsibilities of the LTM. In a general case, this is impossible because the data server may lack the necessary interfaces. It may be possible in specific cases, with a limited set of data server commands allowed, and by enabling the Agent to perform the necessary forward/backward recovery in the server.

11.1.5   Comparing Recovery Techniques

When comparing various commitment and recovery methods, one needs some criteria for assessing how "good" they are. We propose the following criteria:

- *Restrictiveness:* This is a (so far) intuitive measure telling, relatively, what portion of all transactions executable in a failure-free environment is rejected or delayed because of the applied method. For example, a method is highly restrictive if it allows only one global transaction to execute at a time in an MDBS. In the literature, there are some measures for the restrictiveness of diverse concurrency control algorithms. These are usually based on the set of histories the algorithms allow [Pap86]. If there is a proper inclusion relationship among the (R-W) histories they allow, say, CCA1 allows all the histories that CCA2 allows and more, then CCA1 is less restrictive than CCA2.

  This idea could be used as a starting point in defining the restrictiveness of different recovery methods. It could be based on the inclusion relationships between sets of histories allowed in the failure-free situation. Unfortunately, no exact measures to assess the method's restrictiveness formally have been presented so far. In any case, it is clear that if a method is too restrictive, it has little practical potential.

- *Centralization:* If the algorithms of the MTM include a single critical section, the MTM is said to be *centralized*. In such a case, there is only one Master entity. On the other hand, for example, a basic 2PC-based commitment method is decentralized because there may be more than one autonomous 2PC Coordinator-Masters in the system. A centralized method is considered inferior because of possible bottlenecks and introduction of a single point of failure.

- *Correctness level:* Each method preserves a certain correctness criteria. We consider the view serializability [BHG87] that encompasses all global and local transactions the highest and best correctness criterion, and we call it the *overall serializability*. Typically, the more the serializability requirement is relaxed, the less restrictive and less centralized a method tends to be.

11.2
A Formal Recovery Model

In the previous sections, we have discussed various problems related to recovery in heterogeneous autonomous database systems. We have seen that preserving local autonomy jeopardizes the atomicity of global transactions; i.e., they end up in a state where not all local subtransactions are committed that should be; or some of them are committed, although all should be aborted. Achieving atomicity is the basic problem of the multidatabase recovery.

There are two basic strategies to achieve atomicity. We see transaction-based recovery in this case as a continuation of a transaction execution to a successful or nonsuccessful completion. Backward recovery aims at continuing the transaction, after some of the failures above, to a nonsuccessful completion, i.e., in such a way that all its effects caused so far to the durable data are made nonvisible or irrelevant to the subsequent transactions.

Forward recovery aims at continuing the transaction to a successful completion, i.e., in such a way that a semantically consistent set of its effects on persistent data will become visible to the subsequent transactions in spite of the failures. In transaction models that assume a hierarchical or other graph structure for transaction specification, these approaches can also be combined. Thus, a global transaction can try forward recovery, but if this fails, it can roll back the operations tried so far. That is, it can recover backward the successful subtransactions or operations performed during the forward recovery attempt and try another, alternative path (also called contingent path) to recover forward, and so on. Finally, if it cannot recover forward, it can recover backward. This approach has been extensively studied in [Vei90, VEH92].

11.2.1   Recoverability and Serializability in the R-W Model

How is recovery activity modeled in the traditional theory based on the R-W model? Forward recovery is not explicitly modeled. Backward recovery is captured by a "pruning approach"; i.e., the aborted operations are pruned or projected away from the overall history, and the correctness of the resulting pruned history is then considered. This corresponds to the intuition that an aborted operation "never happened." Papadimitriou [Pap86] presents criteria based on view serializability, called reliability and *rollback reliability*, that guarantee correctness of the history in case of failures. The latter allows cascading aborts as a means to achieve the serializability; the former does not. Thus, there exists a uniform theory based on view serializability that covers all possible concurrency anomalies. Unfortunately, recognizing reliable histories is a PSPACE-complete problem, and recognizing rollback reliable histories is an NP-complete problem (see page 319). Thus, there is not much hope for efficient scheduling algorithms that would allow exactly either of the classes. The question is, rather, how to approximate the classes.

In [BHG87], the pruning is technically achieved by defining the committed projection $C(H)$ of a history that prunes incomplete and aborted transactions. Whereas reliability is a criterion based on view equivalence, [BHG87] introduces an orthogonal set of characterizations. R-W histories are classified according to their recovery properties (recoverable histories and their subclasses) and serializability properties (conflict and view serializable histories). The classes are incomparable and overlapping. Is this a good way to approximate the (rollback) reliable histories? What is the lesson for heterogeneous transaction processing? How is (backward) recovery performed in real systems, and how does the modeling based on pruning reflect it? A further question is When are the results based on the pruning idea adequate?

We elucidate the issues with the following example. What is wrong with the following (conflict) serializable but nonrecoverable history?

$$H_1 = W_1[X]R_2[X]W_2[Y]C_2$$

The problem lies in the fact that when the fate of C_2 is decided by the scheduler, it does not know whether T_1 will later be aborted or committed. Thus

$$H'_1 = W_1[X]R_2[X]W_2[Y]C_2A_1$$

is a possible completion of the history after C_2. H'_1 is serializable but not recoverable [BHG87] (because C_1 should precede C_2, which is not the case), and this is also the real problem. In this case, T_2 writes into the database value Y, which is based on the value of X that is later overwritten by the implementation of abort A_1. The theory in [BHG87] ignores the implementation of abort A_1. Modeling the situation in detail, based on the idea above that recovery is a continuation of a transaction, we can write

$$H'_1 = W_1[X]R_2[X]W_2[Y]C_2A_1 - W_1[X]C_1$$

T_1 was continued by the automatic backward recovery action $-W_1[X]C_1$, which implements the semantics of abort action A_1. In this case, $-W_1[X]$ can be modeled as a read-write operation pair $R_1[X_r]W'_1[X_r]$, where the value of X_r is first read from the log and written by the $W_1[X_r]$ operation. Which value X_r should be used here? The first intuitive answer is the before-image of item X that was effective before $W_1[X]$. In this special case, the value is the initial value of X, written by a hypothetical initial transaction T_0. Thus, making T_0 explicit and denoting the versions of data written by W_i by the corresponding index, and denoting the special recovery action with W' we can rewrite H'_1:

$$H''_1 = W_0[X]W_0[Y]C_0W_1[X]R_2[X]W_2[Y]C_2A_1R_1[X_0]W'_1[X_0]C_1$$

This is evidently a "nonserializable" history. By looking at the reads-from relationship, one sees that both in $T_0T_1T_2$ and $T_0T_2T_1$ the standard version function [Pap86]—which always selects the latest version to be read by a read operation—is different from H''_1. The same can be said if indices are pruned from data items X and Y, thus yielding $W_1[X]R_2[X]W'_1[X]$ and, consequently, a cycle in the serializability graph of H''_1.

A serial history is both recoverable and serializable according to any reasonable serializability criterion. Thus, nonrecoverability and nonserializability of a history are both concurrency anomalies. How should an on-line scheduler behave in order to avoid them both? Look at

$$H'''_1 = W_0[X]W_0[Y]C_0W_1[X]R_2[X]W_2[Y]C_2C_1$$

H_1''' is clearly a complete history and conflict serializable in terms of [BHG87]. It is, at the same time, another possible completion of H_1 above. If H_1 could always be completed into H_1''', there would be no problem for the scheduler. Thus, it could also allow C_2 to precede C_1 above and H_1 to develop to H_1'''. The usual, and reasonable, assumption is that an on-line scheduler does not know the whole future and must thus be prepared for aborts and commits at any time. It can refuse commits but not aborts. Thus, it must guarantee that all possible continuations of the history that might result from aborts guarantee durability and preserve database consistency. This observation leads to analysis of occurrence of aborts.

Abort can be issued for three reasons:

1. Because of a crash, in which case all incomplete transactions are aborted by the recovery system and collectively continued into completion; in this case, the scheduler can only arrange the aborts in suitable order, if necessary.

2. Because the application decides to abort the transaction; in this case, the scheduler can delay the abort and perform first the resulting cascading aborts, if necessary.

3. Because the database scheduler decides to abort a transaction, e.g., because of a deadlock or because aborting a transaction guarantees serializability; in this case, it can choose which transaction to abort and when.

An on-line scheduler must, at any moment, ask, If this operation is scheduled, can the transactions that are currently incomplete be run to completion in a serializable and atomicity preserving way in cases 1 and 2 above, possibly using case 3 as an option?

The above history H_1 shows that after the scheduler has decided to schedule C_2, there is a problem. Depending on what happens in the future, history H_1'' or H_1''' might result. In particular, the scheduler cannot guarantee that A_1 is not issued in the future, and because abort cannot be prohibited by a scheduler and delaying does not help in this case, it must take into account H_1'', too. Thus, H_1'' is a possible future of H_1, and additionally, a scheduler cannot prohibit the history to continue into H_1'' should a crash happen after C_2 has been scheduled or should the application abort T_1. The whole situation for H_1 is shown in Figure 11.3. It shows that H_1 can be finalized both in a serializable or nonserializable way.

A sufficient condition for recoverability of history H in the sense of [BHG87] is the following forward conflict serializability, meaning that there is a serializable, correct, enforceable (crash) completion $C_f(H^p)$ for every prefix H^p of history H.

Crash completion of history H, $C_f(H)$ models the situation where a crash occurs at the end of H and the recovery system aborts all incomplete trans-

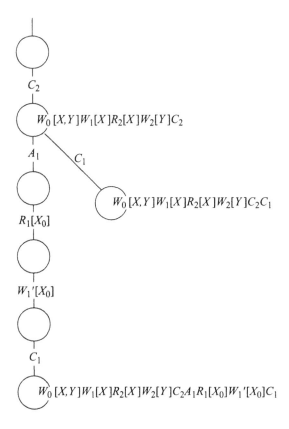

FIGURE 11.3
Possible continuations of H_1.

actions in H, running them into aborted completions. Because a crash can happen at any time, an on-line scheduler must always behave in such a way that the incomplete transactions can be aborted without endangering serializability at the end. Further, it is easy to see that if forward conflict serializability is guaranteed, then individual aborts are already covered.

The word *enforceable* above refers to the fact that the recovery system and scheduler can choose between operation orders and abort/commit orders. It can also select from history the values it will restore during recovery. Referring to the latter point, the crash completion $C_f(H)$ is not unique, because different kinds of policies could be used to select the before-images that are read from the earlier history, and because the abortion of the transactions and their operations to be aborted can be done in different orders.

One simple policy is to abort the transactions in the reverse order of their last operations in H, combined with the reading of the closest value written by

$W_j[X_j]$ preceding $W_i[X]$. We call this preceding-W policy. Taking H_1 above as an example, a crash completion under the above policy is H_1'', which is not conflict (nor view) serializable.

Are there other reasonable crash continuations? One is where the recovery policy is as above, but it does not read the value preceding $W_i[X]$, but it reads the committed value closest to A_i. We call this preceding-A policy.

In H_1, the latter policy would again select $W_0[X]$. The only differing policy would be to read instead $W_1[X]$, resulting in

$$H_1'''' = W_0[X]W_0[Y]C_0W_1[X]R_2[X]W_2[Y]C_2A_1R_1[X_1]W_1'[X_1]C_1$$

This is (view[2]) equivalent with $T_0T_1T_2$, but it is not correct in the sense that the results of T_1 are not abolished from the database as they should be, should the semantics of A_1 be correctly implemented. Because there are no other possibilities to implement the abort for $W_1[X]$, and because all existing ones lead to nonserializable continuation, one can say that H_1 is not forward conflict serializable.

In the above example, nothing could be done, and the same holds for any unrecoverable history in the sense of [BHG87], if the transaction corresponding to T_1 above is aborted after T_2 is committed.

Is the forward conflict serializability, as outlined above, a necessary condition for recoverability [BHG87]? Consider

$$H_2 = W_0[X_0]W_0[Y_0]C_0W_1[X_1]W_2[X_2]C_2A_1$$

The simple preceding-W policy reading the value X_0 preceding $W_1[X]$ and writing it would result in

$$H_2' = W_0[X]W_0[Y]C_0W_1[X]W_2[X]C_2A_1R_1[X_0]W_1'[X_0]C_1$$

In this history, the recovery of an aborted transaction T_1 would overwrite a committed X_2, which destroys durability of T_2. That something is wrong is indicated also by the fact that H_2' is not forward conflict serializable under the above policy. The scheduler could still allow the above schedule H_2 if it recovers in a reasonable way, i.e., if it would use the closest committed value fetched by the preceding-A policy:

$$H_2'' = W_0[X]W_0[Y]C_0W_1[X]W_2[X]C_2A_1(R_1[X_2]W_1'[X_2])C_1$$

H_2'' is not forward conflict serializable because of $W_1[X]W_2[X]W_1'[X]$. This shows that forward conflict serializability is not a necessary condition for recoverability, because H_2 is recoverable. Still, the database contains, at the end, the correct committed value X_2, and the effects of T_1 are gone. Actually,

---

[2]This holds, because we know that $W_1'[X_1]$ writes back X_1, which is subsequently read by $R_2[X]$.

the recovery of T_1 above could also be empty, because T_2 overwrote all results of T_1 and because no other transaction read the results; T_1 is thus dead (cf. [Pap86]). The case of empty recovery corresponds to H_2'' without the two operations in parenthesis in it; a history that is clearly forward conflict serializable. Thus, one can conclude that H_2'' is indeed correct.

The approach is an optimization of the preceding-A policy, where the originally produced value $W_i[X]$ is already overwritten by an operation $W_j[X]$ and is not restored during recovery. Only those values $W_i[X]$, which are not overwritten by an operation $W_k[X]$, are restored by $R_i[X_j]W_i'[X_j]$, where $W_j[X]$ is committed and precedes $W_i[X]$. Notice that, in general, allowing overwriting of uncommitted values leads to histories that are not forward conflict serializable, no matter which of the above three policies is chosen.

How much concurrency can be allowed in a history so that it remains, in general, forward conflict serializable? It is easy to see that rigorous histories are such that they are forward conflict serializable under all the policies above (see Theorem 11.4 later in the chapter).

Complexity of Generating the Recovery Actions

The approach grasped above, where the R-W history is continued with concrete actions deduced from the history, is clearly polynomial in terms of computational complexity. This is because the automatic generation of backward recovery actions is essentially a write action that writes back a suitable before-image, usually the committed one preceding the W operation that overwrote it. To find it requires scanning back the history once, using either policy above.

In a heterogeneous environment, finding the backward recovery action is much more complicated, in fact, impossible if the transaction model relies on compensation for application-level operations as the way to roll back [Vei90, KLS90]. Forward recovery actions in the sense of "redoing" actions are usually easy to generate automatically, because often the original database commands, a stored procedure call, or the entire application program can simply be reexecuted, or its execution continued where it stopped, to achieve this. However, the task becomes impossible, in general, if the system should continue an aborted transaction beyond a point the system knows of.

It is generally not well understood when it is possible to automatically generate the forward or backward recovery operations and their parameters by the execution mechanism and how complicated this is algorithmically. Papadimitriou's results in [Pap86] show that if the recovery uses view serializability as the correctness criterion and pruning the aborted transactions from history as a modeling metaphor for recovery, finding all so-defined reliable histories is PSPACE-complete. Rollback reliability—which allows cascading aborts and uses as the correctness criterion view serializability as above—is NP-complete.

Concluding Remarks on Forward-Oriented R-W Recovery

The main lesson from the above examples is that recovery can threaten correctness of the history, causing concurrency anomalies. Modeling the backward recovery exactly and defining suitable serializability concepts for crash-continued histories is necessary. The key question is What can a scheduler enforce in the future? The scheduler must always behave in such a way that a crash might happen at any time, and yet the history scheduled so far can be run to a correct completion, where all incomplete transactions are complete.

This raises the issue of correct modeling of recovery in histories. Indeed, history

$$H_1 A_1 = W_1[X]R_2[X]W_2[Y]C_2 A_1$$

where A_1 is catenated into H_1 is conflict serializable according to the definition of [BHG87]. This is because its committed projection prunes T_1, and the remaining part is conflict equivalent with T_2. But as the thorough analysis above shows, the recovery of T_1 in $H_1 A_1$ is such that the database state cannot be obtained in any serial history. As was shown in [VWP+97], the "pruning" approach—i.e., the correctness based on committed projection—allows histories that are conflict serializable but not even state equivalent with a serial history. Thus, the backward serializability, as we call it below, which is based on projections on complete transactions, is not necessarily a sufficiently restricting correctness criterion taken alone.

The second lesson is that recovery might be context dependent. That is, the correct backward recovery strategy depends on the preceding history and actions performed.

Third, the eventuality is an important issue. The scheduler must really be able to run each transaction to an aborted or committed completion. In a centralized case, this is not so much a problem, although a series of crashes can cause the recovery to start again and again, and theoretically one cannot show that it will ever end.

These are the problems to be addressed by the recovery and concurrency model in a heterogeneous environment.

11.2.2   A General Framework Model

Two distinct problem areas must be addressed when a comprehensive recovery model is designed for heterogeneous autonomous multidatabases. First, due to unilateral aborts or unilateral commits of local subtransactions, atomicity of individual global transactions can be jeopardized. As a consequence, forward or backward recovery must be performed. The recovery model must thus be able to characterize as to when an individual transaction is complete and when incomplete.

Second, the recovery in a heterogeneous autonomous environment often happens as a concurrent activity with normal operation, because local component systems cannot usually be stopped and because only single global transactions might become aborted or single local systems might crash. Thus the model must address concurrency anomalies that might be caused by operations belonging to recovery parts of global transactions. In practice, this means that the model must be able to express completely a concurrency control theory and the issues pertaining to failure of atomicity. It also requires the ability to model eventuality—in the context of recovery—because recovery actions must be generated again and again, and it is not as simple as it is in a centralized case to guarantee termination of the recovery process. Thus, the recovery leads to diverse multiple local subtransactions per site, i.e., the *MSS schemes*.

The work here is a generalization of [Vei90, VW92b, SWY93, VHYBS97] and [TA94].

The Basic Model Tree

Let us look at the problem from the perspective of a scheduler. When can it schedule operation for execution? Evidently, when it is certain that the overall history will satisfy the serializability (and other) criteria given and known to the scheduler. The problem is that the scheduler does not know the future in this case, because it cannot predict system or transaction aborts. So, in order to be safe, it must schedule operations in such a way that whatever crashes will happen in the future, the overall history will satisfy the given criteria.

The modeling incentive is as follows: The basic structure is a finite (or infinite) directed tree **Sx** whose root is empty and whose arcs are labeled by the operation instances O_i to be modeled. We call the tree the *model tree*. The operations might be transactional operations that can be scheduled—for example, Begin transaction (B), Commit (C), Abort (A), Unilateral Abort (UA), Prepare (P), or some more complicated operations, such as methods, or marks for site crashes, which are of interest for the transaction management. As concerns the real-time order of operations, the order of operations $S_<$ on the path S models it, that is, operation O_i appearing on the path before O_j has started before O_j in the real (Newtonian) time. Notice that the relationship $O_i S_< O_j$ does not imply any particular real-time order for the end of operations. The only exceptions are elementary operations R and W, if they conflict.

We assume that at any moment, there are a finite number of transactions T_i in execution in the overall system to be modeled. On the outgoing arcs of a node N are all operations viable for execution in some incomplete transaction occurring in N, and a finite set of starting operations of new transactions, if any. We assume that in a particular transaction a finite number of operations are viable for execution at any particular moment and an abort is viable for any transaction at any moment (because a crash might happen at any moment). Thus, any node N in the model tree **Sx** has a finite, albeit not fixed, out-degree.

Each node N of **Sx** contains the complete computation of interest, performed based on the requests occurring on the path to the node N. In general, we assume that requests for all operations occurring in N are visible on the path from the root to the node N; i.e., there are no "hidden" operations, albeit the computation model might require some other structures to be generated (e.g., an R-W history, a computation forest, serialization graphs, etc.). In addition, a node content in N is constructed from the preceding adjacent node on the path by applying the operation addition rule of the computation model x applied in the nodes of the model tree. The index x above denotes the particular computation model applied. Usually, the structure(s) modeling the computations in the nodes of the model tree grow with time, i.e., while going further away from the root, in our case.

We get different instantiations of the overall model by applying different computation models at nodes and, correspondingly, different operation requests on the arcs. In Figure 11.3 we have already an instance of the R-W model as defined in [BHG87]. We can have not only the R-W model, with or without [Pap86] explicit commit (C) and abort (A), but also the multilevel transaction model [Wei91], open nested transactions [Mut94], the S-Transaction model [Vei90], and the 2PCA model [VW92b]. In the R-W model case, the operation requests on the arcs are R, W, C, and A, indexed by the transaction identifiers.

The general correctness criteria for the computations modeled in **Sx** can be expressed based on the computation model instances, i.e., the structures in the nodes of the model tree. These are predicates expressed, e.g., in a modal logic. We use Computation Tree Logic (CTL) below.

Model Tree and Some Results of the R-W Model

As an example of an application of the model tree approach, let us consider a centralized R-W model with C and A, as in [BHG87]. The operation addition rule is: Catenate the operation request O_i on the arc leading to N to the end of the sequence H' (or to the set H') occurring in the preceding node N'. Thus, the history in a node N occurs on the arcs leading to the node.

To exemplify the correctness criteria, let us denote the predicate for conflict serializability by CSR and that for the view serializability by VSR. Let CSR(**Srw**) and VSR(**Srw**) denote those nodes in **Srw** where the history satisfies CSR and VSR, correspondingly. Then CSR(**Srw**) $\subset$ VSR(**Srw**) (cf. [BHG87], p. 40). For the set of paths leading from the root to the nodes in the above node sets in **Srw**, denoted by pths(CSR(**Srw**)) and pths(VSR(**Srw**)), the same relationship holds.

Formulating the above relationship in CTL [CES86] is as follows: The model of the predicates above is the history H in a node N of **Srw**. We denote the truth value of predicate P at node N by P(N). Now, $CSR(N) = $ true iff $C(H)$ in N is conflict serializable, as defined in [BHG87]. Correspondingly, $VSR(N) = $ true iff $C(H)$ in N is view serializable, as defined in [BHG87]. The above relationship among the paths in **Srw** can now be formulated as

$$AG(CSR \to VSR)$$

Prefix-Closed Predicates

Both CSR and VSR are *prefix-closed* on the committed projections. This means that if predicate P holds at N—i.e., $P(N) = true$—then $P(N')$ holds for every node N' on the path $pth(N)$ leading to N. In CTL, this can be expressed by

$$AG(EX(P) \to P)$$

Notice that view serializability, as defined in [Pap86], does not have this property, because the definition allows prefixes that are not view serializable.

For prefix-closed predicates, it holds in general:

THEOREM 11.1

If P is a prefix-closed predicate, then the following holds: $AG(\neg P \to AG(\neg P))$. In other words, if $P(N) = false$ for N, then P does not hold at any successor node N' of N in **Sx**.

PROOF

Let N' be a successor node of N, and P a prefix-closed predicate in **Sx**. Assume $P(N') = true$. Because N precedes N' on the path and $P(N) = false$, by definition P is not prefix-closed. This is a contradiction. Thus, $P(N') = true$ does not hold.   ∎

A prefix-closed property holds either for a complete prefix of a path or for the whole path.

General Atomicity Predicates for Transactions

We might also have properties P, which hold for a tail of a path or for a set of paths emanating from node N. A typical interesting one is the Completion Predicate, $CMP(T) =$ "transaction T can be run into completion on a finite path, emanating from any node N, where T is incomplete, with certainty." In CTL [CES86], this can be formulated by

$$CMP(T) = AG(Incompl(T) \to EF(Compl(T)))$$

where Incompl(T) means "transaction T is incomplete (in node N)," and Compl(T) means "transaction T is complete (in node N)."

Another predicate, Global Completion Predicate, GCP(**T**,N) = "all transactions incomplete in N can be run into completion from N and from all its successors," is stronger than the Completion Predicate. This predicate is the implicit goal of all real-life algorithms. In CTL, it could be written

$$GCP(T_1, \dots, T_k) = AG(Incompl(T_1) \land Incompl(T_2) \land \cdots \land Incompl(T_k)$$
$$\to AF(Compl(T_1) \land Compl(T_2) \land \cdots \land Compl(T_k)))$$

The difference between the two predicates is that even if $CMP(T_i)$ would hold in a node for all T_i, there need not be a common path on which all of them become true, whereas in the GCP case, they will be completed on each path emanating from a node in which they are incomplete.

It is further possible to define a predicate that is weaker than $GCP()$ but stronger than $CMP(T)$. This predicate says there is a path on which all incomplete transactions become completed, i.e., the Global Completion Predicate on some Path is

$$GCPP(T_1,\dots,T_k) = AG(Incompl(T_1) \wedge Incompl(T_2) \wedge \cdots \wedge Incompl(T_k)$$
$$\rightarrow EF(Compl(T_1) \wedge Compl(T_2) \wedge \cdots \wedge Compl(T_k)))$$

where T_1, $\dots$, T_k are the transactions occuring on a path $pth(N)$. This is interesting for cases where the computation can be kept on such a path by the overall system.

Remembering some general properties of transactions, one can formulate further invariants, e.g., "if a transaction once becomes complete, it will never become incomplete again" (i.e., the same transaction never starts again):

$$Unique(T) = AG(Compl(T)) \rightarrow AG(\neg Incompl(T))$$

We assume below that $AG(Unique(T))$ for any transaction T.

11.2.3   Correctness Criteria for Sx

As stated above, the goal of the transaction management is to guarantee that each transaction is run to completion and that the overall execution is in some sense "correct." The correct scheduling policy is evidently one that guarantees at any time that any transaction can be run into completion and the overall computation, modeled as a history, a computation forest, etc., remains correct.

Forward and Backward Serializability

In the model tree proposed in the previous section, the forward serializability can be formulated in the following way: Let CR be a predicate called *correctness criterion*, typically some form of serializability, for overall computations occurring in the nodes of **Sx**. Then, a path $pth(N)$ is *forward CR correct*, fCR, if for each node N' on the path $pth(N)$ it holds: for each set of transactions incomplete at N', **T**, there is a finite path $pth(N'')$ passing through N' for which it holds: $CR(N'') = true$ and $Compl(N'',T) = true$ for all transactions in **T**. In other words, all transactions incomplete at N' are complete at N'', and the overall computation at N'' is correct. In CTL, this can be expressed as

$$fCR = AG(EF(GCPP \wedge CR))$$

Notice that correctness criterion CR does not need to hold on the whole path from N' to N''; it is enough that it holds at N''. Actually, it does not need to hold on the forward CR-correct path pth(N) itself at all. Also notice that the definition requires that any subset of the incomplete transactions, **T**, can be run into completion from any node on a forward CR-correct path. This corresponds to the crash completion $C_f(H)$ discussed in Section 11.2.1.

Another (weaker) notion of correctness is the following: A path $pth(N)$ is *backward CR correct, bCR*, if $CR(C(N')) = $ true for all N' on the path $pth(N)$, where $C(N')$ is the projection of the history H on the complete transactions in node N' (similar to or equivalent with a committed projection $C(H)$). In CTL, this can be expressed as

$$bCR = AG(Compl(T_1, T_2, \ldots, T_r) \rightarrow CR|C)$$

where $CR|C$ means that the criterion is only applied to the completed projection, and $Compl()$ is a shorthand notion for

$$Compl(T_i) \lor \cdots \lor Compl(T_r)$$
$$\lor (Compl(T_1) \land Compl(T_2)) \lor \cdots \lor (Compl(T_i) \land Compl(T_j))$$
$$\vdots$$
$$\lor (Compl(T_1) \land Compl(T_2) \land \cdots \land Compl(T_r))$$

In other words, $Compl()$ is a disjunction over any possible conjunctions $Compl(T_i)$ of the transactions $T_1, \ldots, T_r$ occurring for a node N in **Sx**.

In general, it is not possible to relate the two sets of paths defined above in a particular way. This is because CR can be true in a node N even if it is not true on a path leading to N. However, if the property CR is prefix-closed, then more can be said.

THEOREM 11.2

If CR is a prefix-closed property, then pths(fCR($\mathbf{Sx}$)) $\subset$ pths(bCR($\mathbf{Sx}$)), i.e., fCR $\rightarrow$ bCR.

PROOF

Let $pth(N)$ be a forward CR-correct path and N' a node on it. Because pth(N) is fCR, there is a path $pth(N'')$ passing through N', and at N'', $CR(N'') = $ true holds. In addition, all transactions incomplete at N' are complete at N''. Because CR is by assumption a prefix-closed property, it holds on the whole path to N'', $pth(N'')$. But N' is on this path by construction. Thus, $CR(N') = $ true must hold. Because N' was arbitrary, the same holds for any node on the path $pth(N)$. Now, backward serializability is defined based on the completed projection of the history H in each node on the path $pth(N)$. This projection is thus a part of a history H for which CR yields true.

We have two cases: either H does or does not contain incomplete transactions. If it does not, H is the node contents for which $CR(N') = $ true, and we are done. If it does, H contains complete transactions, say $T_1, \ldots, T_k$, and incomplete transactions, say $T_{k+1}, \ldots, T_{k+r}$. By the definition of fCR, there is a node N'', reachable from N', where all these are complete and $CR(N'') = $ true. It is not possible in this case (because CR is a serializability criterion and a prefix-close one) that by removing $T_{k+1}, \ldots, T_{k+r}$ from the history H'' in N'' to obtain a projection $H''|T_1, \ldots, T_k$ would cause $CR(H''|T_1, \ldots, T_k) = false$ to occur. But $H''|T_1, \ldots, T_k$ is exactly the completed projection occurring in N'. Thus, $CR|C(N') = $ true. And, by definition, bCR holds. This holds for the whole path $pth(N)$.   ∎

THEOREM 11.3

For CSR and VSR, it holds: $pths(fCSR(\mathbf{Srw})) \subset pths(bCSR(\mathbf{Srw}))$ and $pths(fVSR(\mathbf{Srw})) \subset pths(bVSR(\mathbf{Srw}))$.

PROOF

As was shown above, CSR and VSR are both prefix-closed criteria. Theorem 11.1 can thus be applied in an obvious way.   ∎

When is the converse inclusion true; i.e., when are the path sets equivalent? In this situation, the correctness criterion is so tight that the scheduler can keep the computation on such future paths, where the criterion itself is guaranteed at any moment, irrespective of the crashes.

Trivially, at least if only serial histories are allowed by the scheduler. But how many more interleavings can be allowed such that the scheduler can guarantee a certain correctness criterion is an invariant, i.e., valid on any path (in addition to SR)?

Let us reanalyze history H_1 in Section 11.2.1 (see Figure 11.3). As was shown, H_1 has the continuation H_1'', which is not conflict serializable. Thus, bCSR does not guarantee fCSR as such (even if $C(H_1 A_1)$ is conflict serializable; see the discussion at the end of Section 11.2.1).

Do recoverability in the sense of [BHG87] and bCSR guarantee $fCSR$? No, as history H_2 in Section 11.2.1 shows. H_2 is recoverable and serializable in the sense of [BHG87], but the crash continuations are not conflict serializable.

These examples show that backward conflict serializability is not a sufficient condition for the history to be forward conflict serializable, assuming any polynomial semantics for aborts, where the backward recovery actions are simply generated based on the known history in time polynomial with regard to length of the history.

How about rigorousness RS [BGRS91]? It requires that if two operations $O_1[X]$ and $O_2[X]$ conflict, then there is C (in the model above) in the history between them. Indeed, this is a sufficient condition, even under the straightforward backward recovery policy that fetches committed before-images preceding W operations (see Section 11.2.1).

THEOREM 11.4

Let bRS(pathsSrw)) and fRS(pathsSrw)) be the rigorous path sets. Then bRS(pathsSrw) = fRS(pathsSrw).

PROOF

It is evident that rigorousness is a prefix-closed property. Therefore, the inclusion bRS(paths**Srw**) $\supset$ fRS(paths**Srw**) holds by Theorem 11.1. To show the converse inclusion, we assume in our computation model that rigorousness means there is always a C between two conflicting operations, i.e., that an eventual recovery has been completed before a conflicting operation is scheduled. Let N be a node for which $RS(N)$ = true holds. We must show that from any node N' on the path pth(N) there is a path to a node N'' for which $RS(N'')$ = true and $CMP(N'', T_i)$ for any incomplete transaction T_i occurring in any set **T** of incomplete transactions at N'. Let us first assume that there are no incomplete transactions at N'. Then putting $N' = N''$ satisfies the conditions stated above for N''.

Assume next that there is a nonvoid set **T'** of incomplete transactions at N', and let **T** be its nonvoid subset. Let T_1 and T_2 be two transactions at N'. Because RS is a prefix-closed property, it holds at N'. Thus, if T_1 and T_2 have conflicting operations $O_i[X]$ and $O_j[X]$, then they are separated by C, i.e., either $O_i[X] < C_i < O_j[X]$ or $O_j[X] < Cj < O_i[X]$. This means that only one of them can be incomplete. Further, the incomplete one must follow the complete one in the serialization order of the history. Immediately from this it follows that in **T** there can only be nonconflicting transactions.

A path required by the definition is found in the following way. Take an arbitrary T_i in **T** and follow a path from N', where the first operation on the arc emanating from N' is A_i, and subsequently, all its update operations $W_i[X]$ have been compensated by writing back the before-images by $-W_i[X]$ operations in the reverse order, and finally T_i is closed by C_i. In the node N''', where C_i points to, every operation $-W_i[X]$ follows the corresponding $W_i[X]$ in the history. In addition, the generation of the backward recovery operations does not cause new conflicts to arise between the complete or incomplete transactions and the one to be rolled back, because no new data items X are touched upon during recovery. Thus, at N''', $Compl(N''', T_i)$ = true and $RS(N''')$ = true. One can continue from N''' in the similar way as from N' by taking another transaction T_j incomplete in N' and N'''' and rolling it back, and so on, until all in **T** have been rolled back at the node, say N''. But at N'', $Compl(N'', Ti)$ for all transactions in **T** and additionally, $RS(N'')$ = true. Because **T** was arbitrary, the claim holds for N'. Because N' was arbitrary, the claim holds for the whole path pth(N). From this, it follows that the overall claim holds, i.e., bRS(paths**Srw**) = fRS(paths**Srw**). ∎

Actually, the simple recovery policy above is not optimal. In a rigorous history, $-W_i[X]$ should be interpreted "retrieve the closest committed before-image occurring before $-W_i[X]$," as was already discussed in Section 11.2.1 while discussing H_2.

From this example, we again see that (backward) recovery and the correctness criteria are closely related: using a certain kind of backward recovery policy determines which kind of correctness criteria are reasonable and vice versa.

11.2.4   Computation Model for Heterogeneous Transaction Management in Srw

We could use the basic R-W model with R, W, C, and A operation sequences in this case, too. We need, however, to model unilateral aborts (UA) along with the additional local subtransactions caused by them and the resulting concurrency anomalies. This cannot be reasonably done with the basic R-W model because there might be a commit and abort operation in transaction, and thus the axiom valid in a traditional case about exactly one of them is not valid. Furthermore, to reason about the functioning of the overall system, we need to model prepare operations explicitly.

We model a real transaction execution as a sequence of execution trees, $\mathbf{T_k} = T_{k(0)}, T_{k(1)} \ldots$, where a later tree always contains all the previous ones. Each individual tree belonging to the same transaction appears in a different node N of the model tree **Srw**. Conceptually, the sequence grows at the same pace as the real transaction advances. A new tree is added into the sequence and thus another node in **Srw** is reached, whenever the execution of the real transaction advances to a point where the principles below require this to happen.

The nodes of an execution tree $T_{k(i)}$ refer to the computation done at different levels of the reference architecture in Figure 11.1. The root and intermediate nodes contain a sequence of individual operations. An operation is the execution of a DML command, or request sent by the MTM or issued locally. It contains the actual parameters and result data. An empty intermediate node, along with an arc connecting it upward and a transaction ID, appears in an execution tree when processing of an individual (sub)transaction begins at the corresponding interface. The request for the execution appears on the arc leading to N, or earlier on the path leading to N, where the $T_{k(i)}$ is contained.

The leaves of the tree $T_{k(i)}$ are R and W operations. At the higher levels there are DML operations (denoted by O_y^x), prepare operations (denoted by P_y^x), commit operations (denoted by C_y^x), and abort operations (denoted by

A_y^x). Abort operations can be decomposed at a lower level to DML operations or R and W operations.

A DML operation appears in an execution tree once it becomes ready at the interface. Global commit (C_k) and abort operations occur at the root whenever the fate of the transaction has been decided and recorded persistently by the Master Manager.

Transaction history $H(T_{k(i)})$ is a sequence of operations formed by taking the leaves of $T_{k(i)}$, the commit and abort operations at all levels, and the P operations, in the order they first appear in the sequence $T_{k(0)}, \ldots, Tk(i)$. Their order is denoted by $<_{H(T_{k(i)})}$.

A complete local (sub)transaction history is always closed by a local commit. If the corresponding transaction history also contains an abort, then the corresponding local (sub)transaction is considered aborted.

Let $\mathbf{T} = \{T_{1(r)}, \ldots, T_{n(s)}\}$ be a set of execution trees. A history over $\mathbf{T}$, H, is an interleaving of $H(T_{k()})$, where

1. Each operation of $H(T_k())$ occurs exactly once in H.

2. The total order $<_H$ is compatible with each $<_{H(T_{k()})}$.

3. $O_i <_H O_j$ iff O_i was complete before O_j in real time.

An example of two global transactions, together with their execution trees, is shown in Figure 11.4. The transaction T_1, which executes at two sites a and b, illustrates a case when a subtransaction T_a^1 becomes locally aborted (A_{10}^a), then resubmitted (T_{11}^a), and, eventually, locally committed (C_{11}^a). The operations are depicted as seen at the interfaces of the generalized architecture. Both trees represent globally committed and complete (local commits have been executed) transactions.

Because the transactions run (eventually) to completion, their operations can be seen at one leaf node of the model tree illustrating a parallel execution of the two transactions. In the following section, we will see that the presence of T_2 may affect the recovery operations in T_1.

11.2.5 Completeness and Correctness Predicates for Heterogeneous Transaction Management in Srw

For the resubmission scheme, we have the following definition of the completeness predicate, $Complf(T_k)$: For a local transaction, $Complf(T_k) = $ true iff $H(T_k)$ contains C_k or A_k. A global transaction $T_{k(i)}$ is complete, i.e., $Complf(T_{k(i)}) = $ true, if one of the following is true:

1. If global commit C_k occurs in $H(T_{k()})$, then there is a local commit C_{kr}^s for each original local subtransaction T_k^s in $H(T_{k()})$.

2. If global abort A_k occurs in $H(T_{k()})$, then each local subtransaction T_{kr}^s contains both A_{kr}^s and C_{kr}^s (here we use the explicit Abort notation for aborted local (sub)transactions introduced above).

Global transaction T_1

O_1^a: SELECT C FROM TAB_A WHERE ID = 'X';

O_2^a: UPDATE TAB_A SET C = C+1 WHERE ID = 'Y';

O_1^b: UPDATE TAB_B SET C = C+1 WHERE ID = 'Z'.

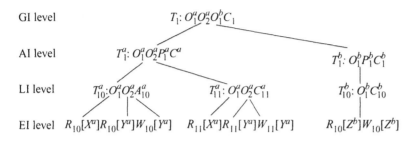

Global transaction T_2

O_1^a: DELETE TAB_A WHERE ID = 'Y';

O_2^a: UPDATE TAB_A SET C = C+1 WHERE ID = 'X';

O_1^b: SELECT C FROM TAB_B WHERE ID = 'Z'.

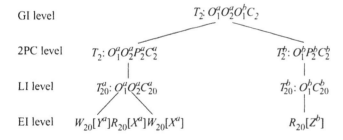

FIGURE 11.4
Two global transactions: an instance of a node in the Srw.

Notice that the compensation-based approaches to backward recovery require a different definition of the completeness predicate. Assuming that a local subtransaction can be committed at some point of time and afterward the global abort is issued, a compensating local subtransaction must be run successfully. Thus, such a predicate differs from *Complf* above in that if the original local subtransaction was already committed, the compensating local subtransaction must also become committed. [VEH92] contains a more detailed discussion of complicated completeness predicates.

Figure 11.5 shows an example of the model tree for the **Srw**. In this case, it is assumed that only two transactions (T_1 and T_2) can be active in the environment at any time. Thus, the out-degree of the initial node is 2. For simplicity, it is assumed that at most one operation in each transaction can be active at a time, and the always eligible abort operations are not shown unless we are interested in unilateral aborts. Thus, the out-degree in any node is usually 2.

Each arc in Figure 11.5 carries an operation of a particular transaction, and in each node is a forest of the trees. The corresponding history grows as one goes farther away from the root.

The leaf node shown in Figure 11.5 represents a possible history of the interleaved execution of T_1 and T_2. Note that the recovery operations marked with dotted lines in Figure 11.4 are not present in the final history. This is because the decomposition of the operation O_2^a has changed since the first time it was executed. In the meantime, T_2 deleted the item Y_a, and thus, the UPDATE statement yields an empty operation.

11.2.6 Correct Transaction Scheduling in a Heterogeneous Autonomous Environment Under Rigorousness

First, we must consider what the reasonable correctness critera are for a scheduler or set of schedulers in such a heterogeneous environment. And second, under which policies and assumptions are these criteria guaranteed? How much knowledge does the scheduler have of the future in order to decide when a history is enforceable? In light of the preceding discussion, the scheduler should strive for a particular forward serializability that is in harmony with the recovery policy and the knowledge of what can and cannot be enforced in the environment.

How is this achieved in a heterogeneous autonomous environment? There are several problems. First, the global scheduler(s) does not know the overall computation, only those parts that belong to global transactions. Second, not all local transactional operations are enforceable by the global scheduler, this being usually true for local commits. Third, there might be local operations, especially locally initiated unilateral aborts or commits, which cannot be prevented from occurring by the global level schedulers. In the computation model above, the UA_k, or UC_k, is in this case always enabled for any incomplete local subtransaction T_k^i, i.e., UA_k^i occurs on one arc emanating from a node N if there is a local subtransaction T_k^i active at site i.

To prove that a certain correctness criterion CR() is preserved, one must show that the set of global and local schedulers can keep the computations on paths where CR() holds.

As shown above, rigorousness RS is a correctness criterion for which the forward recoverable and backward recoverable paths coincide. But this holds only for local histories. We define an overall history H above as *locally rigorous,*

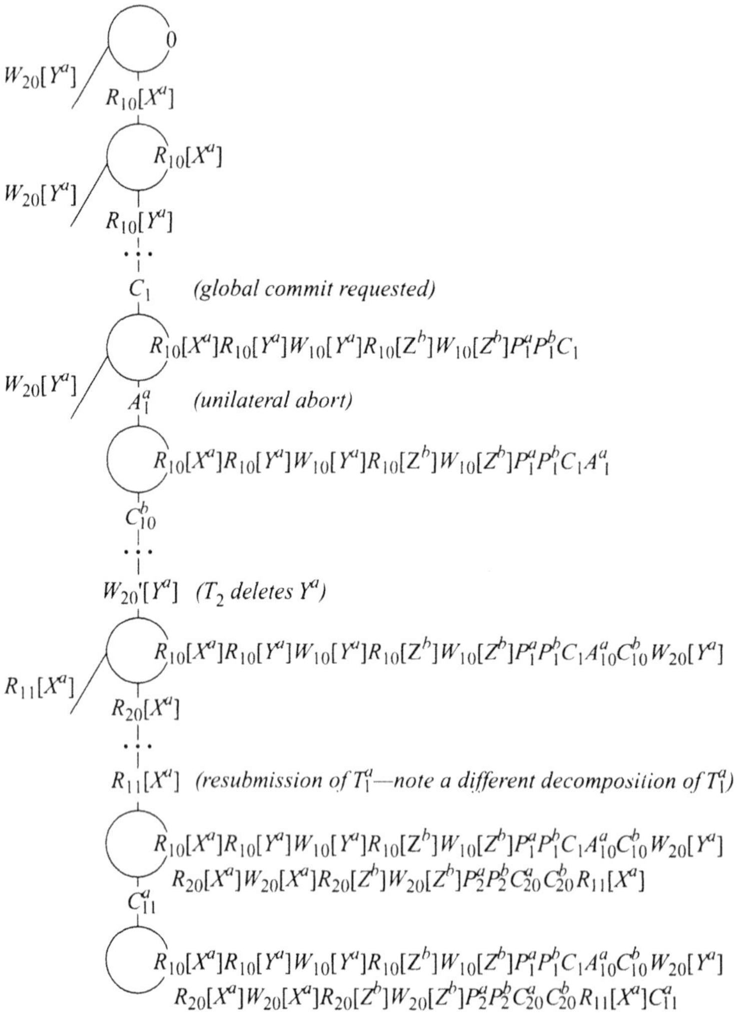

$W_{20}[Y^a]$ ／   0

$R_{10}[X^a]$

$R_{10}[X^a]$

$W_{20}[Y^a]$ ／

$R_{10}[Y^a]$

$\cdots$

C_1 *(global commit requested)*

$R_{10}[X^a]R_{10}[Y^a]W_{10}[Y^a]R_{10}[Z^b]W_{10}[Z^b]P_1^a P_1^b C_1$

$W_{20}[Y^a]$ ／

A_1^a *(unilateral abort)*

$R_{10}[X^a]R_{10}[Y^a]W_{10}[Y^a]R_{10}[Z^b]W_{10}[Z^b]P_1^a P_1^b C_1 A_1^a$

C_{10}^b

$\cdots$

$W_{20'}[Y^a]$ *(T_2 deletes Y^a)*

$R_{10}[X^a]R_{10}[Y^a]W_{10}[Y^a]R_{10}[Z^b]W_{10}[Z^b]P_1^a P_1^b C_1 A_{10}^a C_{10}^b W_{20}[Y^a]$

$R_{11}[X^a]$ ／

$R_{20}[X^a]$

$\cdots$

$R_{11}[X^a]$ *(resubmission of T_1^a—note a different decomposition of T_1^a)*

$R_{10}[X^a]R_{10}[Y^a]W_{10}[Y^a]R_{10}[Z^b]W_{10}[Z^b]P_1^a P_1^b C_1 A_{10}^a C_{10}^b W_{20}[Y^a]$
$R_{20}[X^a]W_{20}[X^a]R_{20}[Z^b]W_{20}[Z^b]P_2^a P_2^b C_{20}^a C_{20}^b R_{11}[X^a]$

C_{11}^a

$R_{10}[X^a]R_{10}[Y^a]W_{10}[Y^a]R_{10}[Z^b]W_{10}[Z^b]P_1^a P_1^b C_1 A_{10}^a C_{10}^b W_{20}[Y^a]$
$R_{20}[X^a]W_{20}[X^a]R_{20}[Z^b]W_{20}[Z^b]P_2^a P_2^b C_{20}^a C_{20}^b R_{11}[X^a]C_{11}^a$

FIGURE 11.5
An instance of an overall model tree for Srw.

LRS, iff each of its local projections is rigorous. Based on this, one can show that in this sense, correct recovery is possible under UA.

THEOREM 11.5

fLRS is a prefix-closed property, and rigorous local schedulers are able to enforce LRS irrespective of the global scheduling policies.

PROOF

Prefix-closeness follows from the assumption that each local projection is fRS and RS is a prefix-closed property. As concerns the enforcing claim by local rigorous schedulers, it follows from the fact that irrespective of the global transaction scheduling policies, each local scheduler can at each step keep the computation on a locally rigorous path.   ∎

THEOREM 11.6

Global scheduler(s) are able to enforce atomicity, i.e., enforce GCP and preserve fLRS, provided TWR is valid and local aborts enforceable by the global scheduler.

PROOF

We must show that from any node N, there is a path, denoted $pth(N)^f$, on which the completion predicate GCP is satisfied, and which can be enforced by the global schedulers. Assume first that the GCP can be enforced by issuing a finite set of local aborts. Because the local aborts are uniformly enforceable, there is a finite path in **S**, passing N and ending at N', where all necessary aborts have been chosen by the global scheduler. This is the path $pth(N)^f$.

Assume then that at least one local commit C_i must be enforced for a global subtransaction T_k^i. The impossibility of enforcing it would mean that there is an infinite path, where resubmission or retry T_{kj}^i occurs infinitely and always ends with A_{kj}^i, and that the global scheduler cannot prevent this path from being followed in the model tree.

But TWR means[3] that the scheduler can enforce the computation to follow the path, including C_{kj}^i from some node N', where T_k^i occurs. We must further show that there is a path where all incomplete transactions will become complete. This follows from the fact that the resubmissions are independent of each other at a site and between sites. Thus, they can be performed one after the other. Additionally, global considerations cannot cause a global livelock, nor can local transactions cause a livelock under TWR.   ∎

---

[3]In CTL, TWR can be expressed as $TWR = AG((C_k \wedge A_{k0}^i) \rightarrow AF(C_{kj}^i))$.

11.2.7   Recovery under FMSS Serializability

It is evident that requiring only fLRS as the correctness criterion is too weak as a global correctness criterion for a resubmission-based MSS variant, as was shown in [VW92b]. A correctness criterion, called from here on *MSS serializability*, or FMSS for short, is defined in [VW92b]. It captures the two special concurrency anomalies found, global view distortion and local view distortion, occurring in a resubmission scheme.

The FMSS conflict is defined in the following way: Two operations $W_i[X]$ and $O_j[X]$ conflict if i $\neq$ j and $O_j = R_j$ or $O_j = W_j$, which is not locally aborted, i.e., not followed by a local abort operation aborting the local subtransaction to which W_j belongs.

FMSS is based on FMSS conflict equivalence between two histories. History H is (backward) FMSS serializable if its completed projection $C(H)$ is FMSS conflict equivalent with a serial history. The criterion has a serializability graph characterization (see [VW92b]).

The following theorem shows that applied alone to a history, fFMSS is stricter than bFMSS.

THEOREM 11.7

bFMSS is a prefix-closed property. Paths(fFMSS(Srw)) is a proper, non-void subset of paths(bFMSS(Srw)) for GCP completeness predicate.

PROOF

The first part follows from the fact that on the path to N, the history in the computation model at N' is a prefix of the history in N. The serializability graph, being acyclic at N, is thus acyclic at N'.

bFMSS is a proper superset of fFMSS for GCP. To see this, assume that H contains two complete global transactions T_1 and T_2, which both have a local subtransaction T_i^a and sites a and b. Assume T_1^a and T_2^a conflict through $W_2[U]W_1[U]$, and thus the serialization order is $T_2 \rightarrow T_1$ because of it. Assume further that the local history at site b is

$$H^b = R_1[X]W_1[X]R_3[X]W_3[Y]R_2[Y]W_2[Z]C_2^bC_1^b$$

Now, H is bFMSS serializable, because the local transaction L_3 is not complete and is thus dropped from the completed projection $C(H)$. Continuing L_3 by A_3 causes a cycle $W_3[Y] \rightarrow R_2[Y] \rightarrow -W_3[Y]$ in the serialization graph during recovery (because H^b is not recoverable). Continuing L_3 by C_3 causes cycle $T_2 \rightarrow T_1 \rightarrow L_3 \rightarrow T_2$. Thus, H is itself a history that cannot be completed without violating the FMSS serializability. This shows the claim concerning the relationship between bFMSS and fFMSS.

Finally, let us grasp the claim that there are fFMSS histories. Let H be serial and contained in node N. H is itself clearly fFMSS serializable.

Assume that a prefix of H, H' in node N' is continued in a different way from H, e.g., by resubmitting some local subtransactions of T_k or aborting T_k instead of committing it. Because in H' only one transaction can be incomplete, it must be T_k. Thus, all possible continuations yield a completeness predicate value true in some node N'', where T_k becomes complete. At N'', the serializability graph of H'' is acyclic, and identical with that of H', or contains additionally T_k. There are still no cycles in it, because H'' is also serial. This shows that the set paths(fFMSS(Srw)) is nonvoid. ∎

Theorem 11.7 shows that FMSS serializability is a rather permissive correctness notion. On the other hand, if the serial histories would be the only ones in the enforceable set, it would be useless, for obvious reasons. The really fFMSS-enforceable paths are a proper subset of bFMSS, which contains the serial histories and much more.

We have deduced from the architectural considerations the following restrictions, which guarantee that the nodes are on the fFMSS paths and at the same time are enforceable under realistic assumptions.

DEFINITION 11.1

History H obeys PSI (prepare state invariant) if, in each local history, H^i, if P_k^i and A_{k0}^i occur, then the former precedes the latter; and if two global subtransactions T_k^i and T_j^i occur in $C(H)$ and have conflicting operations in some of the local subtransactions T_{jx}^i generated from them, then either $C_k^i <_H P_j^i$ or $C_j^i <_H P_k^i$.

$$PSI = AG((P_k^i \wedge A_{k0}^i) \to (P_k^i H_< A_{k0}^i)$$
$$\wedge confl(T_k^i, T_j^i) \to (C_k^i <_H P_j^i \vee C_j^i <_H P_k^i))$$

P_x^i denotes the moment when the Agent has decided to move the global subtransaction into the prepared state.

Intuition tells us that the above restrictions mean a global subtransaction must not be moved into a prepared state if the local subtransaction is "dead"; i.e., the normal response to the coordinator should be "refuse." Furthermore, no conflicting local subtransactions should be allowed to be executed in an interleaved way, otherwise a cycle results in the serialization graph.

Unfortunately, the above restriction is not yet enough. We need to restrict the local transactions because they might intrude between the original and the last one (committed local subtransaction) and cause different kinds of problems. We call the restriction *denied local updates for reread data in the prepared state*, or DLRP. It can be formulated in the following way: Whenever P_k^i, $R_{ks}[X]$, and local $W_j[X]$ occur in $C(H)$ for some $s \geq 0$, then either $W_j[X] <_H P_k^i$ or $R_{ks}[X] <_H W_j[X]$ for all $s \geq 0$.

This says that a local transaction should not update data items that are read during resubmission, i.e., if they are bound (are in the read-write set of a global subtransaction that is in the prepared state). Reading them is allowed even if they would be bound. Notice also that the restriction neither addresses aborted transactions, nor does it deny updates in general, but only for the period of time that the data is bound.

DLRP can be replaced by stronger conditions, such as *denied local updates in the prepared state*, DLUP, which adds to DLRP the denial of conflicting updates to data items that are updated by the global transaction being in the prepared state. Further, *denied local conflicting access in the prepared state*, DLCP, adds to DLUP the restriction that a local committed transaction should not read data written by a transaction in a prepared state. And finally, the strongest requirement, *denied local access in the prepared state*, DLAP, denies local access to any data during the time a global subtransaction is in the prepared state.

THEOREM 11.8

Assuming PSI and fLRS to hold on a path, DLRP is a necessary condition for the computations to be kept on paths where fFMSS = true. It is not a sufficient condition.

PROOF

Necessity. We negate the DLRP assumption, keeping PSI, bFMSS, and fLSR at node N for H. Assume first that there is no view distortion in H, i.e., each decomposition $D(T_{ks}^a)$ is equivalent with the original one. Negation of DLRP means in this case that at node N there is the history

$$H = R_{10}[X^a]P_1^a A_{10}^a C_{10}^a W_2[X^a]C_2^a R_{11}[X^a]C_1 C_1^a$$

Clearly, PSI, LRS, and bFMSS are obeyed. Now, continuing the global transaction T_1 can only happen by committing it, otherwise the completeness predicate would yield false. But putting C_{11}^a into the history causes a cycle into $SG_{FMSS}(H')$ at node N', where T_1 becomes complete. Thus DLRP is in this case a necessary condition for the claim. Assuming that there is a decomposition distortion—i.e., $R_{11}[X^a]$ does not appear in the original transaction—one can deduce that there must be another locally committed $W_k[Y]$ operation that caused the local decomposition distortion. Based on fLRS and PSI, one can show that this must belong to a local transaction. Again, the continuation of T_1 yields a cycle into $SG(H')$. Thus, DLRP is a necessary condition for fFMSS to be kept under PSI, fLRS.

Insufficiency. Let N be a node where PSI, fLRS, DLRP, and FMSS hold for H. It has been shown in [VW92a] that the only cycles in $SG(H)$ under the above assumptions are intersite cycles that result from different orderings of the local commits of the local subtransactions. It was also shown that under the assumptions above, $SG(H)$ is a subgraph of the commit-graph,

$CG(H)$, which is formed by drawing arcs between transactions T_i and T_j iff they both have a local commit at the same site. They need not be complete. The arc follows the order of local commits. $CG(H)$ and $SG(H)$ coincide if all transactions are complete and each of them has a conflicting operation pair at each site. Thus, in order to show the insufficiency of the condition, one should show that there is a path from N to a node N'', where the local commits all occur and where $CG(H'') = SG(H'')$ is cyclic, albeit $SG(H')$ is acyclic at N'. In addition, PSI, fLSR, and DLRP should hold at N''.

The cycle is always possible because the order of the local subtransaction commits cannot be guaranteed to be the same under the assumptions made. Now, a transaction T_k involved in a cycle of $CG(H)$ at N' must be committed on every path, and thus it becomes part of the $SG(H)$ whenever $Complf(T_k)$ yields true at a node. Because $SG(H'')$ is part of $CG(H'')$, and has the same arcs as $CG(H'')$ at those places where there are directly or indirectly conflicting operations at sites, by completing all transactions incomplete at N'', the cycle will eventually emerge into $SG(H'')$. Thus, DLRP is not a sufficient condition for the computation to be on fFMSS paths. ∎

It is difficult to dynamically enforce all fFMSS serializable histories. Which of them are dynamically enforceable under the architectural assumptions we have—i.e., on which paths of the model tree should the schedulers keep the computation in order to be able to complete any set of incomplete transactions? Certainly, this is a proper subset. Taking into account Theorem 11.8 one can deduce the following result.

THEOREM 11.9
Under DLRP, PSI, fLRS, 2PC protocol, unilateral aborts, and TWR, there is a global scheduler that is able to enforce fFMSS from bFMSS.

PROOF
It is sufficient to restrict the paths that will be followed to those that only contain nodes N, where in addition to the above assumptions, CG(H) is kept acyclic. From this, it immediately follows that SG(H) is acyclic as its subgraph and can be invariantly kept as such. [VW92b] describe an algorithm that achieves this in the presence of failures and unilateral aborts. In [VW92a], the proofs are given. ∎

11.2.8 Generalizing FMSS

As stated above, the completeness predicate and the correctness criteria are in a close relationship, assuming that a global transaction can have local subtransactions that are unilaterally committed. Aborting the global transaction in that case requires generation of a compensating local subtransaction for each successful original local subtransaction. The completeness predicate states in this case that there must be local commits for both of them. In the transaction history $H(Tk)$, we thus have two local commits, C_{k0}^i for the original transaction and C_{kj}^i, $j \geq 1$ for the compensating one. Assuming that the compensation can also be locally rolled back and retried, j might be greater than one. The conflict definition of FMSS in the previous section is enough also in this case to guarantee overall correctness. What happens is that it adds to the conflicting operations the W operations of the original local subtransaction. Otherwise, the syntactic structure is the same as in the resubmission case above; i.e., first comes the original transaction $D(T_{k0}^i)$ in H, last the compensating subtransaction $D(T_{kj}^i)$, and between them zero or more resubmissions/retries $D(T_{ks}^i{}')$ for the compensating subtransactions, $D(T_{k0}^i) \ldots D(T_{ks}^i{}') \ldots D(T_{kj}^i)$.

It is easy to see that DLRP is also a necessary condition in this case for the computation to remain on an fFMSS path, provided the decomposition of the compensating subtransaction $D(T_{kj}^i)$ only contains such read operations, which access the data items occurring in $D(T_{k0}^i)$, and PSI, fLRS hold and SG(H) is acyclic.

As was shown above, PSI (named CI in [VW92a]) can be enforced in the forward recovery scheme, based on LRS. In the presumed commit scheme with compensation the algorithms presented in [VW92b] seem to function, but they might also unnecessarily abort global transactions in a failure-free situation, as the early commit is deemed a local subtransaction failure by the algorithms.

Only further study will reveal to what extent and how the problem can be remedied by applying direct conflict resolution schemes at the Agent level. It will also take further study to determine what can be guaranteed if the decomposition of the compensating local subtransaction contains data items other than those accessed by the original subtransaction.

Replacing DLRP by semantically oriented notions is also possible. In this case, the correctness criterion includes, e.g., commutativity of the local transactions/local subtransactions. The node model must also be more complicated than the R-W variant above, in order to capture the commutativity. Some work in this direction has been done in [Mut94, MVN93].

11.2.9   Enforcing DLRP

DLRP is a problematic assumption in the sense that if the local transactions, or the LTM's ability to issue UAs, are not restricted in any way, it cannot be guaranteed. On the other hand, as Theorem 11.8 shows, it is a necessary condition. There are several ways of approaching the issue:

1. Enforce DLRP. This is possible, e.g., under the following conditions:

   a. if the LTM, during normal operation, does not abort an individual local subtransaction, provided it has been completely decomposed, but performs UA only because of LTM crash;

b. during crash recovery, the LTM can be ordered by the MTM to resubmit the local subtransactions in the absence of local transactions.

2. Do-nothing approach. In this case, DLRP is not specifically enforced in failure situations. Because fFMSS serializability is guaranteed, provided there are no global transaction failures, the question is how much effort should be put in guaranteeing DLRP for failure situations. If global transaction failures are rare and the DLRP violations even more rare, and if, additionally, the applications are not disturbed by the DLRP failure, then let them run.

   This approach requires a thorough understanding of the semantics of the global and local transactions when the global transactions are introduced (see the discussion on the intersite correctness problem in [Vei93]).

3. If the first two approaches are deemed impossible, then globalize those local transactions—intruders—that might cause the DLRP to be violated. This means restriction of local LT autonomy and maybe big costs. This is, however, a panacea, because it guarantees DLAP, which always guarantees DLRP.

4. Divide the local database permanently into globally updatable and locally updatable sets, as proposed, e.g., in [BST90], and design transaction programs accordingly. This guarantees DLUP, so the commit order certification is still needed.

5. Time division. Divide, using administrative or technical means, the data usage time into distinct local and global update usage time intervals. Specifically, if the intruders are of higher priority, they may preempt the usage time interval by shutting down temporarily the 2PCA. In the opposite case, the intruders are run only if no dangerous global transactions are run. This guarantees DLAP, so commit order certification is not necessary.

6. Enforcing DLCP algorithmically. As DLCP implies DLRP, enforcing DLCP would be satisfactory, too. This may be achieved by adding a new certification function call to the program of each potential intruder and replacing the local commit command with the following constant sequence:

```
if DLCP-certification = OK then
        commit;
else
        rollback;
```

The Agent algorithms have to be modified accordingly.

7. Approximate methods. If a UA is detected, then either the LTM or the Agent is shut down and the site recovery is performed. This is not a fully safe approach because an intruder might commit before a UA is detected.

One might also try to detect global view distortions by comparing the results the retrieval operations returned originally and during resubmissions. This does not work for UPDATE-type operations. Also, the approach would require appropriate algorithms at the Agent level. The necessary corrective actions would require human intervention.

It is difficult to evaluate the practical relevance of the presented alternatives. Which of these approaches are applicable, if any, depends on the real system's circumstances and the local autonomy requirements,

The model tree approach presented here is new in several senses. It formalizes the possible futures of a history and gives an exact characterization of the invariants in CTL. Basically, all existing serializability results can be subsumed by the model, as the node model can capture exactly those criteria.

11.3
Related Work

One of the earliest works [GPZ86] addressing the issue of recovery in a heterogeneous database required that an atomic commitment protocol be used and that LTMs externalize the prepared state. The requirement stemmed from the viewpoint that the overall serializability should be guaranteed in the system, in a general case, and that it could only be achieved if SSS could be maintained. It took some time before more relaxed approaches appeared. The main body of the literature is based on the implicit or explicit adoption of the SSS paradigm.

11.3.1   MSS Orientation Due to Backward Recovery

Atomic commitment protocols reveal, in autonomous environments, two deficiencies: (1) inferior data availability (due to prolonged isolation of global transactions) and (2) violation of local execution autonomy, because in the prepared state, the participating system has to obey the decision of the Master. Thus, it has to wait for the Master to announce the decision. If the Master fails, the participant is blocked from continuing with the transaction. The delay cannot be specified in advance in either case.

A way to an MSS-type transaction model was paved by suggesting that *semantic atomicity* and *semantically consistent history* [GM83] would suffice in place of traditional atomicity and syntactic serializability. The approach was essentially based on compensation, although the compensating actions were called *counter steps*. More generally, a *compensating* transaction is a corrective action taken after the original (forward) transaction has been locally committed. It is used to revert the effect of the transaction. Compensation, based either on a compensating operation, action, or transaction, has surfaced as a main technique to achieve the semantic atomicity. As traditional (syntactic) serializability could not be achieved any more [KS88], new correctness criteria had to be defined, starting from semantically consistent schedules in [GM83] to [BR87, SWS91, VHYBS97].

Several technical methods were proposed for implementation of compensation-based recovery. In *global procedures* of [AGMS87], based on *Sagas* [GMS87], the Global Procedure Manager has the knowledge of both the original request (a subtransaction program) and the corresponding compensating transactions. It may decide whether to retry the failed subtransaction or to compensate the ones that succeeded. Note that compensation may be applied in the case of any failure under consideration.

The *optimistic commit* method [LKS91] applies a modified version of the distributed 2PC, the *optimistic 2PC* (O2PC). The subtransactions are committed immediately once they are executed, and they are compensated if they have to be completed nonsuccessfully. A correctness criterion that is non-R-W serializable is also proposed. An important feature of compensating transactions is that they undo the effects semantically without causing the cascading aborts of transactions that have read the data written by the transaction to be compensated. In [MR91], the UC is defined as *local commitment before global decision*. The cascading compensations among global transactions are avoided by applying global locks, but local transactions are not taken care of.

The common problems of compensation-based approaches are: (1) difficulties in generating compensating transactions automatically (e.g., at an SQL-based interface, how to compensate a predicate-based UPDATE) and (2) difficulties in avoiding cascading compensations. In reality, both the dynamics and the generality of transactions are under scrutiny [Vei90].

11.3.2 MSS Orientation Due to Forward Recovery

If the LTM offers a single-phase transactional interface and UAs are allowed, the Agent is required to simulate the prepared state. The subtransaction failures, caused by unilateral aborts, are handled by redoing or resubmitting the failed local subtransaction, resulting in the MSS structure of local subtransactions. The idea of the prepared-state simulation appeared, within the same time frame, in [WV90, BST90, Bar90, Geo90, BO91, Geo91].

The main problem with this approach is how to deal with UAs causing global and local view distortions [VW92b]. In particular, indirect conflicts [DE89] inflicted by local transactions in the presence of failures of local subtransactions are difficult to deal with.

Many of the proposed methods did not deal with UAs or local transactions at all. These are dealt with in the *2PC Agent* method [WV90, VW92b], the *commit graph* method [BST90], and also in [KK93].

[VW92b] propose prepare and commit certification algorithms. The first algorithm allows rejection of an unprepared transaction if it may endanger global serializability, in the presence of a unilateral abort. The second one effectively enforces a global commit ordering [Raz92]. In [LHL97], a global transaction manager guaranteeing global commit ordering is assumed, whereby a simpler algorithm is proposed, based on the Context-Sensitive Recovery Rule and the Late Redo Recovery Rule.

[VHYBS97] present a rather extensive model based on the explicit continuation approach to recovery and special correctness criteria. These criteria are possible alternatives in the model tree approach presented here, and thus the model tree subsumes the model of [VHYBS97].

To improve data availability at the LTM, the immediate commit and compensation was proposed in [Per91].

Methods based totally on forward recovery may be used in some circumstances. In the *unilateral commit paradigm* [HS91], the subtransactions are assumed to succeed eventually. The subtransactions are update-only, so there are no value dependencies among them. The failure atomicity of the global transactions is ensured with *persistent pipes*, which are recoverable command queues. The subtransactions are submitted to the pipes, where they are provisionally committed.

In the *asynchronous commitment* method [HLS93], the subtransactions are retried when they fail. The global transaction program is assumed to be of *fixed structure*, meaning the commands are the same in each retry and there is at most one update subtransaction. The subtransactions are committed (by the Master) in the order defined by a dependency graph, in order to avoid cascading aborts when retrying the subtransactions.

A more general model of [EJKB96] also applies retries and dependency analysis. The transactions have to be both intra- and intercommitable, meaning no dependency cycles are allowed or among global transactions. If the subtransaction fails, all the dependent transactions are aborted, and then all of them are retried. Here, as in other retry methods, the local transactions are unrestricted because they will serialize with the retried transactions in a normal way. In the *reservation commit* method [MJSA93], neither compensation nor retry/resubmit is needed because the only failure type considered is a command failure caused by the violation of an explicit database constraint. Once all the commands have been executed successfully, the Master may unilaterally commit subtransactions (and they have to commit flawlessly). In reality, the failures of types UA and LCF would deem the method infeasible.

11.3.3   SSS Orientation, Two-Phased LTMs

[MKSA92] argue that implementation of an atomic commitment protocol is not possible because of violation of local autonomy. If the autonomy can be restricted to the point an LTM will comply with a protocol like 2PC, various appealing possibilities appear. The Agent layer in the architecture is not needed as a transactional one, and we deal with SSS types of local subtransactions. If the LTMs are rigorous [BGRS91], the overall serializability is trivially achieved.

Various mixed transaction models allowing for different recovery schemes in the same system have also been proposed, starting with [RELL90] and then, for example, in [ELLR90, CBSA93].

11.4
Summary

In this chapter, we have discussed the recovery problems in heterogeneous autonomous multidatabases. We show that they are rather complex and mainly result from autonomy of the component systems and its ramifications. The crucial issue is whether the global atomicity can be reached by issuing only one local subtransaction per site or whether multiple local subtransactions (MSS) are needed. In the "single subtransaction per site" (SSS) scheme, recovery problems are solved by simply using the 2PC as a global protocol, as in a homogeneous distributed database, and backward recovery within the local subtransactions.

We first deduce a reference architecture reflecting the autonomy requirements and discuss the issues in an intuitive way, defining the basic concepts and problems. Allowing local transaction managers to unilaterally abort or commit local subtransactions threatens atomicity of the global transactions. In the latter case, the only remedy is to try backward recovery, which leads to the need to use compensating local subtransactions. The unilateral aborts require forward recovery, which leads to the need for resubmitting original commands or retrying global procedures. In all cases, the global subtransaction has more than one local subtransaction per site; i.e., the MSS scheme is needed.

The recovery is treated here, in a systematic way, as a continuation of the transaction to an acceptable successful or nonsuccessful completion. Nonsuccessful completion means that the global transaction is aborted and all local subtransactions have been locally aborted (or compensated). The successful case is one with global commit and exactly one locally committed local subtransaction at each site where there is a local subtransaction.

Besides atomicity, a problem area is the concurrent execution of the transactions, happening also during global recovery. In a heterogeneous autonomous environment, this is especially problematic because there is no way to prohibit concurrent activity during recovery. This poses the question, Which is the correct interleaving of recovery and other transactions, and how can it be enforced? The answers are rather complicated, especially for the MSS schemes. We concentrate on what we call FMSS serializability as a correctness criterion for interleaved executions. It is based on the R-W model. The main body of the analysis concentrates on the syntactical forward recovery based on resubmissions.

Methodically, we present a formal framework model that can be applied for any kind of concurrent recovery. We show that the same correctness criterion can be applied both "backward" or "forward" and that rigorousness is one criterion where the concepts coincide. The model also makes it possible to express livelocks and autonomy properties by making representation of the possible computations visible.

We know that much work must be done before we can apply the concepts precisely to models other than the R-W model. We believe, however, that the framework model can be used in many contexts. And we hope a powerful "transactional logic" can be developed in connection with the model.

Bibliography

[AGMS87]   R. Alonso, H. Garcia-Molina, and K. Salem. Concurrency control and recovery for global procedures in federated database systems. *Quarterly Bulletin IEEE Technical Communications on Database Engineering* 10(3):5–11, September 1987.

[Bar90]   K. Barker. *Transaction Management on Multidatabase Systems* (PhD thesis). Edmonton, Alberta, Canada: Department of Computing Science, The University of Alberta, August 1990.

[BGMS92]   Y. Breitbart, H. Garcia-Molina, and A. Silberschatz. Overview of multidatabase transaction management. *VLDB Journal* 1(2):181–239, October 1992.

[BGRS91]   Y. Breitbart, D. Georgakopoulos, M. Rusinkiewicz, and A. Silberschatz. On rigorous transaction scheduling. *IEEE Transactions on Software Engineering* 17(9):954–960, September 1991.

[BHG87]   P. Bernstein, V. Hadzilacos, and N. Goodman. *Concurrency Control and Recovery in Database Systems*. Reading, MA: Addison-Wesley, 1987.

[BO91]   K. Barker and M. T. Özsu. Reliable transaction execution in multidatabase systems. In *Proceedings of the First International Workshop on Interoperability in Multidatabase Systems (IMS'91)*, pages 344–347, April 1991.

[BR87]   B. R. Badrinath and K. Ramamritham. Semantics-based con-
            currency control: Beyond commutativity. In *Proceedings of the
            IEEE Third International Conference on Data Engineering*, pages
            304–311, February 1987.

[BST90]   Yuri Breibart, Avi Silberschatz, and Glenn R. Thompson.
            Reliable transaction management in a multidatabase system.
            *Proceedings of the ACM SIGMOD International Conference on
            Management of Data*, pages 214–224, 1990.

[CBSA93]   J. Chen, O. A. Bukhres, and J. Sharif-Askary. A customized
            multidatabase transaction management strategy. In *Proceedings
            of the DEXA'93 Conference*, pages 92–103, September 1993.

[CES86]   E. M. Clarke, E. A. Emerson, and A. P. Sistla. Automatic ver-
            ification of finite state concurrent systems using temporal logic
            specifications. *ACM TOPLAS* 8(2):244–263, 1986.

[CP84]   Stefano Ceri and Giuseppe Pelagatti. *Distributed Databases:
            Principles and Systems*. New York: McGraw-Hill, 1984.

[DE89]   Weimin Du and Ahmed K. Elmagarmid. Quasi serializability: A
            correctness criterion for global concurrency control in InterBase.
            In *Proceedings of the 15th International VLDB Conference*, pages
            347–355, 1989.

[EJKB96]   A. K. Elmagarmid, J. Jing, W. Kim, and O. Bukhres. Global
            committability in multidatabase systems. In *IEEE Transactions
            on Knowledge and Data Engineering*, 1996.

[ELLR90]   A. K. Elmagarmid, Y. Leu, W. Litwin, and M. Rusinkiewicz. A
            multidatabase transaction model for InterBase. In *Proceedings
            of the 16th International Conference on VLDB*, pages 507–518,
            1990.

[EV87]   F. Eliassen and J. Veijalainen. Language support for multi-
            database transactions in a cooperative, autonomous environment.
            In *Proceedings of the TENCON 87 Conference*, pages 277–281,
            August 25–28 1987.

[Geo90]   D. Georgakopoulos. *Transaction Management in Multidatabase
            Systems* (PhD thesis). Houston, TX: Department of Computer
            Science, University of Houston, December 1990.

[Geo91]   D. Georgakopoulos. Multidatabase recoverability and recovery. In *Proceedings of the First International Workshop on Interoperability in Multidatabase Systems (IMS'91)*, pages 348–355, April 1991.

[GM83]   H. Garcia-Molina. Using semantic knowledge for transaction processing in a distributed database. *ACM TODS* 8(2):186–213, June 1983.

[GMS87]   H. Garcia-Molina and K. Salem. SAGAs. In *Proceedings of the ACM Conference on Management of Data (SIGMOD)*, pages 249–259, 1987.

[GPZ86]   V. Gligor and R. Popescu-Zeltin. Transaction management in distributed heterogeneous database management systems. *Information Systems* 11(4):287–297, 1986.

[GR93]   J. Gray and A. Reuter. *Transaction Processing: Concepts and Techniques*. San Francisco: Morgan Kaufmann, 1993.

[GRS91]   D. Georgakopoulos, M. Rusinkiewicz, and A. Sheth. On serializability of multidatabase transaction through forced local conflicts. In *Proceedings of the Seventh International Conference on Data Engineering*, pages 314–323, 1991.

[HLS93]   S.-Y. Hwang, E.-P. Lim, and J. Srivastava. Asynchronous transaction commitment in federated database systems. In *Proceedings of the International Conference on Parallel and Distributed Systems*, 1993.

[HR83]   Theo Haerder and Andreas Reuter. Principles of transaction-oriented database recovery. *ACM Computing Surveys* 15(4):287–317, December 1983.

[HS91]   M. Hsu and A. Silberschatz. Unilateral commit: A new paradigm for reliable distributed transaction processing. In *Proceedings of the Seventh International Conference on Data Engineering*, pages 286–293, April 1991.

[II90]   ISO/IEC 9804. *Information Technology, Open Systems, Interconnection-Service Definition for the Commitment, Concurrency and Recovery Service Element*. Technical report, 1990.

[II92]   ISO/IEC 9075. *Information Processing Systems—Database Language SQL, International Standard, third edition.* Technical report no. ISO 9075 : 1992 (E), 1992. Also as ANSI X3.135-1992, Database Language SQL.

[KK93]   I. E. Kang and T. F. Keefe. Supporting reliable and atomic transaction management in multidatabase systems. In *Proceedings of the 13th International Conference on Distributed Computing Systems (DCS-93)*, pages 457–464, May 1993.

[KLS90]   H. F. Korth, E. Levy, and A. Silberschatz. A formal approach to recovery by compensating transactions. In *Proceedings of the 16th International Conference on VLDB*, pages 95–106, August 1990.

[KS88]   H. F. Korth and G. D. Speegle. Formal model of correctness without serializability. In *Proceedings of the ACM SIGMOD International Conference on Management of Data*, pages 379–386, June 1988.

[LHL97]   S. Lee, C. Hwang, and W. Lee. A uniform approach to global concurrency control and recovery in multidatabase environments. In *Proceedings of the Sixth International Conference on Information and Knowledge Management (CIKM'97)*, pages 51–58, November 10–14 1997.

[LKS91]   E. Levy, H. Korth, and A. Silberschatz. An optimistic commit protocol for distributed transaction management. In *Proceedings of the ACM SIGMOD Conference*, pages 88–97, May 1991.

[MGG86]   J. E. Moss, N. D. Griffeth, and M. H. Graham. Abstraction in recovery management. In *Proceedings of the 1986 ACM SIGMOD Conference*, pages 72–83, May 28–30 1986.

[MJSA93]   J. G. Mullen, J. Jing, and J. Sharif-Askary. Reservation commitment and its use in multidatabase systems. In *Proceedings of the DEXA'93 Conference*, pages 116–121, September 1993.

[MKSA92]   James G. Mullen, W. Kim, and J. Sharif-Askary. On the imposibility of atomic commitment in multidatabase systems. In *Proceedings of the Second International Conference on Systems Integration*, pages 625–634, June 1992.

[MR91]   P. Muth and T. Rakow. Atomic commitment for integrated
            database systems. In *Proceedings of the Seventh International
            Conference on Data Engineering*, pages 296–304, April 1991.

[Mut94]   P. Muth. *Transaction Management in Heterogeneous and Au-
            tonomous Database Systems* (PhD thesis). Darmstadt, Germany:
            University of Darmstadt, May 1994. In German.

[MVN93]   P. Muth, J. Veijalainen, and E. Neuhold. *Extending Multi-
            Level Transactions for Heterogeneous and Autonomous Database
            Systems*. Technical report 739. Germany: GMD-IPSI, March
            1993.

[Pap86]   C. Papadimitriou. *The Theory of Database Concurrency Control*.
            Rockville, MD: Computer Science Press, 1986.

[Per91]   W. Perrizo. Transaction management in HYDRO: A multi-
            database system. In *Proceedings of the First International
            Workshop on Interoperability in Multidatabase Systems (IMS'91)*,
            pages 276–279, April 1991.

[Raz92]   Y. Raz. The principle of commit ordering, or guaranteeing serial-
            izability in a heterogeneous environment of multiple autonomous
            resource managers using atomic commitment. In *Proceedings
            of the 18th International Conference on Very Large Databases*,
            August 23–27 1992.

[RELL90]   M. E. Rusinkiewicz, A. K. Elmagarmid, Y. Leu, and W. Litwin.
            Extending the transaction model to capture more meaning. *ACM
            SIGMOD Record* 19(1):3–7, March 1990.

[SBCM95]   G. Samaras, K. Britton, A. Citron, and C. Mohan. Two-phase
            commit optimizations in a commercial distributed environment.
            Distributed and Parallel Databases 3(4):325–360, October 1995.

[SWS91]   H.-J. Schek, G. Weikum, and W. Schaad. A multi-level transac-
            tion approach to federated DBMS transaction management. In
            *Proceedings of the First International Workshop on Interoper-
            ability in Multidatabase Systems (IMS'91)*, pages 280–287, April
            1991.

[SWY93]   H.-J. Schek, G. Weikum, and H. Ye. Towards a unified theory
            of concurrency control and recovery. In *Proceedings of the ACM
            Principles of Database Systems (PODS)*, 1993.

[TA94]   A. Tal and R. Alonso. Commit protocols for externalized-commit heterogeneous database systems. *Distributed and Parallel Databases* 2(2), April 1994.

[VEH92]   J. Veijalainen, F. Eliassen, and B. Holtkamp. The S-transaction model. In A. K. Elmagarmid, editor, *Transaction Management for Advanced Database Applications*, pages 467–513. San Mateo, CA: Morgan Kaufmann, 1992.

[Vei90]   J. Veijalainen. *Transaction Concepts in Autonomous Database Environments* (PhD thesis). Munich, Germany: R. Oldenbourg Verlag, 1990.

[Vei93]   J. Veijalainen. Heterogeneous multilevel transaction management with multiple transactions. In *Proceedings of the DEXA'93 Conference*, pages 181–188, September 6–8 1993.

[VHYBS97]   R. Vingralek, H. Hasse-Ye, Y. Breitbart, and H. J. Schek. Unifying concurrency control and recovery of transaction with semantically rich operations. To appear, 1997.

[VW92a]   J. Veijalainen and A. Wolski. *The 2PC Agent Method for Transaction Management in Heterogeneous Multidatabases, and its Correctness*. Technical report J-10. Helsinki, Finland: Technical Research Centre of Finland (VTT), Laboratory for Information Processing, June 1992.

[VW92b]   J. Veijalainen and A. Wolski. Prepare and commit certification for decentralized transaction management in rigorous heterogeneous multidatabases. In *Proceedings of the Eighth International Conference on Data Engineering*, pages 470–479, February 1992.

[VWP+97]   J. Veijalainen, J. Wäsch, J. Puustjärvi, H. Tirri, and O. Pihlajamaa. Transaction models in cooperative work—an overview. In W. Klas and J. Veijalainen, editors, *Transaction Management Support for Cooperative Applications*, chapter 3, pages 27–58. Norwell, MA: Kluwer Academic Publishers, 1997.

[Wei91]   G. Weikum. Principles and realization strategies of multi-level transaction management. *ACM Transactions on Database Systems* 16(1):132–180, March 1991.

[WV90]   A. Wolski and J. Veijalainen. 2PC agent method: Achieving serializability in presence of failures in a heterogeneous multidatabase. In *Proceedings of the IEEE PARBASE-90 Conference*, pages 321–330, 1990.

[WV91]   A. Wolski and J. Veijalainen. 2pc agent method: Achieving serializability in presence of failures in a heterogeneous multi-database. *Databases: Theory, Design and Applications*, pages 268–287, 1991. A revised version of [WV90].

Bibliography

[A+89]   M. Atkinson et al. The object-oriented database system man-
            ifesto. In *Proceedings of the First International Conference on
            Deductive and Object-Oriented Databases*, December 1989.

[AAK+93]   J. Albert, R. Ahmed, W. Kent, M. Ketabchi, W. Litwin, A. Rafii,
            and M. Shan. Automatic importation of relational schemas in
            Pegasus. In *Proceedings IEEE RIDE-IMS*, April 1993.

[AAM97]   G. Alonso, D. El Abbadi, and C. Mohan. Functionality and lim-
            itations of current workflow management systems. *IEEE Expert*,
            1997.

[ABGM90]   R. Alonso, D. Barbara, and H. Garcia-Molina. Data caching
            issues in an information retrieval system. *ACM Transactions on
            Database Systems* 15(3):359–384, September 1990.

[ACHK93]   Y. Arens, C. Y. Chee, C. Hsu, and C. Knoblock. Retrieving
            and integrating data from multiple information sources. *Interna-
            tional Journal of Intelligent and Cooperative Information Systems*
            2(2):127–158, June 1993.

[AFS81]   S. Al-Fedaghi and P. Scheuermann. Mapping considerations in
            the design of schemas for the relational model. *IEEE Transactions
            on Software Engineering* Se-7(1):99–111, 1981.

[AGMS87]   R. Alonso, H. Garcia-Molina, and K. Salem. Concurrency control
            and recovery for global procedures in federated database systems.
            *Quarterly Bulletin IEEE Technical Communications on Database
            Engineering* 10(3):5–11, September 1987.

[AHC96]   Y. J. Al-Houmaily and P. K. Chrysanthis. Dealing with incompat-
            ible presumptions of commit protocols in multidatabase systems.

In *Proceedings of the 11th ACM Annual Symposium on Applied Computing*, pages 186–195, 1996.

[AM89]   H. Afsarmanesh and D. McLeod. The 3DIS: An extensible, object-oriented information management environment. *ACM Transactions on Office Information Systems* 7:339–377, October 1989.

[ANRS92]   M. Ansari, L. Ness, M. Rusinkiewicz, and A. Sheth. Using flexible transactions to support multi-system telecommunication applications. In *Proceedings of the 18th International Conference on Very Large Databases*, pages 65–76, 1992.

[AS96]   G. Alonso and H. Schek. Research issues in large workflow management systems. In *Proceedings of the NSF Workshop: Workflow and Process Automation in Information Systems*, May 1996.

[ASD⁺91]   R. Ahmed, P. De Smedt, W. Du, W. Kent, M. A. Ketabchi, W. A. Litwin, A. Rafii, and M.-C. Shan. The Pegasus heterogeneous multidatabase system. *IEEE Computer* 24(12):19–27, December 1991.

[ASSR93]   P. C. Attie, M. P. Singh, A. Sheth, and M. Rusinkiewicz. Specifying and enforcing intertask dependencies. In *Proceedings of the 19th VLDB Conference*, pages 134–143, 1993.

[AT93]   P. Atzeni and R. Torlone. A metamodel approach for the management of multiple models and the translation of schemes. *Information Systems* 18(6), June 1993.

[B⁺97]   B. Bohrer et al. Infosleuth: Semantic integration of information in open and dynamic environments. In *Proceedings of the ACM International Conference on Management of Data (SIGMOD)*, 1997.

[Bar90]   K. Barker. *Transaction Management on Multidatabase Systems* (PhD thesis). Edmonton, Alberta, Canada: Department of Computing Science, The University of Alberta, August 1990.

[Bar93]   K. Barker. Quantification of autonomy on multidatabase systems. *The Journal of System Integration* 1-26, 1993.

[BB97]   B. Benatallah and A. Bouguettaya. Data sharing on the web. In *Proceedings of the First International Enterprise Distributed Object Computing Workshop—EDOC'97*, October 1997.

[BBMR89]   A. Borgida, R. Brachman, D. McGuinness, and L. Resnick. Classic: A structural data model for objects. In *Proceedings of the ACM SIGMOD*, 1989.

[BC86]   J. Biskup and B. Convent. A formal view integration method. In *Proceedings of the ACM SIGMOD*, pages 398–407, 1986.

[BCW90]   M. Bouzeghoub and I. Comyn-Wattiau. View integration by semantic unification and transformation of data structures. In *Proceedings of the Ninth International Conference on Entity-Relationship Approach*, pages 381–398, 1990.

[BE96]   O. Bukhres and A. K. Elmagarmid, editors. *Object-Oriented Multidatabase Systems: A Solution for Advanced Applications*. Englewood Cliffs, NJ: Prentice Hall, 1996.

[BEK93]   O. Bukhres, A. Elmagarmid, and E. Kuhn. Implementation of the flex transaction model. *IEEE Data Engineering* 16(2):28–32, 1993.

[Ber91]   E. Bertino. Integration of heterogeneous data repositories by using object-oriented views. In *Proceedings of IMS'91—The First International Workshop on Interoperability in Multidatabase Systems*, pages 22–39, 1991.

[BGM90]   D. Barbara and H. Garcia-Molina. The case for controlled inconsistency in replicated data. In *Proceedings of the Workshop on the Management of Replicated Data*, pages 35–42, 1990.

[BGM92]   D. Barbara and H. Garcia-Molina. The demarcation protocol: A technique for maintaining arithmetic constraints in distributed systems. In *Proceedings of the International Conference on Extending Data Base Technology*, pages 371–397, March 1992.

[BGML+90]   Y. Breitbart, H. Garcia-Molina, W. Litwin, N. Roussopoulos, M. Rusinkiewicz, G. Thompson, and G. Wiederhold. Final report of the workshop on multidatabases and semantic interoperability. In *First Workshop on Multidatabases and Semantic Interoperability*, November 1990.

[BGMS92]   Y. Breitbart, H. Garcia-Molina, and A. Silberschatz. Overview of multidatabase transaction management. *VLDB Journal* 1(2):181–239, October 1992.

[BGRS91]   Y. Breitbart, D. Georgakopoulos, M. Rusinkiewicz, and A. Silber-schatz. On rigorous transaction scheduling. *IEEE Transactions on Software Engineering* 17(9):954–960, September 1991.

[BH91]   M. W. Bright and A. R. Hurson. Linguistic support for semantic identification and interpretation in multidatabases. In *Proceedings of IMS'91—The First International Workshop on Interoperability in Multidatabase Systems*, pages 306–313, 1991.

[BHG87]   P. Bernstein, V. Hadzilacos, and N. Goodman. *Concurrency Control and Recovery in Database Systems*. Reading, MA: Addison-Wesley, 1987.

[BHP92]   M. W. Bright, A. R. Hurson, and Simin H. Pakzad. A taxonomy and current issues in multidatabase systems. *IEEE Computer* 25(3):50–60, March 1992.

[BKW+77]   F. C. Bernstein, T. F. Kötzle, G. B. Williams, E. F. Mayer, M. D. Bryce, J. R. Rodgers, O. Kennard, T. Himanouchi, and M. Tasumi. The protein databank: A computer-based archival file for macromolecular structures. *Journal of Molecular Biology* 112:535–542, 1977.

[BL84]   C. Batini and M. Lenzerini. A methodology for data schema integration in the entity-relationship model. *IEEE Transactions on Software Engineering* Se-10(6):650–664, 1984.

[BLN86]   C. Batini, M. Lenzerini, and S. B. Navathe. A comparative analysis of methodologies for database schema integration. *ACM Computing Surveys* 18(4):324–364, December 1986.

[BO91]   K. Barker and M. T. Özsu. Reliable transaction execution in multidatabase systems. In *Proceedings of the First International Workshop on Interoperability in Multidatabase Systems (IMS'91)*, pages 344–347, April 1991.

[BOH+92]   A. Buchmann, M. T. Özsu, M. Hornick, D. Georgakopoulos, and F. A. Manola. A transaction model for active distributed object systems. In A. K. Elmagarmid, editor, *Database Transaction Models for Advanced Applications*, pages 123–158. San Mateo, CA: Morgan Kaufmann, 1992.

[BOT86]   Y. Breitbart, P. Olson, and G. Thompson. Database integration in a distributed heterogeneous database system. In *Proceedings of the Second IEEE Conference on Data Engineering*, February 1986.

[BPK95] A. Bouguettaya, M. Papazoglou, and R. King. On building a hyperdistributed database. *Information Systems, an International Journal* 20(7):557–577, 1995.

[BPS89] E. Bertino, G. Pelagatti, and L. Sbattella. An object-oriented approach to the interconnection of heterogenous databases. In *Proceedings of the Workshop on Heterogenous Databases*, December 1989.

[BR87] B. R. Badrinath and K. Ramamritham. Semantics-based concurrency control: Beyond commutativity. In *Proceedings of the IEEE Third International Conference on Data Engineering*, pages 304–311, February 1987.

[Bre93] M. Bregolin. *Extensions of MSQL: Notes on an Implementation*. Technical report. Houston, TX: University of Houston, Department of Computer Science, March 1993.

[BS81] F. Bancilhon and N. Spyratos. Update semantics and relational views. *ACM Transactions on Database Systems* 6(4), 1981.

[BS88] Y. Breitbart and A. Silberschatz. Multidatabase update issues. In *Proceedings of the ACM SIGMOD International Conference on Management of Data*, pages 135–142, 1988.

[BS95] M. L. Brodie and M. Stonebraker. *Migrating Legacy Systems: Gateways, Interfaces, and the Incremental Approach*. San Francisco: Morgan Kaufmann, 1995.

[BST90] Yuri Breibart, Avi Silberschatz, and Glenn R. Thompson. Reliable transaction management in a multidatabase system. *Proceedings of the ACM SIGMOD International Conference on Management of Data*, pages 214–224, 1990.

[BT85] Y. Breibart and L. R. Tieman. Adds—heterogeneous distributed database system. In F. Schreiber and W. Litwin, editors, *Distributed Data Sharing Systems*. Amsterdam: North-Holland, 1985.

[BW77] D. G. Bobrow and T. Winograd. An overview of KRL, a knowledge representation language. *Cognitive Science* 1(1):10–29, 1977.

[C⁺]   M. J. Carey et al. *Towards heterogeneous multimedia information systems: The garlic approach.* Technical report RJ9911.

[Cas93]   M. Castellanos. Semantic enrichment of interoperable databases. In *Proceedings of the RIDE-IMS*, April 1993.

[Cat94]   R. Cattell, editor. *The Object Database Standard: ODMG-93.* San Francisco: Morgan Kaufmann, 1994.

[CB⁺89]   S. Chakravarthy, B. Blaustein, et al. *HiPAC: A research project in active, time-constrained database management.* Technical report. Cambridge, MA: XEROX (XAIT), July 1989.

[CBSA93]   J. Chen, O. A. Bukhres, and J. Sharif-Askary. A customized multidatabase transaction management strategy. In *Proceedings of the DEXA'93 Conference*, pages 92–103, September 1993.

[CES86]   E. M. Clarke, E. A. Emerson, and A. P. Sistla. Automatic verification of finite state concurrent systems using temporal logic specifications. *ACM TOPLAS* 8(2):244–263, 1986.

[CFM90]   U. S. Chakravarthy, D. Fishman, and J. Minker. Logic-based approach to semantic query optimization. *ACM Transactions on Database Systems* 15(2):162–207, 1990.

[Che76]   P. P. Chen. The entity-relationship model: Toward a unified view of data. *ACM Transactions on Database Systems* 1(1):9–36, 1976.

[Chr91]   P. K. Chrysanthis. *ACTA, A Framework for Modeling and Reasoning About Extended Transactions* (PhD thesis). Amherst, Massachusetts: Department of Computer and Information Science, University of Massachusetts, 1991.

[CHS91]   C. Collet, M. Huhns, and W. Shen. Resource integration using a large knowledge base in carnot. *IEEE Computer*, December 1991.

[Chu90]   C. W. Chung. Dataplex: An access to heterogeneous distributed databases. *Communications of the ACM* 33(1):70–80, 1990.

[CL88]   T. Connors and P. Lyngbaek. Providing uniform access to heterogeneous information bases. In *Proceedings of the Second International Conference on Object-Oriented Database Systems*, September 1988.

[CMG90]   G. Chierchia and S. McConnell-Ginet. Meaning and grammar: An introduction to semantics. chapter 6. Cambridge, MA: MIT Press, 1990.

[Cod73]   CODASYL Data Description Language Committee. *CODASYL Data Description Language Journal of Development*, June 1973. NBS Handbook 113.

[CP84]   S. Ceri and G. Pelagatti. *Distributed Databases: Principles and Systems*. New York: McGraw-Hill, 1984.

[CP86]   A. Cardenas and M. Pirahesh. Data base communication in a heterogeneous data base management system network. *Distributed Systems* 2:386–390, 1986.

[CR84]   B. Czejdo and M. Rusinkiewicz. Query transformation in an instructional database management system. In *Proceedings of the ACM SIGCSE Conference*, 1984.

[CR90]   P. K. Chrysanthis and K. Ramamritham. ACTA: A framework for specifying and reasoning about transaction structure and behavior. In *Proceedings of the ACM-SIGMOD International Conference on Management of Data*, pages 194–203, 1990.

[CR91a]   P. K. Chrysanthis and K. Ramamritham. A formalism for extended transaction models. *Proceedings of the 17th International Conference on VLDB*, pages 103–111, 1991.

[CR91b]   B. Czejdo and M. Rusinkiewicz. Generation and translation of database queries in an instructional DBMS. *The Journal of Computer Information Systems* 31(4), 1991.

[CR92]   P. K. Chrysanthis and K. Ramamritham. ACTA: The SAGA continues. In A. K. Elmagarmid, editor, *Database Transaction Models for Advanced Applications*, pages 349–398. San Mateo, CA: Morgan Kaufmann, 1992.

[CR93]   P. Chrysanthis and K. Ramamritham. Impact of autonomy requirements on transactions and their management in heterogeneous distributed database systems. In *Proceedings DBTA Workshop on Interoperability of Database Systems and Database Applications*, 1993.

[CR94a]   P. Chrysanthis and K. Ramamritham. Autonomy requirements in heterogeneous distributed database systems. In *Proceedings of the Conference on the Advances on Data Management*, pages 283–302, 1994.

[CR94b]   P. K. Chrysanthis and K. Ramamritham. Synthesis of extended transaction models using ACTA. *ACM Transactions on Database Systems* 19(3):450–491, 1994.

[CRE87]   B. Czejdo, M. Rusinkiewicz, and D. Embley. An approach to schema integration and query formulation in federated database systems. In *Proceedings of the Third IEEE Conference on Data Engineering*, February 1987.

[CS91]   A. Chatterjee and A. Segev. A probabilistic approach to information retrieval in heterogeneous databases. In *Proceedings of the First Workshop on Information Technology Systems*, pages 107–124, 1991.

[CSGS91]   M. Castellanos, F. Saltor, and M. Garcia-Solaco. *The Development of Semantic Concepts in the BLOOM Model Using an Object Metamodel*. Technical report LSI-91-22. UPC, 1991.

[CT91]   B. Czejdo and M. Taylor. Integration of database systems using an object-oriented approach. In *Proceedings of IMS'91—The First International Workshop on Interoperability in Multidatabase Systems*, pages 30–37, 1991.

[CT92a]   B. Czejdo and M. Taylor. Integration of information systems using an object-oriented approach. *The Computer Journal* 35(5), 1992.

[CT92b]   B. Czejdo and M. Taylor. Integration of object-oriented programming languages and database systems in kopernik. *The Data and Knowledge Engineering Journal* 7, 1992.

[CV83]   M. A. Casanova and M. V. P. Vidal. Towards a sound view integration methodology. In *Proceedings of the ACM SIGACT/SIGMOD*, pages 36–47. New York: ACM, 1983.

[CW90]   S. Ceri and J. Widom. Deriving production rules for constraint management. In *Proceedings of the 16th VLDB Conference*, pages 566–577, 1990. Also appears as Technical Report RJ 7348 (68829), IBM Almaden.

[CW92]   S. Ceri and J. Widom. Production rules in parallel and dis-
              tributed database environments. In *Proceedings of the 18th VLDB
              Conference*, pages 339–351, 1992.

[CWB93]   I. Comyn-Wattiau and M. Bouzeghoub. Constraint confrontation:
              An important step in view integration. In *Proceedings of the
              Fifth International Symposium on Advanced Information Systems
              Engineering, CAiSE'93*, pages 507–523, 1993.

[DAT87a]   S. M. Deen, R. R. Amin, and M. C. Taylor. Data integration in
              distributed databases. *IEEE TSE* 13(7), 1987.

[DAT87b]   S. M. Deen, R. R. Amin, and M. C. Taylor. Implementation of a
              prototype for Preci*. *Computer Journal* 30(2):157–162, 1987.

[DB82]   U. Dayal and P. Bernstein. On the correct translation of update
              operations on relational views. *ACM Transactions on Database
              Systems* 7(3), 1982.

[DBB⁺88]   U. Dayal, B. Blaustein, A. Buchmann, U. Chakravarthy, M. Hsu,
              D. McCarthy R. Ladin, A. Rosenthal, M. J. Carey S. Sarin,
              M. Livny, and R. Jauhari. The HiPAC project: Combining active
              databases and timing constraints. *SIGMOD Record* 17(1), March
              1988.

[DBM88]   U. Dayal, A. Buchmann, and D. McCarthy. Rules are objects
              too: A knowledge model for an active, object-oriented database
              system. In *Proceedings of the Second International Workshop on
              Object-Oriented Database Systems*, September 1988.

[DE89]   W. Du and A. K. Elmagarmid. Quasi serializability: A correct-
              ness criterion for global concurrency control in InterBase. In
              Proceedings of the 15th International VLDB Conference, pages
              347–355, 1989.

[DeK86]   J. DeKleer. An assumption-based truth maintenance system.
              Artificial Intelligence 28, 1986.

[DEK91]   W. Du, A. Elmagarmid, and W. Kim. Maintaining quasi seri-
              alizability in HDDBSs. In *Proceedings IEEE Data Engineering*,
              1991.

[DEKB93]   W. Du, A. Elmagarmid, W. Kim, and O. Buhkres. Supporting
              consistent updates in partially replicated multidatabase systems.
              Very Large Data Bases 2(2), 1993.

[Dem68]   A. Dempster. A generalization of the bayesian inference. *Journal of the Royal Statistical Society, Series B* 30, 1968.

[DeM89a]   L. DeMichiel.   Performing operations over mismatched domains. In *Proceedings of the Fifth IEEE International Conference on Data Engineering*, pages 36–45. Los Alamitos, CA: IEEE Computer Society Press, February 1989.

[DeM89b]   L. DeMichiel. Resolving database incompatibility: An approach to performing relational operations over mismatched domains. *IEEE Transactions on Knowledge and Data Engineering* 1(4):484–493, 1989.

[DeS86]   J. M. DeSouza. Sis—a schema integration system. In *Proceedings of the Fifth British National Conference on Databases*, pages 167–185, 1986.

[DG+95]   A. Daruwala, C. Goh, et al.   The context interchange network. In *Proceedings of the IFIP WG2.6 Conference on Database Semantics, DS-6*, May 1995.

[DGH+95]   A. Daruwala, C. Goh, S. Hofmeister, K. Hussein, S. Madnick, and M. Siegel. Context interchange network prototype. In *Proceedings of the Sixth IFIP International Conference on Database Semantics*, 1995.

[DH84]   U. Dayal and H. Hwang.   View definition and generalization for database integration in a multidatabase system.   *IEEE Transactions on Software Engineering* 10(6):628–644, 1984.

[DHL90]   U. Dayal, M. Hsu, and R. Ladin. Organizing long-running activities with triggers and transactions. In *Proceedings of the ACM SIGMOD Conference*, pages 204–214, June 1990.

[DKS92]   W. Du, R. Krishnamurthy, and M. Shan. Query optimization in a heterogeneous DBMS. In *Proceedings VLDB*, 1992.

[DL87]   P. Dwyer and J. Larson. Some experiences with a distributed database testbed system. In *Proceedings of the IEEE*, volume 75, May 1987.

[DSD95]   W. Du, M. Shan, and U. Dayal. Reducing multidatabase query response time using tree balancing. In *Proceedings ACM SIGMOD*, 1995.

[DSW94]   A. Deacon, H. J. Schek, and G. Weikum. Semantics-based multilevel transactions management in federated systems. In *Proceedings of the 10th International Conference on Data Engineering*, pages 452–461, 1994.

[ECR87]   D. Embley, B. Czejdo, and M. Rusinkiewicz. An approach to schema integration and query formulation in federated database systems. In *Proceedings of the Third International Conference on Data Engineering*, February 1987.

[ED90]   A. Elmagarmid and W. Du. A paradigm for concurrency control in heterogeneous distributed database systems. In *Proceedings of the Sixth International Conference on Data Engineering*, February 1990.

[EGLT76]   K. Eswaran, J. Gray, R. Lorie, and I. Traiger. The notion of consistency and predicate locks in a database system. *Communications of the ACM* 19(11):624–633, 1976.

[EH88]   A. K. Elmagarmid and A. A. Helal. Supporting updates in heterogeneous distributed database systems. In *Proceedings of the IEEE Fourth International Conference on Data Engineering*, pages 564–569, 1988.

[EJKB96]   A. K. Elmagarmid, J. Jing, W. Kim, and O. Bukhres. Global committability in multidatabase systems. In *IEEE Transactions on Knowledge and Data Engineering*, 1996.

[ELLR90]   A. K. Elmagarmid, Y. Leu, W. Litwin, and M. Rusinkiewicz. A multidatabase transaction model for InterBase. In *Proceedings of the 16th International Conference on VLDB*, pages 507–518, 1990.

[Elm92]   A. Elmagarmid, editor. *Database Transaction Models for Advanced Applications*. San Mateo, CA: Morgan Kaufmann, 1992.

[EMLN86]   R. El-Masri, J. Larson, and S. B. Navathe. *Schema Integration Algorithms for Federated Databases and Logical Database Design*. Technical report. Honeywell Systems Development Division, 1986.

[EMN84]   R. El-Masri and S. Navathe. Object integration in logical data-
           base design. *IEEE Transactions on Data Engineering*, pages
           426–433, 1984.

[EMW79]   R. El-Masri and G. Wiederhold. Data model integration using
           the structural model. In *Proceedings of the 1979 ACM SIGMOD*,
           pages 191–202, 1979.

[EMW81]   R. El-Masri and G. Wiederhold. Gordas: A formal high-level
           query language for the entity-relationship model. In *Proceedings
           of the International Conference on Entity-Relationship Approach*,
           1981.

[EP90]   A. Elmagarmid and C. Pu, editors. Heterogeneous databases:
           Special issue. *ACM Computing Surveys* 22(3), September 1990.

[Etz92]   O. Etzion. *Active interdatabase dependencies*. Technical report
           ISE-TR-92-1. Haifa, Israel: Technion, January 1992.

[Etz93]   O. Etzion. PARDES—a data driven oriented active database
           model. *SIGMOD Record* 22(1):7–14, March 1993.

[EV87]   F. Eliassen and J. Veijalainen. Language support for multi-
           database transactions in a cooperative, autonomous environment.
           In *Proceedings of the TENCON 87 Conference*, pages 277–281,
           August 25–28 1987.

[FBC⁺87]   D. Fishman, D. Beech, H. Cate, E. Chow, T. Connors, T. Davis,
           N. Derrett, C. Hoch, W. Kent, P. Lyngbaek, B. Mahbod,
           M. Neimat, T. Ryan, and M. Shan. Iris: An object-oriented
           database management system. *ACM Transactions on Office
           Information Systems* 5(1):48–69, January 1987.

[FHMS91]   D. Fang, J. Hammer, D. McLeod, and A. Si. Remote-Exchange:
           An approach to controlled sharing among autonomous, heteroge-
           nous database systems. In *Proceedings of the IEEE Spring
           Compcon*. Los Alamitos, CA: IEEE Computer Society Press,
           February 1991.

[FKN91]   P. Fankhauser, M. Kracker, and E. Neuhold. Semantic vs. struc-
           tural resemblance of classes. *SIGMOD Record, Special Issue on
           Semantic Issues in Multidatabases* 20(4), December 1991.

[FN92]   P. Fankhauser and E. Neuhold. *Knowledge based integration of heterogeneous databases.* Technical report. Technische Hochschule Darmstadt, 1992.

[Fre91]   K. Frenkel.   The human genome project and informatics. *Communications of the ACM* 34(11):41–51, 1991.

[FS83]   A. Ferrier and C. Stangret.   Heterogeneity in the Distributed Database Mangagement System SIRIUS-DELTA. In *Proceedings of the International Conference on Very Large Databases*, 1983.

[G⁺91]   S. Ghandeharizadeh et al.   *Design and Implementation of OMEGA Object-Based System.* Technical report USC-CS. Los Angeles: Computer Science Department, University of Southern California, September 1991.

[GB94]   P. C. J. Graham and K. Barker.   Effective optimistic concurrency control in multiversion object bases. In *Proceedings of the International Symposium on Object-Oriented Methodologies and Systems*, pages 313–328, September 1994.

[GCO90]   R. Gagliardi, M. Caneve, and G. Oldano.   An operational approach to the integration of distributed heterogeneous environments. In *Proceedings of the IEEE PARBASE-90 Conference*, 1990.

[Geo90]   D. Georgakopoulos. *Transaction Management in Multidatabase Systems* (PhD thesis). Houston, TX: Department of Computer Science, University of Houston, December 1990.

[Geo91]   D. Georgakopoulos. Multidatabase recoverability and recovery. In *Proceedings of the First International Workshop on Interoperability in Multidatabase Systems (IMS'91)*, pages 348–355, April 1991.

[GK93]   S. Gantimahapatruni and G. Karabatis.   Enforcing data dependencies in cooperative information systems. In *Proceedings of the International Conference on Intelligent and Cooperative Information Systems*, May 1993.

[GL84]   V. D. Gligor and G. L. Luckenbaugh.   Interconnecting heterogeneous database management systems. *Computer* 17(1):33–43, January 1984.

[GLN92]   W. Gotthard, P. C. Lockemann, and A. Neufeld. System-guided view integration for object-oriented databases. *IEEE Transactions on Knowledge and Data Engineering* 4(1):1–22, 1992.

[GLPT75]   J. N. Gray, R. A. Lorie, A. R. Putzulo, and I. L. Traiger. Granularity of locks and degrees of consistency in a shared database. In *Proceedings of the First International Conference on Very Large Databases*, pages 25–33, 1975.

[GLRS91]   J. Grant, W. Litwin, N. Roussopoulos, and T. Sellis. An algebra and calculus for relational multidatabase systems. April 1991.

[GM83]   H. Garcia-Molina. Using semantic knowledge for transaction processing in a distributed database. *ACM TODS* 8(2):186–213, June 1983.

[GMGK⁺91] H. Garcia-Molina, D. Gawlick, J. Klein, K. Kleissner, and K. Salem. Modeling long-running activities as nested SAGAs. *Bulletin of the IEEE Technical Committee on Data Engineering* 14(1):14–18, 1991.

[GMP⁺92] J. Geller, A. Mehta, Y. Perl, E. Neuhold, and A. P. Sheth. Algorithms for structural schema integration. In *Proceedings of the Second International Conference on Systems Integration*, pages 604–614, 1992.

[GMS87]   H. Garcia-Molina and K. Salem. SAGAs. In *Proceedings of the ACM Conference on Management of Data (SIGMOD)*, pages 249–259, 1987.

[GPZ85]   V. D. Gligor and R. Popescu-Zeltin. Concurrency control issues in distributed heterogeneous database management systems. In F. Schreiber and W. Litwin, editors, *Distributed Data Sharing Systems*. New York: Elsevier Science, 1985.

[GPZ86]   V. Gligor and R. Popescu-Zeltin. Transaction management in distributed heterogeneous database management systems. *Information Systems* 11(4):287–297, 1986.

[GR93]   J. Gray and A. Reuter. *Transaction Processing: Concepts and Techniques*. San Francisco: Morgan Kaufmann, 1993.

[Gra78]   J. N. Gray. Notes on database operating systems. In R. Bayer, R. M. Graham, and G. Seegmuller, editors, *Operating Systems: An Advanced Course*, volume 60, pages 394–481. New York: Springer-Verlag, 1978.

[Gra81]   J. Gray. The transaction concept: Virtues and limitations. In *Proceedings of the Seventh International Conference on Very Large Data Bases*, pages 144–154, September 1981.

[GRS91]   D. Georgakopoulos, M. Rusinkiewicz, and A. Sheth. On serializability of multidatabase transaction through forced local conflicts. In *Proceedings of the Seventh International Conference on Data Engineering*, pages 314–323, 1991.

[GRS94]   D. Georgakopoulos, M. Rusinkiewicz, and A. Sheth. Using tickets to enforce the serializability of multidatabase transactionns. *IEEE Transactions on Knowledge and Data Engineering*, February 1994.

[Gru93]   T. Gruber. A translation approach to portable ontology specifications. *Knowledge Acquisition, An International Journal of Knowledge Acquisition for Knowledge-Based Systems* 5(2), June 1993.

[GSCS]   M. Garcia-Solaco, M. Castellanos, and F. Saltor. Semantic heterogeneity in multidatabase systems.

[GSCS93]   M. Garcia-Solaco, M. Castellanos, and F. Saltor. Discovering interdatabase resemblance of classes for interoperable databases. In *Proceedings of the RIDE-IMS*, April 1993.

[Guh90]   R. V. Guha. *Micro-Theories and Contexts in Cyc Part I: Basic Issues*. Technical report ACT-CYC-129-90. Austin, TX: Microelectronics and Computer Technology Corporation, June 1990.

[HAB+92]   Y. Halabi, M. Ansari, R. Batra, W. Jin, G. Karabatis, P. Krychniak, M. Rusinkiewicz, and L. Suardi. Narada: An environment for specification and execution of multi-system applications. In *Proceedings of the Second International Conference on Systems Integration*, June 1992.

[HBP94]   A. R. Hurson, M. W. Bright, and H. Pakzad. *Multidatabase Systems: An Advanced Solution for Global Information Sharing*. Los Alamitos, CA: IEEE Computer Society Press, 1994.

[HC96]   G. Hammilton and R. Cattell. *JDBC: A Java SQL API.* 1996.

[HFG87]   D. I. Howells, N. J. Fiddian, and W. A. Gray. A source-to-source meta-translation system for relational query languages. In *Proceedings of the 13th VLDB Conference*, pages 227–234, 1987.

[HFLP89]   L. Haas, J. Freytag, G. Lohman, and H. Pirahesh. Extensible query processing in Starburst. In *Proceedings of the ACM SIGMOD Conference*, pages 377–388, May 1989.

[HJK⁺92]   M. Huhns, N. Jacobs, T. Ksiezyk, W. Shen, M. Singh, and P. Cannata. *Enterprise information modeling and model integration in carnot.* Technical report Carnot-128-92. MCC, 1992.

[HK87]   R. Hull and R. King. Semantic database modeling: Survey, applications, and research issues. *ACM Computing Surveys* 19(3):201–260, September 1987.

[HLM88]   M. Hsu, R. Ladin, and D. McCarthy. An execution model for active data base management systems. In *Proceedings of the Third International Conference on Data and Knowledge Bases*, June 1988.

[HLS93]   S.-Y. Hwang, E.-P. Lim, and J. Srivastava. Asynchronous transaction commitment in federated database systems. In *Proceedings of the International Conference on Parallel and Distributed Systems*, 1993.

[HM81]   M. Hammer and D. McLeod. Database description with sdm: A semantic database model. *ACM Transactions on Database Systems* 6(1):351–386, 1981.

[HM85]   D. Heimbigner and D. McLeod. A federated architecture for information systems. *ACM Transactions on Office Information Systems* 3(3):253–278, July 1985.

[HM93]   J. Hammer and D. McLeod. An approach to resolving semantic heterogeneity in a federation of autonomous, heterogeneous database systems. *International Journal of Intelligent and Cooperative Information Systems* 2(1):51–83, March 1993.

[HNSD93]   D. K. Hsiao, E. J. Neuhold, and R. Sacks-Davis, editors. *IFIP DS-5 Semantics of Interoperable Database Systems.* New York: Elsevier Science, 1993.

[HR83]   T. Haerder and A. Reuter. Principles of transaction-oriented database recovery. *ACM Computing Surveys* 15(4):287–317, December 1983.

[HR90]   S. Hayne and S. Ram. Multi-user view integration system (MU-VIS): An expert system for view integration. In *Proceedings of the Sixth International Conference on Data Engineering.* Los Alamitos, CA: IEEE Computer Society Press, February 1990.

[HS90]   M. Hsu and A. Silberschatz. Persistent transmission and unilateral commit—a position paper. In *Workshop on Multidatabases and Semantic Interoperability*, October 1990.

[HS91]   M. Hsu and A. Silberschatz. Unilateral commit: A new paradigm for reliable distributed transaction processing. In *Proceedings of the Seventh International Conference on Data Engineering*, pages 286–293, April 1991.

[HS94]   M. Holsheimer and A. Siebes. *Data Mining: The Search for Knowledge in Databases.* Technical report CS-R9406. Amsterdam: CWI, 1994.

[Hu95]   X. Hu. *Making Multidatabases Active* (Master's thesis). Houston, TX: University of Houston, May 1995.

[II90]   ISO/IEC 9804. *Information Technology, Open Systems, Interconnection-Service Definition for the Commitment, Concurrency and Recovery Service Element.* Technical report, 1990.

[II92]   ISO/IEC 9075. *Information Processing Systems—Database Language SQL, International Standard, third edition.* Technical report no. ISO 9075 : 1992 (E), 1992. Also as ANSI X3.135-1992, Database Language SQL.

[Inm95]   W. Inmon. Data warehouse defined. *Computerworld*, March 1995.

[Jac85]   D. Jacobs. *Applied Database Logic*, volume 1. Englewood Cliffs, NJ: Prentice Hall, 1985.

[JCV84]   M. Jarke, J. Clifford, and Y. Vassiliou. An optimizing prolog front
             end to a relational query system. In *Proceedings of the SIGMOD
             Conference*, June 1984.

[JDEB94]   J. Jing, W. Du, A. Elmagarmid, and O. Buhkres. Maintain-
             ing consistency of replicated data in multidatabase systems. In
             Proceedings IEEE Distributed Computing Systems, 1994.

[Joh93]   P. Johannesson. Schema transformation as an aid in view in-
             tegration. In *Proceedings of the Fifth International Symposium
             on Advanced Information Systems Engineering, CAiSE'93*, pages
             71–92, 1993.

[Joh94]   P. Johanneson. A method for translating relational schemas into
             conceptual schemas. In *Proceedings of the 10th International
             Conference on Data Engineering*, 1994.

[JPSL⁺88]   G. Jacobsen, G. Piatetsky-Shapiro, C. Lafond, M. Rajinikanth,
             and J. Hernandez. CALIDA: A knowledge-based system for inte-
             grating multiple heterogeneous databases. In *Proceedings of the
             Third International Conference on Data and Knowledge Bases*,
             pages 3–18, June 1988.

[Kai90]   G. E. Kaiser. A flexible transaction model for software engineer-
             ing. In *Proceedings of the Sixth International Conference on Data
             Engineering*, pages 560–567, 1990.

[Kar95]   G. Karabatis. *Management of Interdependent Data in a Mul-
             tidatabase Environment: A Polytransaction Approach* (PhD
             thesis). Houston, TX: University of Houston, May 1995.

[KBC⁺87]   W. Kim, J. Banerjee, H. T. Chou, J. F. Garza, and D. Woelk.
             Composite object support in an object-oriented database system.
             In *Proceedings of the Conference on Object-Oriented Program-
             ming Systems, Languages, and Applications*, pages 118–125,
             1987.

[KCGS93]   W. Kim, I. Choi, S. Gala, and M. Scheevel. On resolving
             schematic heterogeneity in multidatabase systems. *Distributed
             and Parallel Databases* 1(3):251–279, July 1993.

[KDN90]   M. Kaul, K. Drosten, and E. J. Nuehold. Viewsystem: Integrat-
             ing heterogeneous information bases by object-oriented views.

In *Proceedings of the Sixth International Conference on Data Engineering*, pages 2–10, 1990.

[Ken89]   W. Kent. The many forms of a single fact. In *Proceedings of the IEEE Spring Compcon*. Los Alamitos, CA: IEEE Computer Society Press, February 1989.

[Ken91a]   W. Kent. The breakdown of the information model in multi-database systems. *SIGMOD Record, Special Issue on Semantic Issues in Multidatabases* 20(4), December 1991.

[Ken91b]   W. Kent. Solving domain mismatch problems with an object-oriented database programming language. In *Proceedings of the International Conference on Very Large Databases*, pages 147–160. Los Alamitos, CA: IEEE Computer Society Press, September 1991.

[KIGS93]   W. Kim, C. Injun, S. Gala, and M. Scheevel. On resolving semantic heterogeneity. *Distributed and Parallel Databases* 1(3), 1993.

[Kin81]   J. J. King. Quist: A system for semantic query optimization in relational databases. In *Proceedings of the Seventh VLDB Conference*, pages 510–517, 1981.

[KK93]   I. E. Kang and T. F. Keefe. Supporting reliable and atomic transaction management in multidatabase systems. In *Proceedings of the 13th International Conference on Distributed Computing Systems (DCS-93)*, pages 457–464, May 1993.

[KLK91]   R. Krishnamurthy, W. Litwin, and W. Kent. Language features for interoperability of databases with schematic discrepancies. In J. Clifford and R. King, editors, *Proceedings of the ACM SIGMOD*, pages 40–49. New York: ACM, May 1991.

[KLS90]   H. F. Korth, E. Levy, and A. Silberschatz. A formal approach to recovery by compensating transactions. In *Proceedings of the 16th International Conference on VLDB*, pages 95–106, August 1990.

[KP91]   E. Kühn and F. Puntigam. *The VPL Vienna Parallel Logic Language*. Technical report TR-185-91-1. Vienna: University of Technology, Institute of Computer Language, January 1991.

[KP92]   G. Kaiser and C. Pu. Dynamic restructuring of transactions. In A. K. Elmagarmid, editor, *Database Transaction Models for Advanced Applications*, pages 265–295. San Mateo, CA: Morgan Kaufmann, 1992.

[KR88]   J. Klein and A. Reuter. Migrating transactions. In *Future Trends in Distributed Computing Systems in the 90's*, 1988.

[KR93]   M. Kamath and K. Ramamritham. Performance characteristics of epsilon serializability with hierarchical inconsistency bounds. In *Proceedings of the Ninth International Conference on Data Engineering*, pages 587–594, 1993.

[KRS93]   G. Karabatis, M. Rusinkiewicz, and A. Sheth. Correctness and enforcement of multidatabase interdependencies. In N. Adam and B. Bhargava, editors, *Advanced Database Systems*. New York: Springer-Verlag, 1993.

[KS]   V. Kashyap and A. Sheth. Semantic and schematic similarities between database objects: A context-based approach. *The VLDB Journal*. To appear; *http://www.cs.uga.edu/LSDIS/~amit/66b-VLDB.ps*.

[KS88]   H. F. Korth and G. D. Speegle. Formal model of correctness without serializability. In *Proceedings of the ACM SIGMOD International Conference on Management of Data*, pages 379–386, June 1988.

[KS91]   W. Kim and J. Seo. Classifying schematic and data heterogeneity in multidatabase systems. *IEEE Computer* 24(12):12–18, December 1991.

[KS94]   V. Kashyap and A. Sheth. *Semantics-Based Information Brokering: A Step Towards Realizing the Infocosm*. Technical report DCS-TR-307. New Brunswick, NJ: Rutgers University, March 1994.

[KSS95]   V. Kashyap, K. Shah, and A. Sheth. Metadata for building the multimedia patch quilt. In *Multimedia Database Systems: Issues and Research Directions*. New York: Springer-Verlag, 1995.

[L+88]   V. Linnemann et al. Design and implementation of an extensible database management system supporting user defined data types and functions. In *Proceedings of the International Conference on Very Large Databases*, pages 294–305, 1988.

[L+90]   W. Litwin et al. MSQL: A multidatabase language. *Information Sciences* 49(1-3):59–101, October–December 1990.

[LA86]   W. Litwin and A. Abdellatif. Multidatabase interoperability. *IEEE Computer* 19(12):10–18, December 1986.

[LA87]   W. Litwin and A. Abbellatif. An overview of the multi-database manipulation language MDSL. *Proceedings of the IEEE*, May 1987.

[LBE+82]   W. Litwin, J. Boudenant, C. Esculier, A. Ferrier, A. M. Glo-rieux, J. La Chimia, K. Kabbaj, C. Moulinoux, P. Rolin, and C. Stangret. SIRIUS system for distributed data management. In *Distributed Databases*, pages 311–343. Amsterdam: North-Holland, 1982.

[LC94]   W. S. Li and C. Clifton. Semantic integration in heterogeneous databases using neural networks. In *Proceedings of the 20th Conference on Very Large Data Bases*, pages 1–12, 1994.

[LDS92]   B. Liskov, M. Day, and L. Shira. Distributed object management in thor. In *The International Workshop on Distributed Object Management*, 1992.

[LE90]   Y. Leu and A. Elmagarmid. A hierarchical approach to concurrency control for multidatabase systems. In *Second International Symposium on Databases in Parallel and Distributed Systems*, July 1990.

[LERL90]   Y. Leu, A. Elmagarmid, M. Rusinkiewicz, and W. Litwin. Extending the transaction model in a multidatabase environment. In *Proceedings of the 16th International Conference on Very Large Databases*, August 1990.

[Leu91]   Y. Leu. Composing multidatabase applications using flex transactions. *IEEE Data Engineering Bulletin* 14(1), March 1991.

[LHL97]   S. Lee, C. Hwang, and W. Lee. A uniform approach to global concurrency control and recovery in multidatabase environments. In *Proceedings of the Sixth International Conference on Information and Knowledge Management (CIKM'97)*, pages 51–58, November 10–14 1997.

[Lit85a]   W. Litwin. Implicit joins in the multidatabase system MRDSM. In *Proceedings of the IEEE-COMPSAC*, October 1985.

[Lit85b]   W. Litwin. An overview of the multidatabase system MRSDM. In *Proceedings of the ACM National Conference*, pages 495–504. New York: ACM, October 1985.

[Lit86]   W. Litwin. A multidatabase interoperability. *IEEE Computer* 19(12):10–18, December 1986.

[Lit88]   W. Litwin. From database systems to multidatabase: Why and how. In *Proceedings of the British Conference on Databases*, pages 161–188. Cambridge: Cambridge University Press, 1988.

[Lit94]   W. Litwin. *Multidatabase Systems*. Englewood Cliffs, NJ: Prentice Hall, 1994.

[LKS91]   E. Levy, H. Korth, and A. Silberschatz. An optimistic commit protocol for distributed transaction management. In *Proceedings of the ACM SIGMOD Conference*, pages 88–97, May 1991.

[LLPS91]   G. Lohman, B. Lindsay, H. Pirahesh, and K. B. Schiefer. Extensions to Starburst: Objects, types, functions, and rules. *Communications of the ACM* 34(10):94–109, October 1991.

[LM84]   P. Lyngbaek and D. McLeod. Object management in distributed information systems. *ACM Transactions on Office Information Systems* 2(2):96–122, April 1984.

[LM88]   Q. Li and D. McLeod. Object flavor evolution in an object-oriented database system. In *Proceedings of the Conference on Office Information System*. New York: ACM, March 1988.

[LMR90]   W. Litwin, L. Mark, and N. Roussopoulos. Interoperability of multiple autonomous databases. *ACM Computing Surveys* 22(3):267–293, September 1990.

[LNEM89]   J. Larson, S. B. Navathe, and R. El-Masri. A theory of attribute equivalence and its applications to schema integration. *IEEE Transactions on Software Engineering* 15(4):449–463, April 1989.

[LR86]   T. Landers and R. Rosenberg. An overview of multibase. *Distributed Systems* 2:391–421, 1986.

[LRO96]   A. Levy, A. Rajaraman, and J. Ordille. Querying heterogeneous information sources using source descriptions. In *Proceedings of the 22nd International VLDB Conference*, 1996.

[LRV88]   C. Lecluse, P. Richard, and F. Velez. O_2, an object-oriented data model. In *Proceedings of the ACM SIGMOD International Conference on Management of Data*. New York: ACM, June 1988.

[LS93]   E.-P. Lim and J. Srivastava. *Attribute value conflict in database integration: An evidential reasoning approach*. Technical report TR 93-14. Minneapolis: University of Minnesota, Department of Computer Science, February 1993.

[LS$^+$93]   E.-P. Lim, J. Srivastava, et al. Entity identification in database integration. In *Proceedings of the Ninth IEEE International Conference on Data Engineering*, pages 294–301. New York: Austrian Computer Society, IEEE Computer Society Press, April 1993.

[Mad96]   S. E. Madnick. Are we moving toward an information superhighway or a tower of Babel? The challenge of large-scale semantic heterogeneity. In *Proceedings of the 12th International Conference on Data Engineering*, pages 2–8. Los Alamitos, CA: IEEE Computer Society Press, 1996.

[MAGW95]   C. Mohan, G. Alonso, R. Gunthor, and X. Wang. Exotica: A research perspective on workflow management systems. *Data Engineering Bulletin* 18(1):19–26, March 1995.

[MB81]   A. Motro and P. Buneman. Constructing superviews. *ACM SIGMOD Record*, pages 56–64, 1981.

[MBP95]   S. Milliner, A. Bouguettaya, and M. Papazoglou. A scalable architecture for autonomous heterogeneous database interactions. In *Proceeedings of the VLDB Conference (VLDB)*, September 1995.

[McL93]   D. McLeod. Beyond object databases. In *Datenbanksysteme in Büro, Technik, und Wissenschaft*. New York: Springer-Verlag, 1993.

[MD89]   D. McCarthy and U. Dayal. The architecture of an active data base management system. In *Proceedings of the ACM SIGMOD Conference*, pages 215–224, 1989.

[ME84]   M. V. Mannino and W. Effelsberg. Matching techniques in
            global schema design. In *Proceedings of the First International
            Conference on Data Engineering*, pages 418–425, 1984.

[ME93]   J. G. Mullen and A. K. Elmagarmid. InterSQL: A multidatabase
            approach to federated databases. In *The 1993 Workshop on
            Database Programming Languages*, 1993.

[Mel96]   J. Melton. An SQL snapshot. In *IEEE 12th International
            Conference on Data Engineering*, February 1996.

[MGG86]   J. E. Moss, N. D. Griffeth, and M. H. Graham. Abstraction in
            recovery management. In *Proceedings of the 1986 ACM SIGMOD
            Conference*, pages 72–83, May 28–30 1986.

[MHG$^+$92] F. Manola, S. Heiler, D. Georgakopoulos, M. Hornick, and
            M. Brodie. Distributed object management. *International Jour-
            nal of Intelligent and Cooperative Information Systems* 1(1),
            March 1992.

[Mic94]   Microsoft. *ODBC 2.0 Programmer's Reference and SDK Guide*.
            Redmond, WA: Microsoft Press, 1994.

[Mil89]   J. Mills. *Semantic Integrity in OSCA of the Totality of Corporate
            Data*. Technical report TM-STS-014112. Bellcore, August 1989.

[Mis93a]   P. Missier. *Extending a Multidatabase Language to Resolve
            Schema and Data Conflicts* (Master's thesis). Houston, TX: De-
            partment of Computer Science, University of Houston, September
            1993.

[Mis93b]   P. Missier. *Extensions of MSQL: Notes on an Implementa-
            tion*. Technical report. Houston, TX: University of Houston,
            Department of Computer Science, March 1993.

[MJSA93]   J. G. Mullen, J. Jing, and J. Sharif-Askary. Reservation commit-
            ment and its use in multidatabase systems. In *Proceedings of the
            DEXA'93 Conference*, pages 116–121, September 1993.

[MK]   E. Mena and V. Kashyap. Observer: An approach for
            query processing in global information systems based on in-
            teroperation across pre-existing ontologies. Working paper;
            http://www.cs.uga.edu/LSDIS/infoquilt.

[MKS97] S. Mehrotra, H. F. Korth, and A. Silberschatz. Concurrency control in hierarchical multidatabase systems. *VLDB* 6(2), 1997.

[MKSA92] J. G. Mullen, W. Kim, and J. Sharif-Askary. On the imposibility of atomic commitment in multidatabase systems. In *Proceedings of the Second International Conference on Systems Integration*, pages 625–634, June 1992.

[Mon93] S. Monti. *Query Optimization in Multidatabase Systems* (Master's thesis). Houston, TX: University of Houston, December 1993.

[Mos85] J. E. B. Moss. *Nested Transactions: An Approach to Reliable Distributed Computing*. Cambridge, MA: MIT Press, 1985.

[Mot87] A. Motro. Superviews: Virtual integration of multiple databases. *Transactions on Software Engineering* 13(7), 1987.

[MR91] P. Muth and T. Rakow. Atomic commitment for integrated database systems. In *Proceedings of the Seventh International Conference on Data Engineering*, pages 296–304, April 1991.

[MR95] P. Missier and M. Rusinkiewicz. Extending a multidatabase manipulation language to resolve schema and data conflicts. In *Proceedings of the Sixth IFIP International Conference on Database Semantics*, 1995.

[MRB+92] S. Mehrotra, R. Rastogi, Y. Breitbart, H. F. Korth, and A. Silberschatz. The concurrency control problems in multidatabases: Characteristics and solutions. In *Proceedings of the ACM SIGMOD International Conference on Management of Data*, pages 288–297, June 1992.

[MRKS91] S. Mehrotra, R. Rastogi, H. F. Korth, and A. Silberschatz. Non-serializeable executions in heterogeneous distributed database systems. In *Proceedings of the First International Conference on Parallel and Distributed Systems*, December 1991.

[MRKS92] S. Mehrotra, R. Rastogi, H. F. Korth, and A. Silberschatz. Relaxing serializability in multidatabase systems. In *Proceedings of the Second International Workshop on Research Issues on Data Engineering: Transaction and Query Peocessing*, 1992.

[MSOP86]   D. Maier, J. Stein, A. Otis, and A. Purdy. Development of an object-oriented DBMS. In *Proceedings of the Conference on Object-Oriented Programming Systems, Languages, and Applications*, pages 472–482. New York: ACM, 1986.

[MU83]   D. Maier and J. Ullman. Maximal objects and the semantics of universal relation databases. *ACM Transactions on Database Systems* 8(1):1–14, March 1983.

[Mul92]   J. G. Mullen. Fbase: A federated objectbase system. *International Journal of Computer Science and Engineering* 7(2), April 1992.

[Mut94]   P. Muth. *Transaction Management in Heterogeneous and Autonomous Database Systems* (PhD thesis). Darmstadt, Germany: University of Darmstadt, May 1994. In German.

[MVN93]   P. Muth, J. Veijalainen, and E. Neuhold. *Extending Multi-Level Transactions for Heterogeneous and Autonomous Database Systems.* Technical report 739. Germany: GMD-IPSI, March 1993.

[MY98]   S. Mazumdar and G. Yuan. Localizing global constraints: A geometric approach. In *Proceedings of the Ninth International Conference on Computing and Information*, 1998.

[NEML86]   S. Navathe, R. El-Masri, and J. Larson. Integrating user views in database design. *IEEE Computer* 19(1):50–62, 1986.

[NG82]   S. B. Navathe and S. G. Gadgil. A methodology for view integration in logical database design. In *Proceedings of the Eighth VLDB Conference*, pages 142–162, 1982.

[NRC88]   National Research Council. *Mapping and Sequencing the Human Genome.* National Academy Press, April 1988.

[NWM93]   J. R. Nicol, C. T. Wilkes, and F. A. Manola. Object orientation in heterogeneous distributed computing systems. *IEEE Computer* 26(6), June 1993.

[NZ84]   M. Nodine and S. Zdonik. Cooperative transaction hierarchies: A transaction model to support design applications. In *Proceedings of the International Conference on Very Large Data Bases*, pages 83–94, 1984.

[OAB94]   M. Ouzzani, M. Atroun, and N. Belkhodja. A top-down approach to two-level serializability. In *Proceedings of the 20th International Conference on VLDB*, 1994.

[ON93]   A. Ouksel and C. Naiman. Coordinating context building in heterogeneous information systems. *Journal of Intelligent Information Systems*, 1993.

[OV91]   M. T. Özsu and P. Valduriez. *Principles of Distributed Database Systems*. Englewood Cliffs, NJ: Prentice Hall, 1991.

[Pap86]   C. Papadimitriou. *The Theory of Database Concurrency Control.* Rockville, MD: Computer Science Press, 1986.

[PC93]   C. Pu and S.-W. Chen. ACID properties need fast relief: Relaxing consistency using epsilon serializability. In *Proceedings of the Fifth International Workshop on High Performance Transaction Systems*, September 1993.

[PDBH97]   M. Papazoglou, A. Delis, A. Bouguettaya, and M. Haghjoo. Class library support for workflow environments and applications. *IEEE Transactions on Computers* 46(6), June 1997.

[Per91]   W. Perrizo. Transaction management in HYDRO: A multidatabase system. In *Proceedings of the First International Workshop on Interoperability in Multidatabase Systems (IMS'91)*, pages 276–279, April 1991.

[PGMU96]   Y. Papakonstantinou, H. Garcia-Molina, and J. Ullman. Medmaker: A mediation system based on declarative specification. In *12th International Conference on Data Engineering*, February 1996.

[PGMW95]   Y. Papakonstantinou, H. Garcia-Molina, and J. Widom. Object exchange across heterogeneous information sources. In *Proceedings of the International Conference on Data Engineering*, 1995.

[PKH88]   C. Pu, G. Kaiser, and N. Hutchinson. Split-transactions for open-ended activities. In *Proceedings of the 14th VLDB Conference*, pages 26–37, 1988.

[PL91]   C. Pu and A. Leff. Replica control in distributed systems: An asynchronous approach. In *Proceedings of the ACM SIGMOD*

International Conference on Management of Data, pages 377–386, 1991.

[PLC91] C. Pu, A. Leff, and S. F. Chen. Heterogeneous and autonomous transaction processing. *IEEE Computer* 24(12):64–72, December 1991.

[PLS92] M. Papazoglou, S. Laufmann, and T. Sellis. An organizational framework for cooperating intelligent information systems. *International Journal of Intelligent and Cooperative Information Systems* 1(1):169–202, 1992.

[PRSL93] S. Prabhakar, J. Richardson, J. Srivastava, and E. P. Lim. Instance-level integration in federated autonomous databases. In *Proceedings of the 26th Annual Hawaii International Conference on System Sciences*, volume III, pages 62–69, 1993.

[Pu88] C. Pu. Superdatabases for composition of heterogeneous databases. In *International IEEE Conference Management of Data*, pages 548–555, 1988.

[Pu91] C. Pu. Key equivalence in heterogeneous databases. In *Proceedings of IMS'91—The First International Workshop on Interoperability in Multidatabase Systems*, pages 314–317, 1991.

[PV88] J. Pons and J. Vilarem. Mixed concurrency control: Dealing with heterogeneity in distributed database systems. In *Proceedings of the 14th International Conference on Very Large Databases*, pages 445–456, 1988.

[Rad95] A. Radding. Support decision makers with a data warehouse. *Datamation*, pages 53–58, March 1995.

[Rap68] B. Raphael. A computer program for semantic information retrieval. In M. Minsky, editor, *Semantic Information Processing*. Cambridge, MA: MIT Press, 1968.

[Raz92] Y. Raz. The principle of commit ordering, or guaranteeing serializability in a heterogeneous environment of multiple autonomous resource managers using atomic commitment. In *Proceedings of the 18th International Conference on Very Large Databases*, August 23–27 1992.

[RB91]   S. Ram and E. Barkmeyer. The unifying semantic model for
            accessing multiple heterogeneous databases in a manufacturing
            environment. In *Proceedings of IMS'91—The First International
            Workshop on Interoperability in Multidatabase Systems*, pages
            212–216, 1991.

[RC85]   M. Rusinkiewicz and B. Czejdo. Query transformation in het-
            erogeneous distributed database systems. In *Proceedings of the
            Fifth International Conference on Distributed Computer Systems*,
            1985.

[RC87]   M. Rusinkiewicz and B. Czejdo. An approach to query processing
            in federated database systems. In *Proceedings of the 20th Hawaii
            International Conference on System Sciences*, 1987.

[RC91]   M. Rusinkiewicz and B. Czejdo. Processing of queries involving
            data and knowledge base systems. In *Proceedings of the Third In-
            ternational Conference on Software Engineering and Knowledge
            Engineering*, 1991.

[RC94]   K. Ramamritham and P. K. Chrysanthis. In search of acceptabil-
            ity criteria: Database consistency requirements and transaction
            correctness properties. In M. T. Özsu, U. Dayal, and P. Val-
            duriez, editors, *Distributed Object Management*, pages 212–230.
            San Mateo, CA: Morgan Kaufmann, 1994.

[RC96]   K. Ramamritham and P. K. Chrysanthis. A taxonomy of cor-
            rectness criteria in database applications. *Journal of Very Large
            Databases* 4(1):181–293, 1996.

[RCE91]   M. Rusinkiewicz, B. Czejdo, and D. Embley. An implemen-
            tation model for multidatabase queries. In *Proceedings of the
            International Conference DEXA '91*. New York: Springer-Verlag,
            1991.

[RELL90]   M. E. Rusinkiewicz, A. K. Elmagarmid, Y. Leu, and W. Litwin.
            Extending the transaction model to capture more meaning. *ACM
            SIGMOD Record* 19(1):3–7, March 1990.

[REMC+88]   M. Rusinkiewicz, R. El-Masri, B. Czejdo, D. Georgakopoulos,
            G. Karabatis, A. Jamoussi, K. Loa, and Y. Li. OMNIBASE:
            Design and implementation of a multidatabase system. *Dis-
            tributed Processing Technical Committee Newsletter* 10(2):20–28,
            November 1988.

[REMC+89] M. Rusinkiewicz, R. El-Masri, B. Czejdo, D. Georgakopoulos, G. Karabatis, A. Jamoussi, K. Loa, and Y. Li. Query processing in a heterogeneous multidatabase environment. In *Proceedings of the First Annual Symposium on Parallel and Distributed Processing*, 1989.

[Reu89] A. Reuter. Contract: A means for extending control beyond transaction boundaries. In *Proceedings of the Third International Workshop on High Performance Transaction Systems*, September 1989.

[Rin95] D. Rinaldi. Matadata management separates prism from data warehouse pack. *Client/Server Computing*, March 1995.

[Ris89] T. Risch. Monitoring database objects. In *Proceedings of the 15th International Conference on Very Large Databases*, pages 445–453, 1989.

[RP95] K. Ramamritham and C. Pu. A formal characterization of epsilon serializability. *IEEE Transactions on Knowledge and Data Engineering* 7(6):997–107, 1995.

[RR95a] S. Ram and V. Ramesh. A blackboard based cooperative system for schema integration. *IEEE Expert* 10(3):56–62, 1995.

[RR95b] V. Ramesh and S. Ram. A methodology for interschema relationship identification in heterogeneous databases. In *Proceedings of the Hawaii International Conference on Systems and Sciences*, pages 263–272, 1995.

[RR97] V. Ramesh and S. Ram. Integrity constraint integration in heterogeneous databases: An enhanced methodology for schema integration. *Information Systems* 22(8):423–446, 1997.

[RR98] S. Ram and V. Ramesh. Collaborative database design: A process model and system. Forthcoming ACM Transactions on Information Systems, 1998.

[RS91] M. Rusinkiewicz and A. Sheth. Polytransactions for managing interdependent data. *IEEE Data Engineering Bulletin* 14(1), March 1991.

[RSK91] M. Rusinkiewicz, A. Sheth, and G. Karabatis. Specifying interdatabase dependencies in a multidatabase environment. *IEEE Computer* 24(12):46–53, December 1991.

[RW91]   A. Reuter and H. Wächter. The ConTract model. *IEEE Data Engineering* 14(1):39–43, 1991.

[S⁺84]   P. Selinger et al. The impact of site autonomy on R*: A distributed relational DBMS. *Database—Role and Structure*, 1984.

[SAD⁺95]   M. Shan, R. Ahmed, J. Davis, W. Du, and W. Kent. Pegasus: A heterogeneous information management system. *Modern Database Systems*, 1995.

[Sal89]   G. Salton. *Automatic Text Processing*. Reading, MA: Addison-Wesley, 1989.

[SANR92]   A. Sheth, M. Ansari, L. Ness, and M. Rusinkiewicz. Using flexible transactions to support multidatabase applications. In *US West–NSF–DARPA Workshop on Heterogeneous Databases and Semantic Interoperability*, February 1992.

[SBCM95]   G. Samaras, K. Britton, A. Citron, and C. Mohan. Two-phase commit optimizations in a commercial distributed environment. *Distributed and Parallel Databases* 3(4):325–360, October 1995.

[SBD⁺81]   J. Smith, P. Bernstein, U. Dayal, N. Goodman, T. Landers, K. Lin, and E. Wong. Multibase: Integrating heterogeneous distributed database systems. In *Proceedings of the National Computer Conference*, pages 487–499. AFIPS, June 1981.

[SC83]   P. M. Stocker and R. Cantie. A target logical schema: The acs. In *Proceedings of the Ninth VLDB Conference*, 1983.

[Sch93]   F. Schwenkreis.   APRICOTS: A prototype implementation of a contract-system managing of the control-flow and the communication-system. In *Proceedings of the 12th Symposium on Reliable Distributed Systems*, pages 12–22, 1993.

[SG89]   A. Sheth and S. Gala. Attribute relationships: An impediment in automating schema integration. In *Proceedings of the NSF Workshop on Heterogeneous Databases*, December 1989.

[SGMS94]   K. Salem, H. Garcia-Molina, and J. Shands. Altruistic locking. *ACM Transactions on Database Systems* 19(1):117–165, 1994.

[SGN93] A. Sheth, S. Gala, and S. Navathe. On automatic reasoning for schema integration. *International Journal on Intelligent and Cooperative Information Systems* 2(1), March 1993.

[Sha76] G. Shafer. *A Mathematical Theory of Evidence.* Princeton, NJ: Princeton University Press, 1976.

[She91a] A. Sheth. Federated database systems for managing distributed, heterogeneous, and autonomous databases. In *Tutorial Notes— the 17th VLDB Conference*, September 1991.

[She91b] A. P. Sheth. Issues in schema integration: Perspective of an industrial researcher. *ARO Workshop on Heterogeneous Databases*, 1991.

[She91c] A. Sheth. Semantic issues in multidatabase systems. *SIGMOD Record, Special Issue on Semantic Issues in Multidatabases* 20(4), December 1991.

[She96] A. Sheth, editor. *Proceeding NSF Workshop: Workflow and Process Automation in Information Systems*, May 1996.

[Shi81] D. Shipman. The functional data model and the data language DAPLEX. *ACM Transactions on Database Systems* 2(3):140–173, March 1981.

[SHKC93] S. Shekhar, B. Hamidzadeh, A. Kohli, and M. Coyle. Learning transformation rules for semantic query optimization: A data-driven approach. *IEEE Transactions on Knowledge and Data Engineering* 5(6):950–964, 1993.

[SHP88] M. Stonebraker, E. Hanson, and S. Potamianos. The POST-GRES rule manager. *IEEE Transactions on Software Engineering* 14(7):897–907, July 1988.

[SJB92] W. W. Song, P. Johannesson, and J. A. Bubenko. Semantic similarity relations in schema integration. In *Proceedings of the 11th International Conference on the Entity-Relationship Approach*, pages 97–120, 1992.

[SK92] W. Sull and R. L. Kashyap. A self-organizing knowledge representation scheme for extensible heterogeneous information environment. *IEEE Transactions on Knowledge and Data Engineering* 4(2):185–191, 1992.

[SK93]   A. Sheth and V. Kashyap. So far (schematically), yet so near (semantically). In *Proceedings of the IFIP TC2/WG2.6 Conference on Semantics of Interoperable Database Systems, DS-5.* Amsterdam: North-Holland, November 1993.

[SKdM92]   E. Simon, J. Kiernan, and C. de Maindreville. Implementing high level active rules on top of a relational DBMS. In *Proceedings of the 18th VLDB Conference*, pages 315–326, 1992.

[SKS91]   N. Soparkar, H. F. Korth, and A. Silberschatz. Failure-resilient transaction management in multidatabases. *IEEE Computer* 24(12):28–36, December 1991.

[SKS97]   A. Silberschatz, H. F. Korth, and S. Sudarshan. *Database System Concepts (Third Edition).* New York: McGraw-Hill, 1997.

[SL90]   A. Sheth and J. Larson. Federated database systems for managing distributed, heterogeneous, and autonomous databases. *ACM Computing Surveys* 22(3):183–236, September 1990.

[SLCN88]   A. Sheth, J. Larson, A. Cornelio, and S. B. Navathe. A tool for integrating conceptual schemata and user views. In *Proceedings of the Fourth International Conference on Data Engineering*, pages 176–183. Los Alamitos, CA: IEEE Computer Society Press, February 1988.

[SM91]   M. Siegel and S. Madnick. A metadata approach to resolving semantic conflicts. In *Proceedings of the 17th VLDB Conference*, September 1991.

[SM92]   A. P. Sheth and H. Marcus. *Schema Analysis and Integration: Methodology, Techniques and Prototype Toolkit.* Technical report TM-STS-019981/1. Bellcore, 1992.

[SP94]   S. Spaccapietra and C. Parent. View integration: A step forward in solving structural conflicts. *IEEE Transactions on Knowledge and Data Engineering* 6(2), April 1994.

[SPAM91]   U. Schreier, H. Pirahesh, R. Agrawal, and C. Mohan. Alert: An architecture for transforming a passive DBMS into an active DBMS. In *17th VLDB*, September 1991.

[SPD92]   S. Spaccapietra, C. Parent, and Y. Dupont. Independent assertions for integration of heterogeneous schemas. *Very Large Database Journal* 1(1), 1992.

[SR86]   M. Stonebraker and L. Rowe. The design of POSTGRES. In *Proceedings of the ACM SIGMOD Conference*, pages 340–355, June 1986.

[SR90]   A. Sheth and M. Rusinkiewicz. Management of interdependent data: Specifying dependency and consistency requirements. In *Proceedings of the Workshop on Management of Replicated Data*, pages 133–136, 1990.

[SR91]   Y. Shim and C. Ramamoorthy. Monitoring of distributed systems. In *Symposium on Applied Computing*, pages 248–256, 1991.

[SRK92]   A. P. Sheth, M. Rusinkiewicz, and G. Karabatis. Using polytransactions to manage interdependent data. In A. K. Elmagarmid, editor, *Database Transaction Models for Advanced Applications*, pages 555–581. San Mateo, CA: Morgan Kaufmann, 1992.

[SRL93]   L. Suardi, M. Rusinkiewicz, and W. Litwin. Execution of extended multidatabase SQL. In *Proceedings of the Ninth IEEE International Conference on Data Engineering*, 1993.

[SSG⁺91]   A. Savasere, A. Sheth, S. Gala, S. Navathe, and H. Marcus. On applying classification to schema integration. In *Proceedings of IMS'91—The First International Workshop on Interoperability in Multidatabase System*, pages 258–261, 1991.

[SSKS95]   L. Shklar, A. Sheth, V. Kashyap, and K. Shah. Infoharness: Use of automatically generated metadata for search and retrieval of heterogeneous information. In *Proceedings of CAiSE-95*, 1995.

[SSKT95]   L. Shklar, A. Sheth, V. Kashyap, and S. Thatte. Infoharness: the system for search and retrieval of heterogeneous information. In *Database Application Semantics, Proceedings of the Sixth IFIP Working Conference on Data Semantics*, 1995. Extended version in *Proceedings of the ACM SIGMOD*, 1995.

[SSR92a]   E. Sciore, M. Siegel, and A. Rosenthal. Context interchange using meta-attributes. In *Proceedings of the CIKM*, 1992.

[SSR92b]   E. Sciore, M. Siegel, and A. Rosenthal. Using semantic values to facilitate interoperability among heterogeneous information systems. *Transactions on Database Systems* 17(12), 1992.

[SSS92]   M. Seigel, E. Sciore, and S. Salveter. A method for automatic rule derivation to support semantic query optimization. *ACM Transactions on Database Systems* 17(4):563–600, 1992.

[SSU91]   A. Silberschatz, M. Stonebraker, and J. F. Ullman. Database systems: Achievements and opportunities. *Communications of the ACM* 34(10), October 1991.

[Sto79]   M. Stonebraker. Concurrency control and consistency of multiple copies of data in distributed INGRES. *Transactions on Software Engineering* 3(3), 1979.

[Sto86]   M. Stonebraker. Triggers and inference in database systems. In M. Brodie and J. Mylopoulos, editors, *On Knowledge Base Management Systems.* New York: Springer-Verlag, 1986.

[Sto94]   M. Stonebraker, editor. *Readings in Database Systems.* San Francisco: Morgan Kaufmann, 1994.

[Sua92]   L. Suardi. *Execution of Extended MSQL* (Master's thesis). Houston, TX: Department of Computer Science, University of Houston, June 1992.

[SV86]   E. Simon and P. Valduriez. Integrity control in distributed database systems. In *Proceedings of the Hawaii 20th International Conference on System Sciences*, 1986.

[SWS91]   H.-J. Schek, G. Weikum, and W. Schaad. A multi-level transaction approach to federated DBMS transaction management. In *Proceedings of the First International Workshop on Interoperability in Multidatabase Systems (IMS'91)*, pages 280–287, April 1991.

[SWY93]   H.-J. Schek, G. Weikum, and H. Ye. Towards a unified theory of concurrency control and recovery. In *Proceedings of the ACM Principles of Database Systems (PODS)*, 1993.

[SYE+90]   P. Scheuermann, C. Yu, A. Elmagarmid, H. Garcia-Molina, F. Manola, D. McLeod, A. Rosenthal, and M. Templeton. Report on the workshop on heterogeneous database systems. In *SIGMOD Record*, volume 19, pages 23–31. New York: ACM, December 1990.

[SZ91]   P. Shoval and S. Zohn.   Binary-relationship integration methodology. *Data and Knowledge Engineering* 6:225–250, 1991.

[T⁺86]   M. Templeton et al.   An introduction to aida—a front-end to heterogeneous databases. *Distributed Systems* 2:483–490, 1986.

[TA94]   A. Tal and R. Alonso.   Commit protocols for externalized-commit heterogeneous database systems. *Distributed and Parallel Databases* 2(2), April 1994.

[TBD⁺87]   M. Templeton, D. Brill, S. K. Dao, E. Lund, P. Ward, A. L. P. Chen, and R. MacGregor. Mermaid: A front-end to distributed heterogeneous databases. *Proceedings of the IEEE* 75(5):695–708, May 1987.

[TCY93]   F. Tseng, A. Chen, and W. Yang. Answering heterogeneous database queries with degrees of uncertainty. *Distributed and Parallel Databases, An International Journal* 1(3), July 1993.

[TRV96]   A. Tomasic, L. Raschid, and P. Valduriez.   Scaling heterogeneous databases and the design of disco.   In *Proceedings of the International Conference on Distributed Computer Systems*, 1996.

[TS93]   C. Thieme and A. Siebes. Schema integration in object-oriented databases. In *Proceedings of the Fifth International Symposium on Advanced Information Systems Engineering, CAiSE'93*, pages 54–70, 1993.

[US91]   R. Unland and G. Schlageter. A flexible and adaptable tool kit approach for transaction management in non-standard database systems. *IEEE Data Engineering Bulletin*, March 1991.

[UW91]   S. Urban and J. Wu. Resolving semantic heterogeneity through the explicit representation of data model semantics. *SIGMOD Record* 20(4):55–58, December 1991.

[VEH92]   J. Veijalainen, F. Eliassen, and B. Holtkamp. The S-transaction model. In A. K. Elmagarmid, editor, *Transaction Management for Advanced Database Applications*, pages 467–513. San Mateo, CA: Morgan Kaufmann, 1992.

[Vei90]   J. Veijalainen. *Transaction Concepts in Autonomous Database Environments* (PhD thesis). Munich, Germany: R. Oldenbourg Verlag, 1990.

[Vei93]   J. Veijalainen. Heterogeneous multilevel transaction management with multiple transactions. In *Proceedings of the DEXA '93 Conference*, pages 181–188, September 6–8 1993.

[VH93]   V. Ventrone and S. Heiler. *A practical approach for dealing with semantic heterogeneity in federated database systems*. Technical report. The MITRE Corporation, October 1993.

[VHYBS97]   R. Vingralek, H. Hasse-Ye, Y. Breitbart, and H. J. Schek. Unifying concurrency control and recovery of transaction with semantically rich operations. To appear, 1997.

[VW92a]   J. Veijalainen and A. Wolski. *The 2PC Agent Method for Transaction Management in Heterogeneous Multidatabases, and its Correctness*. Technical report J-10. Helsinki, Finland: Technical Research Centre of Finland (VTT), Laboratory for Information Processing, June 1992.

[VW92b]   J. Veijalainen and A. Wolski. Prepare and commit certification for decentralized transaction management in rigorous heterogeneous multidatabases. In *Proceedings of the Eighth International Conference on Data Engineering*, pages 470–479, February 1992.

[VWP+97]   J. Veijalainen, J. Wäsch, J. Puustjärvi, H. Tirri, and O. Pihlajamaa. Transaction models in cooperative work—an overview. In W. Klas and J. Veijalainen, editors, *Transaction Management Support for Cooperative Applications*, chapter 3, pages 27–58. Norwell, MA: Kluwer Academic Publishers, 1997.

[WCH+93]   D. Woelk, P. Cannata, M. Huhns, W. Shen, and C. Tomlinson. Using carnot for enterprise information integration. In *The Second International Conference on Parallel and Distributed Information Systems*, 1993.

[Wei91]   G. Weikum. Principles and realization strategies of multilevel transaction management. *ACM Transactions on Database Systems* 16(1):132–180, March 1991.

[WF90]   J. Widom and S. Finkelstein. Set-oriented production rules in relational database systems. In *Proceedings of the ACM SIGMOD Conference*, pages 259–270, May 1990.

[Wie92]   G. Wiederhold.   Mediators in the architecture of future information systems. *Computer* 25(3):38–49, March 1992.

[WNC91]   W. K. Whang, S. B. Navathe, and S. Chakravarthy. Logic-based approach for realizing a federated information system. In *Proceedings of IMS'91—The First International Workshop on Interoperability in Multidatabase Systems*, pages 92–100, 1991.

[Woo85]   W. J. Wood. What's in a link?: Foundations for semantic networks. In R. Brachman and H. Levesque, editors, *Readings in Knowledge Representation*. Los Altos, CA: Morgan Kaufmann, 1985.

[WQ87]   G. Wiederhold and X. Qian. Modeling asynchrony in distributed databases. In *Proceedings of the Third International Conference on Data Engineering*, pages 246–250, February 1987.

[WR92]   H. Wächter and A. Reuter. The ConTract model. In A. K. Elmagarmid, editor, *Database Transaction Models for Advanced Applications*, pages 219–264. San Mateo, CA: Morgan Kaufmann, 1992.

[WS96]   D. Worah and A. Sheth. What do advanced transaction models have to offer for workflows? In *Proceedings of the International Workshop in Advanced Transaction Models and Architectures (ATMA)*, 1996.

[WV90]   A. Wolski and J. Veijalainen. 2PC agent method: Achieving serializability in presence of failures in a heterogeneous multidatabase. In *Proceedings of the IEEE PARBASE-90 Conference*, pages 321–330, 1990.

[WV91]   A. Wolski and J. Veijalainen. 2pc agent method: Achieving serializability in presence of failures in a heterogeneous multidatabase. *Databases: Theory, Design and Applications*, pages 268–287, 1991. A revised version of [WV90].

[WYP92]   K.-L. Wu, P. S. Yu, and C. Pu. Divergence control for epsilon serializability. In *Proceedings of the Eighth International Conference on Data Engineering*, pages 506–515, February 1992.

[YSDK91]   C. Yu, W. Sun, S. Dao, and D. Keirsey. Determining relationships among attributes for interoperability of multidatabase systems. In *Proceedings of the First International Workshop on Interoperability in Multidatabase Systems*, April 1991.

[YWH82]   S. B. Yao, V. E. Waddle, and B. C. Housel. View modeling and integration using the functional data model. *IEEE Transactions on Software Engineering* Se-8(6):544–553, 1982.

[Zad78]   L. Zadeh. Fuzzy sets as a basis for a theory of possibility. *Fuzzy Sets and Systems* 1(1), 1978.

[ZCT91]   R. Zicari, S. Ceri, and L. Tanca. Interoperability between a rule-based database language and an object-oriented database language. In *First International Workshop on Interoperability in Multidatabase Systems*, pages 125–134, April 1991.

[ZE93a]   A. Zhang and A. Elmagarmid. On global transaction scheduling in multidatabase systems. In *Proceedings of the Second International Conference on Parallel and Distributed Information Systems*, pages 117–124, 1993.

[ZE93b]   A. Zhang and A. Elmagarmid. A theory of global concurrency control in multidatabase systems. *VLDB Journal* 2(3):331–360, 1993.

Index

rollback reliability, 314, 319
rule-based approach to schema
  integration, 139
rule-based language (RL) in language
  translations, 164–165
rules
  Context-Sensitive Recovery Rule, 342
  for integration of objects, 137
  for integration of paths, 137
  Late Redo Recovery Rule, 342
  in STARBURST, 243
running states, 307
R-W model, 322, 343–344
  histories, 314–319
  pruning within, 314–315
  recoverability and serializability in,
    314–320
  results of, 322

S

Sagas transaction model, 16, 19, 209,
  256, 287–289, 341
schedulers, 258
  interschema relationship identification
    (IRS), 142
  on-line, 316–318
  schema generation (SGS), 143
schedules, local, 46
schema conversion phase
  in semantic abstractions approach, 81
  steps in, 81
schema elements, mappings between, 60
schema generation, improving integrated,
  147–148
schema generation scheduler (SGS), 143
schema integration, 13–15, 92, 120–148
  automating, 140–145
  classification of strategies, 125–132
  constraints on, 14
  defined, 120–121
  framework for, 122–132
  future directions in, 145–148
  generating integrity constraints, 148
  identification techniques for, 133–140
  problems in, 148
  rule-based approach to, 139
  steps in, 122–125
schema integration approaches, 131–132
  based on logic, 132
  based on object-oriented models, 131
  based on relational models, 131

based on semantic models, 131
schema integration methodology, 123
  also integrating object-oriented
    schemas, 138
  steps in, 141
schema integration phase
  heterogeneous data models, 38–39
  query and update translation, 41
  reconciliation of data values, 40
  resolution of schematic discrepancies,
    39–40
schema integration toolkits, 140–146
schema isomorphism conflicts, 179
schema knowledge
  combining with fuzzy terminological
    knowledge, 60
  methods using, 93
schema-level conflict resolution, 180
schema manager, 180
schema mapping generation, 125, 133
schema mismatches, 93–94
schema object creation construct, 189
schema optimization, 21
schema reconciliation, 189
schema restructuring methodologies, 127
schemas
  conceptual unified, 38
  imported, 38, 40
  native, 38
  standardizing, 139
schematic conflicts, solutions to, 40
schematic differences, classification
  taxonomies of, 58
schematic discrepancy
  incompatibility in, 178–179
  resolution of, 39–40
schematic interschema relationship
  generation, 122–124
schema translations, 8, 122, 158–171
  into an ER model, 159
  into an object-oriented model, 161
  characteristics needed, 122
  developing mappings during, 139–140
  example of, 161–162
  into a functional model, 159–160
  into a relational model, 158
security in multidatabase environments,
  218
SELECT
  basic evaluation in MSQL+, 204–205
  multiqueries in MSQL language, 184
SELECT clause, 191, 195, 199